Forty Years in a Missouri Classroom

" TEACHER, TEACHER,
I DONE IT! I DONE IT!
I DONE DONE IT! "

Library of Congress Cataloging in Publication Data

FORTY YEARS IN A MISSOURI CLASSROOM

"TEACHER, TEACHER, I DONE IT! I DONE IT! I DONE DONE IT!"

by GRACE BACON FERRIER

The Westphalia Press
Loose Creek, Missouri
1986

THE HORSE SHOE BEND REGION

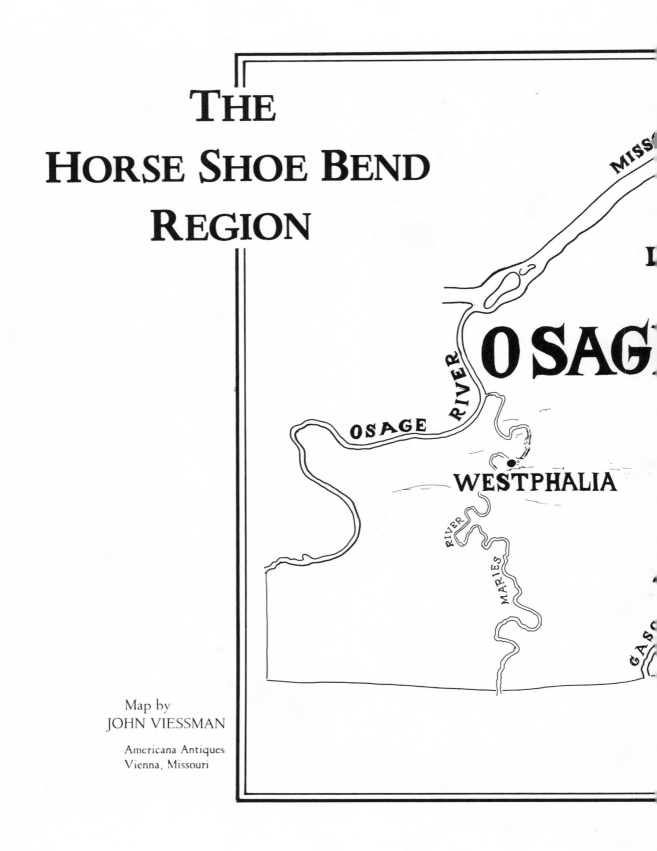

Map by
JOHN VIESSMAN

Americana Antiques
Vienna, Missouri

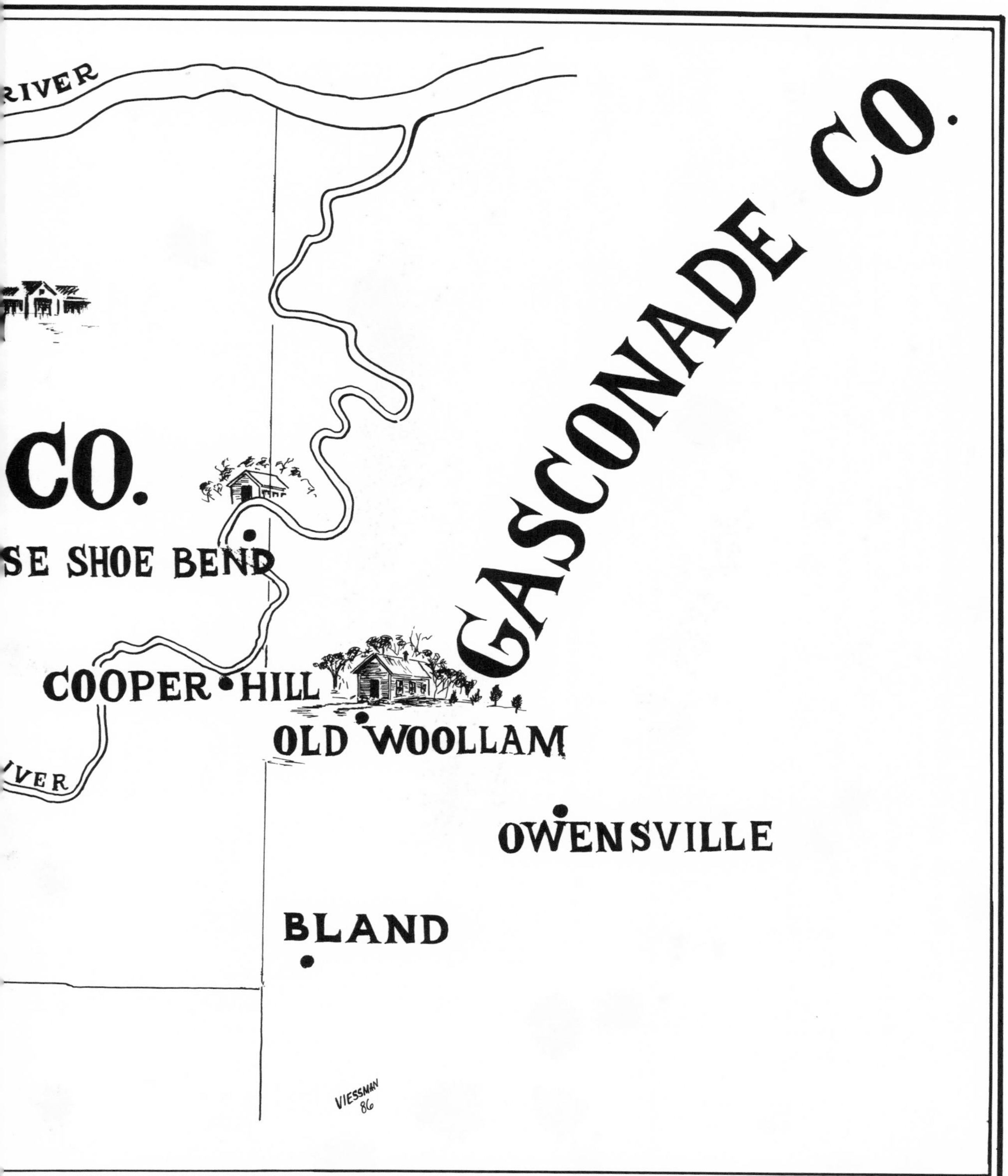

RIVER

GASCONADE CO.

CO.

SE SHOE BEND

COOPER • HILL

OLD • WOOLLAM

IVER

OWENSVILLE
•

BLAND
•

VIESSMAN
86

Courtesy *School and Community Magazine*

CONTENTS

PART ONE

PART TWO

PART THREE

PART FOUR

PART FIVE

Period illustrations and Problems are from books used in the Third Grade by Alice and Clarence Haslag of Loose Creek, Missouri.

Titles: *Common-Word Spellers: A Two-Book Course in Spelling for the Common Schools*, by Ervin Eugene Lewis, Ph.D., published in 1921 by Ginn and Company, and *Elements of Arithmetic: For Primary and Intermediate Classes in Public and Private Schools*, by William J. Milne, Ph.D., L.L.D., first published in 1893 by American Book Company.

She also rang the bell

The one-room schoolhouse...

The words conjure up one of America's best loved images. It's a small building, nestled at the edge of a clearing with woods all around it. It's red — faded red — on the outside. Inside an old potbellied stove purrs with warmth. The young schoolmarm stands in front of the blackboard, filled with perfect cursive writing, Palmer style, imparting knowledge and character building to a dozen or so eager-eyed students clad in clean overalls and starched gingham dresses...

Horse Shoe Bend, where Grace Ferrier taught her first classes, did look somewhat like that. It was white, though, not red. But nestled it was, far back in the wooded hills above the Gasconade River in the steep slopes of central Missouri's Osage County. Just a short crow's flight over the hills to the north, the Missouri River sang boisterously. And just a nose smell away lay Herman Lipskoch's pig pen.

The year was 1932, another Depression year, and Grace was lucky to find a job — especially one that paid $40 a month. She had graduated from high school with some "teacher training." She had obligingly "visited" the board members on their farms. She had been "offered" room and board (for $20 a month) by the president's wife. And she was scared to death.

That first morning she walked from Jim Hollandworth's farm through the woods to the schoolhouse. It was 7:15 a.m. and the new teacher went to work:

"First, I raised the windows and propped them up with the sawed-off broom handles lying on the sills. A blackboard was nailed to the back wall. In front of it sat an old-fashioned teacher's desk...Rows of desks were fastened to the floor with large bolts, and between the rows were two long recitation benches...

"At the back of the room was a large potbellied cast iron woodstove wearing a galvanized metal jacket around it..."

And at 8:30 a.m., on the dot, she rang her first school bell.

Only this far into Grace Ferrier's manuscript, I knew I was reading much more than nostalgic reminiscings. I read on, finding places I knew and people whose names still identified mailboxes all over the region and rediscovering days of my childhood — with a German flavor. Some 400 onion skin pages later, in the wee small hours of the morning, I knew I had read not only an authentic account of 40 years of teaching but a detailed reporting of a way of life in a region that still clings to its unique history and culture.

At first, I thought perhaps I was lured on by knowing the places she knew and enjoying finding out about the "real people" behind the names so common in this

By Bill Nunn

The Westphalia Press
The Dohman-Boessen House
Loose Creek, Missouri

place where we now live. Then I decided the lure was universal, that everybody knows people like these ... the people she lived with, the students she taught and the parents who raised them, the school board members — whose wives really run things, the good teachers who can't find enough time and ways to help any student who wants to learn, and the poor teachers who never learn that daily lesson plans and daily discipline are prerequisites to acquiring an education.

I came to know Grace Ferrier as an unsure, self-conscious young schoolmarm growing into a capable, dedicated dispenser of discipline and learning. And I came to know the people she knew. Some she loved, some she disliked, some she admired. Some were simply "characters." But all were worth knowing.

There was Mama, always right and always ready to advise; Dad, like Mama once a teacher, too, but at home on the land now; Dell, her rooming-mate colleague who sagely "wants my money when I sells my pigs;" Log and Birdie, whose room was a home away from home; Rosie, who needed a friend more than a teacher, and Bessie, who finally "done it;" Buell, the "Clay Dog" who became her rock and died too soon...

With Grace, I lived with these people through the Depression — eating "Coolige Custard" with Uncle John and Aunt Ida; through World War II with families — including hers — who sent sons and brothers and husbands all over the world to fight a war they didn't quite understand, under a president they disliked and somehow distrusted. Some of them didn't come home. Some returned to a world they'd helped change, a world never to be like the one they and their fathers and mothers had grown up in. But they learned to live in it.

Grace Ferrier's stories are real. They are true, with her living of them. They are sad with the troubles and the deaths of loved ones. They are funny, with the sanity-saving humor a teacher needs to survive. They are about people you will recognize, because the sorrows and the joys, the successes and the disappointments of their lives are of our own.

Grace Ferrier had written her memories mostly for her nieces. The manuscript had languished in her dresser drawer where she put it when she moved back to her beloved home place across Mistaken Creek south of Cooper Hill, Missouri. Some ten years later she summoned up the courage to mail it, with the self-deprecating comment that perhaps "I should forget about it and become interested in real estate."

You'll be glad with me that she didn't. More than a piece of real estate, she has given us an entertaining and enduring piece of Americana, wherever we live.

This book is dedicated
to my mother and father,
who had the determination to rescue me
from the fate of becoming
a "one year teacher";

to the Ferrier family,
for a few years of true happiness.
I am truly thankful.

to my nieces,
Yvonne, Anna Lo and Jennie Mae,
who insisted I write it,
and especially
to Debra Bacon,
who typed the first copy; and

to all the people
who taught me so much
in my forty-three years as a classroom teacher.
I am deeply grateful.

*"Perhaps the most valuable result
of all education is the ability
to make yourself do the thing you have to do,
when it ought to be done,
whether you like it or not."*

THOMAS HUXLEY

PART ONE

HORSE SHOE BEND

1

"... and don't forget da fancy vine glasses, by Gott."

It was the first of more than forty such Augusts in my life, but I wasn't thinking about beginning a lifelong career that last Sunday of the month in 1932.

As was usual in the 30s, the summer had been one long, hot, droughty day and today was no change. I had dreaded this time all summer long, ever since early in the spring when I had signed the contract to teach the Horse Shoe Bend School. I had had trouble getting anyone on school boards to "hire me." I was young, I weighed less than a hundred pounds and I had no experiece. I was caught in that eternal chicken-or-the-egg dilemma of employment: How do you get experience when you've had no chance to teach?

Getting oneself employed was quite a chore in those days of the Depression because there were numerous teachers hungry for each school job. Sometimes there would be 40 to 50 applicants for a school reputed to be changing "personnel." So I made application, along with the other 49, for this teaching job.

This one did by calling on each member of the school board. So early that spring Dad, brother Bud and I went calling on Jim Hollandworth (the President), John Topel, Lafe Beller and Herman Lipskoch. Usually the august personnage was found somewhere "about the place." Sometimes I jumped fences and loped over freshly-plowed furrows to where the desired lord of the manor would be resting his team of mules.

The interview I remember best was the one with Mr. John Topel. We turned off Highway 50 at Pin Oak Creek, just east of Mt. Sterling, and headed north toward Bay. Soon another road came in from the left. That was the only road into and out of Horse Shoe Bend.

Just after leaving the main road, we crossed Pin Oak Creek, and lying just north of it was the lovely farm belonging to Mr. Topel. (Cap Hoehne lives there now). Wide river bottom land lay on one side and creek bottom on the other. There was a beautiful old stone house, and well kept barns and machine sheds.

Rain was pouring down the day we visited him. We must have awakened him from his nap because he met us at the door yawning and running his hand through his thick black hair as if to comb it quickly. He was a short, stocky man with a typical Falstaff nose, and extremely courteous in an oldfashioned Germanic way.

We had hardly explained our business when he slapped his knee excitedly and exclaimed, "Mandy, Frieda, out vith the vine! And don't forget da fancy vine glasses yet, by Gott."

Mandy and Frieda were the two young daughters who did the housework, and out they soon came with the "vine" and the fancy "vine" glasses and some delicious crisp sugar cookies on a beautiful plate on which was written in gold letters, "Give us this day our daily bread."

All this time I could see Mrs. Topel lying in a bed in a darkened room just off the kitchen. Before long I was ushered into the bedroom to say, "Hello to Mama." I am sure it was so Mama could get a look at the prospective

eacher turned authoress iven prestigeous award

Grace Bacon Ferrier was a cher, not an author. She didn't end to write a book; she was just ting down stories which her ces enjoyed hearing. And the ion skin manuscript lay un-ched in her bureau drawer for ten ars . . . until she read in the ekly Linn <u>Unterrified Democrat</u> out book publishing by The estphalia Press.

Now her book-that-wasn't--eacher, Teacher, I Done It! I ne It! I Done Done It!"--is the st place winner for nonfiction in e 1987 Society of Midland thors competition.

Mrs. Ferrier's book--a detailed, rsonal account of her experiences d way of life in 43 years of aching--covers her career in veral Osage County schools and Winfield in Lincoln County and rkwood in suburban St. Louis. st year the society's prestigious vard went to Dr. Franklin onzalez-Crussi's <u>Notes of an natomist,</u> published by Harcourt, race & Jovanovich of New York.

<u>"Teacher, Teacher . . ."</u> received st place amid "heavy com-tition," according to Susan eston, awards chairwoman of the ciety, headquartered in Evanston, . Mrs. Ferrier will accept the vard at the society's annual dinner d ceremony May 14 at the Drake otel in Chicago.

It is the second national recog-tion for the <u>"I Done It! I Done</u> " book within a month. In late arch it won a finalist award the annual "Best Book" mpetition sponsored by the ational Association of Independent blishers. In announcing the inners, the NAIP commented, he sub-title of this book is

"Forty Years in a Missouri Classroom,' and it's wonderful, preserving an era of Americana in fine style."

The Society of Midland Authors was formed in 1915 by a group of authors that included Hamlin Garland, Harriet Monroe and Vachel Lindsay. Among its charter members were James Whitcomb Riley, Edna Ferber, George Ade, Clarence Darrow and Zona Gale. Today it "seeks to preserve a literary tradition that has included a significant proportion of the important Midland authors of the twentieth century."

The two awards from professional authors and critics and fellow publishers, said Bill Nunn of The Westphalia Press, "verify our belief that Grace's book has national interest and appeal--and lasting value--far beyond the borders of Osage County and Missouri."

Now in its second printing, the book is available at many bookstores or directly from The Westphalia Press, Loose Creek, Missouri, 65054. Paperback copies are $12.95; hardbound copies are $18.95. Mail orders should include $1.70 for postage and handling.

schoolmarm. She was pale and white, like the beautiful linens around her, but her smile was simply angelic.

She was paralyzed from the waist down, I found out later. People in the neighborhood said she had worked too hard helping out in the fields by day and doing her housework at night. I also found out later that it was a trite statement — and probably untrue — in the neighborhood to say, "My house is as clean as Mrs. Topel's." And that was followed up, truthfully, with, "You can't scrape up two teaspoonsful of dirt in the whole place." I'll never forget the scoured floors in that house; they were really almost as white as snow.

On the visit Lady Luck was with me. Mr. Topel had heard "goot 'tings about me, by Gott," and he was going to "wote for me by Gott" when the board members "came togedder to wote."

With that, the thunder and lightning came together in a drenching thunderstrom, and Dad and I both knew we had better get back across Pin Oak Creek or be marooned in Horse Shoe Bend. As we were leaving, Mrs. Topel called from her bedroom, "Give them something to put on to keep them from being drowned on their way back to the car."

"Youst a little somesing to hang over your het, by Gott," Mr. Topel kept saying as he pressed rain gear and extra coats on us.

After I had been chosen and my contract was signed, I was fair game for the women in the district to bid for my board. There I'll have to hand it to Mrs. Hollandworth. She was slyer than the others — and she was first.

A few days after my approval by the board, I looked out the front door at home and saw Mr. and Mrs. Hollandworth and their small daughter, Lillian, alighting from their Model T Ford. I was in the midst of doing the family laundry and looked my worst, with soap suds sliding down my arms and a big wet spot covering my tummy.

I comforted myself with the thought, "Oh, they won't stay long since it's morning. They've just come by to pay a friendly call." But I didn't know what I was in for.

Mom and Dad came into the living room to help out and we all worked hard at entertaining. It was especially hard on Dad because Mr. Hollandworth's conversation was spare. He held Lillian on his lap and puffed on his pipe as he stared at the floor.

Dinnertime was approaching, and if you've lived through a time of drought and depression, you know company food was never prepared in advance unless people had notified you earlier. So I'm sure that Mama had been planning a dinner as she talked garden and chickens with Mrs. Hollandworth. It was very apparent that they were certainly "staying on for a while."

Eventually Mom and I made our exit and headed for the kitchen. Mom began to give orders: "Grace, you bake a cake while I go catch a couple of chickens and dress them!" And while we were planning she was raking the stove catch through the coals in the wood stove and laying dry chips and split oak kindling on top to hurry the fire along. And the teakettle was filled with water and set on the front burner so we would have boiling water to scald the chickens.

For once, I would rather have picked those chickens with their smell of hot feathers. This was in BCM Days — Before Cake Mix — and absolutely no cook could tell how her cake was going to turn out until it was out of the oven. I shook with fear as I mixed and creamed and beat the shortening, sugar, eggs, and flour ... And I thought to myself that they might revoke my contract if my cake came out "flatter'n a pancake."

But my guardian angel was with me that day. I don't know what I did differently, but for once in my life a cake turned out perfectly. It raised just right, and it was baked perfect brown, and the texture was moist and light — something I had never beheld in one of my cakes before. I even made seven-minute frosting that didn't run off the cake and onto the floor. That cake became the household epitome of perfection: Mom would say, "Do you suppose you could make a cake like that one you made the day Hollandworths were here?" But I never did again .. "By Gott."

Finally, we got the meal together. When the boys came in from the field they were overjoyed to find fried chicken and cake on the weekday menu. Then the long, hot fidgety afternoon began.

"No, you've done all of the cooking," I insisted to Mama. "Now you go visit with Mrs. Hollandworth and I'll do the dishes."

I could see Mom's eyes flashing daggers at me, but Mrs. Hollandworth jumped into the fray with, "I see you have a piano. Won't you play something for us?"

My musical ability was something less than that of Beethoven or Brahms so I hesitated. That was just what Mrs. Hollandworth wanted. "Would you mind if I tried it out?" she hurried to say. "I've always wanted to try a piano."

I was delighted to let her "try it out." Anything was better than having to play it myself. She sat down and began "trying out" first one familiar hymn and then another. She had a nice alto voice and I didn't mind singing, so I joined in. Dad sang bass very well, and his eyes twinkled as he and I tried to keep up with Mrs. Hollandworth's mixture of fast and slow time as she haltingly picked out the sharps and flats of "The Old Time Religion." She certainly "tried out" Dad and me as well as the piano.

It was getting dark when we finally wound up entertaining the Hollandworths. They had really come, it seems, to tell me that I was elected to board with them...because, as Mrs. Hollandworth said, "Jim really had done all the talking in your favor." And he had "persuaded all the other board members" to vote for me.

I could picture that. Jim had hardly opened his mouth all day except to move his pipe from one position to another.

But Horse Shoe Bend was a job and I was young and $40 a month looked like riches after a long depression. What if I did pay $20 of it for board?

All that summer thoughts of my riches-to-come had helped balance out my dread of its end and the beginning of school. Now is was Sunday and tomorrow was Monday...and school was to open. Having made all of the arrangements for board, there was only one thing to do: Get the family's one and only suitcase and put in my few little necessities and leave.

Packing was simple; my worldly goods could have fit into a grocery sack. I had a faded yellow voile dress — a hand-me-down from Jennie Hancks; a bright red and white printed percale dress, one that I had made myself; and two print percale dresses that were really sister Mae's. But she wasn't teaching and I might as well wear them, so Mama thought.

I had one extra white cotton slip (home-made), one extra pair of hose, a bar of Palmolive soap, my small compact containing "Three Flowers" face powder, and a very small container of rouge — which belonged to Mae. I had one pair of cotton pajamas — I made them myself — and a few assorted pieces of a more personal nature. At that time, I found these items sufficient for my needs. Today we have much more than we need.

All morning that Sunday, as I placed these carefully washed and ironed pieces of clothing in the old brown leather suitcase, I gazed out upon the beloved hillsides around the house. We were all worried. No rain had fallen. The crops were short. Corn, so tenderly and hopefully placed in the ground that spring, had sprouted and grown only about waist high, then withered without even entertaining an idea of getting an ear on it. Pastures were burned brown and gardens, long past the fruitful stage, were dried and crackly. The only bright spot for us had been my "school teaching job" — and its $40.

"That'll get us through another winter," Mama would say.

After our noon dinner — that was the big meal on Sunday — I went upstairs to change from my everyday dress into my going-away one. It wasn't much better but it was considered a sensible school dress. I brought down the suitcase — my Dad's old Gladstone, a handsome piece in its day — and fastened the outside straps. With my meager belongings, I certainly didn't need the straps for support but I couldn't just let them hang loose. There were fancy leather holders for them to fit into on each side of the case and I thought it looked slouchy without the straps brought around and buckled on top.

We were ready for the slaughter. Bud brought the old Model T sedan up from the cowbarn hallway. Mom and I climbed in the back seat. The old brown suitcase sat between us, straps and all. Dad rode on the little jump seat up front.

You pushed the back rest down and climbed over it to get into the back seat and we always thought it was fine and dandy that the driver got to sit over the gas tank. It was a handy arrangement: All you did to fill up was to take off the cushion, unscrew a metal fruit jar type lid and refill the tank — or get a stick and measure the gas, if you wished. No one really thought of it as being dangerous.

Then we were off. Bud herded the old Ford up our hill and out onto the main road. And all I could think of as we got farther and farther from home was, They will all be coming back home tonight but me. I'll be sleeping in a strange house, in a strange bed. I'm a teacher now. I have to do this. I'm getting paid to do a job. And, after all, Bud and Pete were in high school and we had to have the money.

The drought had hit even harder in the areas we passed through, and Mom and Dad talked about how much worse it seemed. Bud was silent. I'm sure now they all knew what I was thinking, but at the time I was sure my thoughts were a secret.

After leaving the highway, the road ran before us like a picture postcard. We crossed Pin Oak Creek and started up the hill toward the real bend in the Gasconade River and we could see again the beautiful Topel farm on the right. And far off to the left, over the tops of the trees as the road skimmed along the bluff, we could see the river making a huge curve.

We passed the school house — "Well, there's *your* school" Mama said. I nodded. A lump in my throat wouldn't go away.

We made a right angle turn onto the Hollandworth land, and had to stop at a gap, one of those always to be opened in Missouri farming sections. A gap is a makeshift gate — usually three strands of barbed wire (usually with cow hair twisted around the barbs where the cows have scratched themselves) attached to a pole at each end. One pole is firmly tied to a post and the other swings loose to facilitate opening — such opening and closing being not without its dangers, especially in closing. One usually finds it expedient to place the ground end of the pole in the wire loop attached to the post first; then with all your might and main, if your might and main are strong enough, you place the upper wire hoop over the

OUR MODEL T FORD

The driver got to sit over the gas tank. To refill with gasoline, you took off the cushion, unscrewed a metal fruit-jar type lid and stuck in a stick to measure the gas.

CROSSING A GAP

A gap is a makeshift gate, usually three strands of barbed wire (with red cow hair twisted around the barbs where the cows have scratched themselves) attached to a pole at each end. Passage through it is not without its dangers.

upper end of the stick attached to the wire. In the next two years I would fight many a battle of the "loop and stick."

We drove through the gap onto a private dirt road — quite good now when the weather was dry, but I was to discover it quite obnoxious in rainy seasons. The house sat at the bottom of a steep slope. Beyond that stretched the farm land, and far across to the hills must be where the river came around to form the "bend."

The house was always lonesome looking to me, and never more so than that afternoon. It had never been painted and it left the impression that it just had to hold together because so many people were depending on it for shelter. As we drove up the Hollandworths came to meet us. In addition to Mr. and Mrs. Hollandworth (Jim and Caroline), there were eight children, ranging in age from twenty to four years. Louis, the eldest, was a short roly-poly fellow; he served part time as his father's farm hand and worked parttime as a Watkins salesman. Anna was the second in line. Then like stairsteps came Oliver, George, Frieda, Eugene, David and Lillian.

Mom and Dad and Bud didn't tarry long with me. I'm sure they saw no need to prolong the misery. I watched the old "T" sail over the hump out of sight and knew I was really along. And the whole world seemed to descend on my shoulders.

I was shown to my little room. It opened out onto a porch from one door; another opened into the "separator room" where the cream separator was bolted to the floor. From the minute I spotted that piece of machinery, milk lost all food value. Each of its spouts was encased in a man's sock foot. To this day, I'm not sure why. But they were there. And all milk and cream had to pass through them into the containers thereof.

It's pretty hard — especially for a born-and-raised farm girl — to eat only non-milk foods for two years, more so during a drought and when you're one in a household of twelve people (Anna married Fred Heidbrink a little later and they lived there.) But I worked hard at it.

The only door from the separator room led into the kitchen. Along the north kitchen wall was a huge black range-type cook stove. On one side a small door opened into an enclosed stairway, and on the other side a door led into what I called "the dark room." On occasion Anna would be sent to bring out some treasure, but when she approached *the door* she always turned sideways and executed something of an invisible act. And when she came back out, the door was firmly closed almost before she got through.

The remainder of the kitchen was plain — a kitchen safe, full of heavy white everyday china and black wooden handled knives and forks; a large, plain, wooden kitchen table, covered with a blue and white oilcloth. And behind it was a bench for all of the small fry to sit on.

(A momentous discussion ensued one night over whether Oliver, 15 years old, was eligible to graduate from the bench to a split bottom chair. Oliver resolved the issue by simply getting his chair, moving his plate and ordering Louis to move over so both could sit at the end of the table.)

At the end of the kitchen looking toward the river was a sink — really a drain, because plumbing in country houses was almost unheard of.

One outside door led from the kitchen to the porch. This porch joined my room on one side; thus, my room the separator room, and the kitchen formed an "L" around the porch. For the two years that I lived there, this constituted all of the territory over which I moved.

My room was…well, small. As I entered it from the porch, it struck me as more like a large closet. It was filled with furniture — a wash stand on which stood a large white Alfred Meakin pitcher and bowl; an organ; a small bed without headboard or footboard — more like a cot than a bed; a small Franklin stove; a table, the kind we designated as a stand table. And on it were a small kerosene lamp, about half full of kerosene, and some religous tracts. Out in the center of the room were an upholstered divan and chair; they had been purchased by Anna earlier in the summer at a sale and were being stored here until after the wedding.

All of these pieces of furniture caused me to make some wrenching decisions: Was it easier to squeeze between the washstand and organ to get to the bed and then crawl from the foot to the head, or simply climb over the back of the divan and drop into bed? I found that my answer varied with my fatigue.

There was one other thing in that room that I've never seen since — a framed and glass-fronted picture called "Tree of Life." On the trunk of the tree were written the Ten Commandments, and on the branches reaching out and upward the good people were entering the pearly gates and receiving golden harps and being fitting with jeweled crowns. But, mercy, on the lower half of the picture, sinners were falling through a sort of funnel at the root of the tree into a fiery furnace where the Old Boy himself was spearing a victim with his pitchfork. In the far lower right, these poor tortured souls were being ferried across the River Styx — to enter Hades, I suppose.

I felt for them. I was certain that these were to be the most lonesome days of my life. But I was earning my own living, I told myself, and I would grow up and I would feel secure…some day. I had been taught to "bear up" under any situation, and so began the testing of my teaching.

2

At home with the sock foot separator

All summer, at regular intervals, Mama and Aunt Ida had warned me that a teacher must be prompt, so I set myself a strict schedule for arising and getting to school early.

I didn't have much preparation to make. My biggest problem was getting around the furniture. My second one was fear — fear that my watch might stop and I would be late to school. This would undoubtedly ruin my reputation forever, according to Mama.

I found out soon that I need have no worries about a time piece. On the other side of the wall and above my head (in the separator room) was a huge, ancient clock. It bonged out — faithfully — every hour of the day and night with no respect for the living or the dead.

I slept very little that first night. I was tense with fear of the unknowns of tomorrow. That stupid old clock kept me awake when fear didn't. I never heard such loud ticking. But finally light crept into my room and I came to a sitting position on the foot of my cot. (You'll remember I was blocked in from sitting on the sides.)

I looked out the window where I could see the road leading up the hill — the hill over which our Model T had disappeared yesterday afternoon, leaving me in this dreadful, forlorn place. There were trees and hills on every side — and rocks. Rocks of every size, manner and description on that hill just outside my window. I sat there so long that I thought it must be noon. But the only sound — the "bong bong" of that clock — assured me it was still only morning when its bong coincided with my watch.

Finally I heard someone stirring in the kitchen, then someone taking long steps across the porch and out on "the cement" to get a bucket of fresh water. I heard the sound of wood being laid in the big, old wood range. I figured it was safe to move around now, to wash my face and to put on my school clothes ... for my first day.

While I dressed I could hear various sounds. Then I heard Caroline going to the stairway, opening the small door and calling ...

"Louis!

"Oliver!

"George!

"Eugene!

"*Da-vid!*"

She put a special accent on *Da-vid* because he was the hardest to arouse. But he was usually the first to the table.

I could hear the rattle of knives and forks being laid out, and the clunk of heavy china being placed on the table. The big kitchen table had been moved onto the porch for more comfort in the summer heat, so I could look out my window and see this breakfast taking form. After what seemed like a year, there was a rapping on my door from the separator room and Caroline announced, "You can come out now."

I went out through the separator room, glancing again at the machine to see if I had dreamed that sock foot episode. Much to my disappointment, I hadn't.

I don't remember anything outstanding about the breakfast. There wasn't anything outstanding about any of our meals in those days. The drought had taken care of that! The standard fare was home baked bread, rather heavy but good tasting, with home made apple butter, home made butter, and coffee.

I announced when the butter was passed that I didn't often eat it. From that day forward "No butter" was going to be my motto — nothing that went through *that separator!* I also had to decide quickly that I liked black coffee.

As soon as breakfast was finished, I picked up my lunch box and went back to my room. I dabbed a bit more powder on my nose and washed my hands before letting myself out the porch door. Then I walked onto "the cement", across the slanting path to the tired old gate and across the road to a beautiful path which was a "short cut" to the school house.

Because of the warm, dry summer, the oak leaves had begun to fall early, and they crunched consolingly under my feet. They seemed friendly, trying to tell me everything was going to be all right. The world wasn't going to come to an end just because I was "hemmed in," "One road in, one road out," I kept thinking.

The beauty of that path was astonishing. Bright sunshine on this morning had brought out all of the forest life for my companionship: squirrels, both the grey and the red fox; rabbits; bluebirds and red birds, a flashy combination; woodpeckers, the common redheads and a lone, scrawny-necked pileated; doves...and mockingbirds flashing back and forth from one tree limb to another.

I had to jump over a small stream (called a "branch" in Missouri) and clamber up a bank on the other side. Immediately I started climbing the steep slope that would bring me out on the road just opposite the school house. Of course, there was a barbed wire fence to crawl through — so a decision had to be made.

I was no stranger to barbed wire fences. And with two people there's no problem. One simply puts one foot on the lower wire and holds up the second wire while the first person crawls through. Then the process is repeated on the other side of the fence. But a lone person has to decide whether he (or she, in this case!) would rather have a hole torn in his middle front torso or in his middle rear, because it's impossible to hold one wire up and one wire down and scramble through between them all at the same time.

Stooped over to protect both front and back interests, I was mastering the barbed wire when an old hoot owl suddenly startled me by demanding, "Who? Who? Who? Who?" I thought for a minute that someone was questioning my right to be there. Then I saw the shadow of the big, silent wings pass lazily over the road and slide off into the deeper part of the woods. I'm afraid I said a few unkind and uncomplimentary phrases about the nosey old bird as I crossed the road, jumped the ditch and fitted the key into the lock on the school house.

This door was on the east side of a special little vestibule built around the front door of the school. Inside it was as bare as your hand except for several large black iron clothes hooks, fastened securely into the wall. These were to hold the outer garments the children wore in the winter. Another door led into the "inner sanctum."

I stook still for a minute, just surveying my new domain. I was plenty early; in fact, too early. It was only 7:15, but there was work to do. It was a routine I was to repeat — with variations — many days of many years and places to come.

First, I raised the windows and propped them up with the saw-off broom handles provided for that purpose and left lying on the sill — one for each, of course! There were three windows along each side of the room. A blackboard was nailed on the wall along the end. In front of it sat an oldfashioned teacher's desk; on it stook a round-faced, two-legged bodacious looking alarm clock. The desks were lined up in orderly rows and fastened to the floor with large bolts. They faced the teacher's desk, and between the rows were two long recitation benches.

At the back of the room was a large, potbellied cast iron wood stove with a jacket around it. The jacket was a galvanized metal skin wrapped around the stove on an iron frame. Supposedly, its purpose was to help distribute the heat more evenly, but my experience with these things was quite opposite. I grew to dislike this one especially because the door handle had been bent until it was almost impossible to either open or close the door.

On the wall in the east corner was a glass-doored kitchen type cupboard. This was our library. I can truthfully say after all of these intervening years that I truly enjoyed the contents of that cupboard. It contained many volumes of good reading material. My thirst for reading has never been quenched, and such books as "In His Steps," "That Printer of Udells," "The Calling of Dan Mattews," and "Ten Nights in a Bar Room" helped me spend many otherwise dull hours over the next two years. These pieces, together with a small table holding a water bucket, a dipper and a tin wash pan, completed our furnishings. On this first morning, I noted the freshly scrubbed floor and the new broom which had been carefully propped in the corner by the stove, handle down. These people had all been taught thrift and letting the broom rest on the straw end was considered wasteful and extravagant, I soon found out.

In the school yard, back towards the woods, stood two outhouses — one for each sex. On the seat between the two necessary openings in each one was a Sears Roebuck Catalog. (Oh, if Sears and Montgomery Ward had only made their paper a little softer! But they really did the population of our rural areas a big favor all those years before indoor plumbing.)

Opposite the privies was the woodshed. The wood had been stored in it so many years that the dirt floor was covered with rotted chips, bits of newspaper and large pieces of bark. My eyes almost bugged out of my head when I spotted a snake skin clinging to the cracks between the boards that formed the back wall of this building. Well, so long as it was only a skin. I hoped the owner wasn't around close!

My tour of inspection finished, I returned to the center of learning. It was now 8:30 a.m. Time to RING THE BELL! This was really the test of a teacher: A good one always rang the bell "on time," according to Mom and Aunt Ida. I grabbed the bell rope hanging through a hole in the ceiling just inside the "inner sanctum," and with one eye on my watch and the other on the old "potbelly" clock sitting on my desk, I waited until they synchronized on 8:30 exactly and began to ring that bell as if there were a fire! I soon found out that I could hear the bell being rung at the Hope School across the Gasconade River, and sometimes the bells at Possum Town and Pin Oak. But the wind had to be just right for me to hear them. I'm sure, though, that they could hear the Horse Shoe Bend teacher ringing the bell that first day.

It now seemed an eon since I had crawled out of bed and sat on the foot of my bed early that morning. The ringing of the bell seemed to be the signal that now all was in order and the teacher was ready to receive her subjects. Not long after the last peal rolled out over The Bend, figures began to appear along the road. There were Emma and Myrtle Lipskoch and their brother, Virgil. They were accompanied by their cousins, Fred and Bessie Leimkuehler. Up out of the beautiful woods came the Hollandworth children — Oliver, George, Frieda, Eugene and David. Down the river road beyond the school house came the Beller children — Carl, Steele and Esther. The Bellers were the only ones not related to the three other families.

All of them were anxious to see the new schoolmarm. That first morning before starting our studies was a rather strained affair. We stood around and smiled at each other. I went to my desk and checked my watch with old "Potbelly": It showed nine o'clock. Time to begin the intellectual part of the ritual. Lunch pails were dropped unceremoniously on the floor out in the entry room. That floor was concrete and the lunches would stay cooler there.

I had my day all planned, not on paper exactly but in my mind. A good way to break the ice in any stiff situation is to sing. And since I remembered this an enjoyable experience in my own days of going to a one-room school, I passed out song books.

The book was "The Golden Book of Favorite Songs" and on that first morning we sang most of them — "Aunt Laurie," "Old Folk at Home," "The Star Spangled Banner," and a dozen more. We finished and I was collecting the golden books, wondering what to begin first, when suddenly I heard that same deep, masculine owl voice across the road hooting, "Who? Who? Who?" I thought to myself *What? What? What?* But I would soon get used to questions from both children and owls.

THE FIRST MORNING

The book was "The Golden Book of Favorite Songs" and we sang most of them — "Annie Laurie," "Old Folks at Home," "The Star Spangled Banner..."

Next came the lessons. Emma Lipskoch was what we referred to as a post graduate. She had graduated from the eighth grade the spring before, but since she wasn't going to high school, she wanted to "pick up a little more learning." Oliver Hollandworth was also a post graduate. Both were sixteen — almost as old as I. Myrtle Lipskoch and George Hollandworth were in the seventh grade, so all four of these students recited in the same class. Since the advanced books were all the same for grades 7 and 8, Carl Beller and Frieda Hollandworth were in the 6th grade, Steele Beller was in the 5th, Virgil Lipskoch in the 4th, Eugene Hollandworth and Esther Beller and Fred Leimkuehler were in the 3rd, and Bessie Leimkuehler and David were my beginners.

The morning passed quickly. It was almost gone by the time books were distributed and lessons assigned in all the various departments — Arithmetic, Language, History, Civics, Physiology and Agriculture for the older students), and Reading, Numbers and Alphabet Drill for the younger ones. And, of course, Spelling for everyone. We also had a 15-minute recess about the middle of the morning and before I knew it, it was noon and time for everyone to stop lessons and have lunch.

I was hungry, too. We all shared the tin wash pan and dried our hands by slinging them around in the warm outside air. Then we sat down anywhere we were comfortable to eat. The boys went outside and sat in the shade of the trees. Myrtle, Emma and I sat on the recitation bench to spread out lunches on my desk.

I opened the lunch box to see what Mrs. Hollandworth had prepared. There was a nice bread and butter sandwich and a bread, butter and jelly sandwich. I started to munch the bread and butter. Suddenly, the butter stuck in my throat. Oh, yes, the butter. Was I going to starve because of that cream separator?

I laid the sandwich aside and reached for the Thermos bottle. I needed a sip of something while I debated my sandwich problem. I poured the liquid into a little cup-top container and halfway to my lips I realized that liquid was milk — milk that had gone through the same process — the same separator — as the butter.

Now I was really in trouble, because I had told Myrtle and Emma when I opened the box that I was "hungry as a bear." But my appetite — at least as far as bread and butter were concerned — was gone. I discovered a small apple in the bottom of the lunch box and took small bites of it so it would last a long time. I also pretended to be eating the sandwiches because I already knew that there were no secrets in this neighborhood. Mrs. Hollandworth, Mrs. Lipskoch and Mr. Leimkuehler were all offspring of the elder Leimkuehler, so Mrs. Hollandworth would know before I got home that evening that I hadn't eaten the lunch.

During the afternoon Lesson period, it came to me that I could dispose of the milk easily. Just pour it out. But the sandwiches presented more of a problem. I didn't dare just toss them away casually. Someone would find them. But first day luck was with me. Soon after I had dismissed the children I saw this long, lean, hungry hound come bolting out of the woods. I was saved!

I didn't know then that John Fent came out of the woods two or three times a week to get his mail, but while I was gone to get the sandwiches John emerged from the trees. He, his clothes and his dog were all the same color as the dusty road. I came out of the school building calling, "Here, here, here, hound dog, here, here..."

Hound Dog loped up, snapped up the bread and butter in one gulp and nosed my hand for more. Then I saw John, and realized that I had been caught in the first criminal act of the year at Horse Shoe Bend.

Luckily, I had had a slight acquaintance with John previously. Dad had known him through their Masonic work, so he came well recommended. We stood and stared at each other for several minutes...while I wondered, Would he tell?

John broke the silence with a string of sentences: "Sure glad to meetcha. Know your dad real good. Hope you like us well enough to stay around a spell. Have a good mind to start back to school myself."

Without giving me a chance to say anything, he slipped back into the woods. I finished sweeping the floors, lowered the windows and wound old Potbelly. Then I sat down on the stone step to read for a while before I headed back through the woods to Hollandworth's ... old, gray, rundown, *slanty-floored porched house.* The adjectives tumbled out, reflecting my state of mind as much as the house.

It was getting late when I reached it. The sun was setting on another of those miserably hot, brassy days we were becoming accustomed to. As I came near the house, even in the heat it seemed cold and unfriendly — I noticed again the sagging gate. And it ended my reverie.

To open it from the outside, you grabbed hold of the top picket. Then you had to step lively because it banged shut behind you swiftly and with great force because of the old contraption rigged to it. This was an old, blue and white enamelware kettle filled with rocks and hung on a chain fastened to the gate post and the gate itself. This worked as a sort of automatic gate closer, and although it was not attractive, it certainly performed the task required of it.

Mrs. Hollandworth took my mind off the gate, calling, "Da-vid...Yo-gene...You boys come here. Da-vid...Yo-gene...it's time to go to the be---an pa--t-ch."

David and Eugene were typical small boys. They would hide from their mother and pretend not to hear. But she knew their hiding places, and she soon dispatched them to the truck garden somewhere "below the hill" to bring in green beans, tomatoes, onions and potatoes for supper.

With that chore under control, she wanted to "question me out," as she aptly termed it:

"How did the children behave?

"Was it warm in school?

"Did we sing?" And what.

"Had anyone passed the school beside the mail carrier?

"Was the clock keeping good time?

"Was Herman Lipskoch starting to plow for wheat in the big river bottom field?"

Then came the inevitable, "How was your lunch? Did it taste good?"

It was fine, I replied, and I was sure it had tasted good. But I neglected to mention to whom.

During my "questioning out," Anna had brought some fresh water into the kitchen, and I filled my enamel pitcher and retreated to my little closet room to wash my hot, dusty face. To fill in the leisure moments, I had brought my quilt pieces (the little "Flower Garden" I spent about 20 years putting together...with no two blocks alike) and I sat down on the divan in the middle of my room to stitch some pieces together. Soon Anna came to the door which opened onto the slanted porch and invited me to "Come sit awhile and cool off." She had Fred's guitar and we would strum and sing, she said.

She picked out the melody for "When the Work's All Done This Fall," and I sang along when we could hit the same key. The world didn't seem half so sad and dry and dusty as she strummed and we sang. It was long after dark when finally we were all called to supper.

The kerosene lamp was perched on a bracket attached to the window facing, but its pale little flame failed to add anything to the gloomy atmosphere. Jim (Mr. Hollandworth) always ate with Lillian on his lap — and out of the same plate. She was a sweet, pale child and very quiet like her father.

This night was a typical one, I soon found out. We never ate supper until 8:30 or 9 o'clock. That was why David and Yo-gene were just being sent to pick the beans when I came home. Even so, the beans were never done; they squeaked between your teeth. But the mealy, shook-down potatoes and the sliced tomatoes were good. I declined the milk, saying I preferred water to drink.

While we ate, a stiff little breeze came up from toward the river and blew out the lamp. We sat in darkness while Louis fumbled his way into the kitchen for a match, burned his fingers on the hot glass globe and succeeded in restoring the feeble little flame.

Soon after supper, I felt very tired so I retired to my room. I lighted my own little green glass lamp and read for a while. Then I climbed over the back of the divan and dropped into the arms of Orpheus, occasionally aware of "Big Ben" ticking and bonging on the outside wall.

I awakened much later to hear the sound of the mill dam in the distance...soothing and musical and mystical sounding. This was originally Heckman's Mill. A century or more earlier when steamboats were the region's principal means of transportation a dam had been built here at the bend in the river. (Now the building is gone — the mill machinery was purchased the same year I started teaching school and huge trucks hauled away the parts — and only a small part of the fine stone masonry is visible along the river bank.)

I had heard Mama tell about her father, Grandpa LeFevre, rafting ties on the river down from Rollins Ferry and they always "tied up the first night at Heckman's Mill." Remembering the story gave me a friendly feeling of family sharing, knowing Grandpa had been there and had listened to the same soothing sound only several years earlier than I.

As I dozed off, I was startled to hear the separator begin to grind. Sure enough, the Hollandworths were already bringing in the milk to put it through the "sock process." Well, I certainly wasn't going to let a little thing like that bother me. I had to teach school! I dozed off again and fell into a deep sleep — after a day that I was sure had had at least 36 hours in it.

Every morning for the remainder of the week I awoke early and sat on the foot of the bed gazing out at the road, the trees, the rocks and the scorched grass of that autumn. Every morning I was sure that I was going to be late to school. Every morning I carefully synchronized my watch with Old Bong-Bong on the wall of the separator room. Every morning I waited for the rap on my door and the announcement, "You can come on out now." Every morning I had to eat bread and jelly washed down with black coffee to avoid anything with milk. Every day I had to dispose of my lunch in some diplomatic, surreptitious manner. If John Fent's Old Drum didn't appear, I put the sandwiches in a bag to carry home with me over the weekend.

Along with being late to school, that was another mortal fear I carried with me always: Would the river get over the road and would I have to spend a whole weekend in Horse Shoe Bend?

137

LESSON 155

CONVERSATION LESSON

How are our homes lighted?

How were houses lighted many years ago?

How were candles made?

Describe a coal-oil lamp. How many parts has it? Of what use is the chimney?

Where does gas come from? How is it carried to a house?

How is gaslight put out? What happens if it is blown out?

How is electricity brought into homes? How are electric lamps lighted? How is the light put out?

LESSON 156

REPRODUCTION—ORAL AND WRITTEN

THE STORY OF CLYTIE

Once there was a little girl named Clytie. She had long golden hair and she always wore a green dress.

Her home was not on land. It was in the sea. She had a pretty carriage drawn by four goldfishes.

PART TWO

Bessie

3

She wouldn't say the words

Within a few weeks things sort of settled into place. I was a strict teacher. Too strict. I hardly allowed the kids to move except when I called on a class to recite. This was another carry-over from Mama and Aunt Ida (Both considered themselves past masters of the teaching arts.) You must be strict, never let the children get the "upper hand," they called it. In this settlement of mild-mannered, well disciplined Germanic descendants there was no need to fear that anyone would try to get the upper hand. But I didn't know that yet.

Bessie Leimkuehler gave me quite a time. She was enough to challenge any teacher. She was a fat, pudgy, little blonde, six years old. She never left her brother Fred's side. She wouldn't sit in a seat by herself. She wouldn't talk to me. She wouldn't say the words in her primer when I read them aloud to her. But when I would ask her if she knew them, she would nod her head affirmatively.

I tried everything in my bag of tricks — some from my high school teacher training, some from common sense — to get Bessie to say something to me. Nothing worked. Finally in desperation I enlisted Fred's help. He kept reassuring me, "Yes, ma'am, she knows her words good. She reads for us at home all the time."

Fred was a very bright boy, so I knew he knew what he was talking about. But I saw no evidence of Bessie's knowing her words "real good" at school. Bessie's mother and father each made a call to school to see if they could help, but to no avail. Bessie simply wasn't ready to vocalize. She wouldn't talk to any of the other children, either. She simply followed Fred around like a plump shadow.

The Beller children were different from the other students — more like the kind of people I'd grown up among. All three were good looking — Carl and Esther in a brown-eyed, blond pattern and Steele in a very dark-haired, dark-eyed way. He tended toward the plump side. His eyes were always merry and he wasn't bashful, so he became my favorite pupil.

I remember one recitation period when we were studying the American Colonies. I was vividly describing the plight of Roger Williams being driven out of the Massachusetts Bay Colony and making his way into Rhode Island. Our book had a small black and white drawing of Williams clutching his cloak about him as he struck out through deep snow to set up the new colony.

HOPE IN HARD TIMES

"We won't starve. There's always persimmons."

Steele looked worried as he studied the drawing with great concern. But he looked up and announced quite cheerfully, "But Roger Williams wouldn't starve, would he? There's always persimmons!"

For a long time, these were household words in my family: "We won't starve. There's always persimmons." (Writing this more than 50 years later, I wonder how many suburban children would know what a persimmon is.)

Every day had its fine moments. I didn't have to worry now about not eating my lunch. With my permission, the Lipskoch children went home for lunch since we had a full hour and they lived so near to the school. Bessie shadowed Fred and Frieda ate outside with the boys, so no one was around to notice that I ate no lunch. I could get by with this just fine until winter came and everyone would be eating inside...

I was constantly aware that winter was not far away even though the sun was still very warm, the earth was quite parched and everyone was very saving with water. I really wasn't aware of how saving, though, until Mrs. Hollandworth eyed my enamel pitcher one evening and reminded me that "Later on we might be using river water yet." She also reminded me that I needn't pull the shades in my little closet-like bedroom. "It wears them out, and besides, no one is going to bother to look in."

I knew better. "Yo-gene" and David delighted in looking in as they passed my window. Even Jim was not above a little "lookin' in" to see what I was doing when he went "on the cement" to pump a bucket of water.

Thirdly, I was "burning too much kerosene." I had begun to wonder why, when I came back after a weekend at home, my lamp would have no more kerosene in it than when I left on Friday. I decided that someone had forgotten to take the kerosene jug when the family went to the store, but after repeated failures to have a lamp full of kerosene I took charge myself.

There was a large kerosene jug at school. It was to be used to start fires, but since I didn't use it for that purpose I filled a bottle, brought it home and filled my lamp with it. I was spending most evenings after school and also after supper in my room, and I was so fond of reading and piecing quilts that I had to have light. After I solved that kerosene problem, however, I was told that it was "hard on the wick" to burn the light so long!

I spent my evenings pumping the old organ. I could — if I inhaled my body to fit — squeeze between the window and the end of the divan and seat myself on the red velvet-covered organ stool. There I sat and pumped until my legs wore out.

The only books were hymnals, but the songs were easy to play. Sometimes Mrs. Hollandworth came in and stood in the center of the room — she couldn't get any closer — and lent her alto to my soprano. Sometimes she said, "I couldn't stand it any longer. I just had to help out." I was never sure about the first part of that remark.

Grandpa and Grandma Leimkuehler lived across the pasture and over a low hill from the Hollandworths. Grandpa was sick but the family decided to celebrate the elderly couple's 55th wedding anniversary anyway. And I was to find a surprising cause for celebration myself.

The family had made no great or exciting plans, but all of the chidlren were to come home and the dinner to be served by Miss Rieka, the only Leimkuehler who had not married. Miss Rieka was "educated," having gone to high school and to the state teachers college at Warrensburg. She had taught at Horse Shoe Bend School for a few years, and was disappointed now because someone else was teaching there. She wrote long, tiring religious poems, all beginning and ending with "I shall lift up mine eyes unto the hills, from whence cometh my help." Poor Reika. Everyone in the neighborhood laughed about her eccentricities.

On the evening of the celebration when I came home from school, Anna asked me if I would like to "walk along to Gramp's" with her. I'm sure the invitation was only an excuse to let Gramp see me, but I was happy to accommodate her — and Gramp. So away we went, out the back gate, down through the rocky hog pasture — where George and Oliver playfully threw ears of corn at us from the crib. We ran quickly out of the way and soon arrived at the barbed wire fence. We lay down and rolled under it and worked out way up the rocky knoll to Gramp's house.

It was a low, rambling house, spread out along the top of the knoll. Its shutters and roof were freshly painted green and the weatherboarding was a beautiful white white. On the hill above Gramp's stood a smaller house, painted gray and looking more like a shed than a house. Their son, George, and his wife, — Fred and Bessie's parents — lived there.

Anna and I approached the kitchen quietly because Gramps might be sleeping. Our rather timit knock was answered by Grandma. Grandma was an attractive, very Germanic-looking woman — wide at the shoulders and hips. But that bulk could have been all of the clothes she wore. Her skirts went to her ankles and heavy woolen knit stockings showed where her skirts failed to meet her shoes. She wore a kerchief on her head and had a short jacket thrown over her shoulders. She was so glad to see us — and Gramp would be, too, she said. Gramp couldn't move around the way he wanted to, she explained. He got so tired of lying in bed all day. Rieka was massaging his back now. We could go in to see him soon.

Suddenly something caught my ear, something with a familiar, school-ish ring to it.

"Jack be nimble, Jack be quick, Jack jumped over the candlestick..."

Then "Once upon a time this old lady lived all alone in the forest"...And on and on.

The words were, oh, so well known. But the voice...

Grandma glanced at me. "Ack!" she said proudly. "That's *our* Bessie. She loves to read to Grandpa. That Bessie, she's the smart one!"

Somehow, wisely, I made myself not tell her that I agreed with her, halfway.

FRINGE BENEFITS
"Dey all say like you been a real good teacher."

Anna and I were ushered into the sickroom where Gramp lay propped up on his pillows. He was fully dressed in a white, starched, tucked-front shirt and dark woolen trousers. His mind was alert, and he held my right hand with his and patted it with his left hand. "I shure want to t'ank you for what you done for our Bessie," he said. "She shure does read real good. Dey all say like you been a real good teacher."

I wasn't at all sure about that, but he had given me a taste of the real fruits of teaching.

Gramp began telling me about how well he knew my Grandfather Bacon. They had served together in the Civil War. But he soon became tired after the long, exhausting day and Anna and I said goodby to him and slipped out of the cool, darkened bedroom into the kitchen.

"Fetch some plates," Grandma instructed Rieka, "and give the girls to eat."

Rieka fetched two lovely china plates from the glass-doored safe and began fishing in the big stew pot on the stove with a large, **slotted spoon**. She looked exasperated when the spoon brought up only the wing of a chicken and a few bones. Grandma siezed the spoon and spoke sharply to Rieka in German, "Ack, ack, what for you so slow."

But Grandma, too, failed to come up with anything so she turned to Anne and me and said, "Ack, ack, you poor things. You just have to go home empty yet." She laughed with that and began setting out pretty painted china cups and saucers for coffee. We drank and chatted, and it was obvious that Grandma was glad to have had all of her children home for the day.

On the way back to the Hollandworths Anna and I talked about the family and Grandma's and Gramp's big day. And I remembered Bessie. Somewhere in the middle of all this and the day was Bessie. Bessie could read! She *did* know her words "real good," like Fred said. I made up my mind: Tomorrow, I vowed, I'd begin a new lesson I'd learned for myself. I was tired of reading and re-reading "Once upon a time there lived an old lady…"

The warm sunshine continued to pour down on us, day after day cut from the same pattern: Wake up, sit on the foot of the bed, watch feverish Old Sol rise out of his hiding place and come roaring at us with all of his strength — and heat, eat a bite of breakfast, then relish the cool quiet of the beautiful walk along the path to school.

I resented Louis asking me to "ride the road around." This meant riding up the slope, opening the gap and being dropped off at the schoolhouse, so I usually tried to leave while Louis was still at the barn. I didn't want to hurt his feelings, but I didn't want to be teased about him, either. On most mornings I succeeded in giving him the slip, but I couldn't forever. His determination, I'm sure, must have served him well in selling Watkins products — and Louis was determined to haul me to school in his blue Model A Ford.

One morning I went into the kitchen to pick up my lunch and there sat Louis, grinning. "Well," he said, "just looks like we're ready to leave at the same time."

I'm sure my face dropped at least a foot. We walked across the screened-in porch, out onto the cement, and across the yard where the blue enamel stewpot held the rocks for ballast. Louis held the gate open for me…and out of nowhere Lady Luck came flying. The stiff baling wire holding the pail of rocks broke loose and caught Louis somewhere in the vicinity of the seat of his pants, accompanied by the sound of ripping cloth.

Louis, of course, was *so* embarrassed. He wouldn't turn around. But he was not to be outdone.

"Why don't you just sit in the car for a few minutes while I run in and draw this hole shut," he said.

But I wasn't about to wait for Louis to "draw the hole shut." I walked to school that beautiful morning along my beautiful path — and never enjoyed it more.

My days at school, once I arrived there, had become routine: Singing in the morning, hearing the classes recite, recess, more classes, noon and disposing of my lunch, more classes… We seemed to always have Arithmetic in the morning, followed by English and Reading, and all of the dull things, like Civil Government and Animal Husbandry in the afternoon.

One afternoon Steele Beller had to instruct me. The room was quiet and serene when a sudden loud pecking on the tin roof startled all of us. The rapid rapping nearly shook the schoolhouse. I couldn't imagine what the loud racket was, and I guess I showed my fright and puzzlement.

"Ain't nothin', Miss Bacon," Steele Beller blurted out. "Just one of them damned old red-headed woodpeckers."

If Steele hadn't explained that to me, I'd probably still be wondering.

These were the days of the Depression, and the learning equipment of this little group was less than sufficient. I had seen slates brought to school before, but only as a novelty. But these kids brought them to use. The Beller children had tablets and pencils and, my, how the other children envied them!

The Hollandworth children used all kinds of scrap paper — the reverse sides of calendar pads, the backs of handbills. Any piece of paper was precious. "Yo-gene" had a unique school tool — a thick-leaded, flat, carpenter's pencil, borrowed from Oliver. He used it all winter to write his spelling words. That pencil was Eugene's pride and joy — and the object of considerable covetousness, sinfully so, perhaps, in another day and time. But understandable then.

After school let out, I had another pattern: I swept the schoolhouse floor and sat down at my desk to read for a while and listen to old Pot Belly tick. The silence was deafening. Sometimes the friendly old hoot owl across the road would come out of hiding and "Who, Who" at me as I locked up the business for the day and headed back down the green, mossy slope, jumped the branch and crossed the road to the Hollandworth house.

4

Hard on the wick

One afternoon when I came home a little early Mrs. Hollandworth, Anna, Aunt Esther and Reika were out in the yard canning corn. Down in the corner of the yard, a huge black, iron kettle sat on the fire and water boiled up around a wooden frame in which the glass jars were placed for cooking the corn.

The process went on far into the night — cutting the corn off the cobs, stuffing the kernels into jars, sealing and cooking them in the kettle, "chunking up" the fire under the kettle, then twisting the jar lids to make sure they were sealed. This was a common practice; farmers always planted at least one acre of corn for roasting ears and canning.

There was always a pleasant air about the old house now in spite of the huge number of people occupying it. Mrs. Hollandworth kept things in reasonably good order. Of course, there wasn't much furniture to keep (It was all piled in the middle of my room), but on most days the floors were swept neatly. She didn't dare use any water for scrubbing them.

Water became so scarce that Jim and the boys rigged up a wagon with big metal barrels, and every day as soon as George and Oliver came home from school they were dispatched to the river to haul water for the hogs. About dark they would return home with the barrels about half full. The would unload one barrel "on the cement" for dishwater and laundry.

In the two years I boarded there I never saw a "regular wash" being done. Sometimes I saw Jim, with a plumber's plunger, loosening the soil in a pair or two of blue jeans which had soaked overnight in a bucket behind the cook stove. Occasionally Mrs. Hollandworth would explain that Jim would soon have to wash out the necessary pieces.

Standing and using the plunger, I guess, didn't hurt Jim. But there seemed to be lots of work Jim couldn't do. Mrs. Hollandworth referred to "that what had happened to Jim", and she divided time into two periods — before "that what had happened to Jim" and after "that what had happened to Jim." But beyond that I never knew what it was "that had happened to Jim."

The evening meals continued to be principally bread, potatoes, green beans, and sometimes a baked chicken with dressing. But there were also some dishes foreign to me.

There was a concoction of stale bread crumbs dipped in beaten eggs and seasoned with salt and pepper and fried in bacon grease.

There was turnip kraut — turnips sliced thin and soured in a stone jar, like souring cabbage for kraut.

There was milk soup. This was simply sweet milk scalded, sweetened slightly, with a handful of barley or rice added. I steered away from this for a long time, but finally seeing that the milk wasn't fatal to any of the Hollandworths, I began eating a bite or two of it.

I simply couldn't eat many of these things, and one evening Mrs. Hollandworth pointedly asked me what I *could* eat. I'm sure I didn't do a very good job of fooling her.

I had always been very fond of potato soup. We made it frequently at home. We simply boiled potatoes until they were well done, removed them from the water and mashed them with cream and butter until they were fluffy. Then we put them back in the potato water, added rich sweet milk, salt, pepper and some finely diced onions and, behold, we had a dish fit for a king!

I supposed everyone made potato soup the same way., And, smart me, I forgot about the milk. So I told Mrs. Hollandworth that I like potato soup better than anything. She looked rather surprised and a day or so later I found out why. Mrs. Hollandworth's potato soup was cubed potatoes, cooked in water and bacon grease with turnips and green beans added. Backing away from that took some explaining!

Often she invited me to help with the household chores. "Now, maybe just to be different," she would say, "You'd like to make supper for us all."

I wasn't about to take that on — not with her charging me half of my salary for board.

In the evening I usually read or sewed by the light of the little green class lamp as I sat in my closet-size bedroom. When I lifted my eyes there was always the "Tree of Life" staring down at me from its place of honor above the door.

Sometimes Anna would bring her embroidery and sit with me. She was near my age and fun to be with. She had been away from home most of the last year caring for an elderly Mrs. Poehle who lived across the river. This had educated Anna somewhat; she knew that not all people lived as her folks lived. Her mother seemed glad that Anna was going to marry Fred and have a "chance at better ways of livin'." Sometimes Anna and I would sing and play the organ. That always brought Mrs. Hollandworth from the kitchen — and always with the same remark: "I couldn't stand it any longer. I just had to help out."

On many evenings all of the neighbors gathered in one of the homes to sing. They took this singing seriously and worked at it. Mrs. Hollandworth was always "working up a special." And it mattered not a whit what the other person sang because she or he was never heard, anyway. On special occasions, Mrs. Hollandworth would forsake her alto and announce, "I'll take the lead part" on account of Anna or Rieka — or whoever — might break down and "We want the *lead* to come through."

These singings were Herman Lipskoch's idea of an evening well spent, too. How he loved to sing! Everyone worked for Herman's approval. And if Herman said it was good, believe me, it was good. Or at least loud. For my part, it seemed that Herman equated good with volume.

Wherever we were Mrs. Hollandworth usually played the organ. Herman took his place to her right, the song books were passed around...and all Hell tore loose. (Even the redheaded woodpecker couldn't make more racket.)

One hymn always amused me. It was called "I Shall Not Be Moved" and it began like this:

"Just like a tree that's planted by the water, I shall not be moved." The accent was on the *not*.

Then came the chorus:

"I shall not be, I shall not be moved. I shall not be, I shall not be moved. Just like a tree that's planted by the water, I shall not be moved."

We always sang several verses of this song, and the nearer we came to the end, the faster Mrs. Hollandworth jumped and played — and the faster Herman beat the time and patted his foot. Herman's front teeth were gold, and the flame from the coal oil lamp reflected on them, shooting little flecks of light as he opened and closed his lips.

When we finally came to the end of a hymn, Herman would praise all of us: "The time was just great. You did a fine job keeping up." Then he would sit down in a split bottom chair to catch his breath before he and Mrs. Hollandworth started on another song.

Herman was a fine farmer and a wonderful provider for his large family. On these singings, he always wore a suit of matching buff-colored cotton trousers and shirt. The shirt sleeves were held in place above the elbow by elastic sleeve bands — old-fashioned even then. I never saw him without these accessories, and when he and Mrs. Hollandworth sang a "special" he really dressed up by adding a red necktie.

Jim Hollandworth always went along to these singings, but he never ventured near the organ. He always sat in the kitchen holding Lillian on his lap and smoking his pipe. The two older Lipskoch boys, Walter and Harvey, joined in the music making. Walter played the banjo and Fred Heidbrink added his guitar on the occasions when he would "walk along" with us to be with Anna. Some of the popular songs were actually recognizable when those two tried their luck at harmony.

Mrs. Hollandworth always worried about her younger children's lack of musical ability. "Looks as if they just don't take after me when it comes to singing," she would say. "Well, I guess some of them have to be like Jim. Ack! Ack!"

We would sing everything in the hymnal. Then Anna would take over the organ and Mrs. Hollandworth and Herman would stand up to sing a special. Afterwards, we would take ourselves home. By now I had learned to let the waters of the mill dam put me to sleep. The constant sound of the rushing water had a soothing quality about it that made it a powerful sedative for me.

5

Friday, the delightful day

The singings usually were Thursday night affairs. Then came Friday, by far the most delightful day in the week for me: I was either going home for the weekend or heading over to Uncle John's and Aunt Ida's home. Their farm was directly across the river from the schoolhouse, but when they came for me they drove around the road by way of Mt. Sterling.

At times during the week I made myself miserable for no good reason. I would arrive at school early, open the windows to air and cool the building. Then I would go to the back of the room and stare into the distance. First, I would pick out Uncle John's house, a glossy white, then the big red barn on top of the hill, and another metal-covered barn at the foot of the hill. This made me so homesick I was really ill.

But on Friday the nausea left me. I sang louder. I could reach the upper octave "F" in the "Star Spangled Banner" without half trying. I didn't even notice the odor of Herman Lipskoch's pigs in the nearby pen.

I led the children through Fridays with a hop, skip and a jump. But I never dared to dismiss early. This ruined a beginning pedagogue's reputation. One never, never dismissed early, Mama said, so even if Uncle John and Aunt Ida arrived a few minutes before four o'clock, I went right on with my subject matter. Sometimes we passed out the "Book of Golden Songs" and sang again. This always drew Uncle John from the front seat of the four-door Chevrolet sedan into the schoolhouse--especially when we sang "Long, Long Ago." He had a musical bass voice and the kids loved to hear him sing.

Finally old Pot Belly rolled his hands around to exactly four o'clock. I gave the dismissal sign and almost magically the kids were out of sight. I shut the windows, locked the door (safeguarding the sandwiches for the dogs) and we were on our way. Oh, happy day! Away we went--along the bluff road, across Pin Oak Creek, out the flat county road to the highway. We stopped at the Mt. Sterling Store for a soda or an ice cream cone, checked the car tires, crossed the bridge, left the highway and finally came to the grove of trees leading to the house. And the crunch of loose gravel on the driveway told me: We were home! I always felt as much at home with Uncle John and Aunt Ida as I did with Mom and Dad. Uncle John was Dad's oldest brother. He and Aunt Ida had no children, so all of the nieces and nephews loved to go there--to get a little special attention, I suppose.

When I opened the gate, their dog, Jeff, almost knocked me down. He was always so wiggly glad to see us return. And Tom and Puss vied for attention in their catty ways. Tom was a huge, gray and white cat, lazy as all get-out. He preferred to sit on the flat top of a gate post by the chicken yard and growl at Puss. Puss and Tom fit Uncle John and Aunt Ida perfectly. They never produced offspring either. Aunt Ida always said they were modern: I think she meant the felines.

Every Friday there was the same. By the time we arrived dusk had fallen so Uncle John hurried away to do the chores. He always whistled as he worked, so it was easy to locate him. When we didn't hear his whistling, we knew he had gone to the lower barn below the hill to feed the calves. His last chore was to milk "Old Jers" and separate the milk, so when we heard his whistling at the big red barn, Aunt Ida trotted out with her buckets and a damp wash rag to wipe Jers's bag. Soon she came back to the house with two big buckets of fresh, warm, foamy milk. Uncle John even whistled as he worked up a head of steam turning the milk through the big, black De Laval separator. (And it didn't have a sock foot tied over its spout!)

After the chores, we began to relax. Uncle John got his glasses and the St. Louis *Globe-Democrat* and pulled his wicker rocker, covered with flowered blue and red cretonne, under the light in the center of the kitchen. The light was one bulb hanging on a cord from the ceiling and powered by a Delco plant in the basement. While he read the paper, Aunt Ida set out the supper appointments. I was sent to the cellar room to get cool milk while she cut slices of home made bread and chunks of store-bought cheese. Or country ham, or something else equally good.

They always had a huge mold of country butter. Both Uncle John and Aunt Ida were especially fond of it. They cut great hunks of it from the mold and spread it thickly on their bread--especially when we came to the strawberry preserves, a staple on Aunt Ida's table.

She kept a crock full of sweet cream, too, which she spooned into the bottom of glasses in copious quantities before she filled them with separated milk for drinking. When she was satisfied that everything was ready, we put Grandma Bacon's china plates on the table, set the glasses of milk at each plate and began the most pleasant part of all. Eating.

I remember, often as we sat there, watching the last faint rays of an autumn sun filtering through the grove and throwing shadows of the window frames on the east wall of the kitchen. This big, clean kitchen with its dark green enameled range, its huge dining table in the center, a small sink and cook table meant security to me. I was never worried or afraid of anything when I was there. Even Horse Shoe Bend was far, far away. It would not take on real proportions until Monday morning.

Bedtime came early on the farm. As soon as the dishes were done (the separator was covered with a clean, white cloth to be washed in the morning) and Uncle John had read all of the news in his *Globe*, we retired. Or headed toward bed. Sometimes visiting prolonged the process.

Often I entertained them all evening with funny incidents from Horse Shoe Bend. Or if the big Atwater-Kent radio was in working order, we sat in the sitting room and listened to the Friday night Old Fiddlers' Contest from Jefferson City.

THE RADIO

Uncle John was wholly to blame when there wasn't any 'good speakin' on it.

Uncle John managed the radio. Aunt Ida seemed somewhat awed by it, but that didn't keep her from directing Uncle John to "Get some good speaking" on it. And she acted as if he were wholly to blame when no "good speaking" was on.

I've never seen another radio like that one. The tubes fit on top of a long polished board which held the whole shebang. The little knob, pulled straight up, turned it on. And many little red and green-covered wires connected the various exposed necessary mechanisms. The table on which it sat was especially made for the contraption, and the battery for it was concealed in a compartment below. I'm sure that Uncle John and Aunt Ida were very proud of this newfangled radio-table combination. And it was pretty, but I don't ever remember hearing anything much out of it--not even any "good speaking." I do remember Uncle John putting the battery "on to charge" when he ran the Delco about once every two weeks.

All of us slept upstairs in the room over the kitchen. This was a cozy "boudoir," sparsely furnished with two beds, an old marble-topped dresser, an open closet (with a cretonne curtain hung in front to keep out dust), and one split-bottom chair by Aunt Ida's side of the bed. She had asthma and frequently sat up all night on the side of the bed. Often in the middle of the night if I awoke I saw her, fighting for breath with her head leaned on the back of a chair as it sat in front of her.

Sleep came quickly--and luxuriously--in those young days. I never had to count sheep or hypnotize myself to lose consciousness. The bed was wonderful--a featherbed under me and fine lightweight covers over me, a down pillow under my head, no furniture to crawl over and around and then drop over a cliff to get to bed.

I also indulged in the luxury of sleeping just a little later in the morning. Aunt Ida and Uncle John got up early, had their good strong coffee with sugar and the thickest of Old Jers's yellow Jersey cream stirred into it. Aunt Ida prepared the coffee cups by dipping the cream into the cup before she poured the coffee on top of it.

I felt as if I were watching an artist mix his paints for a masterpiece: Aunt Ida bent over the pan of cream with a fine silver berry spoon and skimmed off only the very topmost layer of yellow gold cream into each large cup. Then she went to the range and carefully picked up the big gray enameled coffee pot. Tipping it most carefully so as not to disturb the grounds, she poured the coffee with her right hand and stirred the cream into it with her left. When the concoction was exactly the right color she put the coffee pot back on the stove and usually added a little more water, because the "second cup doesn't need to be so strong."

This work of art, with Aunt Ida's French toast, was our usual breakfast. She made the French toast from more huge, thick slices of home made bread dipped in egg beaten well, sweetened slightly with a pinch of salt and rich milk added. She beat all of this together to mix it well, then she dipped the bread slices in it, and let them soak up some of the mixture before she put them in a skillet to fry--in butter which had been melting and browning while she prepared the batter. She fried each slice until it was brown, turned it with a spatula and browned the other side. With her strawberry or peach preserves, this was simply ambrosia.

After breakfast they went outside to do the usual farm chores--water and feed the chickens, feed Jim Tom and Old Bell, the mules, and, of course, milk. If Uncle John had his fishing lines set, he got up extra early and trotted down to the river to see if he had "anything" on his hooks. "Anything" was the ultimate in positive thinking, because most of the time "anything" wasn't on his hooks.

I remember how mad he became when turtles ate all of his bait or if he caught a gar. These were "trash" fish, considered highly inedible by people who knew good fish, so he carried the gar to the hog pen.

One morning, I remember, I came down to breakfast and found a plate of beautiful, perfectly browned fish ready for me. Uncle John and Aunt Ida kept making trips through the kitchen and looking wise as I ate...and they kept inquiring how I liked the fish. I liked it just fine. Much later they informed me, with much delight, that I had eaten gar.

Those Saturdays were straight from Heaven. Aunt Ida always saved little errands and chores for me to do. She and Uncle John made me think I did them better than anyone else--and my ego soared. I put my tiniest stitches into Uncle John's work socks as I darned them because he said my stitches didn't hurt his feet and Aunt Ida's did. I hemmed dish towels and table cloths for Aunt Ida and

pillow shams for her mother (Lanteen Benson). I churned the buttermilk, mopped the kitchen floor, swept the walks, watered the flowers. And I made sure I had time left over to scratch the cats' bellies and make them wrap themselves around my hand as we sat on the cement cistern block and soaked up the late afternoon sunshine.

Aunt Ida was a meticulous housekeeper. Not having a family, everything she placed "stayed put." Everything was so neat and clean I almost ached. I loved my visits there, but being so orderly and precise was difficult for me. I went upstairs to comb my hair, then walked carefully downstairs, across the porch and outside to brush my shoulders. I washed my hands a hundred times a day if I helped in the kitchen, as I often did.

Aunt Ida liked my pie crust, so almost every Sunday morning we made pies. I made the crust and put them in the pans. She made the fillings--usually gooseberry, apple, peach or custard. She liked them thick and fat with lots of filling. If they boiled out into the oven, she told me I didn't stick the two crusts together tightly enough.

DEPRESSION DELIGHTS

For Uncle John, it had to be Coolidge Custard. Or Aunt Ida's Old Black Cake.

We usually had a little crust left over; this we used for Uncle John's favorite, "Coolidge Custard." My mother and Aunt Stella (Bacon) judged it not really good custard. But Uncle John wouldn't eat a bite of anybody's custard unless he was definitely assured it was "Coolidge Custard." Then the world became rosy and gay for him.

"Oh, fine pie. Mighty fine pie. Can't be beat, that Coolidge Custard." His comments were always hearty and predictable. "I was never very long on apple pie," he would add. But at Aunt Ida's or at Mom's there was never just one kind of pie. For lovers of custard or apple, there was always a second or third choice because pie was the one dessert everyone liked.

Uncle John and Aunt Ida frequently had company for Sunday dinner. Often Mom and Dad and the boys came to visit. Mama and Aunt Ida were both of French descent; Mama was a LeFevre and Aunt Ida was a Benson but her mother was a very Frenchy Maire. Sometimes Uel and Pearl Benson, Aunt Ida's youngest brother, their daughter, Hope, and Mrs. Lanteen Benson came over from Linn to spend the day. These big get-togethers were highlights of my young life.

Aunt Ida didn't like unexpected company, so dates were set up ahead of time. This suited the younger people fine; we knew we could expect her typical table-groaning dinner. It usually consisted of her specialty: Smothered chicken, mashed Irish potatoes, sweet potatoes, green beans or stewed tomatoes, cottage cheese, home baked bread, butter, pickles, peach preserves, strawberry jam...And for dessert she set out pies, or what she called her "old black cake."

This was a reddish, chocolate cake, and I can still see her making it: She cooked the eggs, sugar and shortening together with the chocolate beforehand and let it cool thoroughly before she added the baking powder, flour, milk, flavoring and so on. After the layers were baked and cooked, she went to the cellar and skimmed off the thickest of the rich cream from the big crock. This she whipped to just one beat short of butter. She spread the whipped cream on the layers as thick as it would hold, then she sliced bananas over the cream between the layers and on the top to finish the job. And she usually served it with a Jello fruit salad--also topped with whipped cream. The adults always helped themselves to more cream for their coffee, but we young people drank "Old Jers's" milk--only half cream!

Once, I recall, while we were eating this dessert Uel Benson remarked that the cream just "set the whole thing off." In a few minutes Dad called for the pitcher of rich coffee cream and proceeded to pour unwhipped cream on top of his whipped cream. "Well, Uel," he explained, "you said the cream just set it off, so I thought I'd just try some."

I was so embarrassed. But maybe this will show the future generations of Bacons why they are all so fond of milk and anything made from it.

The afternoons were spent visiting. People didn't see other people everyday in those Depression times, so anything new in the family or in the various neighborhoods was thoroughly discussed. There was no gossip; no one was criticized; sometimes funny incidents were related. Aunt Ida was particularly good at these-- always telling things on herself.

While the women visited, Dad and Uncle John, Uel and the boys went "prospecting", as they called their walk over the farm. I never knew two men who loved the soil and what it grew as much as Dad and Uncle John. It was the same wherever they were: They inspected everything--the grass, the trees, the prospects for the corn, the wheat, the cattle, the need for rain, how deep the dry soil went. And when they came to the house they reported to Mom and Aunt Ida what they had found.

Sometimes the report was sad, like this fall of '32. Corn, even in the river bottom, was hardly worth gathering; grains were uneven and thin on the ears and most ears were small and crooked. If they prospected in the spring or early summer, they looked over the blackberry or gooseberry crop and found where the first and largest berries grew so Mom and Aunt Ida didn't have to hunt for the "best pickin'" place. In early summer of a good crop year, they brought in heads of the wheat stalks to show the size of the grains. I suppose this was a kind of masculine pride in knowing the farm crops would provide food for the family and the animals. And there was a direct connection to feeding the family, because we hauled our wheat to mill in those days to have our flour ground.

After the inspection tour was ended and the crop prospects fully discussed, Dad rolled his eyes toward the car parked on the gravel drive and said, "Jennie, better get your trottin' harness on. It's time we were headin' for home."

That meant the weekend was about over for me. After Mom and Dad and the boys were gone, I felt so lonely. Sunday always gave me a queer feeling, anyway. It was a Holy Day, and even though you worked some, it was light work and there was time to concentrate on the beauty of nature, whether it was dry and brown or green and moist. Usually as those Sunday afternoons ended, while Uncle John and Aunt Ida left the house to do the chores, I sat on the front porch and read until darkness blurred the words.

Sunday night suppers were like a light lunch, with leftovers "set out" from the refrigerator or uncovered from their noontime midday "puttin' away" and grouped in the middle of the table. Then we went to bed "with the chickens" because we had to roll out early Monday morning to get to Horse Shoe Bend on time.

Monday mornings were terrible for me. The taste of Sunday was still fresh in my mouth. But I didn't complain. I always had that almighty dollar in the back of my head. Soon a month would be gone and that $40 would be mine. Or so I thought.

On those mornings Uncle John got up earlier than usual--even for him--and hurried with his milking. Aunt Ida always fixed a big breakfast--ham and eggs, French toast and coffee. Just one thing was missing--my appetite. I simply couldn't eat while contemplating another week in the Bend. Aunt Ida always fixed a huge lunch for me. (This later got me into trouble with Mrs. Hollandworth.) I counted on the usual big slices of buttered home made bread, cold meat, pickles, with fruit and slices of leftover pie or cake. Sometimes this sumptuous fare lasted me for two or three days, with careful nurturing.

With breakfast finished, Uncle John brought the car from the garage. Aunt Ida got in the front seat with him. I sat in the back, holding onto my precious lunch and my clean clothes packed in a small, flat cardboard box, and away we went. The drive was beautiful, even in a dry year when the dust lay so thick on the goldenrod that the bloom and the foliage all looked grayish green.

Some strangers had come into the Bend during the first month, finding their way in over newly-finished Highway 50. Bill and Clarence Riechert from Tennessee (They pronounced it "Dennezzee.") had married sisters (also from "Dennezzee") and had bought a small tract of wooded land from John Topel on the west side of the main road just past the Pin Oak Creek crossing. They cleared out the trees and built three small log cabins. The wives' parents, Mr. and Mrs. Williamson, came along with them and occupied the third cabin.

The young husbands were hard workers. They cut and sawed wood into fireplace and stove lengths and sold it in town and they worked for farmers in the neighborhood. But few farmers could hire help then, and all of us wondered how they could get along. I'm sure I stared at those cabins as we drove past, because I had never seen people living in that kind of rough house.

Uncle John always drove up on the school ground with a flourish when we arrived. More accustomed to mules, he never was a good driver of cars. I never was sure where he was going to stop. He always drove at the same speed and never slowed down one iota before swinging up onto the bank and into the school yard. The results of his feat were always the same: He threw Aunt Ida up against the dashboard and me against the top of the car.

This brought Aunt Ida to life. (She usually slept all the way.) "John Bacon," she yelled, "What's the matter with you? You're going to turn this thing bottom side up and kill us all yet."

She always made Uncle John go in the schoolhouse with me and see that everything was all right. And in the winter he started the fire for me. Then we carefully synchronized our watches and clocks with old Pot Belly and they were gone. And I was left with my nauseous feeling and my memories of a lovely weekend--and wondering when the rewards of this lofty calling of teaching would overcome the tug of home and family.

By the time I dusted the room and got my lesson plan book in order, the children began to appear, with Fred and his shadow, Bessie, appearing last of all. And remembering the lesson I'd learned at Gramps and Grandma Leimkuehlers' celebration, I stopped reading--over and over--"with" Bessie. I stood in the back of the room while Bessie read her lesson to Fred.

I learned other things, too. I learned not to jump out of my skin when the woodpecker sat up his woodchopping block on the roof. I curbed my laughter, also. These kids thought school was a serious matter and there must be something amiss with a teacher who laughed--especially with my gusto. I even learned to leave the window closed on the east side near my desk so the pig odor didn't drift into the room directly under my nose.

I discovered there's nothing like teaching to teach a teacher things she should have known before she started to teach.

As the end of the fourth week approached, my excitement heightened: I would have $40 and half of it would be mine. On the Friday payday Mrs. Hollandworth asked me for the $20 board money in full. In wondered where she thought I'd get $20 before I got my warrant from the school board. I hadn't had one red cent I could call my own in my whole life, so I explained to her that if I got my warrant from the board, I could have the $20 for her on Monday.

That put her plainly out of sorts. She wanted to "go to town" on Saturday. After much planning and maneuvering, we decided to meet at Mt. Sterling on Friday evening. I'd get my warrant cashed and she could claim her $20 board money, all in one huge financial process.

I made one big purchase with my money--a pair of scissors. I had been borrowing Mrs. Hollandworth's scissors--lent to me grudgingly--to cut quilt blocks. Now I had a pair of my own; they cost 75 cents at the Mt. Sterling store, and I still have them, a souvenir of my first warrant.

I also ordered a box of Houbigant face powder from Sears & Roebuck, along with a cheap brand of cold cream which came packed in a large one-pound size glass jar. Aunt Ida thereafter called it my "pink lard." (It was tinted a delicate pink.) I treasured these purchases greatly and the boxes made my little shed-like bedroom a bit brighter.

Autumn was fading--or drying away. No rain had fallen and we crunched the dead brown leaves under our feet as we walked to and from school. Water became an even more precious commodity. The boys dreaded the daily hauling of barrels of water from the river and any water drawn from the cistern on the cement was practically rationed.

The evenings were too cool now to eat on the porch so the big kitchen table was moved inside. The last of the truck patch vegetables were brought up and stacked on the porch. One afternoon when I came home Anna and her mother were slicing green beans crosswise to make what they called sour Schnitzel beans. Another day they were making sandwich spread--a thick, yellow base with green beans and pickles diced into it. I don't remember ever eating any of this. It seemed as if everything they cooked ended up with green beans in it and in those days I wasn't especially fond of them.

The cool evenings called for a fire in my little Franklin stove. Mrs. Hollandworth waited until I came home each day to start the fire. The fire compartment was so small that the wood had to be split, or use small round sticks. Above the fire box was an oven-like affair with two doors opening to each side from center. It was a one-of-a-kind stove to me; I never saw anything like it before nor since.

Wood was rationed, too. Each evening about one good armload would be placed in the small woodbox beside the stove. There was never a surplus of nice, split, dry sticks such as we always had at home. Mrs. Hollandworth must have split the wood herself, because often at night after I'd gone to bed (because I'd burned up my supply of wood) I heard the rhythmical whack of an axe chipping a block or stump into stove-size pieces. I know Jim didn't split it. Out my window and across the porch into the kitchen I could see him sitting at the end of the table, holding Lillian on his lap and pulling at his pipe.

For some time I sensed that Fred and Anna were making plans for their wedding. I sensed, too, that I wasn't supposed to know this. Not that either Fred or Anna were secretive about it, but Mrs. Hollandworth didn't want "the others" to know. They--her brothers and sisters--were "too nosey." In a family where everybody could see everybody else just by looking out the window--and with only one entrance and exit in use--I couldn't see how anything could be very secretive.

I did notice more activity going on, with much opening and careful closing of the door to the "dark room." But the clincher was being asked to help tack a comfort.

We ate supper early that evening. The quilting frames were brought down from upstairs and laid on the kitchen floor. The lining was stitched in with heavy twine binding it to the frame. Wool which had been washed and carded was spread evenly in a cheesecloth covering and laid on the lining. Over this was placed the bright diamond pattern print for the top.

It doesn't take long to tack a comfort when many hands work at it. We soon finished and were cutting the twine which had held the material while we were tacking when we discovered that Reika had caught her dress in the tacks she had made. Before we knew what had happened, we were shaking our scraps of threads off the comfort when lo and behold, Reika's skirt was up around her waist and she stood horrified in our midst while we all stared at her all stitched up in the center of the comfort and her dress.

Fred and Anna planned to live in the Heckman Mill house by the dam. Water kept them from marrying sooner. They were waiting for rain or snow. Nobody had lived there for several years and they had cleaned the cistern sometime earlier and now had no water for household use.

One morning long before daybreak, I was sitting on the bed in my usual early morning station when I noticed much stirring in the kitchen. This was unusual. I watched the goings-on through my porch window, looking directly into the kitchen.

Jim sat, as usual, in his appointed place, holding his pipe. Before long I heard soft footsteps on the squeaky porch floor, the screen door squawked on the door step and I looked out toward the road. There was Anna--all fitted out in her white wedding finery striding quickly along the cement, gliding through the gate with the blue enamel pot holding the rocks. Louis was already in the car. He released the clutch and away they went, grinding up the steep slope and over the hill out of sight.

At breakfast and all day at school I had to think twice before I said anything because I wasn't supposed "to know."

THE "LINE FENCE" CALL

"Ach, ach, now let it go in "German."

There were other things I wasn't supposed to know, either, things I found out via the telephone--sort of. The phone hung in the separator room on the same wall with old Bong-Bong. I suppose it was a convenience, in emergencies at least, but these people were so convinced that everybody else was listening in on their conversations that they only used the telephone to make appointments.

These confabs were always held at the "line fence." If the two sisters, Mrs. Hollandworth and Mrs. Lipskoch, wanted to talk over something that they didn't want Rieka or George's wife, Esther, to hear, she would give the other one a ring and say, "Meet me at the line fence in ten minutes."

Nothing made Mrs. Hollardworth move quite so quickly as a call to the "line fence." These sessions generally were held in the evening, sometimes late. I'd hear the phone ring and know that someone was calling an exclusive meeting.

I suspected that I was the reason for some of them because when Mrs. Hollandworth was really bogged down in work and couldn't attend a line fence get-together, she'd say, "Ack, ack. Now, let it go in German!" Then she would reply in German.

She didn't know that I could understand everything she was saying. But that remained my secret for two years. I didn't want to miss anything, either!

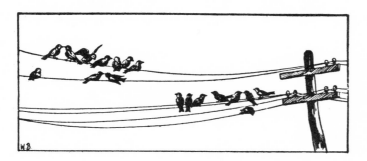

After Fred and Anna's wedding there were twelve of us at the table, numbers and noise enough to qualify as a public gathering. But the dark room was more secretive than ever. It was occupied by the newlyweds only.

The weather turned really cold and in the mornings I had no fire in my bedroom. I climbed out of bed shivering, stumbled around the extra furniture and dressed as quickly as possible. I washed my face and hands in one quick, icy swipe, then sat down on the end of the bed again to await the tap on my door. When it came, I dashed across the separator room and into the big, bare, but warm kitchen.

In the winter we usually had cornbread for breakfast. It was baked in a huge, rectangular tin pan and usually it was sitting in a warm place on the back of the big black range awaiting the finishing touches of its accompanying dish. This usually was home made sausage, crumbled very fine and browned--somewhat--in a big iron skillet. When it was browned sufficiently, water was poured over it and allowed to come to a boil. This was poured into a large ironstone bowl, a huge iron spoon was placed in the bowl and breakfast was served.

The pieces of cornbread were more than enough for me. Everyone took a piece and cut it carefully sideways, thus doubling the number of slices on his plate.

Oliver was very exacting about this operation. He would lean his head far to one side so his eyes were almost on a level with his plate and slice through the bread very deliberately.

After this the gravy dipping process began. Beginning with Jim, it proceeded around the table as each person tipped the bowl on edge and strained the fried sausage crumbles out of the bottom of the bowl. This was spread evenly around over the cornbread. Then the knife and fork were brought into use; the fork was to hold the bread in place and the knife did all of the cutting and carrying to the mouth.

I had been taught to use my fork for the latter process, but I felt out of place and embarrassed when David was reproved for trying to follow my example. He dropped a couple of wedges off his fork onto the floor and Mr. Hollandworth said, rather softly, "Davie, ain't you got no knife?"

David also held the gravy dish longer than anyone else. And to this day when I try to picture him, I always see him with that ironstone bowl and that big iron spoon and he is always fishing for another crumble of sausage.

Early in the winter a revival was held at the Mt. Sterling Baptist Church. At first when the services were announced I had no intention of lending my presence to the nightly meetings, but I soon found my desires subjugated to the family tradition. Mrs. Hollandworth "had to go" to either play the organ or "sing the lead," whichever she felt was most necessary. Jim "had" to drive the car. He simply reveled in this necessity, his face aglow when Louis gave him permission to take the car and go. The younger fry were sort of divided up--sometimes George and Frieda would be elected to attend, sometimes David and Eugene, but never all of them together.

Supper was served a little earlier than usual, and as soon as the last crumb was swallowed we put on our coats, Mrs. Hollandworth grabbed her song book because she was always singing a "special" and away we'd go. Jim bent over the steering wheel as if his life depended on getting Mrs. Hollandworth to the church on time. But when he delivered all of us, his duty ended. He curled up on the front seat of the car and slept until we came trooping out after all of the singing and shouting were over.

These revivals were tremendously overpowering. The minister preached fire and brimstone and the members would sing and pray and respond with a loud "Amen" when he uttered a particularly fine bit of Biblical wisdom. People who were not members of that church--or any other--occasionally attended. I always felt sorry for them because Hell took on such hideous proportions. Each night it became warmer and less attractive. After two weeks the minister called the deacons together to ask their advice: Do you think "So and So" is about ready to "capitulate"? If so, perhaps we should continue another week. Usually Mrs. Hollandworth and Herman Lipskoch voted to go on another week; at least it gave them a chance to work up another special.

School suffered during these nightly adventures, but Mrs. Hollandworth gave me no chance to stay home. Nor the kids. Frieda was especially tired. Since her mother was so wrapped up in the church going and the specials, the children had more home chores to do. Supper dishes were often left to be done when we return-ed home.

About this time Frieda discovered a nook to stand in and how to sleep there. The space between the separator and the sewing machine fitted her just right; the separator served as a prop and there she stood, sound asleep. At school, too, while one class recited, I looked around to find Frieda sound asleep with her head on the desk.

Mrs. Hollandworth led in prayer at least once per evening during the whole revival. Her voice came through loud and clear, even though her poorly fitting dentures caused her to lisp slightly while the moisture trickled from the corners of her mouth and into the wrinkles leading away from her lower lip.

Sometimes she hinted broadly that I should pray. "Just cut right in," she said. "Don't wait to be called on."

I lived in mortal fear for several days that she would call on me. Finally I got up enough nerve one evening when she was grilling me to tell her that if she ever called on me, I'd pretend not to hear. Then she told me to listen carefully when Johnie Brown Branson prayed. Johnie Brown's prayers, she said, "just lift you right into Heaven," she said.

This tickled Dad and Uncle John almost to helpless laughter. They had grown up with Johnie Brown Branson. They knew him especially for his "taking ways." He had stolen a complete set of harness from Dad when he worked for us. And Mrs. Hollandworth never understood why Johnie didn't attend those revivals the years I did. I wonder if the Bacon harness had anything to do with it.

At long last the revival was over and we settled into the routine of a long winter. I worried constantly that a big rain would fall and I'd have to spend a weekend "cooped up" in my shed bedroom, because any extra water in Pin Oak Creek made it impossible to cross. Uncle John kept telling me he could always come for me in his "skiff" and "set me across" the river again on Monday morning. But this didn't allay my fears one bit. Often I stood on the bluff above the river and wondered how in the world I could get through the brambles and briars to the water's edge. Thank goodness, I never had to find out.

With very little rain falling, Fred and Anna continued living at home, but since Anna was a married woman her mother put fewer chores on Anna's list. Almost every evening she and Fred came into my room and we would play the organ and sing. Fred would "second" on the guitar. Louis, too, often joined us after he figured up his Watkins sales for the day.

I soon realized that the singing was only a ruse to use me as a fourth partner in a game of euchre. The Horse Shoe Bend Baptists strongly opposed card playing of any kind. Fred, however, wasn't a Baptist and Anna thought it was a huge joke to pull this card playing over on her mother. Lacking a proper card table, we used the organ stool, and when the kerosene lamp ran out of oil we lighted Fred's old "coon huntin' " lantern and went right on playing euchre.

Sometimes Harvey and Walter Lipskoch or Ben Ritter, a cousin from Owensville, dropped by on their way to or from the river and played a hand or two. And there was the unpredictable Bill Shelly, Lafe Beller's hired hand. Bill was always full of fun. His one enemy was Rieka. She wanted Bill to join "the church"-- meaning the Mt. Sterling Baptist Church. And Bill wasn't about to join any church.

School was running along smoothly, I thought. Several visitors dropped in, as was the custom in those days. Dr. Leach from our home neighborhood was one of the first. I was a little surprised one afternoon to see Doc's Model A Ford go puffing past the school, and I was worried too. I thought someone at the Hollandworths or Bellers was sick. But in about a half hour he came back by and stopped. He was puffing on his cigar and grinning from ear to ear.

Later I found out he had been successful in collecting his bill from Mrs. Hollandworth. He had "waited on her" four years earlier when Lillian was born and had been waiting ever since for his $15.

Doc complimented me on having "good order" and a "clean school room." As he left he motioned me to come out in the little entry room where he whispered rather loudly, "Now, you're doing a good job. It looks like you've got things under your thumb. I'll be dropping in occasionally when I'm down this way."

Rieka, everyone told me, would ruin my complacency, though. Her frequent visits had discouraged hardier souls than I. She had a bachelor of science degree from Central Missouri State College and she had taught the school five terms in a row sometime previously. But all of the students except the Beller children were her nieces and nephews and they had paid no attention to her as a teacher.

I was afraid, anyway, that Rieka would come to visit and "show me up" since she had so much experience. But either she had given up hope of teaching there again or she was too busy writing poetry to pay me a visit. Whatever the reasons, she never showed up in the two years I taught there.

However, Bessie's mother, Aunt Esther, visited several times. She was not a woman of great intelligence, but she was interested in the welfare of her children. She couldn't understand why Bessie wouldn't read "out loud" for me when she was so vocal at home. Neither could I. Bessie, I supposed, was to be my cross as a school teacher. Or perhaps a constant reminder to be humble despite my growing confidence.

Aunt Esther showed the ravages of hard, rough work. She was in her early thirties, but her hands were the largest, coarsest, reddest I'd ever seen. Her face and hair were the same color--bright red--and most of her teeth were gone. When she came to visit she always carried Emil, a fat two-year-old boy, on her hip. She always seemed so happy; I guess she was glad to get away from home.

George never left the house, Mrs. Hollandworth told me, unless Esther went along to do the work. So sometimes Esther would be so worn out with carrying Emil that she sat on the step outside the schoolhouse and fanned herself with her bonnet until I dismissed for afternoon recess. When I called the children back inside, Esther put her hand over her mouth to hide the ugly, gaping spaces and said, "Please, let's sing like you do in the morning."

Esther wasn't musical like her husband's sisters, but she loved to hear the children sing. So out would come the "Golden Book" and we'd really put our souls into "singin'" for her.

Another character in the neighborhood was Henry Poehle (pronounced Pel'le). He lived across the river on a good farm but he considered himself a sort of self-appointed community judge. Nothing was quite legal without Henry Poehle's approval. He always signed his name to documents "Henry Poehle," and under his signature he would write, "Otherwise known as H.F.P. (Henry Fritz Poehle)."

Several times Mrs. Hollandworth asked me, "Hasn't Henry been to school to visit you? Ack, I can't understand. He always visits the school two or three times a year anyway."

I really couldn't see what business he had visiting. But one day in early winter Henry appeared, seemingly out of nowhere. He was a big, stout fellow, wearing clean blue bib overalls, a blue work shirt and a blue denim jacket that farmers referred to as a "jump jacket."

He didn't bother to knock. He came in quietly and appropriated for himself a vacant desk near the stove. Rather at a loss to know what to do, I introduced myself and invited him--unnecessarily--to make himself comfortable. As I played hostess, Henry busily got his steel-rimmed, oval spectacles out of a Bull Durham tobacco sack and perched them on his big red nose. Then he eyed me up and down several times before he spoke.

Finally he said, "Young lady, you don't look big enough to kill a flea, but just hand me a book like the one you're using and I'll follow right along."

Not another word did he say during the whole hour-long period, but I could see that the kids were all amused by Henry's presence. He stayed until I dismissed school at four o'clock, following along as best he could through Spelling, English,

Reading and the works. And when the kids scrambled out the door, he picked up his hat, put his spectacles back in the Bull Durham tobacco sack, stuck them in his bib pocket and announced, "As far as I can see, you're not doin' such a bad job." And off he went, clambering down the side of the bluff to his skiff tied to a tree.

Henry came to visit several times during the next two years--always with the same approach, always the same routine. The visits didn't bother me, but they bothered Aunt Ida. She couldn't see what business that "old lout" had coming across the river to stick his nose into someone else's business. She was sure he must have some ulterior motive, so when I reported that Henry visited school again, she would roll her eyes and moan, "That old cuss is everywhere except home, where he should be."

I guess Aunt Ida knew then what I didn't find out for years: Henry's wife, so they said, refused to sleep with him unless he paid her $5.00. But Henry was smart, too. He wouldn't sleep with her unless she paid him $5.00. The neighbors said the $5 bills were worn quite well.

We had official visitors, too. M.O. Reed was then superintendent of all county schools and it was his duty to visit each school at least once a year. He had held the office for years, and I remembered his coming to our home school, Post Oak. He always told a story, chatted with the kids a little while and went on his way.

His most memorable attribute were his eyes. Such eyes I've never seen. They were very dark, with an almost oriental slant, and compelling when they wanted you to listen. He was a short, stocky man, always well dressed, always driving a late model car, and always wearing a flat-crowned, straw hat far back on his head. Even though I knew him well, I dreaded having him sit and judge me. But I was no exception and the inevitable day arrived.

Soon after noon I spied a blue Chevrolet Landau sedan sliding swiftly between Herman Lipskoch's house on the right and the odiferous pig pen on the left, and in an eyelash M.O. Reed drove up on the playground and parked his car in the shade of the building. I was thankful then that I had had so much company. Aunt Esther, Henry Poehle and all the rest had given me practice in teaching under supervision.

I took pride in the way the children ran through the history facts and the spelling tests. Then all of a sudden that "damned" old woodpecker started trying to bore a hole in the tin roof. He was in a hurry to get his drilling done; he didn't stop to rest at all. He kept on with his "Rat-a-tat-ta-, rat-a-tat-tat" in thunderous tones.

Steele Beller's hand went up over his mouth and his brown eyes twinkled, but I didn't see anything funny.

M.O. Reed's eyes lost some of their slant and I saw a big question mark in them. "What in the world is that?" he asked.

The kids and I all started to explain, "It's just our old woodpecker. He does this every day." M.O. jumped up and ran outside to see for himself. Then he removed his blue serge suit coat, folded it and laid it on the front seat of his car, picked up some medium-sized rocks and heaved them at the naughty bird which was disturbing our learning processes.

After dispersing the noisy fellow from the ridgepole, M.O. put his coat back on, re-entered the schoolroom, told the students a funny story about three little monkeys and started on his way. I accompanied him to the entry and thanked him again for coming. I felt he had sized up the situation quickly and fully when he replied, "Between that old woodpecker and Herman Lipskoch's pig sty, I don't see how you stand it!''

With a wave of his flat straw hat, he was gone, and I had one more big stone rolled off my shoulders for another year.

That afternoon when the children were gone I sat at my desk for a long time, reading Charles Sheldon's ''In His Steps.'' The roar of the mill dam was the only sound. I had thoroughly enjoyed the tranquillity and was turning the key in the lock on the front door when all of a sudden there it was again: ''Rat-a-tat-tat, rat-a-tat-tat.'' That old redheaded monster was back at it again.

I guess he was telling me that even important people like M.O. Reed didn't tell him what to do! I couldn't help laughing as I crossed the road and crawled between the barbed wires for my pleasant hike through the woods pasture to the Hollandworth house.

Teaching school wasn't so bad after all.

6

That winter of '32-'33

During that first year I'm sure I learned much more than the pupils I was teaching. Now, more than a half-century later, I wonder how I shifted gears several times daily — from first grade to third, to fourth and sixth and seventh and post-graduate courses. If I made an error, it was heard and repeated at every home in the community by 4:30 that afternoon. Mrs. Hollandworth was notified and in due time I was told exactly how the situation should have been handled.

I soon came to recognize Mrs. Hollandworth as the executive council of the entire district. (How in the world she managed all her chores I'll never know.) She always wanted to know several days in advance if I planned to dismiss school for teachers' meetings or Thanksgiving holidays; if I scheduled a vacation, she planned to visit her sisters in Saline County. This meant that she and Jim and the "youngest three" would drive Louis's car there.

I understood her love for going — "travel" she called it — but I was under pressure to get eight months of school taught and go to summer school so I could qualify for a first grade teacher's certificate. I had a second grade certificate from having taken teacher's training in high school. This plus ten hours of college would qualify me for the first grade.

At times we disagreed on the holidays. In those cases Jim (the president of the board) would step aside and utter three words: "Let Herman decide." So I would put my case before Mr. Lipskoch and he usually agreed with me. I still find him an exceptionally fine character, with ideals of honesty and a reputation for good judgment uppermost in my memory. He always had my paycheck — a teacher's warrant — ready promptly. Usually he brought it to me at exactly 4 p.m. each Friday ending the month.

Early in December I began to tackle the problem of putting on a Christmas program for the parents. With so few pupils, this required some planning. I could count on only the upper graders because I still couldn't depend on Bessie to vocalize before an audience. She was making some progress, though, I told myself. She had adjusted enough to stand close to me when she read. (Too close, when winter underwear and garlic sausage combined into a strange aroma I called Schoolhouse No. 7.)

That left six who liked to sing, so we decided to make the program a singing and ask our visitors to join in the Christmas carols. We worked up some appropriate recitations, a short dialogue by the older children and a solo by Virgil Lipskoch. This pleased his father no end; he was so glad that Virgil "could stand on his own two feet and sing before an audience." Herman's gold teeth really flashed in the sunlight that Friday afternoon.

But the crowning achievement was the appearance of Santa Claus. Instead of asking an adult to do the honors, Mama decided that Bud, my 16-year-old brother, could handle the part. From Sears & Roebuck I ordered several yards of red outing flannel, a Santa Claus mask and cap and some quilting cotton. From this raw material my sister, Mae, fashioned a quite good-looking Santa suit.

CHRISTMAS AT H.S. BEND

*A sagging Santa has stomach trouble
and departs hurriedly in a
Model T Ford.*

Our plans called for Bud to dress in Lipskochs' garage and walk to the school where he would deliver sacks of candy to the children as a Christmas treat. But the whole procedure lacked internal logistical control: Bud arrived early, while parents and pupils were still coming in the school yard. He came flying over the top of the hill in our yellow Model T Ford sedan, parked it in full view of the gathering and shattered any hopes of concealing his real identity with his Santa Claus suit and false face. Mama had supplied him with a couple of large feather pillows to round out his paunch but, alas, she had given him nothing to secure them in the proper belly region.

I rang the bell early — and a bit frantically — and tried to herd everyone inside but they were difficult to herd because they were all loudly laughing at our mislaid plans. We started the program early by singing carols. I had asked Herman to lead but he could hardly get going from laughing.

Finally the songs had been sung and the recitations recited and I fearfully peeped out the window. Bud was fighting his "battle of the bulge." The pillows had fallen dangerously low and the elastic in his Santa suit wasn't strong enough to hold them up. But it was time for Santa to appear. Seeing no alternative, Bud shoved one hand inside his red jacket and tried to hold the pillows. This shifted his stomach to the upper leg, leaving the would-be Santa with one skinny leg, no stomach and one huge, fat leg. I was embarrassed more for Bud than for me.

The candy was distributed quickly. We sang "Silent Night, Holy Night" while everyone stood up. All but Santa. I guess he wasn't sure where his stomach might move to.

As soon as I could push everyone out of the tiny vestibule, Santa disrobed — all of his movable parts — and we headed for home. Ordinarily, I would have thought this episode hilarious but because it had happened to Bud and me, we never mentioned it to anyone at home or to each other. Whenever we were asked how the program was, we replied, "Oh, just great! Exactly as planned," or some such cover-up.

But we got oodles of mileage out of that Santa Claus suit. It was the only one for miles around which looked authentic (when the pillows were secured properly). I can't remember ever using it again but I recognized it for the next 20 years when I attended Christmas plays and programs around the communities. Each fall people would call on the phone and ask, "You still got that suit people use around this time of year?" and off it would go again. But I never heard of another Santa having stomach trouble in it, or having to sit down to keep fallen pillows in place.

During my Christmas week vacation snow fell — not a big, deep, fluffy snow, but a fine, grainy, sleet-like one. It was almost like ice and I worried all week at home about getting back to the Bend. The temperature hung near zero and the snow stayed on the ground. My week of pleasure was soon gone, but I found time to work up a piece of red and white printed percale which Aunt Ida had given me. I now had *one* new dress to wear.

When I returned to the Bend everything seemed dark and dreary for a time. Even the snow under the cedar trees looked black. I noticed this particularly since they were in the upper side yard on my way to the Hollandworths' outside privy. I would watch out my side window before I headed out there, to be sure no one was scraping snow off the ground to melt in the kitchen for household use. But sometimes when I thought I had found just the right moment, I would meet Jim coming from the porch "off the dark room" with his buckets. Sometimes he would back up and slam the door so quickly he would almost catch his pipe in it. Sometimes I would back up and wait until after dark when I was reasonably sure no one was digging snow under the cedars.

I certainly remember some uncomfortable moments from those confrontations. And I suppose that Jim confided in Mrs. Hollandworth about his embarrassment. One Monday afternoon when I returned to my side room bedroom a new white enamel commode was sitting out in plain view, between the organ and my bed — hidden, of course, by the sofa. I *did* feel some relief to know I had a substitute plan in case I just couldn't reach the outside privy.

About this time Fred and Anna moved to the Heckmann Mill House. One evening I came home to find my room almost bare. The overstuffed sofa and chairs were gone. So was the little table I had been using for my quilt pieces, needle, thread and thimble — all of which had been stacked in front of the west window.

I was left with the organ, small bed, Franklin stove, one tiny table for my kerosene lamp and one split-bottom, straight-back chair. And, of course, my new enamel commode. I felt robbed, but there was one improvement: I could get into bed properly, without climbing on the sofa and rolling in.

I continued to smuggle in my kerosene. But my firewood was always limited. Thank goodness, I was not inclined to insomnia in those days because when the wood burned out I had to go to bed.

I was awakened in the mornings by old Bong Bong and the clattering of iron lids on the big black cook stove in the kitchen. I never had a fire in my room in the mornings. Often I broke the ice in the pitcher to pour water into the bowl. You may be sure I didn't tarry long about my dressing.

With no closet in my room, my entire wardrobe hung on one hook on the back of the porch door. This wardrobe consisted of one good, warm flannel coat-style dress which I wore almost continuously on cold days; two cotton print dresses, the red and white one I had made and the hand-me-down from Mae; and two coats. I wore one to school. It was a rubberized, belted, trench coat — also a hand-me-down from Mae. It did have a warm, fleece lining but this garment never appealed to me.

The other coat, also a hand-me-down — from somebody — was a good, black cloth affair with a black and white fur collar. I wore this on Fridays because I was going home or to Uncle John's and Aunt Ida's. I can still see that coat tail flapping in the draft that flowed in the east windows where I hung my coat. I used it as a weather vane: When the wind flapped my coat I heaped more wood on the fire to keep the children warm. That building, surely, was the coldest one I ever experienced in four decades of teaching — and I've held forth in some cold ones. It was "finished" inside with only ceiling strips along the walls and there was no plaster between them and the weatherboarding outside.

The rest of that year proceeded mostly according to Mrs. Hollandworth's direction. We had passed the big traditional holidays, but we had birthday celebrations. These always turned into singin's, with Mrs. Hollandworth and Herman singing a special which they had "worked up, just in case." Usually, we had cake and coffee afterward. That helped some.

My birthday was February 28th but I never suspected that any celebration would be held in my honor. So I almost fell over that evening when a knock sounded on my porch door soon after I had retired to my room. There on the cement well covering stood the whole neighborhood — the Bellers, the Lipskochs, the Leimkuehlers and John Fent, Fred and Anna — and even Reika — and all of them singing "Happy Birthday to you."

I spent most of the evening shaking. I stopped, though, when we got the organ going. Because Mrs. Hollandworth was the hostess, she had delegated Lydia Lipskoch to sing a special with Herman, dedicated to me. Before they took their places in front of the organ, facing me, I knew what it was going to be. And, sure enough, "Just like a tree that's planted by the water" began to roll over me in all the splendor and volume that Herman and Lydia could muster. By the time they reached the chorus, "I shall not be, I shall not be moved," I was positive I was taking root myself and probably never would move.

The cake and coffee afterward was very good. I sampled a piece of each cake as we all sat around the big kitchen table. Jim sat at the head of the table, with Lillian on his lap. With so many people gathered around, I guess Jim's feet became crowded so he took off his shoes and put them by the side of his chair. Lillian, as usual, sat slightly to one side of his lap and as she reached for her glass of milk, she lost her balance and dropped her glass, spilling milk directly into Jim's shoe. Jim wasn't like most men I knew. He smiled at Lillian. "Well, well," he said, "we won't cry over spilled milk."

That was the week for excitement. For several weeks a pet pig had shared the kitchen with us. He was the only one from a litter to survive a severe cold spell, so he was bottled, petted and bedded down in a box behind the kitchen stove each night. By now (February) he had grown into a shoat-sized pest. He practically governed the household — and perfumed his entire domain.

At meal time he put his front feet on the chair rounds and grunted until someone gave him a bite, then he would run around the kitchen chomping and squealing in delight. All of the younger Hollandworths thought this was great fun. Louis always looked down at the floor, embarrassed. Jim looked solemnly at his plate and paid no attention. But whenever "Pig" came close to Mrs. Hollandworth, she gave him a good, solid kick in the rump, after which he would squeal back at her and run for his box behind the stove.

His going in and out of doors, however, brought Pig his biggest trouble. When he was small everyone had helped him up the steps, thinking he was cute. Now he was a hog-sized nuisance. If you opened the kitchen door, he was likely to run right between your feet and throw you flat. And so it happened early one morning as I was climbing out of bed. I heard a monstrous Bang, Bang, Thud, Thud, and then a heavy rolling over followed by Pig squealing happily, "Oink, oink, oink!" I pulled back the window shade just enough to see Jim sprawled full length on the slanted porch floor, the water bucket on his head. And Pig was scampering merrily about as if he had achieved the greatest moment of his life.

Evidently Pig and Jim had tried to get out the kitchen door at the same time. But the hog-feet affair was never mentioned. I suppose only Jim, Pig and I know what had happened — and perhaps the fun-loving Overseer of Pig Heaven.

That winter of '32-'33 was a long, hard one, made even harder for farm people by the lack of moisture. I became more and more wary of the water in the Hollandworths' bucket, afraid it was either river water or melted snow. Milk, I finally concluded, might be more sanitary, even if it has passed through a sock foot. So I started drinking the hot chocolate Mrs. Hollandworth made each evening for supper. She used some of Louis's samples of Watkins chocolate to make a very good tasting concoction.

Often we had other good things to eat. The Lipskoch boys, Louis and Ben

Ridder and a cousin often went duck hunting on the river and brought home beautiful wild ducks. Mrs. Hollandworth baked these in the oven with a bread crumb dressing and made a really exceptional dish. Often, too, we had rabbit, for which I could work up no appetite.

Usually I could discern what was cooking before the rap on my door but one evening my nose failed me. I had not previously met this aroma. I sensed I wasn't going to like it, and the longer I smelled it cooking, the more positive my convictions became.

By the time the rap sounded on my door, I was tempted to yell out, "No, thank you. I don't believe I care for ... whatever it is we're having tonight." But my female curiosity overcame me. I had to find out what we were having.

As I passed the sink, I caught a glimpse of a well-picked skeleton. Coon, sure enough, I thought, as Mrs. Hollandworth tried to cover it quickly with a dish towel. When the meat was passed, everyone took a generous helping — everyone but Oliver. Always the cautious and particular one, he quickly passed the platter to Louis, saying, "You all can have my share of that ol' coon. I'll eat cornbread and molasses."

He had let the cat — or the coon — out of the bag. Mrs. Hollandworth stood dumbfounded in the middle of the kitchen. Then, redfaced, she harshly reprimanded Oliver. "You know we all agreed not to say what that was," she said. "Ack, Ack. Shame on you."

Once uncovered, the arrangement seemed humorous. All of them had suspected that I wouldn't eat any of the coon, unidentified or not. But I was finally persuaded to put one tiny portion in my mouth. And as small as it was, it choked me for a week.

After that I became overly cautious with unfamiliar meat. Now that I look back on those bitter Depression days, I'm convinced that what I ate for beef sausage was really venison burger, but I had no experience in cooking meats and hadn't learned to detect texture in the various wild meats. I'm also convinced that the sausage crumbled into the watery gravy every morning, which we ate on the cornbread, was venison. But the old saying is right: What you don't know won't hurt you.

At times I was invited out to spend the night with one of the neighborhood families. Late in that first winter, I was invited to "stay the night" with Freida and Amanda at the Topel farm (where Cap Hoehne lives now). As during my first visit there, I was simply amazed at the cleanliness of everything. The board floors were scrubbed as white as snow, and the sheets covering poor, bedfast Mrs. Topel were the same clean white.

I don't remember what we had for supper, but I do remember how long Mr. Topel prayed — before and after we ate. I remember, too, the scrubbing that Amanda and Freida gave the kitchen sink after the dishes were done. How their hands flew! And I can still feel the intense cold when we undressed to go to bed in the big, bare, scrubbed bedroom upstairs.

I got up very early because the Topels lived far from school, so I had to leave before daylight. When breakfast was finished, Mr. Topel lighted a huge, old kerosene lantern and said, "Now, Frieda will walk with you until you can see good, by gott." (Until good, full daylight, he meant.) We set out for the school house, with Frieda leading the way with the lantern. I followed behind her until we reached the county road where we could walk two abreast.

The Reichert houses were located at the junction of the Topels' lane and the

MRS. H'S SURPRISE
*Cornbread and molasses...
and "that ol' coon."*

county road. As we came near them, we noticed lights in the houses. We thought this was a bit strange; we didn't know that one of Clarence Reichert's twin babies was seriously ill. When I returned to the Hollandworths after school I found out that the baby had died.

The Reicherts were living on county "relief funds," as the local people referred to them, so the baby's death posed some problems for the neighbors: Where to get a casket? Where to bury the child?

Herman Lipskoch came though with all of the answers. A neighborhood caucus was held; Hermann would make the little casket. Mrs. Lipskoch and Mrs. Hollandworth brought out their sewing equipment and lined it with quilting cotton. Then from Grandma Leimkuehler's scrap bag came a fine piece of the softest muslin, just big enough to go over the cotton.

Mrs. Hollandworth sat late that night in the kitchen, fashioning a tiny pillow for the head. Just as I was about to blow out my light, she tapped on my door. "Ach," she said, "your stitches are fine and small. Would you help me with the lace around the edge?" We fitted the little lid of the casket and lined it with a bit of lace and went to bed with only a few hours of night left.

It was arranged to bury the baby in the Giedinghagen family cemetery, only a few steps distant from the Reicherts' home. When I came home the following evening, the house seemed lonely and subdued. Mrs. Hollandworth's eyes were still red from the funeral service. She and Anna had sung a special for the baby, "Gathering Flowers for the Master's Bouquet," and Mrs. Hollandworth had sung the lead, afraid Anna might break down.

Spring finally arrived. I had counted the days, marking them on my desk calendar one by one. I felt my spirits rise a notch when we no longer had to build a fire every day in the potbellied stove at the back of the room. But one could never be sure in Missouri: One day might be warm and sunny, the following one wintry and cold.

I really became anxious now for the last day of school, because I was going to Central Missouri State Teachers College at Warrensburg during the summer. I was also happy to have been re-employed by the board of directors. (If a teacher wasn't re-elected, Mama and Aunt Ida told me many times, it was almost a total disaster.) But I wasn't expecting the fringe benefit I received that day.

We worked up an appropriate short program for the last afternoon. It was mostly songs we had sung every day, so we knew all of the words. And we added a dialogue and some recitations to show off the children's accomplishments for the year. Even Bessie got caught up in the spirit of the occasion and was willing to recite. Or so she said. But I wondered what she would do when the time came...

The program was almost over when we came to her part. She had four lines. Behind the curtain, I wondered if she'd remember what I'd tried to drill into her: Walk to the center of the stage and say your lines; don't reel them off as you walk. And speak up.

I peeked out to watch what I feared might be a debacle. Bessie got up and almost ran across the stage, mumbling as she went:

"I'm just a little girl
"And I haven't much to say,
"But I want to let you know
"I'm glad you came today."

She was almost behind the curtain when she mumbled the last word. And with her momentous attempt at speechmaking, she sank on a stack of books and

BESSIE'S LINES

"I'm just a little girl,
and I haven't much to say,
but I want to let you know
I'm glad you came today."

buried her fat, little, round face in her hands. But she kept tugging at my skirt and repeating in a loud stage whisper: "Teacher, teacher, I done it! I done it! I done done it!"

I think she surprised herself almost more than she surprised me. And Bessie's Mama was so proud of this four-line accomplishment that I almost felt that I had performed a miracle, all by myself.

"I never thought she'd do it," Aunt Esther kept saying. "She actually made a speech. I never thought she'd do it."

At last it was all over. And what an ending to my first year, a beautiful surprise ending. I was a teacher and I had taught someone something — even if Bessie's declaration of triumph had been grammatically faulty. And now I was going home.

I was still savoring the good feeling of it all when Bud came flying over the hill in that yellow Model T. (Thy boys in his high Vocational Agriculture class had painted it as a Halloween prank and we drove it that way for years.) Usually he came after me about five o'clock; he was in high school at Belle and it took him about an hour to drive the distance — even when he had no flat tires. In good weather I usually started walking until I met him on the Topel hill. Sometimes I got all the way to Pin Oak Creek, where I usually had to wait for him since there was no bridge to walk on. But today we splashed through the water in the Model T and memories of my first year at the Bend fell away behind me like the creek water dripping off the running board.

For the next three weeks there was much to do at home. Mama always left the house cleaning for me to do. And there also was a beautiful piece of gray Canton crepe to make into a dress-up dress. It was to have a pink collar. And at Mae's urging to make the most of it, I had also ordered a pair of gray shoes from Garland's in St. Louis to match.

A few days later I received a letter from the State Department of Education with astounding news: "Since you have received less than $50.00 per month for your services as a teacher this term" it read, "we are authorized to supplement this sum by paying you $10.00 per month bonus — total $80.00."

Well, you would have thought I had fallen heir to a gold mine. I had been financing Bud and Pete with their high school education, car expense and the few clothes they had. "We can help you next summer," Mama would always explain, "when the old hens lay." At least, the $80 would help me get started at Warransburg ... then those old hens had better come through.

On the strength of this extra money, I ordered a piece of white Canton crepe for another dress and some red and white polka dot silk for a big bow tie to wear with it.

For three weeks I washed, ironed and mended my old clothes to take to summer school, helped put out our big farm garden, cleaned the house. And in between I cared for "Crip." Crip was a quarter-grown brown leghorn rooster who had had the misfortune to catch his foot in a barn door and break it. The folks had brought him into the house and kept him in a shoebox behind the stove in the kitchen. He had almost recovered when I came home and he was swaggering about quite lively until he caught the other leg in the screen door.

I put splints on the leg and carried him around the house as I worked. His favorite place was on my right shoulder; he could peck at my ear lobe and talk to me from there. I even carried him upstairs at night where he slept in a clean shoebox by the side of my bed. He never showed any interest in anyone else.

MAMA WILL HELP

Next summer, "when the old hens lay."

When he began to walk again he always came to the kitchen door and pecked on it for me to let him in, or if he was sleeping in his shoebox he never moved or peeped until he heard my voice.

But I had to leave Crip and my family to go away and get that 10 hours of precious college credit so I could get that first grade teaching certificate.

So off I went to Warrensburg.

THE COMMON-WORD SPELLERS

Phonic Drill: Short *e*

Spell these helpers:			Spell these words:		
d	e	de	de	n	den
f	e	fe	fe	d	fed
k	e	ke	ke	g	keg
l	e	le	le	t	let

Spelling helpers:			Spelling words:		
p	e	pe	pe	n	pen
s	e	se	se	t	set
r	e	re	re	d	red
n	e	ne	ne	t	net

PART THREE

WARRENSBURG

7

Churchill and his "Cabbage Heads"

In my countrified mind, Warrensburg was the ultimate City — a metropolitan Utopia. Several acquaintances, including my brother-in-law to be, Irvin Leach, had gone there, and now for me to be a student of higher learning there ... Well, it was almost unbelievable.

I feared the prospect almost as much as I love it — feared that I wouldn't be able to make good grades, feared professors who knew so much, feared that my poor, country ways and manners would cause other students to laugh at me. What I failed to realize was that nearly everybody else was just like me.

Nearly all freshmen took the same courses. English Composition, American History and Elementary Education I were required. We could choose one elective. I chose Nature Study and it gave me a delightful hour — every day.

Mrs. Maud Nattinger taught it and she put her whole heart and soul into it. She looked somewhat like a bird herself, and she knew more about trees, shrubs, birds and all nature than anyone I've ever known. We identified every tree, shrub and flower on the campus and we took short side trips to surrounding farms to see leaf patterns, bark, blooms and such things. We had to keep a scrap book in which we pressed the leaves and wrote the names of the trees.

The other courses were rather meaningless to me. In English Comp, Professor Ben R. Craig read to us such stories as "The Black Duck Dinner" from "Paul Bunyan's Tall Tales." I had never heard of these stupendous adventures and although I wasn't too impressed at the time, they were mighty useful to me later.

Elementary Education I was the dullest of the dull. Mr. Moreland taught it but all we did was read articles from the Elementary Education Bulletin and report on them in class. These assignments were easy, but I did find it hard to stand before the class and "deliver the goods."

But I did learn a useful theory in that class. We were seated alphabetically and my left hand neighbor was Anna Pearl Broyles from Waynesville, Missouri. She was as smart as they come and she stimulated my ego on the mornings of my oral reports by saying, "Just remember Winston Churchill. He thought of his fellow members of the Parliament as cabbage heads. And that's what I do. I just see cabbage heads when I get up to report."

I used that Cabbage Head theory the rest of the summer and a great many more times in my life.

American History was a very dull, very warm afternoon class. I can't recall the professor's name but he was Dean Morrow's son-in-law. I can't remember one thing I learned in that class and I remember answering only one question: "Who began world travel by journeying to Cathay?"

My two-word response must have been brilliant. "Marco Polo."

The prices we paid for accommodations were simply incredible by today's standards. My $1.25 per week room rent included kitchen and laundry privileges — the "laundry" being a tub, water and wash board. Usually on Saturday mornings there were no classes so all of the girls rooming with the Coopers on

College Avenue gathered in the back yard to do our laundry. My roommate, Geneva Courtright, was terribly particular about the water temperature. "Cold water sets stains and dirt," she said, so she stoked the old coal stove diligently to heat the water.

We had lots of fun doing our laundry because the homes on both sides of us housed boys. And on Saturday mornings they'd be outside, too, rubbing out their week's collection of soiled shirts and towels and a handkerchief or two.

All of us used pieces of brown, home made soap which we had brought from home. Mary Lou Harrington, I remember, always melted her bar of soap in a small sauce pan half filled with water before she poured it in the tub of warm water. Mary Lou was a little older than most of us. She had a degree in Home Economics and was doing extra credit work to be with her younger sister, Rosalie, who, like me, was tussling with her first summer session. It was also in one of these back yard "tub and rub" sessions where I met Bob Stonner, later Dr. Bob Stonner, the dentist. The Stonners were Osage County people who had moved to Saline County.

The eating process was new and different to me, too. Many women in Warrensburg made a living and sent their children to college by renting out rooms at $1.50 a week and adding $3.50 a week for three meals per day — minus Sunday night supper. Geneva and I ate at Mrs. Lena Fisher's place on Tyler Street and her meals were superb. In the early part of the summer we filled two large tables in her huge dining room. Food was served home style, vegetables in large bowls, meat on huge heavy platters and always dessert. Breakfast was whatever you wanted — an egg, bacon and toast, fruit juice, coffee. And always on every table everywhere I ate was a huge dish of peanut butter and white Karo syrup mixture — referred to by all students as "No. 1." "Please pass the No. 1" was the main sentence in the morning. The boys seemed especially fond of it. Some of them ate piece after piece of toast with this mixture spread thickly and gooey-ly on top.

Sunday dinner was quite elegant. Fried chicken with pie and ice cream was the usual menu. I don't see how these women cooked for so many people. Later in the summer another group moved in to eat with us and a large dining table was set up in the living room to accommodate the new eaters.

Fourth of July rolled around quickly. I went home for the holidays. When Bud met me at Belle it was dark and an ugly looking cloud was hanging over us, so we were anxious to get home before the rain poured down. As usual, the lights on the Model T went out almost as soon as we were out of town. The rain came down in torrents and we poked along at the proveribal snail's pace — except when a streak of lightning helped us to see the road. Then Bud poured on the gas to try to make up for lost time. We were used to hardship in those days and thought nothing of such a small thing as this — especially when one was going home.

I had enjoyed my first brush with college living, but I was glad to be at home for a few days. After supper that first evening, the storm had passed and we were sitting on the back porch when suddenly from around the end of the kitchen came a chirping, hopping, very excited "Crip." He hopped up on my lap, then onto my shoulder and snuggled up close to my ear, all the while chirping and trying to crow in his adolescent voice. Everyone was surprised; they hadn't seen him around the house since I left. That night he wanted to come in the house and sleep in his shoe box, but since he had been roosting out in the hen house, we decided he had better stay out.

After the holiday came the real test of the summer's work. Would I get "D" slips? ("Valentines," they were called by the students who "had been around.") If you got one, you were supposed to talk to your professor. I worried for days about getting that piece of paper. Luckily, I escaped.

So my summer was fun. Few students had cars. If we needed anything, we walked the twelve blocks to town and made our small purchases. Rooms were not air conditioned so walking about the campus was a means of cooling off after the lessons were done for the next day.

There were few luxuries. I usually received a $10 bill from Mom every week now that the old hens were laying and this was more than sufficient for my room and board. Nearly always on Sunday nights we went to see a movie ... and eat a ham salad sandwich accompanied by a milk shake. I always paid for mine and Geneva's; she never offered to "go Dutch" and I was too timid then to just walk away and go eat by myself.

The last week of summer school was marked by the excitement when Mary Lou Harrington had a sudden attack of appendicitis. Her father came from Kansas City, called an ambulance and rushed her off to a hospital. I have always wondered if her attack had anything to do with her melting the soap before she poured it in the wash water. But I guess not. Any medical connection escaped me.

Finally my leaves were all pressed and in order for Mrs. Nattinger. My education reports were all outlined for Mr. Moreland. And I guess I passed Mr. What's His Name's history test because I remembered Marco Polo. Ben Craig must have either been very tenderhearted or very lazy, because I don't remember doing one thing in that class but listening to him read. But when my grades were mailed to me later at home, I had four "B's." How proud I was of myself. I never thought I could do it!

In August at home we always canned tomatoes. I soon learned the summer schedule. For several summers to come, it varied little: June and July were the summer session. August was can tomatoes and entertain the Ladies' Aid, clean house and perhaps paper a room or two and get ready for another year of teaching. So the pattern of my life began to take form. I didn't realize this for several years; I wonder if any of us do at the time.

My second term at Horse Shoe Bend was much like the first except I felt much more secure. I didn't dread anything. I had become hardened to being the subject of telephone conversations in German. I knew all of Mrs. Hollandworth's menus by heart. I knew the sock foot would be used for a milk strainer. But I did continue to fret about one big possible calamity — having to spend a whole weekend in the Bend.

RESCUED

The rains come and Pin Oak rises but Herman Lipskoch saves the day and I am "set acrost" the creek.

One Friday morning early in the second term dawned dark and cloudy. We ate breakfast by lamp light, and as I tramped along the pretty little path to school, the rain began to fall in sheets. *This must be Mom's "e-qui' Nox' ial,"* I said to myself. Any rain falling around September was always so named by Mom. The old owl must have been confused by the darkness, too, because he constantly "Who-Who"ed at me.

The clouds hung low and the rain fell heavily all day. We had to keep the windows down and all the odors of all the families and all the lunches in the buckets mingled in an unpleasantly pungent mixture. The nearer the hands of old Pot Belly got to four o'clock, the darker the clouds became and the harder the rain hit on the tin roof.

I didn't know what to do. I was sure that Uncle John would try to come for me; he knew the terrible dread I had of a weekend in the Bend. But if I walked to the creek, would he be gone? I was sure he couldn't cross the creek with the car. And I would be soaked through and through if I walked the three or four miles to Pin Oak Creek.

It was Herman Lipskoch to the rescue again. At four o'clock when I turned the kids loose, there was Hermann with his new Chevrolet. "Now, I called John Kosark to be at the crossing with his team and wagon to set you acrost," he said, "and your uncle will be waiting on the other side."

Herman's plans were as good as his word — and his thoughtfulness. John Kosark was at the creek with his team of big bay mares and a sturdy old farm wagon. He and Herman drove across the creek first, to be sure that no holes had washed out which might tip the wagon over. Returning to the Bend side, they handed me in the wagon and ordered me to sit flat on the bottom of the bed. I obeyed promptly; after all their trouble, I wasn't going to be obstinate.

The water *was* deep. Toward the middle of the creek, it came up in the wagon and I knelt on my knees and hung onto the side. The big bay mares snorted and lunged and finally pulled the wagon up on the south side of Pin Oak Creek. And in a few minutes we were heading for what surely was one of the most beautiful places in the world, Uncle John's farm.

Somehow it never entered my mind that the weather sometime might keep me from getting back *into* the Bend. I suppose Herman would have arranged that, too.

That second year I found myself missing Fred and Anna. They had moved to the Heckman Mill house near the dam. This was about two and a half miles from the school, but on several occasions Anna insisted that I come over after school and spend the night. I found this a pleasant way of relaxing away from old Bong, Bong, Mrs. Hollandworth's questions, and various and sundry small, querying eyes — as well as assorted livestock behind the kitchen stove. We played Euchre and Pinochle again — the games highlighted by the appearance of Louis or Walter Lipskoch who, invariably, were out hunting and just happened "to see a light" and stopped by.

The Bellers, Lafe and Bessie, liked to dance — another activity held in great disdain by Mrs. Hollandworth. She "just couldn't see what anybody wanted with all that shufflin' around to fiddle music." Now, music was fine, but it was made to praise the Lord, and nobody in their right mind would go dragging three kids around to square dances on Saturday night ... And so on and so on. Mrs. Hollandworth had a great deal to learn about her own family!

Bessie often came to the singin's. She had a sweet, husky-toned soprano voice, very pleasing to the ear. She and I went in cahoots to try to drown out Mrs. Hollandworth and Herman. I don't think we ever even came close. But once during a revival the minister asked us to perform a special. When Mrs. Hollandworth found out, she was determined to accompany us on the organ. She immediately wanted to know what we were going to sing so she could "practice up." We hadn't decided, we told her, and probably wouldn't know until the evening of the service.

Mrs. Hollandworth frowned darkly. "Now that's no way to work up a special," she informed me. "Now you take Herman and me, for instance. We practice for weeks."

But Bessie and I sang our special our own way, without accompaniment, much against Mrs. Hollandworth's better judgment. She never voiced an opinion on the quality of the performance to either Bessie or me, much to our amusement. It was tough to measure up to Mrs. Hollandworth's standards where specials were concerned.

One evening in early winter Lafe and Bessie invited all of the younger people in for a party. There weren't many — Fred and Anna, Louis Hollandworth, Walter and Harvey Lipskoch, Ben, me, of course and Bill Shelly. The party meant dancing — for which the girls were woefully outnumbered by the boys. John Fent was there to play the fiddle and Fred seconded on the guitar. But that still left one extra man to be a girl. This improvisation was made by putting one of Bessie's big kitchen aprons on the lucky fellow who "got to be a girl."

Thus we had fun while the big iron range grinned at us through red, glowing open teeth in the grate. The kitchen floor had no covering — and the house not a very good foundation — so the wind blew up through the cracks in the boards, keeping our feet cool. Bessie was a good cook and after we became tired of dancing she served wonderfully thick sandwiches made with homemade bread, boiled ham and homemade cucumber pickles. After that came pie or cobbler with thick, yellow cream whipped and piled on top.

All the time we were dancing the big coffee boiler bubbled away on the back of the wood stove and the aroma of the freshly ground coffee which Bessie measured into the dark blue granite boiler just before we started our last set was enough to make the salivary glands do double duty.

So simple were our pleasures. A little square dancing, a little card playing. No worry about smoking pot, drinking alcohol or sniffing glue.

THE HOPE REVIVAL

Rieka prayed "to the Lord who abideth in the hills"...figuring He didn't mind that she had a portion of the river bank all over her seat.

On another evening our same brave band sallied forth to attend a revival meeting at the Hope Presbyterian Church. "Brave" is, perhaps, a bit strong for the adjective. Foolhardy, I guess, is more accurate, because the church was across the Gasconade River from the Bend. Soon after supper the hardy souls began to gather. The boys inspected the lanterns carefully because it was already dark and we had miles to walk. Herman sent along his extra heavy duty three-cell flashlight but it was slated for emergency use only. The Lipskoch boys each had a fine gas lantern which they carried proudly at the head of the pack. Rieka decided to join this band of religious night-walkers — "Just to return the favor," she said.

The way to the river still comes more clearly to my mind now than it did that dark night: We started out through the Hollandworth backyard (by the privy), opened the gate into the barn yard, then entered the pig pasture where we carefully picked our way through pigs and manure, then out into the cow pasture — with all of this punctuated by eternal gate openings and crawling through wire fences. At the Beller house there were no fences so, hooray, no gates to open.

Bessie and Lafe joined us, and now there was no road, just farm lanes deeply rutted by wagons and other wheeled machinery. This was good corn ground so as we approached the river we selected a corn row and played Follow the Leader for almost a mile to the river bank. Rain had fallen at intervals all day, so we all were wearing boots or overshoes. At the river bank the boys unchained the skiff, dipped water out of it with a tin can and placed the oars in the locks.

At the come-ahead signal, Bessie, Anna, Rieka and I started single file down the slippery bank, with Rieka bringing up the rear. One step away from being safely down the steep incline, Rieka's feet slipped out from under her. I — directly in front of her — went down, too, and knocked Anna down who, in turn, sent Bessie sprawling. But the four of us — one huge, muddy ball — stopped short of the river.

Nothing daunted, we got up and clambered into the boat. We rowed across the river, climbed the steepest, rockiest bluff I had ever seen and finally came out on a country road not far from the church. I suppose the mud dried somewhat on our coats as we completed the walk, but I remember being terribly embarrassed in church and trying to huddle in the center of a group when we stood.

The revival minister had one of the biggest voices I ever heard in song and psalm and he led the service energetically. We joined in singing some rousing good revival hymns and Rieka prayed "to the Lord who abideth in the hills — the hills from whence cometh my help." It didn't bother her at all that she had a portion of the river bank all over her seat.

It must have been after midnight when we straggled back to the Hollandworth house and I rolled into my little bunk bed. When I think now of walking over those hills and through the woods at night, and how we used to take a skiff across the river in all kinds of weather, it rather frightens me. But, as I said, life was so simple then — and more so in retrospect than in actuality.

That simplicity included no bathrooms. Therefore, one didn't worry about taking a bath every night. One simply took off as many clothes as deemed necessary and crawled under the covers.

The covers on my bunk were different than I had had at home. The principal cover was a light feather bed over which was a blue and white plaid flannelette. This always kept me warm on whichever side was up, but in dreadfully cold weather the mattress under me was so thin that I was forever turning over to warm at least one side of me against the feather bed.

Times were hard and Mrs. Hollandworth had many ways of managing food and clothing for her large family. Never one to "look a gift horse in the mouth," she was proud of hand-me-downs. She never called them that, however. About such clothing she would say, "I got it given." Nearly everything she had in the way of clothing, I think, she had "got it given." In many ways she was artistically talented. When she sewed for Frieda and Lillian she would put in late hours stitching some extra little decoration by hand "just so it don't look like all the others have," she would say.

And occasionally she would make her "special dishes." One was dried prunes and apricots cooked together and the juice thickened with pearl tapioca. This was about a once-a-year dish, she would explain. On Valentine's Day she made larger sugar cookies, cutting them with a tin can bent into a heart shape. On them she put pink icing or wrote "I love you" in white icing on the pink. She sent a cookie to each child in class. Of course, all of them were her nieces or nephews except the Beller children. I think she enjoyed "outdoing the others," coming up with something different so, as she said, "Mine wouldn't be just like all the others."

That second spring I decided for sure that I wasn't going to teach the next year. I wanted to go to Warrensburg for a whole winter. If I attended the summer session, the winter term and the following summer, I would have 60 hours. That would qualify me to teach in an elementary school in town. I was sure that's what I wanted to do. So as spring approached, I worried less about Mrs. Hollandworth's questions, the condition of Pin Oak Creek and the sock foot on the cream separator.

An unexpected happening — one all too frequent in farming communities — ended the year sadly for all of us. It was a warm, sunny day in early spring. I was dismissing the children for afternoon recess when Morton's ambulance zoomed past Herman Lipskoch's house, by the school and turned into Bellers' road. An ambulance always meant that something terrible had happened — hospitalization or death. But, surely, not at Bellers...

When I rang the bell ending recess, Carl Beller was missing. He had gone home, the children told me, after seeing the ambulance turn into their road. But brown-eyed Steele and blue-eyed Esther sat there, their eyes fixed on their books. I tried to be calm and we went on with classes as usual. Shortly before four o'clock the ambulance came back. It stopped at the school while the driver poured some water into the steaming radiator — and Bessie told Steele and Esther that their father had been badly burned in an accident.

He died the next day in a Jefferson City hospital. Bessie and the children never came back to Horse Shoe Bend to live. I hadn't realized how much I had depended on the Beller children to help me through classes each day. Now there were only Hollandworths, Lipskochs and Leimkuehlers, all cousins.

Now I religiously crossed off the days on my calendar — in secret, of course, on a small calendar I kept in my desk. My evenings were lonelier, too, knowing no one was living on the Beller farm, and as I raised my window and propped it open with a stick before going to bed, the sound of the rushing water over the mill dam gave me an unsettling feeling.

Without the Beller children I found it hard to prepare an end-of-school program. But, according to Mom and Aunt Ida, I had to. *You must always work so hard at any job that if you ever want it again, they can't turn you down.* So I worked up some specials and we had a program ... immediately after which I left Horse Shoe Bend, vowing never to return.

Almost forty years later I drove back over that "one road route" and found it beautiful. Few changes had been made. The schoolhouse still stood there, empty; the Heckman Mill house was sort of a resort, very modern. Harvey Lipskoch was farming his father's place, and Fred Leimkuehler and his younger brother, Emil, worked the land which their father, George, and Grandfather Fritz once owned.

There was one great and grand improvement. A new road led out of the Bend, so no one had to worry about Pin Oak Creek as I did. And they called it Kings Highway.

I couldn't have named it better myself.

8

My "Grandpa Bacon Year"

Now came one of the greatest years of my life! I was going away — to Warrensburg, to the State Teacher's College — for a whole summer and winter. My dream was coming true.

Grandpa Bacon made it possible. He was still owed a few hundred dollars from a farm which he had sold to Alfred Gove. Grandpa hadn't been able to collect the money, mostly because he was too tenderhearted to push for it. So he told my father if he could get Alfred to "pay up," we could keep half the money.

That was all Dad needed. He made a couple of trips to Linn "on business" and soon Alfred found it convenient to pay up.

The proceeds — $1600 — went into Mom's cigar box. This was a red tin box on which was printed "Hoffman's Fancy Cuban Tobacco Cigars" and its place of safekeeping honor was on the lowest shelf in the kitchen cabinet. Backed by the box, we went to work on the family budget and mine. At least $1,000 had to be paid on "The Principal" which hovered over our farm. That was absolutely, positively not to be questioned. "The Principal" was an invisible but very real member of our household at the time and we were all elated at the thought of our live-in monster being pushed $1000 farther from our doorstep. This left $600 to be budgeted — for taxes and interest and my year at Warrensburg.

The summer at this great institution proceeded much like my first one there. But now I considered myself quite knowledgable about the whole affair — and was not even awestruck by the usual long lines of students enrolling. First I went to the Registrar's office and asked for my previous summer's records. Then for each class I was to take, I stood in line to receive a permit to enroll in the course. This took hours upon hours because 1600 students were doing the same thing. Once I obtained my permit, I had to locate that course's professor and have his OK stamped on my precious permit. This process took all day and part of a second — all under a sun that was beastly hot, early in a summer that was to be a record breaker.

Mrs. Fischer's rooms were all filled, but I found a room on a back street two blocks south of the campus. So I began what was known as "light housekeeping." My bedroom was a little, dark cubbyhole off the downstairs living room; the kitchen we were to use was upstairs. The arrangement was not one to make me happy, but I set about trying to adjust myself to the situation.

Among my fellow "light housekeepers" were three fat, fat Smith sisters with a common claim to fame: They cooked and ate all of the time. No matter how warm the day — or whatever else — they believed in well fortified, strong bodies. Vera, the largest, oldest and fattest, arose early to prepare the breakfast. She would fry a pound of bacon, toast about a loaf of bread, fry a dozen eggs and shout, "Verna, Viola, get out here right now if you know what's good for you." Evidently, Verna and Viola knew, because here they would come, all bundled up in gowns, housecoats and hair curlers, and plop down at the table and tackle Vera's output.

THE SMITH SISTERS
"Viola, I told you to put more water on those damn beans!"

After Vera had finished her breakfast routine, the rest of us could get to the stove. However, those preparations were so many and so prolonged that I never seemed to be able to get the stove long enough to cook anything. I soon decided that a half pint of milk would have to suffice as my breakfast. But I supplemented it well with some supplies I brought from home — such as country cured ham, strawberry preserves and other home canned fruits and vegetables.

While The Three Smiths, as we soon dubbed them, ate breakfast, they planned lunches; while they ate lunch, they planned dinner; and while they ate dinner, they talked about more meals on the morrow. Before Vera left for her first class she always put navy beans or potatoes on to cook. Then she admonished either Verna or Viola to "run home during second hour and put more water on the beans." With a dozen of us trying to prepare ourselves a bite to eat three times a day, we were always upsetting Vera's schedule.

One noon I came dragging in tired and hungry to find all of the upstairs kitchen windows open and all of The Three Smiths rushing madly about fanning newspapers at a room full of smoke. Vera was yelling crossly, "Viola, I told you to come home the second hour and put more water on those *damn beans*."

After the bean smoke cleared, I took my bottle of milk and ventured up to the kitchen again. I prepared a sandwich and sat down at my small table near the Three V's. As I opened my milk bottle, the cap slipped down into the bottle, spewing milk all over the V's. They couldn't quite fathom what had happend to them — first, their favorite food had burned up in smoke and now they were getting a milk bath!

But they were no unhappier than I. After classes were over that day, I again went by Mrs. Fischer's to ask about a room. Luckily for me, one of the girls had dropped out of school so there was a space for me. I spent the weekend moving — carrying all of my clothes, food, books and, of course, the ham, all by myself to my new rooming house.

Now all things seemed brighter for me. Even my school work seemed easier. I was taking the usual courses prescribed for the 60-hour teaching certificate. These included Elementary Education (6b), American History (Part 2), English Composition and World Geography.

The latter I'll never forget. The textbook was three inches thick and filled with explanations of such strange phrases as summer solstice, horse latitudes and lunar phases. It also listed 300 "Places One Must Know." Our tests were principally over this place knowledge. One place still sticks in my mind: "Christ of the Andes." But the flowery inscription with it defies my power of recall.

I can still picture, however, Dr. Phillips conducting the class, waving his arms and pointer at us like a great maestro pulling music out of an orchestra. He discarded his suit coat and conducted his daily performance in shirt sleeves, perspiring profusely as he strove to put the horse latitudes in their proper perspective and explain to dunces like me what the summer solstice really was — to me, who had always depended on Mama to esplain the "e' qui'nox'ial." I didn't make a very good grade in Dr. Phillips's course, but I thoroughly enjoyed his rousing renditions of the subject matter.

That summer of 1934 was a scorcher. Days in that dreadful heat were almost unbearable. Nights brought no relief. We perspired so much that keeping our clothes odor-free was a problem. We washed our underthings in the bathroom during the week and on Saturdays we all gathered in the back yard to rub our dresses and blouses on the washboard. With my few clothes, washing all of them was no problem.

We could use the iron for ten cents an hour, so each Saturday evening and Sunday we brought Mrs. Fischer's iron and board upstairs and pressed our few pieces of wearing apparel for the next week. I think I had less than any of the other girls — and what I had was homemade. But on one of our leisurely, warm Saturday afternoon strolls to downtown Warrensburg, I made the grand glorious purchase of a white seersucker dress — price, on sale, $1.98. For the next several summers this was my uniform. It was easily washed and required no ironing.

The days boiled on. The Fourth of July meant a brief holiday at home ... followed by more heat. The temperature on a cool day was 112 degrees and 114 on a warm one. With no such thing as air conditioning, we raised the windows to get air. And in came the insects. They danced around the light bulbs as I pored over the life of Horace Greeley or the birthplace of Pestalozzi. And after I retired the bugs crawled over my face as they made their journey through the screen to the outside world from whence they came in hordes.

Finally the last day of summer session arrived. I returned my rented books to the library and received enough money for my bus ticket home. I arranged with Mrs. Fischer to reserve a room for me when I returned in the fall and said goodbye to Warrensburg for a few weeks.

"Wait until Grace comes home," was Mom's favorite expression, "then we'll clean house and can the tomatoes." But August at home was still good in many ways. I didn't have to do my own cooking and there were lots of peaches and tomatoes to eat — as well as to can.

We usually picked the tomato crop by the bushel. Then we brought in the half gallon jars from the smokehouse, washed them and scalded them and turned them upside down to await the brilliant red fruits. For days peaches or tomatoes were household bywords. When we worked up the fruits we often didn't care about eating them, but we never turned down Mom's special peach pie. My mouth still waters as I remember how she made it:

She lined a pie tin with a rather thin, rich crust. Then she placed peach halves — seed side up, but with the seeds removed — on the crust. Over those red-tinged blobs of ripened gold, she sprinkled sugar, butter, flour, cinnamon and nutmeg. Then she dipped spoonful of rich sweet cream over all. She popped this concoction into a piping hot oven and baked it until the crust was crispy brown and the cream, sugar and butter mixture bubbled. Then she knew it was done.

Tomatoes, too, lent themselves to many interesting dishes. Many times a big dish of stewed tomatoes formed our main supper menu. To heighten the flavor of breaded tomatoes, I consider homemade bread a necessity. We stowed away huge quantities of this, with the tomatoes seasoned with sugar, salt, butter, cream and a tiny bit of vinegar to cut the acid. This, poured over homemade bread, is still one of my favorite quick meals.

Sandwiched between the canning and cleaning were such events as entertaining the Ladies' Aid (later called the Women's Guild). That was one of the big days of the summer. It called for cleaning the house from top to bottom and planning a menu for some thirty ladies — plus a few men to drive the cars. Few women in this hilly Missouri country drove cars; fewer had a car *to* drive.

August was Mama's month to "take the Aid." Arriving at this tradition was a very solemn ceremony. At the end of the previous business meeting, the president always discreetly asked the secretary, "Now, where is our next meeting, please?" Running her forefinger down the alphabetical list, the secretary always reported,

MOM'S PEACH PIE

Line a pie tin with a thin, rich crust. Place peach halves seed side up (with the seeds removed) on this crust... And taste pure ambrosia.

AUGUST

It was Mama's month to "take the Aid" — preceded by a whirl-wind of housecleaning and menu making.

"Well, it's really So and So's time, but Mrs. Bacon's time is in August." Then it was Mom's turn to be hospitable and say, "Yes, I'll take them unless someone else wants them."

That was standard procedure: Remind the other members, just in case someone else really coveted the honor in August, but you stood ready and waiting to entertain.

Many times Mom postponed papering a room until she was the August hostess. Then all became bedlam. Barrels were moved in, boards placed across the tops so we could walk the full length of the room, paste was made, the lengths of paper were measured and matched, and hung in place. Usually Dad and I did the work, under Mom's orders. After she selected the paper, she would say, "You and Dad do such a good job I believe I'll just stay out of your way."

Once our best laid papering plans backfired. We were going to splurge and hire our papering done. This time we'd do it right, so we tore off all the old paper in the living room, the hall and front bedroom. And you can probably guess what happened. The paper hanger had previous commitments — he was running for county judge — and he couldn't get to us. August arrived and we entertained the ladies in two rooms — the dining room and the kitchen. Worse, for Mama, they never got to be impressed with our new paper!

Still worse was the time of the lost lunch. We had planned to really "put on the dog." We would serve chicken salad sandwiches and potato salad, along with cake and pie, jelly, preserves, bread and butter, coffee and I can't remember what all. We prepared the salads ahead of time and sank them in the cool spring water to be brought up and put on the table at the last minute.

The business meeting was finished and the next meeting place decided upon and Mom and I started to the spring. Halfway across the yard, I broke into a run, shouting to Mom, "Hurry, hurry, the pigs are in the springhouse!"

The cuplrits were gone, but the damage had been done. The chicken and potato salad were ruined. Each crock had a layer of blue spring mud on top.

We rescued enough cream and butter for the bread and preserves — which we ended up serving with the coffee. The boys thought this little episode was uproariously funny. They had made such pets out of the pigs I'm sure they thought the pigs were justified in their crime — and deserved the goodies more than the Ladies' Aid-ers.

After the canning and cleaning, after the Ladies' Aid, I turned my attention to getting my small wardrobe ready to return to Warrensburg. Even I didn't realize then its meagerness: Mae's worn woolen skirt turned inside out and cut down to fit me, the 98-cent Sears & Roebuck sweater to wear with it, a few other dyed, cut-down and made-over dresses. They were all I had. I had been allowed $9.98 to order a genuine camel's hair coat from Sears and a 98-cent brown and white speckled cotton hat to accompany it.

It wasn't hard to get all of these personal belongings into our one and only suitcase, and one Monday early in September the four of us — Bud, Dad, Mom and I — set out for Warrensburg. We now had a very respectable-looking maroon Ford sedan, a golden chariot compared to the T we had previously owned. About noon I was deposited at Mrs. Fischer's door with my suitcase, a bag of potatoes, home-cured ham, bacon and a few jars of canned goods — such as tomatoes, corn, green beans, and preserves and jellies.

The next morning I began the enrollment process all over again — standing in long lines of students outside the Administration building, waiting my turn to get

"OKs" stamped on my class permits. Mine called for European History, Physiology, Art in the Home, Clothing Selection and Chorus.

What memories come rolling back from the past as I recall European History! Presiding over the class was one Dr. Marti, who read from his notes — hour after hour, day after day — for three months. I can see him now: The tattered pages of his notes were placed upon a small lectern. This in turn was placed on a desk. Upon all of this was placed Dr. Marti's elbows, and on his upturned hands was Dr. Marti's head. This last-named item rolled from side to side as he held it in his hands and extolled the grandeur of old Europe under the "fief" system and praised the practice of "Celibacy." I knew, though, that any question on a test could be beneficially answered by in some way involving these two great ideas. And by so doing, I came out with a B. Not until many years later did I stumble onto the exact meaning of celibacy — after which I began to see why Dr. Marti attributed everything progressive to this sterling quality.

Dr. Marti was a rather small, shy man. He always wore gray suits, kept his gray hair cut short — it stood up like a bristle brush all over his head — and he smoked a pipe constantly. He was considered a great brain on the campus. I'm sure he was. I had so little knowledge — as well as relevant background — that all of the great things he aspired to teach missed me completely.

The most exciting event that ever occurred in European History happened after a football game. The class hour was from 1 to 2 each afternoon. Many football players were struggling through the long day after the night-before game. Most of them were asleep on the back row by the time Dr. Marti finished his droning lecture. Chuck Workman, always full of devilment, and Jack Niebrugge had strapped a burly fellow named Trantwein into his seat by unbuckling the straps of his leather jacket and re-buckling them around the back posts of his chair. When Trantwein arose to leave class he created the greatest rumpus as the chair came up with him. That I remember, oh, so clearly .. but little else, I fear.

Physiology, however, was different. I have always been a bit curious about the functions of the body and why its parts behave as they do. It didn't bother me to cut open a frog and dissect it or bisect it — whichever it is you do. I guess this came from having dressed so many chickens on the farm. I didn't mind slitting an earthworm from stem to stern, either.

But when it came to drawing an illustration of their insides, I was stymied. Drawing anything — much less a frog's insides — just wasn't "my bag." But the class was a pure delight and I worked my heart out on papers and research — and even on drawings that I'm sure couldn't be deciphered.

Art in the Home and Clothing Selection were both taught by Miss Julia Hatz (I'm not making up that name, either!) In fact, Miss Hatz was practically *the* Home Economics Department. Her classes were all girls. We learned lots of valuable homemaking tricks — how to dye old silk hose, cut and braid them into small rugs; how to crochet by pattern, how to hemstitch and do venetian drawnwork. I make several place mats out of plain grocer's cotton twine and Miss Hatz helped me size and stretch them on a form as a wedding gift for Mae.

Chorus was pure fun. We met on alternating days in the auditorium of the Administration Building. We had a large group, boys and girls. Professor Utt led us through all of Handel's "Messiah" and drove us especially hard through its Hallelujah Chorus which we presented in public at both Christmas and Easter. The singing had a therapeutic affect on us and I always came away feeling happy and free from care. But to this day I dream that I have forgotten to go to Chorus

CELIBACY

The great thing Dr. Marti aspired to teach us missed me completely.

and I just know I won't get credit for the course. It's puzzling, because we only received one hour of credit for going all three quarters.

The schedule was easy so the weeks passed by quickly; the weekends were pure gold. One reason was that I was allowing myself to see at least one movie a week. "Little Women," "The Little Minister", "Naughty Marietta" and "Suez" would amuse the youngsters of today by their naivete, but we lived in a world of reality and didn't want to dish out good money for another dose of it for entertainment. Most of the students were going to school on a tight budget so we had respect for a dollar.

I was the only roomer at Mrs. Fischer's house, so I had full sway. She took me under her wing and on Sunday afternoons we went for rides in the country — if she could get her Chevrolet out of the garage. Her driving was far from accomplished and when I think of the chances I took with my life, I shudder, and thank heaven for surviving to maturity.

But if her driving fell short, her cooking more than made up for it. She brought me a plate full of food evening after evening and always on Sunday at noon. I'm convinced that she saw how little I prepared for myself, mostly because the tiny kitchenette was freezing cold. It had been a porch converted into a makeshift kitchen, so it was like going outside to do your cooking.

In due sequence came the winter quarter. I again stood in line and received permits for Elementary Education (4b), English Composition, Interpretation of Poetry and Typewriting — plus Chorus, of course. Course contents and professors of the first two courses completely elude my memory, but Interpretation of Poetry is with me still and it never ceased to be a most valuable asset in my teaching.

Miss Anna Marie Todd took us through "The Odyssey" and "The Aneid" and Dante's "Paradiso," "Purgatorio" and "Inferno," as well as introducing us all of the Greek myths, gods and goddesses and their Roman counterparts. This course I loved. I carefully re-wrote my notes each evening and I frequently repeated the adventures of Ulysses as he encountered Polyphameus, the Cyclops, Circe, Scylla and Chrybdis. I loved the sound of Menelaus and Agamemnon, Achilles, Clytemnestra, Priam and Hecuba as they rolled off my tongue.

Miss Todd told us the stories with a merry twinkle in her eye. When something really struck her as humorous, she would chuckle out loud, and if we didn't laugh, she would look over her glasses and demand to know why we didn't think the incident was funny. For instance, some of the old books called their chapter divisions "fyttes" (pronounced "fit"). Miss Todd would look over her glasses and announce, "Folks, today I'm going to have "fytte" one. Tomorrow we'll have fytte two." At which we had better laugh. (One such book written in "fyttes", I seem to recall, was Thomas Mallory's version of "King Arthur and His Knights of the Round Table."

Typing was a real challenge. Miss Myrtle Downs wouldn't accept anything with a strikeover or an erasure so this meant many and many a copy was made until I finally came up with a perfect run through, "Now is the time for every good man to come to the aid of his country." I enjoyed the finger exercises, though, and came out of the class with an A — and typing 60 to 80 words per minute. I was proud of myself.

Christmas was a big event, for an extra reason this year. Mae and Irvin had set December 23rd as their wedding date. Irvin was teaching Math in the Webster Groves High School and Mae had been working for a dentist and a Mrs. Morris in

MYTHS AND MEMORIES

Agamemnon and Achilles,
Menelaus and Clytemnestra
Priam and Hecuba ... I loved the
sounds as they rolled off my tongue.

St. Louis County. Now they would live in Maplewood at the Brownson Hotel Building at the Loop.

The biggest thing I can remember about the holiday however, is the quantity of divinity I made to treat the neighbors when they dropped in and to pass around to the traditional Charavari Crowd. After a few days Mae and Irvin returned to St. Louis to set up housekeeping in their apartment and the rest of us became busily engaged in butchering pigs.

This was another of Mom's ways of utilizing her family: "We'll butcher during the Christmas holidays while all the kids are home." So while our German neighbors were relaxing and making merrry during the holidays, the Bacons were steeped to their eyebrows in sausage, lard and mincemeat. And Christmas of '34 was no exception.

On the appointed evening Dad stepped to the telephone and rounded up two or three neighbors to help with the lifting. Butchering, like most all farm work in those days, was by manpower. We all rolled into bed early that night, because 4 a.m. was considered the proper time to roll out and get the fire started under the big black iron kettle which had been filled with water for scalding.

Breakfast was a hurried affair on such mornings because a mule had to be harnessed to pull the dead pigs from the hog barn to the butchering site. This usually was just outside the white picket fence on the north side of the house. Sometimes a platform was built and a scaffold erected for hanging the hogs, but this usually was done on the previous day.

When the water felt just right — not too hot because that would scald the skin side too much, not too cold because the bristles wouldn't slip — Dad would come in the house for his .22 and I'd go upstairs and stick my head under a thick pillow. I couldn't stand to think of those nice, friendly pigs being shot. I usually had to do this three or four times, depending on how many pigs we butchered, because only one was killed at a time and dragged up to the scalding barrel.

This barrel was firmly fixed at an angle which allowed the men to push and pull the fat pig in and out of the hot water. When testing determined that the "bristles'll slip," the pig was laid out on the platform and the scraping began. Knives had to be very sharp and their users very careful so as not to sever the skin because that would prevent curing later. When all the pigs had been killed, scalded, scraped and hung on the gambling sticks (sticks stuck through the hock just back of the Achilles tendon), the tubs were set underneath to receive the intestines, liver, stomach and "guts."

While the men hurried to and fro with all this work, Mom and I busily prepared dinner. It was considered necessary to have an early dinner for at least two reasons: One, we had eaten an early and somewhat skimpy breakfast; second, the fat had to be taken off the intestines as quickly as possible. And that was women's work, after the tubs were carried in and set under the big kitchen table.

I never minded the work of separating the "leaf lard" from the intestines, but the odor I *did* mind. For days afterwards the house smelled as we went about the follow-up chores — rendering the fat out of the leaf lard and regular lard, frying down sausage and so on.

But the worst job of all was cleaning the intestines prepatory to stuffing sausage ... and we all liked stuffed sausage. We carried the tubs of intestines (now minus the fat) a distance away from the house, then we cut them into four- to five-foot lengths and turned back the ends an inch or so. Mom or I held the intestine and the other poured warm water into the folded-over end, causing the intestine to

MAMA'S CHRISTMAS
"We'll butcher while the kids are all home."

turn wrong side out and divest itself of the contents. Then Mama ran her fingers the length of the strip to clean away as much of the chime as possible. Sometimes the weather was so cold we would have to go to the house several times to warm our hands. The next day we washed the intestines in several baths of salt water and begin the scraping.

This was done by laying them on a board and scraping — always in one direction — until all the waste and fatty tissue were disposed of. When the intestines from one hog could be put into a teacup, they were considered clean enough to use.

During the afternoon the men cut the hogs in two, sawing down the backbones, and carried them into the smokehouse where it was a little warmer to work. There the huge hind legs were separated from the sides, or middlin', as some people called them. Then the men cut off the front legs, the head and the rest, until each piece was carefully laid out so no two pieces touched. Tomorrow they would trim down the pieces neatly to form hams, shoulders and sides. These trimmings we used for sausage, ground by our hand-turned sausage mill.

This mill was attached to a board placed on the seats of two chairs in the middle of the kitchen. We children all begged to turn the handle. We liked to squeeze the raw trimmings down into the mill and watch as the steel worm pushed the meat against a cross-shaped knife and squirted it out through perhaps 25 little round holes in a piece of steel. The ground sausage fell out into a large, clean pan, and when it was all ground it was seasoned with salt, black pepper and sage.

Mama always seasoned the sausage sparingly because something we were going to eat all year couldn't be ruined by too much salt or pepper. So she seasoned, mixed and fried a small patty to taste. This process contined until we all decided it was just right. Then we stuffed the greater part of it into the clean intestines which had been soaking in warm salt water in the back of the kitchen stove.

The final step was to fry down the patties or the stuffed pieces, seal them in a clean, dry glass Mason jar — to be opened and relished for a delicious meat dish the following summer.

This butchering season was no different than many others except that we put away a few choice pieces for me to carry back to Warrensburg with my meager wardrobe. All packed, it filled a rather good-sized box which Dad tied securely with a long piece of binder twine, stout but rough looking.

I returned as usual on the Missouri Pacific bus, and all the way I was bothered about getting off the bus at the regular depot. At the end of a holiday I feared many other students would be arriving and there I'd be — carrying my big box of meat, tied up with binder twine. Somewhere along the way I had a bright idea. The bus made a stop at the end of Broad Street; if I got off there, only a few would see my box.

I knew this would be much farther to walk, but I didn't know how *much* farther until I got off and started walking. The suitcase was heavy and the box of meat was heavier. The binder twine cut into the palm of my hand. The streets were pitch black and the weather was zero. Somehow — exhausted and cold — I made it to Tyler Street and my room ... only to find that if I had ridden on to the depot Mrs. Fischer was there to meet me!

Such pride. I always had to learn things the hard way.

After the Christmas vacation I settled down to business-like study habits. My little upstairs room was often cold. It was directly over the downstairs bedroom of Mrs. Fischer and her mother, Mrs. Rodgers. At the price I paid per week, I don't see how they afforded to heat the room at all. What little warmth I got, I'm sure, was courtesy of their kindness to me — like those Sunday plates of chicken, mashed potatoes, vegetables and salad Mrs. Fischer brought me. And whatever else she cooked for herself and Mrs. Rodgers.

In my spare moments I started using the needlework knowledge I had learned in Miss Hatz's Art in the Home course. I had learned simple crochet stitches, Italian drawnwork, braiding rugs, how to quilt patterns on chair cushions. I was enamored with all of these things. So on Sunday when I didn't have school work to do, I crocheted. Mrs. Rodgers, quite old, would come upstairs and see me working with my needles and pause at the door just long enough to tell me, "You know, Miss Grace, you're going to have to take all that out with our nose when you get to Heaven." (If that's right, I'll have a busy nose Up There, because needlework remains one of my consuming joys.)

I don't remember any sunshine that whole winter. I'm sure there must have been some sunny days, but my memories of that time are all dark and cloudy and cold. I'm sure I didn't eat properly. There was no money for food; I ate a lot of hot potato salad. I kept the potatoes in my bedroom because they would freeze in the kitchen. I would buy a loaf of bread and a jar of sweet pickles about once a week and this would have "to do me."

At the middle of the spring quarter Hazel Tremaine and Ruth Martin came to live at the house. They could make five hours of credit this way, and by continuing throgh the summer they could make 15 hours. Hazel had been my roommate the summer before, so she moved in with me while Ruth occupied one of the big front rooms.

The quarter was a bad one for me. First of all, one of the requirements for that 60-hour elementary certificate was Art I. For me this was a calamity. Miss Foley was the teacher. I attributed my troubles to being a country bumpkin, but for whatever reason mastering the primary colors and secondary colors and mixing water colors to just the proper hue to make a color wheel just wasn't my cup of tea. I despised it. But both Hazel and Ruth were town girls and had been exposed to all the artistic mediums, so they helped me just enough to get a grade.

American Government and State Government were also required courses, both taught by Professor Calvert. I struggled manfully (woman-fully?) with the Bill of Rights, the constitutions and the various assignments to be memorized from them. We had to keep scrapbooks, too, and I pasted them full of anything having to do with Government. Here Dad came to my rescue. He was always interested in what he called "Civil Government" so he clipped articles from the St. Louis *Globe-Democrat* and mailed them to me for more pasting.

I awoke one morning near the end of the quarter feeling terribly ill. My legs wouldn't support me; my throat was sore and swollen. I was terribly warm, dizzy and miserable. For more than a week I lay in bed, too sick to care what happened to my color wheel or my "Government scraps." When the fever ran high, I saw dreadful things — Miss Foley tearing up my beautiful color wheel and my scrapbook, too, and Prof. Utt waving his baton at me and telling me to sing when my throat was too sore.

After several days my left ear began to ache. The pain was excruciating. Mrs. Fischer had had some nurse's training so she gave me some care. Hazel moved into another room and I was left alone except when Mrs. Fischer brought me a bowl of soup. I couldn't afford the price of a doctor. That was out of the question. But I'm sure Mrs. Fischer recognized strep throat infection. She called

THE FEVER

I saw dreadful things. Miss Foley was tearing up my beautiful color wheel and my scrapbook, too. And Professor Utt was waving his baton at telling me to sing, but my throat was too sore.

an M.D. and got a prescription for some nasty-tasting little black pills which I had to mash up in a teaspoon of warm water and hold them in my throat as long as possible without choking before I swallowed them. All of these things Mrs. Fischer supplied, so you see what I mean about her not making expenses from my $1.50 a week room rent.

Finally one evening I began to feel better. I was hungry, too. Hazel and Ruth were going to Buente Town to eat and they brought me a paper carton of lemon Jello with carrots, pineapple and nuts. Ah, how beautiful that cool Jello felt against my raw throat.

I recovered quickly and plunged into making up the work I had missed. Prof. Calvert informed me that I looked like a ghost and inquired what was the matter. He gruffly insisted I do a "few more things" for my scrapbook. Very kind and considerate he was, because he gave me Bs in both courses, lofty grades I know I didn't deserve.

When I showed up in Chorus, Professor Utt *did* wave his baton at me. But instead of demanding that I sing, he said, in a low tone, "Have you seen the school nurse? You really should if you haven't."

I was called out of Government class the next day and told to report to the school nurse's clinic. She looked at my throat and took my temperature. She filled out some forms and asked who my M.D. was. When I told her I didn't have one, she said, "Well, why didn't you call me?" I didn't know I should have — or could have. She shook her head at my stupidity and looked aghast at me over her spectacles. Ah, the ignorances and fears of youth. Mine, anyway.

But only my Art I grade suffered from my afflictions. Miss Foley wasn't about to lessen the load of all the lettering, poster making and color wheels just because I had had a "little old sore tonsil." *And* I had just better get all those assignments in right now. She doubted I had been sick because my name wasn't on her list from the nurse and her parting shot was, "You just don't like Art I, do you?"

I wanted to fire back that I didn't like Art II or II or IV, either. But I gathered up all my little pieces of paper, paints, water pan, construction paper and everything else I could grab and took it home with me. That night Ruth, Hazel, Mrs. Fischer and I burned the cliched midnight oil getting the posters, the wheels, the water color bits and all into their proper perspective.

Bright and early the next morning I delivered all the darling little projects to Miss Foley. Her funny little thin nose sniffed the air as if to say, "I smell a mouse somewhere" and her long black bangs bobbed up and down furiously as she checked my projects. I prayed silently that she would at least bless me with a D so I could say goodbye to Art I. And that's exactly what she did. So I guess Ruth and Hazel weren't such expert artists either!

How I ever got through the quarter exams I'll never know. I was so weak and exhausted from the bout with strep throat I could hardly cling to the steps to the third floor of the Administration Building where the classes were held. One day as I was creeping along a nice boy I had known from several winter classes caught up and walked along with me. Again, after class, he came along and chatted about some amusing incidents in class. By the time we reached the first floor he had asked me to go with him to a party at the President's home and I had said Yes.

It was routine for each class to have a party at the home, a large colonial house on the outskirts of town, surrounded by a huge lawn, garden and trees. That night a large group of us met on the steps of the Administration Building to walk together to the party. Some of us had a so-called "date" — which meant we had been asked to walk with a boy. Perhaps none in the group was as naive as I, but I thought it was being quite intimate if the boy held my hand.

We had fun stumbling along over broken sidewalks and up the gravel driveway to the front door of the presidential mansion. Until then I hadn't worried at all about my attire, but it seemed that everyone else in the room had on real "dress-up" clothes. The boys wore good dark suits and top coats; the girls, although not formally dressed, had on their best coats and dresses — some even with touches of fur on the collar and cuffs.

So why did I feel out of place? I had on a black silk dress. It originally was the gray Canton silk one that Mae had made for me that first summer at Warrensburg. We had dyed it black for the second go-round and I had attached a pink ruffled chiffon collar that Mom dug up out of one of Aunt Mae's clothing boxes. My coat was the same $9.98 one I had worn to school all winter. My shoes were blonde kid; I had bought them at a fire sale for 75 cents. So, you see, I really was elegant!

I like my cap

I like my cape

However, I was determined not to let a little thing like clothes ruin my evening. We played mostly guessing games, one of which was to place an object in view of the players and give one-word clues to a secret word. One object was an Irish potato and one of the clues given was "common." I immediately guessed this one: "Commentator."

It simply made my evening complete, especially when Dr. Phillips of Geography class fame, asked what the word meant. He had never heard of it! I wanted to tell him there were a few things in this world besides horse latitudes and summer solstice — but I didn't!

We ended the party with the usual refreshments — a dip of ice cream served on a paper plate with a small, hard cookie and a very small cup of red punch, with no "spike" in it, of course. The party ended about 10:30 and we shook hands with President and Mrs. Eliot and Professor and Mrs. Phillips and trooped off down the gravel drive, through the gates and back over the broken concrete sidewalks to home. Thus ended my first college "date."

When I went home at the end of the term Mama and the boys teased me unmercifully about my sore throat — "What color are your spots now?" — because I had written about those badges of my illness. By chance I heard from Hazel that Mrs. Rodgers had died of strep throat; then Mama got around to asking Dr. Leach about it.

"Sure," he told her, "it kills people."

After that I didn't hear so much about the color of my spots.

I faced two problems during this stay at home. One, Alma Homfeldt and Wesley Schulte were to be married the first Saturday in June. If I stayed home for the wedding, I'd be a week late enrolling for summer school.

Number Two was money. My $300 was about gone. I had one asset — my registered Hereford heifer which Uncle John had given me the year before. Mom and Dad were determined to not let me borrow $100; the heifer would have to go.

I had a contract to teach in the Linn Elementary School for the next school year, but the thought of borrowing money left me a little petrified. Mom had brought us all up on the "Interest, mortgage and taxes" theory: "Don't borrow, then you won't owe." When my "return" for the calf arrived, it was a few cents less than $60. That had to last me for an entire summer. Tuition would be $20 and room rent $13.50 for nine weeks. That left me less than $30 for food and incidentals. I ate even less than usual that summer.

THE WEDDING

I saw Alma slip up the back stairs with a stew pan of water; she had given up hope of ever getting the wash pan.

I did stay home for the Homfeldt-Schulte wedding. It was a big affair in our parts. I had crocheted Alma a set of place mats for her gift. I had to work like a Trojan to get them done, sized and wrapped by Saturday.

Mom had been asked to come early in the morning along with other women in the neighborhood to help cook. I stayed home until early afternoon to prepare dinner for Dad and the boys. Then I put on my white seersucker dress and my everyday shoes; I carried my "dress-up" shoes. It was a short walk — along our lower field, over a couple of rail fences and under a couple of wire fences, across a foot bridge over the creek and I was there.

The scene bordered on bedlam. The Homfeldts were a large family, eight boys and Alma, the only girl. This was Before Plumbing and everybody wanted to "wash up" at the same time, so the wash pan and soap were really getting a workout.

When the neighbors began to arrive for the cermony, Mr. and Mrs. Homfeldt stood just inside the front door and welcomed the guests. I was charged with keeping the list of wedding gifts and a complete description of each one. There always were several sets of water glasses and pitchers, embroidered pillow cases and such. So I would write:

"Green glass water set ... Mr. and Mrs. John Doe.

"Pillow cases with birds ... Mr. and Mrs. Joe Doe..."

I was busy with my bookkeeping when I saw Alma slip up the back stairs with a stew pan of water. She had given up hope of ever getting the wash pan. Wesley, the groom-to-be, had shed his blue shirt and bib overalls for a plain dark suit — always described in Sears & Roebuck catalogue as an "all occasion" suit.

A short time later Alma sent word downstairs that she was ready. The minister took his place in the southwest corner of the parlor under a fancy little clock shelf. On it was a snow-clean white, starched scarf with embroidered blue birds carrying a pink rose bud in their bills. Alma's parents and Wesley's father sat in a row of dining chairs placed on a bias back of where Wesley had entered from the kitchen. He took his place, facing the minister. Then everybody crowded into the parlor to see and hear the sacred, age-old words.

Alma descended the front stairs, rustling in her white satin gown, resplendent in her long veil and crown of orange blossoms, and looking quite unlike the Alma I had known for so many years. She took her place by Wesley, and in what seemed an incredibly short time the Rev. Renken read the words and pronounced them "Man and Wife."

I realized that day how the entire remainder of one's life can change in a short time. I felt it a little frightening. One minute you were free and independent; the next you weren't. You belonged soul and body to this man and your children to come.

These good sturdy German descendants knew the meaning of a successful marriage. There were no such things as separations or divorces among them. And such a marriage was this one to be — until death do us part. Now fifty years later, Alma and Wesley have done more than their share of rough, hard farm work. They have been the "salt of the earth" kind of people who put their best into church, school and community. They had been trained from childhood to perform hard, unpleasant tasks in a pleasant, uncomplaining manner, a lesson so lacking in many of our young people today.

Back in the kitchen, Mom and Mrs. Frank Schulte and Loretta Struemph and her mother had been making things fly because as soon as the "I do's" were said, supper was to be served. The menu wasn't fancy, but preparing enough food for at least 100 people wasn't an easy task. I remember the huge dishpan of slaw Mrs. Schulte made, with bits of green pepper and carrots to give it color and the usual country dressing of sugar, vinegar, salt and oil.

The potatoes were boiled, drained and riced. Bread had been baked earlier in the week; the chickens had been baked that morning and Loretta and Mrs. Struemph were now slicing them and laying them out on platters. Cream and butter had been hanging in the well since yesterday. Clarence and George carefully removed the pump top from the well and pulled out the large molds of butter, each with a pattern of sheaves of wheat molded on them. The cream was yellow, sweet and thick as we poured it into the pitchers to be passed with coffee.

There were numerous kinds of pickles, preserves and jellies set around in pretty footed glass compotes. For dessert there was wedding cake and homemade ice cream — both made from scratch. The wedding cake was decorated very simply with small blue blossoms from some fresh flowers. (I believe it was iron weed; I never saw another bloom like it.) These blossoms were perfectly shaped, with four petals spread out in a pattern on both top and sides of the cake.

In those days the Ladies' Aid owned and operated the business of an ancient five-gallon ice cream freezer; anyone having a large gathering could rent the contraption — providing you came for it and returned it promptly and paid 50 cents for its use. (This was always a part of the Aid's secretary's duties, to check on the whereabouts of the freezer at each monthly meeting and report on the "total receipts" derived from the use thereof.)

This monstrosity must have weighed 50 pounds or more. It consisted of the necessary handle and dasher — the mechanical requirements — inside a huge wooden tub. The sometimes drawn-out process of turning the handle to freeze the ice cream was the "catch:" Most of the men would rather do without the traditional delicacy.

But today it held the place of honor in the Homfeldt cellar, covered and packed in damp, clean feed bags to hold the coolness and let the flavor ripen. This delicious creamy concoction was the crowning glory of the wedding feast. Everyone sat down at the table in order of importance — at the "first" table, of course, were the bride and groom, his parents, her parents and grandparents and the minister and his wife.

After the wedding and the dining, it was time for dancing. Willing hands cleared the dining room of chairs and took the table apart and stored it in the kitchen. Someone made sure "the music" had arrived and others shaved thin slices of paraffin on the board floor to facilitate smoother dancing. One of the big chores was to stop the small children from sliding around on the chips. Then the older people moved their chairs to the best vantage points to view the dancing.

By this time darkness had fallen, so we brought in freshly cleaned and filled kerosene lamps. They were lighted and set on the mantle and the musicians were given the sign to begin playing. Only the bride and groom danced the first dance. After that, everybody was welcome and there were dances for everyone — squares, rounds and waltzes. I didn't really care what the music was as long as someone asked me to dance. And I sat out few dances in my young life.

This was Saturday night, so the dancing came to an end shortly before midnight. Everybody lined up outside to contribute his noisiest bit to an oldfashioned charavari. After that the people clambered into their cars, farm wagons and buggies and rolled off down the hill toward home. Mom and I walked. We clung to the sides of the rickety old foot bridge and crept cautiously along the creek bank until we had again conquered all of the fences and gaps. When we reached our own land, we traveled almost to the house without opening any more gates or crawling through more wire fences — for which I was duly thankful.

On Sunday I returned to Warrensburg — to a summer I wish had never been. I was still weak and tired from the throat infection. I knew I didn't have enough money to see me through and Mom had made it crystal clear that I couldn't expect them to help me. So I ate almost nothing. I felt too tired to do my school work and, needless to say, I didn't do very well. Hazel came to my rescue, lending me money for food, and Mae lent me money to repay Hazel, and I reimbursed Mae after school opened and I was earning a salary of $60 a month. Money matters can get complicated!

FRACTIONS.

135. 1. Into how many parts are these squares divided?

2. How do the parts compare as to size?

3. What is each part called?

4. What is a half of anything?

5. How many halves are equal to a whole one?

6. How many halves are there in 2 apples? In 3 pears? In 5 peaches? In 1 orange and a half? In 2 lemons and a half? In 4 and a half plums?

7. Two half melons are equal to how many whole melons? 4 half melons? 6 half melons? 3 half melons are equal to how many whole melons, and how many half melons besides? 5 half melons?

8. Draw a line. Divide it into halves. Then divide each half into two equal parts.

9. Into how many parts is the whole line divided?

10. What is each part called?

11. What do you call 2 of the parts? 3 of the parts? How many thirds are equal to a whole thing?

12. How many fourths are there in any whole thing?

13. How many fourths are there in 2 circles? In 3 squares? In 1 line and 1 fourth of a line? In 2 lines and 3 fourths of a line?

EL. OF AR. — 10   145

PART FOUR

LINN

9

The first fytte, 1935-40

The next five years were among the happiest of my life. Charles Howard, my darling youngest brother, was ready for high school, so he and I were to occupy a "suite" of light housekeeping rooms upstairs at our cousins, Logan Wills and his wife, Birdie. In these two small rooms we had the bare necessities — in the kitchen a kerosene stove, a cook table, a small eating table, two chairs and a small bed (cot) for Charles, a closet on one side where we hung our clean clothes, and two wide board shelves where we stored our groceries, our china and cooking pans.

My bedroom was over the front porch, so it was never overly warm, but Log tried his best to keep it comfortable. He weather-stripped the windows, put on storm windows, and kept the furnace going full blast in the winter. I had a bed, a wash stand and a rocking chair. We used the bathroom downstairs and Log's and Birdie's living room. How they endured all the activity for the next four (five for me) years, I'll never know. But for me, they carried those years 'way past enduring, far into enjoyable.

I was to teach at the McDaniel School, a consolidated, one-room school about five miles out to Linn — in an area known as "The Flat." It was correctly named. As you left Linn on your way to the Flat, you went down a long, steep hill behind the Courthouse, curved around an elbow along an amost sheer drop-off into a creek bed, then climbed hills and more hills until you reached a flat top. On it sat several houses of various and sundry shapes — all the same weathered gray. The barns were all made of logs and loose hay stuck out between the timbers. I had never seen such poor looking country.

I had arranged with George McDaniel, a sort of early pioneer taxi driver, to drive me to school each morning and pick me up each evening. He had similar arrangements with the school board for hauling high school students from that area. I paid him $8 per month for my service.

"Gib" McDaniel was one of the tallest, thinnest, most pessimistic people I've ever known. Nothing was ever right: The weather was always too warm or too cold; at the filling station the gas in his car had been diluted with kerosene or water; you couldn't trust anybody these days; and "that right rear tire most likely'll go flat before we get to the first ditch." I found that it took lots of coaxing to get Gib and his Model A Ford started toward the Flat.

But I was hardly prepared for what I found that first morning. Sam Bacon, Dad's cousin, was on the school board. The small, two-story, gray weatherboard house was his, and at the end of his lane he was waiting for us with his two small daughters, Mary and Orlies ("Sug"). They climbed into the rear seat and we kept on climbing upward until we came to the highest peak on the Flat. There, sitting precariously on an insecure rock foundation was one of the smallest one-room schoolhouses I had ever seen. It, too, was weatherboard gray, and it looked so cold and lonely I felt sorry for it.

Sam, Mary, Orlies and I piled out of the car, all in a heap in the ditch alongside the road. Gib gunned the accelerator a few times to hurry the high school kids along as they sauntered along the road coming from toward Rich Fountain. But they were used to Gib's gunning and didn't hie themselves much.

Sam opened the schoolhouse door with his key, and we entered a pitiful scene — a pathetic conglomeration of broken-down desks and seats, a huge old King Heater stove, and a teacher's desk so old I was sure it must have pre-dated the Mayflower. One leg was completely unattached and, I discovered later, if anything leaned on it or touched it, the leg fell off and the desk wobbled most disconcertingly. It had a high middle compartment. One could lift up the lid and store papers, ink, books and whatever one wished in it — if one were extremely careful to balance it all properly so the leg wouldn't fall off. During the summer Sam had built a big closet in the rear quarter of the room. It now held a dozen tin pie pans. I found out later they were used to serve hot lunches. The previous teacher had tried cooking some simple dishes for the kids. Later I saw why.

This was a rather hurried inspection of my domain for the next nine months, but it was almost too much. Fortunately, the kids began to arrive, mobs of them. And Mary and Orlies were so happy to see all of them. There were the three Kehr children: Faye, large and plump with beautiful red hair; Larry, small and plump with beautiful fire-red hair; and a sweet, blue-eyed, plump little girl with red-gold hair who shall be nameless here because I can't remember her name. The Kehrs lived in a tall, skinny gray house across three or four fields from the school.

Katherine Wilhelmina Gertrude Meyerpeter — Katie — came down the road from Rich Fountain with her brother, Frankie. Nelson and Opal Marie Mertens came across the field with the Kehrs. Clarence and Herbert Nilges came up out of the back pasture behind the school. And Vincent Nilges appeared from out of nowhere.

Vincent had large, dark eyes and a high, thin, whiney voice. He would keep the whole school in stitches, I would discover in due time, asking funny nonsensical things like, "Why does stink hazel stink? Heck, teacher, why does it? Some people call it skunk hazel, only it stinks worse than skunk, huh, don't it, teacher? You don't know why stink hazel stink? Why don't you find out and let me know. Always did want to know why stink hazel stink!"

I noticed an apprehensive twinkle in Sam's eye, and he kept looking up the road toward Rich Fountain. I soon found out why. Here came the children from the "tie woods." These people were known as "tie hackers" because they cut and shaped railroad ties. They had become members of the Mennonite Church and when I knew them they were very devout. But they were less than religious in attending school. They did as they pleased. And today, I suppose, it pleased them to give me a treat, so here they came — Emma Phillips and her nephews, Alfred and Howard Phillips, Leon, John Jr. and Alfred Pearon and others whose names I've forgotten.

The last to arrive were the three McDaniel children — Bob, Virginia, and Jessie Marie. Knowing their father, Willie, the slowest human alive, I wasn't at all alarmed that they were late. I suspected they would be so every day — and most of the time I was right.

All of them I would come to know well — some as rewarding recipients of a teacher's best efforts and intentions, some as exasperating ignorers of knowledge and learning, some as humorous fun lovers with only a secondary interest in schooling, but all as products of ways of living heretofore foreign to me.

About all I got done that first day was to sort out the various grades — Faye Kehr and Bob McDaniel went in the 8th grade. Orlies Bacon was a 6th grader,

275. A pile of wood or stone 8 ft. long, 4 ft. wide, and 4 ft. high is called a **Cord**.

A pile that is 1 ft. long, 4 ft. wide, and 4 feet high is called a **Cord Foot**.

THE TIE HACKERS
It wasn't recorded that these children would attend school. They did as they pleased.

Mary Bacon and Larry Kehr were 3rd graders, Virginia McDaniel was a 5th grader and Jessie Marie McDaniel was a beginner. I couldn't even make a guess as to where Herbert, Clarence and Vincent Nilges belonged. Nor any of the "tie woods" people. I'd just have to wait until I could talk to Frances Huffine, their last year's teacher, to find out.

That made my first few days rugged. Frances had failed some of my "unclassifieds" and they resented my "putting me in the same old book again." I tried to explain that I couldn't help it, but they didn't understand why I couldn't advance them.

In the big closet I found a stack of song books — at least a dozen of the good old standby, "Golden Book of Songs I Love to Sing." So, falling back on what I had learned at Horse Shoe Bend, I passed them out and we began to get acquainted by singing together.

Never had I heard a sweeter voice than that of Emma Phillips. Her tone was' pure and her pitch perfect. Orlies and Virginia also loved to sing and often these three girls would stand alone and sing as a trio or duet. Everyone admired their courage, but the girls loved doing it.

Bob McDaniel and Fay vied with each other in arithmetic, each trying to outdo the other. Bob had a peculiar way of standing at the blackboard, the toe of his left shoe turned sideways and pressing hard on the toe of his right shoe. Mary and Orlies never missed anything funny, and Mary always giggled when Bob got his feet placed just right. Then Bob would glare at her and say, "Teacher, make her stop that there gigglin'. I cain't concentrate without my toes trompin' on each other."

Leon Pearon was a queer character. "Prairie Chicken," the kids called him, because he walked as if he were "stepping on eggs." I tried, with less than complete success, to persuade the worst offenders not to tease him about it. He would implore me to help him and explain: "You see, teacher, I jest cain't walk no other way but this here way." And he would step high and place each foot on the ground real easy-like. That walk made it almost impossible for him to play ball and other games that required fast, firm footing. I suppose he had weak arches and today we would do something about them.

Then there were Jesse and Mary Nell Pennington. Jesse was a half brother to Mary Nell. His mother had burned to death when he was a baby and his father married Nell Vaughan. This made them, as well as the McDaniel and Bacon children, my cousins. With such a colorful assortment, the coming school year should be ... well, interesting.

The evenings were fun. Logan and Birdie treated Charles and me like "family." Log was a deputy game and fish commissioner and Birdie, Charles and I often went to their cabin on the Gasconade River at Rollins Ferry. Or we visited many of the little towns around Linn — Westphalia, Bonnots Mill, Loose Creek and Rich Fountain — to deliver bird feed or on some such trivial errand. Log and Birdie had lived in Linn all of their lives and they knew all of the "Flat people." They were related to most of them — as I was.

Among these relatives was one Lou Kenney. Lou was a woman, and she was considered very strange because she wore men's clothing — bib overalls, blue chambray work shirt and men's heavy brogan work shoes. She preferred the carpenter's trade and she had built a house on her farm near the Flat schoolhouse on the Rich Fountain Road. Now she was helping build a barn at one of the Scheulen farms near Linn ... and she became one of my "regulars."

Soon after I arrived at the schoolhouse each morning, I looked down the Rich Fountain Road and here came Lou, clattering along at a fast pace, swinging her arms and talking to herself. She wore a man's felt hat set well to the back of her head, and her wisps of gray hair straggled from beneath it to her shoulders. Her carpenter's apron — full of nails — was tied around her waist, and she carried her hammer in her hand.

At first I was halfway afraid of Lou. I barely spoke to her if I happened to be outside when she passed by. But gradually I came to know her. After the cool fall weather set in, I usually had a fire going in the King Heater and Lou would stop in to warm her hands and chat a few minutes. During those chats I found that Lou wasn't queer at all; she was simply a female carpenter.

Each morning she shook her head over the deplorable condition of the desks. Finally she said, "I'll just pound a few nails while I'm gettin' warm and I just b'lieve we'll have this here schoolhouse in A-1 shape."

One morning I pointed out my poor crippled teacher's desk, and how I had to balance the contents to keep the loose leg from falling off. Lou looked over the situation and spewed out a few fancy four-letter words. She went to the stove, opened the top lid and spit out a stream of amber tobacco juice between her cracked lips. "Them damn men," she said, "can build a big fancy closet in the back end of a schoolhouse when they ain't got nothin' to put in it, but they cain't nail a leg on the teacher's desk."

The next morning Lou brought the proper screw and in "jig time" had the loose leg in place and the other three legs tightened, so I had no need to fear a total collapse.

I enjoyed Lou's love of walking. All of the Bacons and Vaughans were good walkers and Lou, being a Vaughan, was no exception. She never rode anywhere she could walk. Soon after Lou would warm up a bit and "pound a nail or two," she would take off across the field "by a nic cut" to the Scheulens. About that time her daughter, Mrs. Nell Pennington, would come barrelling down the same road in her Model T Ford roadster (they lived in the same house), deposit Jesse and Mary Nell into my care, and roar on down the Linn Road to her job at the WPA sewing room in the Courthouse basement.

In the afternoon the scene was repeated from opposite directions: Nell would come barrelling in from Linn, pick up Jesse and Mary Nell and roar on homeward. As I swept and dusted, waiting for Gib, Lou would come clattering by on her way home, usually with the same question: "Has that there Nell come by yit?"

"Yes," I usually answered.

And usually Lou would respond:

"Well, I'm shore glad, 'cause I shore don't want nothin' to do with that _____ contraption she scoots around in. I don't see how she stands the noise. Now I can enjoy the walk home."

And she'd swing her axe or her cross-cut saw — or whatever she was carrying — over her shoulder and start walking.

This schoolhouse, I soon learned, was more than just a seat of learning. It was a comfort station, depot and visiting center all rolled into one. At first it bothered me to have adults wandering in and out to warm themselves at the stove, or to "sit a spell, jist t' rest." But Log helped me to understand: These people, he explained, had so little to look forward to that the school was their greatest source of interest. So I grew accustomed to the door opening at odd times and visitors

LOU KEENEY

She wasn't queer at all. She was just a female carpenter...who'd "just pound a few nails while I'm gettin' warm."

THE McDANIEL SCHOOL

It was more than just a seat of learning. It was a kind of comfort station, depot and visiting center all rolled into one.

whispering to me, "Just wanted to drop by a spell and see how things is."

One of the frequent visitors was the Rev. Bowman and, sometimes, his wife. The Rev. Bowman was the Mennonite minister who lived down "in the tie woods." He wore a shoddy, wrinkled, somber black suit, a black wide-brimmed hat and a white shirt with a little black string tie. Mrs. Bowman wore a long black dress, shirt waist, long sleeves, a full gathered skirt, black gloves and, or course, a small black bonnet tied with a black ribbon under her chin. She was a sweet, young, mild-mannered woman and the children all loved to hear her sing. So usually as soon as the Bowmans appeared, Emma appointed herself a committee of one to get the singin' started. We usually sang the hymns to get everyone rolling, then the Rev. and Mrs. Bowman and Emma would sing what Caroline Hollandworth would have called a "special."

The school served as a depot for those wishing to be conveyed to Linn by Gib when he brought me to school. They were a constant source of irritation to Gib, so he never wanted to be on time and he never set a regular time to be there. "Don't want them tie hackers ridin' to and fro with me," he'd say. But try as he might to dodge them, someone usually was waiting to "ride into town" with him.

One morning, though, I thought Gib had won a round. Just as he was setting me out in the ditch in front of the school, Mrs. John Pearon and Mrs. Ralph Phillips came around the bend. Gib lost no time and roared away back toward Linn before the two women could even try to wave him down.

The weather was bitterly cold but Jim Wilson had done his usual good deed by starting a fire for me early in the morning. So we all found a cozy room awaiting us. I insisted that the two visitors get nice and warm before they set off for back home — thinking, of course, they would be going back soon. But my thinking wasn't theirs. The two women had heard about the Bowmans stopping by to visit and to sing. Now they intended to have their day in the sun — or around the warm stove.

I rang the bell and started my usual round of Readin', Writin' and 'Rithmetic. Mrs. Pearon and Mrs. Phillips removed their outer coats and sat up near the stove with their heavy shoes turned so as to "bake the soles of our feet." They didn't remove their little black bonnets like Mrs. Bowman's. Both wore the same uniform-like clothing — a black shirtwaist, a full-gathered skirt-type of dress, and heavy black cotton stockings showing just a bit above their shoe tops.

It soon became apparent that these two had no intention of returning home. Noon came and they shared the cold biscuits and fat meat lunches with their children. Then Mrs. Pearon let the axe fall squarely between my shoulders: "Ain't it about time we got around to some singin'?"

They had had no intention of catching Gib and riding into town. They had come to sing. And sing they did. I never heard two sweeter voices — Mrs. Phillips, soprano, and Mrs. Pearon, alto. Their time was excellent, their pitch true, and as they went through the "Golden Book" and started on the hymns, the children sang with them. And sometimes they sang alone. We must have devoted the whole afternoon mostly to song, but I can't remember anyone complaining.

This visit aroused my curiosity about the exact identity of these two women. Later I found that Mrs. Phillips was the mother of my two youngest pupils, Howard and Charles Phillips. Mrs. Pearon was the mother of "Prairie Chicken" and Alfred Pearon. At the time she was living as the common-law wife of "Chick" Phillips, father of Emma and Ralph and a dozen or so others. This woman who sang hymns so beautifully and dressed in the garb of a dedicated church woman became a never-ending enigma to me. Poor motherless, little Emma seemed to adore her and snuggled up close whenever she could to this large, plump matron. She, in turn, smoothed Emma's straight blonde hair into even tighter braids each time the child came near.

The winter days became colder, grayer and bleaker and the pupils became less interested in getting to school. For daily attendance I could count on only Mary, Orlies Bacon, the three McDaniels and the Kehr children, along with Katie Meyerpeter. The tie woods children weren't about to walk that three miles to school every day. The Nilges and Mertens children came on the days they didn't have to go "to Catechism" at Rich Fountain. Vince Nilges attended regularly — for a part of the day. He might arrive at 10 o'clock with a note from his father saying, "Send Vince home at noon. He has to help sow wheat." Vince hated to leave school; he would have much rather stayed to play games at noon, but he knew his father's temper tolerated no foolishness.

Even not counting his helpful early morning fire starting, Jim Wilson and his sheep were almost as regular at school as some of the pupils. Jim and Eva lived in a small but comfortable little gray frame house just a few hundred yards from the schoolhouse on the Linn end of the road. His land surrounded the school so he was a frequent visitor. He had known me all my life, ever since Mae and I used to stop by their house after school to eat Mrs. Wilson's big fat biscuits with butter and molasses before we trudged on home.

JIM WILSON

"Doggone them sheep. They shore seem to hanker after an ejycation." Looks like they'd gradgeeate some day, don't it?"

Jim always got the wood for the heating stove; this was an important part of the school directors' April meeting. But he delivered more than wood. He brought up chips of bark for kindling, as well as corn cobs in a big burlap bag to "start the for off quick," he said. When winter set in hard, he built my fires because, as he said, "We allus get up before breakfast, anyhow. I jest as well git one more for goin'." (These people all said something that sounded like "for" for fire, "orn for iron, "thout" for without, "nackle" for nickle and other individualistic pronunciations.)

Neighbors laughed about Jim and Eva's farming. Jim always grew just one crop. If he decided it was a good year for pumpkins, he'd put in a huge field of pumpkins. One year he sowed the big ridge field across from the school in turnips. Whatever his crop, he peddled it in town.

In my year on the Flat, the crop was sheep — and if you'll pardon the pun, they gave us all a "baa'd" way to go. Jim never quite found the time to build a "good sheep fence." So almost every day his sheep got out into the road and came up to the school. We might be in the middle of a reading lesson when suddenly outside, under the window, the whole flock would "Baa - aa - aa, baa - aa - aa, baa - aa - aa" so loud they would drown out anything going on inside.

Bob McDaniels, Vince and Prairie Chicken would grab their jackets and caps and run out to chase Jim's sheep home — and try to prop up the fence where they had escaped. Sometimes the sheep would be back at school — via a backwoods path — while the boys were still mending fence.

The first few times the sheep wandered in I was certain the visit was just an accident and would soon be rectified. But I was so wrong. I would dispatch one of the middle-sized boys to go down the road and tell Mr. Wilson his sheep were out. Invariably, the messenger returned with the same message from Eva: "Jim's in town peddlin' turnips, and it'll be awhile before he gits home." In which case all of us — the children with great glee — deserted the schoolroom and drove the sheep down the road.

Sometimes Jim would come at full speed, which was about a snail's pace, and get his wayward animals. In these times, Jim never failed to make his favorite observation: "Doggone them sheep. They shore seem to hanker after an ejycation. Looks like they'd gradgeeate some day, don't it?" Jim never let anything bother him. He was a tall, thin man with thick black hair and bushy black eyebrows — and his black eyes always twinkled mischievously when he spoke of his "ejycated" sheep.

By now my days had settled into an almost unvarying pattern, starting off something like this: Get up, dress, make beds, cook breakfast for Charles and me — and wait uneasily for Gib. I still can hear the phone ringing and the voice on the other end days:

"This is Gib. It's too bad to go out yonder today. Never make it up Hubert Hill."

I interrupt quickly. "No, Gib, it's not that bad. You have to try. I'm ready and waiting."

In another quarter hour Gib comes sliding around the Courthouse lawn and Charles signals me, "Here comes Gib." Off we go, with Gib groaning and fuming every tire-turn of the way, holding the steering wheel with his left hand and wiggling his thin right hand into a fine pair of kid leather gloves all the way down that steep hill behind the Courthouse. Those gloves were his pride and joy. He never drove without them.

At the foot of Hubert Hill, Gib never forgot to point out "that stinkin' dead horse. Don't see why they don't burn it." The old white horse had died in the pasture near the road and all winter the people who traveled the road not only had to look at it but to smell it. Gib's nose was long and thin and it turned up, making his upper lip slip up over his long, yellow front teeth. After we passed the dead horse, Gib would roll down the car window and spit several times — as if to clear the air. I learned later that the Nilges brothers, owners of the dead horse, couldn't agree on the means of disposal. One wanted to burn the horse, the other wanted to call the rendering truck. So while they argued, the passersby reaped the scenery and the perfume.

But all of this torture wasn't necessary; we could have taken another road. It led westward out of Linn by Highway 50 for about three or four miles, then turned left on Strope Lane, went over the cave road and into the same road leading to the school. And it wasn't any farther. I suspect that Gib thought there was a better chance of not getting up Hubert Hill; therefore, he wouldn't have to come back for me at 4 o'clock.

In the evenings the four of us — Logan, Birdie, Charles and I — often played pinochle, with Birdie and I always challenging Log and Charles. It developed into a ritual:

We would come home tired and hungry. Log would say, "Now, hurry up and get your supper eaten. The cards are gettin' cold." Then he'd dispatch "Bant" (our nickname for Charles) up to "The Mercantile" for a dime's worth of hard candy. "Suckin' candy," Log called it. And in a remarkably short time, we would be settled in Log and Birdie's warm, comfortable kitchen around the small, square table, dealing out the "cold cards" and keeping our mouths full of suckin' candy. We usually played with a double deck — which made the losses quite large when we "went set," a euphemistic phrase for "lost."

I recall, too, other enjoyable evenings. A group of women — most of us either teachers or insurance clerks, with some young housewives — formed a club which we called the Etc. Club. The title really nonplussed the gossipy old hens in town;

they kept trying to figure out what the Etc. stood for.

These "girls" were Ina and Sylvia Morton, Mary Bradley, Effie Mahon, Carmen Campbell, Zelda Dubrouillet, Lillian Sawford, Frances and Helen Huffine, Sylvia Garstang, Ada Herndon and others who were members for a shorter length of time. But these were the "regulars," along with me, of course.

We started as a sewing club. All of us were so poor that we usually were making an article of clothing, but sometimes we carried our embroidery, crocheting or knitting to our meetings. Mary Bradley always crocheted — always with the handle part of her crochet hook held in the palm of her hand.

We took turns being hostess to the group, and since none of us was earning more than $60 a month the refreshments were extremely simple. But several were memorable. I especially remember Zelda's vegetable soup and her famous gingerbread. And I recall with mouth-watering vividness Sylvia Garstang's velvety, red chocolate cake full of pecan pieces. This toothsome delight had chocolate frosting with more pecan pieces on top and she served it with coffee and fruit salad. When we went to Ada Herndon's home, on a farm outside of town, her mother always served homemade sausage or cured ham with some kind of homemade pie — apple, peach or raisin.

For other activities I went to O.E.S. (Order of the Eastern Star) where I came in contact with many fine people — and where we pranced around the hall (in these small country towns "the hall" was always located above the drug store) like female fashion plates (we thought), dressed in our finest garbs, accompanied by the one member who could play the piano.

We also went to church, the Methodist — the "other church" besides the Catholic. There were prayer meetings on Wednesday nights and most of the time I went with Birdie. Strange, how satisfied we were to do the simple things. We seldom left town or did anything which required money.

On most weekends Charles and I went home. Sometimes we rode the Missouri Pacific (MoPac) bus to Mt. Sterling ... for 28 cents apiece. Bud would meet us there — with our soiled clothes in our durable old suitcase.

Saturday was wash day. We brought the wash tubs into the kitchen. We set up for business with the washboard, hot soapy water and clear rinse water on the big wide bench by the south window. Mae and Irvin frequently came from St. Louis to spend the weekend, too, so I did the laundry of all of us.

It was quite a day, with soap suds spilling all over the place, boiling water cascading to the floor when I removed the clothes from the big enamel boiler on the stove, stirring the clothes with a broom handle ... But the worst ordeal was in the winter, hanging the clothes on the line. They froze stiff as a board while you were shaking out the wrinkles and getting them ready to hang. Often my hands got so cold I had to go inside to warm them.

After the washing was finished, I took the hot soapy water and scrubbed the floors in the dining room and kitchen. Then I felt satisfied with a big day's work behind me.

In the evening we had a warm, crackling fire in at least three rooms — the living room, dining room and kitchen. I still see the crack in the side of the old box heater in the dining room. No matter how clean you scrubbed the floor, the ashes would sift out through this crack and form a gray miniature mountain on the stove platform below. The crack never seemed to bother anybody else — just me.

On most Saturday nights I made a huge batch of divinity. This we polished off nicely while playing pinochle, hearts or dominoes (with double twelves) around the big dining room table. Dad liked sweet things so well he cracked the walnuts or hickory nuts to make the divinity more palatable. We also had homemade cakes and pies and doughnuts and such goodies — some of which Charles and I carried back to Linn for the next week.

Sunday morning meant ironing — with flat irons heated on the wood cookstove in the kitchen. First I went to the clothes line to discern which pieces were dry enough to iron; then I picked out the pieces which we had to have but which weren't ironing-dry. These usually were undergarments — especially Charles' and Irvin's. These I brought in the house and draped them gracefully over the oven doors, on chairs placed near the stove and over what was already an overburdened clothesline in the kitchen.

For some strange, still unknown reason (to me), Mom kept the slop buckets directly under this line. I would be hanging up Dad's "long handles" and out of the wall would come the hook and "Kerplop!", down everything would go into the slop buckets.

Slop was very important in those days. Nothing was ever wasted. But one of the most irritating procedures of the morning was Mom's setting those big buckets on the stove and warming the mixture of potato peelings, apple peelings, turnip tops, skim milk and wheat to feed the pigs and chickens. I could always count on one leaky bucket to pop and spit this delectable juice out on the stove while I was ironing.

Mom tried to get all the "good" out of everything, so while we had a "good hot fire to heat the irons," she put the slop buckets on the back of the stove. (This was her concession to let me have the "front" of the stove for my three flat irons.) We also got mileage from the wood by baking pies at the same time. So the kitchen was awash with the delicious aromas of apple pies a-baking (our favorite), and clean clothes being ironed. But they were over-powered when the slop mixture oozed out and scorched on the hot stove lids.

As soon as dinner was finished, everyone began to scurry. Suitcases were filled with clean (if slightly damp) clothing; boxes or baskets were packed with meat, pies, and vegetables for Mae and Irvin to take back to St. Louis and for me and Charles to take to Linn. Sometimes Bud took us but usually we rode the MoPac bus; Charles carried the food box and I lugged the suitcase. He couldn't say his "g's"; they came out "d's." So he would ask, "Drace, is the drub ready?" And off we would do — or go, that is — for another week.

The bus stopped at the Star Cafe across Highway 50 from the Courthouse, wo we had only a short block to walk east of the Courthouse and down the slope to Logan's and Birdie's house. Once there, we put away our food (Birdie let us use her refrigerator for perishables), hung our clean clothes in the kitchen pantry upstairs and we were ready for another evening of pinochle.

The weather that winter was severe. In February and early March an ice storm paralyzed most traffic. The thermometer fell to 15 below zero and stayed there. Gib was enormously pleased; he could stay home safe and warm for a few days without trying to trump up any excuse.

As it seems to inevitably happen in extreme cold snaps, the furnace blew up at the high school, so Charles had no school, either. Log had to get out and distribute feed for quail and other wildlife, so Charles went along with him. I cooked and did my household chores in the freezing atmstphere upstairs as quickly as possible and hurried downstairs to sit in Birdie's comfortable living room.

Trying to walk anywhere in town was akin to signing your own death warrant — or risking it, anyway. People crept along the streets holding to fences along the yards or balancing themselves with a stick. One spot in particular we learned to avoid — the entrance to the Aimee Maire Store, the "Mercantile." Its street entrance sported a two-foot wide sheet iron sheathing, impossible to step over from the sidewalk. Now covered with a layer of ice, the sheathing was a killer.

Birdie tried it first. She came home limping, with a gash across her lower knee region. She was a large woman in her upper parts, but she had pretty slender legs and ankles. She and I together bandaged her knee and she sat propped up in the living room, moaning.

But we were still without groceries. Warily, I ventured outside and crept up the sidewalk past the weekly *Unterrified Democrat* office and the bank. I was thankful to have its old iron picket fence to hold on to. But I longed for the other side. There were still hitching posts over there, for those country people who still drove teams and buggies to town. Over there if one fell, the hitching posts would catch you ...

But I felt secure and smart as I rounded the bank corner. I slid past Teen Bradley's Barber Shop and put my right foot on the iron slab. There was nothing to hold to there — just glass store-front windows, set in about three feet from the sidewalk. But, oh, I had it made ...

I was reaching for the iron door handle when — *ka-dip* — down I went. When I managed to get up, my stocking was cut straight across the lower knee — and so was my knee. And blood was streaming down my leg. I was too embarrassed to go in the store for groceries, so I turned around and crept back down the slope to cry and moan with Birdie.

For a few days neither of us could walk. When we tried, our wounds would gape open and bleed. So Log and Charles did the cooking and the housework. Log was a good cook, but he only liked certain things. So we had vegetable soup aplenty, with homemade biscuits and steak (which Charles and I had brought from home), and Birdie's good homemade peach preserves.

Now I couldn't go to school even if Gib and the ice storm decided to let me. My, how that knee did hurt! Nowadays I would have stitches and probably go to a hospital, but in those days the expense warded off any such thought. However, the wounds were never too bad to interfere with our pinochle games. Log rigged up a low stool with a couple of pillows on it and put it under the kitchen table. And there we sat, all afternoon and evening.

With Birdie and I playing partners, the stool worked just fine. She stretched out her big, long leg on the pillows toward me and my smaller, shorter leg faced her. Log used to stoop over, look under the table and bend over laughing. Then Charles would join him. Birdie and I knew we must look pretty comical, too, so we laughed with them. We'd postpone pinochle just long enough to fill our plates with Log's swiss steak, vegetable soup and biscuits. Then as soon as he and Charles washed the dishes, we'd be at it again — bidding, winning and going set.

Finally one day of sun warmed through the ice, the thermometer rose above zero and school was on again. Gib and I made it cautiously down the dangerously steep hill, dropped off into the creek bed and began our upward climb to the Flat. I can't say that my vacation away from this dreary location made me eager to return, but there was no reason to contemplate any other course.

So back I went to the big old King Heater, back to hearing Howard and Charles

HOWARD PHILLIPS
*Of Readin', Writin' and
'Rithmetic... and "maters 'n 'taters
'n roasin' ears."*

Phillips recite their ABC's — only now I was teaching Howard to read a first grade reader. One story involved a garden with its vocabulary including the word "tomatoes," "potatoes" and "roasting ears. The objects were familiar enough but the terms were foreign to Howard. They were, he insisted, " 'maters, 'taters 'n roas'in' ears."

I worked with him endlessly. But he refused to say the words properly. I kept him in after I dismissed all the other children in the afternoon. Still, he never pronounced them correctly — until one day when Emma was completely out of sight around the bend on the Rich Fountain Road. Suddenly he said, all in one long word:

"To-ma-toes — Po-ta-toes — and — Roast-ing Ears!"

Ah, how sweet the Triumph, to me. And how welcome his release to him. He wiggled his fat little legs out of that rickety old desk and ran, tumbling all over himself, to catch up with the other "tie hacks" disappearing down the road.

Time passed quickly and spring, always pleasant in the country, came, bringing its beauties. The little forget-me-nots covered the pastured with a filmy blue haze. Everyone started out with their knives and baskets to pick a "mess of sour dock" or "poke greens." This brought still more visitors to school. Annie Meyerpeter and Eva Wilson would wander by and stop to chat a minute. The breezes were soft and warm and we could have the windows open. And the greatest blessing of all — the children could leave off their long underwear. Some had worn the same set all winter and the children were delighted to shed the garments. But I'm sure I was the gladdest of all — especially when the Phillips boys finally burst out of their flannel cocoons.

We planned a program for the last day of school; it certainly wasn't much but everyone had a part in it. The only thing I remember about it now is Emma Phillips asking me if she could sing a solo. I said, "Yes," of course, thankful to have one more number on my sad little list of presentations.

The entire neighborhood turned out for this big event; not only all the parents of the children came, but grandparents and friends from neighboring districts flocked into the little school. I was amazed at the crowd. I peeped out from behind our makeshift curtains — sheets fastened with safety pins to a strong wire strung the width of the schoolroom — and I saw many familiar faces: the Rev. and Mrs. Bowman in their somber black; Mrs. Phillips and Mrs. Pearon, also in black; Mr. and Mrs. Jim Wilson (without sheep *or* turnips!); Lou Keeney in her overalls and blue work shirt; the Bacons and the McDaniels. Even Gib had come out early to hear the children sing and recite their trite little verses.

I hadn't bothered to ask Emma what the title of her song was, so I was as surprised and amused as my audience when she walked to center stage and announced her own solo: "When I Take My Vacation in Heaven."

Herbert Nilges insisted on reciting his one great accomplishment — "Everywhere Christmas tonight, Christmas in the land of the palm tree and pine ..." and all the rest. He had learned that one and he couldn't learn another one, he had argued. And that was true. I had sweat blood at Christmas teaching him only one verse. So I thought, why not? So Herbert made one speech do for two occasions.

I don't think many people understood much of his oration, though, because he had never mastered the art of eye contact. He recited the verses haltingly while staring at the ceiling from a sideways stance. And I hoped that the audience didn't get the impression that I thought Christmas came in May.

At last it was over. The "monarchs and the kings" departed. Katie and Faye took down the sheets; we folded them to be taken home and washed. I lowered the windows, patted the ink spot on the old wobbly desk goodbye and with a sigh of relief, I put the key in the door.

From the back of the schoolhouse came Prairie Chicken, lifting his feet high but smiling from ear to ear. "I just want to say Thank You for being nice to me," he said. Then he added an extra special verbal bouquet: "You learn us good, too," he said. "You learn us gooder'n anybody else ever did."

"PRAIRIE CHICKEN"

"You learn us good, too. You learned us gooder'n anybody else ever did."

The sentiment was unmistakable, even if its expression made me wonder about the truth of it. And it made me realize that I had learned a great deal from these people, too. I certainly learned that a schoolhouse could be much more than a seat of learning. This drab little school for them was a community center, a place to get away from the tie woods and to see other people — to move in a different world.

I realized, still standing there with the key in my hand, that I had become somewhat attached to all of these children and their problems:

Bob, who still couldn't do Arithmetic "'thout one foot was trompin' on t'other foot.":

Faye, who made the most beautiful figures on the blackboard but counted the tables on her fingers.

Virginia, who simply couldn't read without moving her lips and sounding the syllables.

Howard, who would go right on saying, "'maters, 'taters 'n roasin' ears."

Vince, who probably would ask the next teacher "What makes stink hazel stink?"

And poor Prairie Chicken ... I wondered what would become of him. He needed friends, companionship.

I was a bit sorry I wasn't coming back to the Flat next year. I was going to teach one of the elementary rooms in town. As I turned the key in the door and waved goodbye to Prairie Chicken, Gib gunned the car motor to let me know he had waited long enough. I hurried out to the road and as I got in the car I noticed Jim's sheep grazing contentedly in the pasture. Now that I was through with "ejycational" duties, so were they!

As we headed back to town I recalled my first impression of this high, flat terrain, how all the houses had looked flat and gray to me. But now I knew the people who lived in them and they seemed happy and the houses seemed cozy, not gray.

We were coming to the smallest of the houses, on the edge of the Flat at the east hill. Charles and Tip Laughlin lived there and I wondered if Tip would be outside. Tip was a Bacon, Sam's sister and my father's cousin. She aired her bed clothes at least twice a week and they brightened up the whole Flat — beautiful quilts with star designs and turkey tracks in oldfashioned red and blue calico.

Or maybe she and Charles had hitched up their team of big sorrel mares to the buggy and driven to town to market their eggs. Charles was the last farmer I knew who used those fringed fly nets over his mares' bald faces — only Charles never removed them in winter. They were permanently attached to the harness, so in winter or summer when we met Charles on the road, the fly nets would be dangling over the mares' eyes and faces.

"Don't see why that stingy old So and So don't buy himself a car!" Gib would say. "I know dang well he can afford it."

These farmers from the Flat often drove teams and wagons to town. But they weren't allowed to drive on the highway through town, so they tied their teams to the hitching rack on the slope just above Log's house and just outside the bank. One could always tell who was in town by the assortment of teams, buggies, surreys and wagons at the hitching rack. The manure piles used to infuriate Birdie, especially in summer when the flies swarmed around them and came on down to sit with us on the front porch.

Frank Meyerpeter's car might be "hitched" there, too. He had a new maroon Ford which he parked at the posts. "If they won't let me drive my team and buggy on the concrete," he'd say, "then, by Hell, I won't drive my car on it." And he would walk from the hitching rack to church — at least three long blocks ...

Memories of these people and these places blew over me through the windows of Gib's old car as we left the Flat behind and came into town. In a few short months they all had become a part of me. Perhaps I had become a part of some of them — like Prairie Chicken. Still, I remember from that day a feeling of helplessness, of wanting to do more, but not having the chance now.

10

I overlook the privies.

Now that I would be teaching in town I would have $8 more to spend since I wouldn't be paying Gib to haul me to the Flat. On the basis of that huge sum, I ordered wallpaper for the entire house. Upstairs and downstairs, I meant to paste paper on our walls this summer.

Such a task! But I was young. Nothing was too much. Mercy, though, how I did struggle with those 20-foot strips of ceiling paper! Dad and Bud helped some, but I could justly dub those months "The Pete and Paper Summer."

Pete had a job measuring farm land for one of the early government agricultural programs. He was gone from home, early to late, with the car. One night, just as we were sitting down to supper, he came in, sat down and helped himself to large portions of everything.

"Well, Pete," said Mom, "you seem hungry. Didn't you have any dinner?"

Pete finished his mouthful, swallowed and replied, "No, I didn't have any dinner, but I had a big supper just awhile ago."

We have used that ever since as an excuse for eating a lot. And we used it often that summer. The months passed by too quickly, but things were a little better for all of us. We had decent crops for a change--no droughts, no floods. Pete had saved some money from his job for his first year at the University of Missouri at Columbia, and we'd all had fun shopping in the "Wish Book."

We had ordered his necessary clothes from Sears & Roebuck--a gray, double-breasted wool suit, gray suede shoes, a couple of pairs of dark, serviceable wool trousers for school, and shirts to wear with them. Most of all, though, I remember his peach-colored rayon knit undervest and shorts. They must have worn well, because I'm sure the vest is still around in the rag bag. I saw it last summer.

The famous suitcase now became Pete's property. So all of his worldly goods were packed in it as we prepared to take him to Columbia where he would enroll in the School of Agriculture. He had a job working in the kitchen at Gabler's Black and Gold Restaurant--for three meals a day. This was one of Columbia's best-known dining places. It had taken its name from the pie it featured--and its colors from the University's official colors. The "black" was a layer of dark chocolate topped with the "gold" of a cream custard. And the taste...umm, umm, good.

On a warm, sultry Sunday in early September, Bud, Pete and I set out for Columbia to find a room for the budding scholar.

Mistakenly, we had deemed it unnecessary to find a room in advance. Now we found that all of the good, relatively inexpensive ones convenient to the campus were filled. So we kept going, farther and farther toward the suburban area until we finally found a clean, affordable room at the extreme end of Hitt Street. We left Pete and his suitcase to the tender mercies of Gabler's and the College of Agriculture and headed back to Linn where Bud dropped me off.

Teaching in town upped my exercise quotient considerably. Log's and Birdie's house, where Charles and I took up light housekeeping again, was at the far west end of Linn. The school building (Morton's Funeral Home is located there now) was in "East Linn"--about a mile away. Charles and I walked to school in the morning, back home at noon to eat our lunch, back to school by 1 p.m. and back home again after school was dismissed.

I walked the same distance again many evenings as often a group of us would gather either at Frances Huffine's (Herndon) or at Ina and Sylvia Morton's houses. Ina and Sylvia lived in two rented rooms at Mrs. Annie Monroe's home, two doors east of the school. Lillian Sawford, the principal of the Linn High School, became my inseparable companion. We walked anywhere and everywhere we wanted to go. Lillian boarded with Mrs. Charles Huckstep, in a new brick home about halfway between Log's house and the school. I soon formed a habit of stopping there to walk the last half of the way with Lillian, wherever I was going...to school, a card party or just a fun session.

The Linn "faculty" consisted of six teachers. The high school had three: The superintendent, Irvin Laughlin; Lillian Sawford, the principal; and Mrs. Lucy Annabelle Willeford McMahon, the only one with strictly teaching duties. I had known Irvin, a distant cousin, all my life. Lillian was an only child from well-to-do parents. She had everything, I thought--pretty clothes, plenty of money--and she was getting $100 per month. And saving most of it. Mrs. McMahon lived outside of town in Jim Bryan's farm house with her arthritic, almost invalid husband and adopted nephew. Among them, these teachers taught enough subjects to get about 125 high school students through graduation. Irvin taught English and social studies, Lillian took commercial subjects and Mrs. McMahon handled math.

That left three of us in the elementary school. Mrs. Gertha Duncan taught grades 6, 7, and 8. I was supposed to have 3, 4 and 5, and Frances Huffine was to have 1 and 2. However, the numbers didn't add up right when the children assembled; I had 30-plus pupils in 3, 4 and 5, and Frances had only 15 in 1 and 2. So Supt. Laughlin decreed that the six third graders return to Miss Frances's room.

My room was the middle one--big and old and cold. And it stuck out the back, overlooking the outside privies. As an integral part of this era's "learning experience," these privies merit attention perhaps unwarranted today.

They--two of them, naturally--were built back to back, but even the approaches to them were segregated. At the school's front door, the only entrance and exit, the girls turned east, walked along a narrow sidewalk by the side of the faded red brick building, jumped off the end of the walk and trod a gravel path to the necessary "little house." The boys made a right turn to the west and repeated the route around the west side of the building...to the same "duplex" comfort station.

Linn always had a building problem, built as it is on something resembling a "sweet potato ridge." But I really don't think land was that scarce. Surely, we could have had space for separate privies. But there was no discrimination by status when it came to using them. Everyone shared these fringe benefits--the teachers and "administrators," the students, and the one and only custodian.

The inside architecture accommodated all sizes of users. There was the usual height seat for the grown up high school girls and other adults; there was a lower, smaller-sized round accommodation for the "intermediate sized" girls; and at the farthermost end was a very small seat with a miniature-sized opening for the tiny "beginners."

On each seat between the openings were the traditional Sears & Roebuck and Montgomery Ward catalogs. These catalogs served many purposes other than the

PRIVY CATALOGS

Sears & Roebuck and Montgomery Ward served many purposes other than that for which they were intended.

intended one. Looking at illustrations and reading about "genuine pearl necklaces" or "pure amethyst birthstone rings" has stimulated many a peristaltic wave, with resultant relief.

With only a rough oak partition between the back-to-back privies, teachers were wise to account for all of the big boys before visiting them--or authorizing such visits. Many times my young, intermediate privy patrons--4th and 5th graders-- would come back to the classroom with tears streaming down their cheeks: "Miss Bacon, Tommy was on the other side peeking at me through that big crack in the wall."

For recess and noontime recreation we had an outside basketball court and, farther down the hillside, a lopsided baseball diamond. We never could figure out the best spot for home base. If we located it at the top of the hill, the primary and intermediate boys were so winded they could never make it back "home" after running to first, second and third. If we put home plate to the east (where first base had been), the ball rolled north down the hill, and the batter could walk the bases and arrive home with time to spare. And if we pegged home at the foot of the hill, the pitcher overthrew the batter and the ball rolled so far we had to station a "pigtail" several yards down into the rough.

I can say one good thing, however, for this Linn elementary baseball diamond: When the snows came, it made the finest hill for sledding I've ever seen.

There was little time for games, anyway. Everyone went home for lunch except a few who rode the so-called "school buses." Teachers took turns bringing their lunches and supervising all the students, elementary and high school. We ate in our rooms with the kids, so we got to know them quite well.

We didn't feel obligated to organize any games; there were always older pupils around who felt honored to be put in charge of games. Sometimes the high school boys would get up a game pitching low balls that the small batters could hit; then, everybody stalled and dropped the ball several times to let some little, chubby hitter get on first. There was no strong competition; they played for the fun of playing with each other. When the town boys returned from lunch, a basketball or baseball game was organized and the high school girls and teachers stood around to watch and cheer.

Many of the town boys ate lunch at the "snack bar" in J.P. McDaniel's store, a half block east of school. J.P., a tall, thin, typical southern mountaineer, had run a store in this location all his mature years. He was my father's first cousin; their mothers were sisters, Amelia and Betty Vaughan. J.P. fixed sandwiches for the boys and served them on newspaper "tablecloths" on the back counter.

From J.P.'s menu, one could choose a heady variety--bologna, braunschweiger or cheese. Or a slice of each on the same sandwich. J.P. handled all sandwich makings with his fingers, sometimes carrying a slice of bologna between his thumb and forefinger all over the store before he finally found a piece of bread he had laid down somewhere else--while he was counting out eggs someone had left with him while they performed other chores downtown.

On extremely cold or rainy days, I dispatched Bant to J.P.'s to get us a sandwich. J.P. took special delight in preparing mine. If I specified bologna, he always added a slice of each--bologna, braunschweiger and cheese. If I specified only cheese, he sent one slice of each. If he had a jar of jelly open, he would add a generous blob of it to one piece of bread. So I learned there was no use to "order." Just tell him "the usual," I instructed Bant.

Several times I tried to get my preference across to J.P., but he always interrup-

J.P.'S STORE
From braunschweiger, bologna or cheese — or all of the above — just make it "the usual."

ted. "Ahh-hh, now I know eggsactly how every one of you fine gulls like your sandwiches fixed. Always do every one of 'em mah-self. Nevah let my hi-uhd he'p fix your sandwiches. No, sah. Always fix 'em up mah-self." So for four years I ate J.P.'s sandwiches--fixed just the way "I" liked them. Yes, sah!

Among his inventory, J.P. stored an immense amount of good material for arguments. One winter it was Daniel Webster. And in good time, whenever a newcomer--or anyone not yet exposed--entered the store, J.P. would get around to his opening statement:

"That thar Dan'l Webster, he musta been sum fella in his day. Heard say he knew the Bible back'ards and for'ards. Some say he read the thing from kiver to kiver at the age of fo'."

Some people paid no attention; others stayed to argue. It mattered not to J.P. either way.

Another winter J.P. would open with the age of Methuselah. "That thar Methuselah, now. He musta bin some fella. How d'ya reckon he managed to live to long?"

J.P. had a great and open admiration for the opposite sex. He never missed any occasion when the components were largely women. He was both an Eastern Star and a Mason--but he only attended the former.

On the appointed nights--the second and fourth Thursdays of each month--J.P. donned his navy blue suit, white shirt and black string tie, got in his maroon Ford sedan and escorted all of the Eastern Star ladies from east Linn to the Chapter Hall above the Jones and Ferrier Drug Store. Sometimes this required two trips, especially if we were entertaining dignitaries and dressed formally.

Once, I remember, he had to report that he couldn't find Mrs. Lucinda Gelvin. He had "hunted this place ovah three times," but, J.P. swore, "the lady of the house had 'simply disappid'." Later, near the end of the session, Lucinda finally arrived; her cantankerous Jersey cow had "treed her" in the hayloft. She had yelled her lungs out for help, but the barn was too far away for anyone to hear.

J.P. almost always attended the W.S.C.S. at the M.E. Church. I think he went to everything but the Women's Auxiliary of the Veterans of Foreign Wars. I don't believe he ever qualified for that--or our Etc. Club. And he never made any excuses for appearing at these all-female functions.

"I like pretty gulls," he said. "The gulls are much mo' entertainin' than the men."

He could be descriptively detailed about that entertainin'. One morning when I stopped by his place of business--probably to pay my bill for the sandwiches he knew "eggsactly how to fix"--J.P. began to describe all of the lady teachers:

"I tell you, Miss Grace, that Lillian Sawfud is the cutest homely gull who has evah come to Linn to teach school. And that Miss Mary Catherine Buhdette can sing like a bud ("Sing" was drawn out long and emphatically), and Miss Frances, she is just pew-ah solud gold."

To which Frances replied later, "That must be why I weigh so much."

It was another hard winter. I remember distinctly how cold my ears, hands and feet got as I walked the mile to and from Log's house to school twice a day. More and more, I relied on J.P.'s sandwiches to avoid the noontime walk. Neither Charles nor I had any surplus clothing, but we were young and we walked fast to stimulate the circulation.

There were days when we had no heat in the school. We could count on the good old furnace to blow up whenever Dee Owens, the custodian, decided to have a holiday. Dee was a tiny, wiry, red-eyed, red-nosed fellow who knew exactly when to encourage the old furnace to explode. The furnace room was directly beneath my room, and whenever Dee needed to "shake down the ashes," or "poke up the fire," it was useless to try to teach.

When Dee was finished, he would slam the furnace door, kick it two or three times and throw the big, iron poker into the nearest corner--all the while speaking very unkindly to the poor, old worn-out heap of metal. The children, of course, loved the entertaining interruption so we laughed together. When it was over, everybody usually was willing to go back to work--except Henry. Henry never knew when to stop laughing.

Henry Balkenbusch, Jr. was...well, different...in many ways. He was almost six feet tall and weighed at least 240 pounds. He had a bright mind for memorizing poetry, but he couldn't learn arithmetic at all. He drank the ink, ate the art paste and generally made a nuisance of himself.

HENRY BALKENBUSCH, JR.

"The boy stood on the burning deck whence all but he had fled..." and other interminably long classics.

He was a parttime student at both the public and the parochial schools. Both parents were lawyers. Neither had time for their son, so Henry was the product of the streets. And he was the reason the previous teacher had resigned. I decided--with the helpful advice and counsel of Log and Birdie--not to let him bother me. My job and my salary were too dear to make a jeopardizing issue of Henry. So when Henry laughed at odd things and at odd times, I laughed with him. I even encouraged all the others to laugh. And when Henry discovered I refused to scold him or be bothered by his strange antics, he soon stopped laughing and trying to get constant attention.

For most of the year Henry busied himself with memorizing poetry. He came to school before anyone else. Each morning he would be sitting on the worn wooden steps which ran the width of the front entrance and as I unlocked the door, he greeted me with, "The boy stood on the burning deck...from whence all but him had fled."

This was his favorite poem, until he came across Samuel Foote's "The Mayor of Garratt." Then for weeks he greeted me with, "He made him a hut, wherein he did put The Carcass of Robinson Crusoe. O, poor Robinson Crusoe!"

Henry placed monumental emphasis on that final line. I was always tempted to recite to him the only two lines I know from "A Fable for Critics":

"A reading machine, always wound up and going,
"He mastered whatever was not worth the knowing."

Those lines described Henry to a "t", but I couldn't help feeling pity for him. He never had any underwear or warm outer wear. He wore blue overall pants, usually held up with a sack string, and a blue chambray man's work shirt, usually short sleeved. The shirt tail was never long enough to tuck inside his blue jeans and never covered his navel. Much of the time, the buttons would be off the fly of his pants and Henry would be partially exposed to people and weather. But as long as he had a piece of poetry to memorize, he seemed comfortable.

Henry's mother often returned to her home state of New York for long intervals. During those times he would have been almost totally uncared for if it had not been for Mrs. Peter Gove. Clem's mother, better known in Linn as "Miss Rieka," lived across the street and was always good to him. He came to think of her as his "friend of all seasons."

One of Henry's greater moments came at Thanksgiving time. He was chopping the head off a turkey and lopped off the last joint of his left little finger. He was quite proud of this distinctive accomplishment. The following Monday morning Henry was sitting on the steps as usual when I came to school. But instead of reciting poetry, he said, excited with his showing, "Hey, teacher, look at my finger. See, here it is!"

He reached into a Bull Durham tobacco sack and extracted the severed joint. Pleased by my exclamations and admiration (What else could I do?), Henry displayed the bloody joint to each teacher as they arrived. He promised me he would leave it at home when he went for lunch, but he couldn't think of a safe place to put it. I made a few suggestions--like speaking with his father--but none pleased Henry.

When he came back after lunch he assured me he had found a safe place, but he wasn't going to tell anyone. "No, sir! Don't ask me. I won't tell."

I didn't ask. After four o'clock I was working at my desk and Henry was working on a piece of new poetry. Suddenly he stopped mumbling long enough to say, "Hey, teacher, I'll tell you where I hid my finger. I hid it under the corner of Miss Rieka's living room rug. Nobody'll ever find it there, will they, teacher? Huh, will they?"

I shook my head.

"Funny thing about that turkey, teacher," Henry went on. "Him and me wuz a whole lot alike. He was big and fat and overgrown and smart, but not old enough to be the master of the flock."

That was vintage Henry. A puzzlement.

Besides Henry, there was quite an assortment of other 5th and 6th graders-- Betty Mosby and Patty Flanagan, John Albert Marsh, Robert Turner, Ruth Malan, Rose Mary Patterson, Lorene Malan and Mary Lou McGinnis (Helen Benson's daughter). There must have been 25 or 30; a few names escape me.

I could hardly wait for the Christmas holidays. Mae and Irvin were expecting their first child. Mae was coming home to have the baby. Irvin's father, Dr. Leach, could look after her and the baby. That was comforting because he lived so near--on the top of the hill above us.

During the Christmas holidays I cleaned the house thoroughly. I ordered new pink dotted swiss ruffled curtains for the dining room and a beautiful flowered linoleum rug for the floor. And I really splurged on a set of china. We had never had anything but plain "kitchen white," so this set of dishes excited me. We still keep them on the lower shelf of the china cabinet and use them on special occasions.

After the holidays Mae stayed home to await the arrival of the baby. But the baby decided not to be born until the weather became worse. During the second week of January a heavy snow fell and the thermometer dipped to zero, then sank lower. Snow drifted on the roads; the men walked into town to get groceries and carried them home in a burlap bag, deftly tied at the top and the middle to balance the weight over the shoulder.

Bant and I spent the weekend at home and on Sunday evening Mae began to feel bad. Mama put me to scrubbing the bedroom floor and dusting the downstairs bedroom where Mae was quartered. But as soon as I finished, she hurried Bant and me off to Linn. Irvin didn't return to St. Louis as usual.

When we reached Linn I was stunned to learn that Mattie Bacon Stigall's son, Bobby Monroe, had been killed in an auto accident in California. He and Mattie ("Sis") were on their way home after spending Christmas with her parents, Uncle Al Bacon and Aunt Vi on their farm near Linn.

More snow fell. I was anxious about Mae having her baby while we waited for

Bobbie's body to be brought home by train. It arrived on Friday and a small, sad group gathered at the old M.E. Church to pay respects to Bobby. I remember Grandpa Bacon, in his 90s, saying, "Why couldn't it have been me?" But he was still a hardy soul in his 90s. There was a still smaller gathering at the little snow-covered grave--Log, Birdie, Bobbie's father Bob Monroe, stepfather Jack Stigall, Uncle Al and his son Russell, Grandpa, Uncle Will and Paul, the minister and a few close friends.

There was a bright spot about noon when Uncle Will arrived in town for the funeral. The baby had arrived the previous Sunday night...a little girl...every thing was fine. And if I wanted to go home with them after the funeral, they would take Bant and me to the top of the hill.

After the graveside services, we set out--sliding, skidding, scooting and spinning on the hills. I didn't expect to get anywhere near the top of our hill, because the snow was so deep. But Uncle Will, never one to the hurried, wasn't daunted. We stopped at Mt. Sterling to put on chains.

In the winter Uncle Will always wore four-buckle overshoes, but he never buckled them. And today was no exception. He had worn them all day--into Birdie's spotless, polished living room, into the church, to the cemetery, and now he stomped about in the snow supervising the process of putting on the chains. He kept as his constant companion a mouth-bulging cud of chewing tobacco, from which he spit gobs of amber liquid onto the white snow. With the chains on and riding along surefootedly, he rolled down the car window and without sticking his head out any farther than absolutely necessary, he--with great gusto--let the tobacco juice fly back into my face. With that diversion--and no heaters to warm us up--we stayed awake.

In due time we arrived at the top of the hill. Bant and I climbed out of the car with our boxes of dirty clothes and made our laborious way through the snow drifts to the house. I was so excited I could hardly wait to see the new baby and to hold her. To me that was what babies were for--to hold. But I didn't get to hold her much that weekend. She was too new--and there was too much to do.

I did laundry for Bant and me and for Irvin, who had arrived late Friday evening. I cleaned house and helped with the cooking and general chores. Dr. Leach came every morning with Mrs. Leach to bathe the baby--Yvonne Grace--make up the bed and check Mae. Then off they would go, with Doc wearing his bearskin coat which he always put on when the weather hit zero.

That weekend now is mostly a muddled memory, but I remember clearly how much the baby cried. I hadn't figured on that aspect; I had foreseen only pleasant things. Mae and Irvin had vowed to rear their children "by the book" so Yvonne Grace couldn't be fed unless "the book" said she could be fed. The book, however, was sorely lacking in instructions about how to make her quit crying. The only thing that could quiet her was Pete's big, deep voice. When he held her and talked to her, she would open her dark eyes, look at him and stop yelling immediately.

Yvonne was a pretty baby, with lots of dark hair, fair skin and fine features. We had no baby bed for her, so she was kept wrapped in a pink, fluffy blanket in the big bed with Mae. In about two weeks she and her mother returned to the apartment in the Bronson Hotel in Maplewood and my life resumed its former rather routinized existence--teaching, cooking for Bant and me, attending all the social functions in Linn...

As spring emerged from the biting cold of winter, we had to plan for the

YVONNE GRACE

Babies were to be held. I hadn't figured on her crying — all weekend long.

numerous activities associated with closing school properly: "Properly" involved Mrs. Gertrude Carroll. The bits of "great art"--like the white picket fence which Frances Huffine and I made for an operetta--usually were the brainchild of "Miss Francess" but the culmination of the finished product often was the handiwork of Mrs. Carroll.

"ASK GERTRUDE"

We could never have any school function without the amazing Mrs. Carroll.

She could do anything. She concocted paper roses and green stems out of crepe paper. She cooked and sewed, did all sorts of fancy work, refinished furniture. With her handiwork of the moment, she sat on her front porch (her yard fence edged the sidewalk in the downtown business section) and she intercepted every man, woman and child who passed. "Ask Gertrude" was the stock answer when anyone asked for information--of any kind.

She could buy material for a dress, lay the pattern on it in the store so there would be no lost yardage, take it home and stitch it up and be back with the dress in the same afternoon. She once said she could do all main seams in 45 minutes if she weren't interrupted on her front porch by "people who just want to gossip."

Mrs. Carroll, along with her housework and sidewalk superintending, handled the switchboard for our local communications setups, questionably called the telephone company--a position which undoubtedly added to her store of "information." There was one tale about her I could never quite believe, although the townspeople told it for the gospel truth and laughed about it all the years I taught there. When one of Mrs. Carroll's sons was a baby, they swore, she took in some motherless pups and nursed them at the same time. She might have...She could have.

She did occasionally fail in some of her efforts, however, as in her attempt at neighborly negotiation between Irvin Leach's Aunt Dora Jett and Lanteen Benson, Aunt Ida Bacon's mother. The two women lived across the street from Gertrude and for years each one claimed a beautiful maple tree. They battled all summer about whose yard the tree was in. And righteously spiting themselves, neither would sit under it until the decision was resolved. Mrs. Carroll acted as a go-between, trying to get Mrs. Jett and Mrs. Benson to share the tree and "be thankful" for it. But her efforts went for naught. One night when Mrs. Benson was away from home, Mrs. Jett took her little hatchet and girdled the beautiful tree.

But no school function came off without Gertrude's help, and now at the end of the school term she came into full flower. Who would serve the banquet? Which restaurant would give us the best price? What about proper clothing for some of the less well-off boys and girls who didn't have dress-up clothes?

Just stop by the porch and tell Gertrude. She would manage it all, even bring a small trinket (usually crocheted out of scrap yarn) for each graduate--15 or so, plus guests. At these banquets were about the same number of juniors and seniors, four high school teachers and four elementary teachers and the school board members with their wives.

On this "night of nights" we met at Paul Mattingly's Cafe in the Commercial Hotel on the square. It was exactly what the name implies. On the north side was the hotel, Bill Turner's Garage, a telephone building and a tall, slender, unpainted frame structure where the Leonard Sullins family lived. On the west side was the Star Cafe and the Linn Cafe, owned and operated by Slick Davis. On the east was a filling station, Henry Nilges's saloon and a restaurant and a switchboard type telephone service operated by Mrs. Lueckenhoff and her two spinster daughters. On the south, the Courthouse stuck out and made Highway 50 bend around it.

So, you see, our surroundings were not scenic. However, I had acquired a new beige lace dress for the occasion and I sported beige shoes and--at last--I had a pair of gloves. Beige cotton. I felt truly queenly.

Money to entertain the seniors came from the profit made on the Junior play. The public school had no auditorium, so the play was always presented at St. George's Hall. Most of the work had to be gratis; no wonder we saw the picket fence re-used so many times.

Lillian usually coached the plays--and got permission from Father Fischer to use the hall. For some strange reason, she was afraid of Fr. Fischer--and afraid to go to the Hall at night for rehearsal. So I usually went with her. I would sit in the rear of the hall and either signal or yell whenever the lines became indistinct. When our patrons paid out hard-earned farm money for a seat, they expected to understand every word. If they didn't, the teacher heard about it!

Many times after these evening affairs were over, we walked downtown to the Jones and Ferrier Drug Store and drank a nickel Cherry Coke--chipped ice in a small glass with a squirt of cherry-flavored syrup and a dash of carbonated water. We could easily stretch that five-cent Coke over an hour. Or more.

At other times young men would be waiting to ask us to go for a ride. Clarence Herndon was dating Frances Huffine. I sometimes dated Clarence's older brother, Clifford, who had a car--a Chevrolet touring sedan, we called it. But we didn't consider it necessary to go--if we were asked.

Both Lillian and I liked Irvin Laughlin, the superintendent. But he was my distant cousin and, according to Mama, the whole situation was "running a terrible risk." It was worse for distant cousins to marry than "close kin." Everybody she ever knew who married relatives had children "with eyes set in the sides of their heads"--or "children with no sense at all."

These two horrible visions always popped up in my mind when Irvin asked me to go someplace with him. He was a fine, intelligent young man. Handsome. He was tall, too, more than six feet tall, with dark hair, skin and eyes. In addition to being superintendent, he taught English in high school. He also built much of the furniture around the school building. His father was a carpenter and they spent much of their summer repairing broken desks, tables and chairs. They did everything except fix Old Clank-Clank Pop-Bang, that furnace under my room. No one wanted anything to do with that monstrosity.

ME AND IRVING

Everybody Mom ever knew who married relatives had children "with eyes set in the sides of their heads." Or, worse, children "with no sense at all."

11

A chance for many a hillbilly

With Commencement and Baccalaureate behind me, Bant and I packed our belongings in our boxes and returned to Cooper Hill for the summer. Irvin and I were planning to attend the summer session at Rolla. The University of Missouri had rented the buildings at the School of Mines there and hired the school's professors. By so doing it gave many a hillbilly a chance to get some college work rather inexpensively. Irvin still had two weeks of school at Webster Groves High

School, so I had to find a place to stay in Rolla for two weeks. After that he and I would drive each day, some 50 miles or so each way.

That Monday morning on campus as I was registering I met Mrs. McMahon, a Linn teacher. She was positive that her sister, Mrs. Decker, had a bedroom available. I jumped at the idea. She ushered me to a restaurant her sister operated, introduced me to the "help" and I sat in a booth, waiting to be shown to the bedroom.

I was a bit leery when Mrs. Decker appeared in a frilly dress, a flowery hat and frizzy hair and invited me to follow her. We walked back through the restaurant kitchen into a very dark hallway, up what seemed to me innumerable steps and finally into a dark room. I could barely see a bed. When my eyes became accustomed to the murky light, I spotted a sink on the far side. There were no doors; just a cotton curtain.

Before I could recover my senses, Mrs. Decker said, "That will be ten dollars a week, in advance."

I wanted to say I would prefer a room with doors at least, but before I found my tongue, Mrs. Decker was saying, "There's a community bathroom right down the hall."

"Right down the hall," I discovered, was about a half-mile around the corner. The room smelled musty. No fresh air. One erstwhile window, thanks to a building butted close to the wall, was now a useless ornament filled with dusty, smoky panes of glass laced with spiderwebs.

This strange arrangement frightened me. But my $10 was gone. So were Mrs. McMahon and Mrs. Decker.

As usual, I had almost no money left, so I ate sparingly and went to bed. But to sleep...No. People kept coming and going all night. I had no idea what was "afoot." I was afraid to shut my eyes; I wanted a door. The other rooms seemed to have them. I could hear voices, quite easily, in the room next to mine. One male, one female.

After one week in this smelly, dark dungeon, I was reasonably sure what was going on in the adjoining rooms. I also understood why they were so dark! I was scared to death for two weeks; worse, I was worn out for want of sleep. I'm sure Mrs. McMahon didn't know. Or did she? She might have thought it a big joke.

At any rate, I was plenty happy when Irvin's school was out and he and I could drive each day. For the summer Mae and Irvin rented the Jess Owens house, an old white frame home on the hillside above the Baker place in Cooper Hill.

My days became long. Irvin liked to get everywhere at least an hour before anything was open or anybody was up. This meant I had to get up before 4 a.m., dress, get my books and assignments arranged, walk up the steep hill to the mailbox on the county road and wait for Irvin. Promptly at 5 a.m. he would round the curve in his blue '28 Ford coupe and halt long enough for me to jump in.

The drive to Rolla required a little more than an hour and classes didn't start until seven o'clock. At first we sat in the car and waited for the custodians to open the buildings. Then we started frequenting the little one-room restaurant along the street where we parked. For ten cents we could get a sweet roll and coffee. Irvin sometimes had cereal. I always had the same sweet roll, but I still remember how good that coffee tasted. It was strong and richly lardered with real cow's cream. I could face the world--and the Rolla campus--after a cup of that coffee and forget all about the dreadful experience of those first two weeks.

That summer I reveled in Shakespeare with the notorious Dr. Barley, in the English novel with the still more notorious Mrs. Nadine Sease, and a course called Elementary Education taught by a woman from Northwest Missouri State College at Maryville. Mrs. Sease was Dr. Barley's "girl friend." He was married, but in all the years I knew him I never saw him with anyone but Mrs. Sease.

No matter. He was a really fine professor. He realized, I'm sure, what country bumpkins many of us were, so he prodded us gently through "Macbeth" as a starter. Later we graduated to "Henry IV." In this class I met "Louie" Propst whose life was to be lived in many of the same towns as mine, principally Kirkwood. Dr. Barley delighted in snapping his fingers and asking, "Mr. Propst, Mr. Propst, where are you? Who is Grey Malkin? Come on, tell me, Mr. Propst, who is Grey Malkin?"

Louie would stammer out, "I don't know who Greymalkin is."

Then Dr. Barley would laugh and say, 'Don't you know that's an old grey tom-cat?"

The lively hours passed so quickly in his class, and they were so dull in Mrs. Sease's English Novel. She read to us from a dog-eared notebook (We suspected it was Dr. Barley's notes because she couldn't even read it well). She assigned us boring early English novels to read and to make oral reports on. I remember two: "Pamela" and "Old Wives' Tales" by Matthew Arnold. All we did in Elementary Education was keep a scrapbook, so my school work was very simple.

We were out of class at 10 a.m. and home by 11:30. So I did all of the housework at home in the afternoons. I worked out a weekly schedule: On Monday afternoons I did the family laundry, after building a fire under the big iron kettle outside in the yard. We carried water in buckets to heat, then lugged the clothes back and forth from the kettle to the washtub to the rinse tub, to the clothes line. Such hard work!

On Tuesday I gathered in the clothes, sprinkled and ironed with the old hand irons heated on the wood stove.

Wednesday I went over the whole house with a dust rag and oil mop.

Thursday I reserved for school work--my scrapbook and such.

On Friday many times Mae would want me to help her with some task so I went to Cooper Hill. Yvonne was six months old now and fat and cuddly. I loved to stay with her and hold her while Mae and Irvin had an evening away from home.

In August after summer school ended, I had a little time--to rest an extra bit, to can tomatoes and peaches, reap the farm crops, go to church on Sunday, and to take part in whatever social activities happened along.

The Ladies' Aid always had a picnic--and when they did we always had a good rain. So we would have to grab our pies and fancy work and run for shelter. Once, when we were still holding our picnic in the hollow, the rain came down in torrents and washed our pies and pie cabinet away. Everyone ran for the cars, and some man scurried around from car to car, wagon to wagon, to tell everyone that the picnic would be re-scheduled for the following day, Sunday.

Maybe it was. I knew good and well that Mom and Dad wouldn't go through the process of bringing us again the next day, however.

In September I returned to the school room, feeling rather secure for a change. I had three years of teaching under my belt now. And Bant was becoming less of a worry; he was a junior and really beginning to grow. He had been so terribly small; that's why Dad had always called him Banty Rooster--or Bant for short.

He had an enormous appetite and we ate rather well. It was surprising what a lot of food we could buy for $10 or less. I usually had a "ticket" at Aimee Maires Store ("The Mercantile"). We bought whatever we wanted and usually the ticket was less than ten dollars at the month's end.

We were having life a little easier. Log and Birdie continued to help us out in many ways. When Log made soup we all sat around the kitchen table and stuffed ourselves with it--often along with Birdie's home baked bread. When we butchered beef and hogs at home, an ample portion came to Log. He cooked it and we gorged ourselves again. Once, though, when he made his soup, we didn't eat all we wanted; the top fell off the pepper shaker as Log was seasoning it. The soup was literally black. Just the way he liked it, Log said.

Sometime during this period a new Methodist minister came to Linn--the Rev. E.I. Ailor and his family. And they proved the exception to the oft-repeated "rule" that a preacher's family was "nothin' but trouble." The family consisted of Annie Chloe, Georgia Lee, Mary Frances, James Edward ("Laddie"), Edgar Irvin, William Bartlett and Betty Lois. They made a truly fine addition to the community. Georgia Lee was soon employed as a teacher of Social Studies and was also admitted to our Etc. Club. Mary Frances was employed at Belle as an elementary teacher, and in a year or so, she married John Shanks.

Early in the winter the unbelievable happened. Grandpa Bacon died. The obituary spelled out his full name, which I always loved for the rolling cadence of it--Charles Porter Bacon. He was always so hale and hearty that people laughed and said he'd be around when Gabriel blew his last trumpet call. He was forever cutting sprouts, raising a large truck patch, walking from Uncle Will's house to ours. He was never senile. Even at 93, he never looked old. He looked like Grandpa. I suppose he finally overdid it--getting wet when he was cutting sprouts. Pneumonia, the doctor said.

Uncle Will came to Linn with Scott to make the final arrangements. When I went home at noon that day and heard the words, "Grandpa died," we all sat in Log's living room and cried for those days and those times we could never retrace. It was the weekend of Thanksgiving. Soft snow fell; the cemetery looked like a fluffy white blanket except for the black, gaping hole waiting to receive Grandpa's earthly remains.

That night it snowed again, and when I walked to the cemetery after school on Monday, somehow the all-over white comforted me. It was a warm, cozy coverlet made especially for him. Grandpa had been so much a part of our lives for so long that I couldn't quite picture life without him. This was my first brush with the death of someone I really loved.

The three years in the Linn Public Schools come back to me now, all rolled into one huge educational experience. We had so much plain fun on such a simple basis. We elementary teachers received the monumental sum of $65 per month for our dedicated efforts; the high school teachers were paid $100 to $125 per month. All of us but Lillian Sawford had to stretch our pennies to make them cover what were almost the bare necessities.

As usual in this school business, there were a few changes in the teaching personnel. The Board of Education discontinued two of the outlying one-room schools--Lone Star and Forest Grove. Their two teachers, Clara Holstein and Mary Catherine Nilges, were brought to town to help out, unhappily for Clara. She wanted to stay at Lone Star with her eight pupils. So she came on the condition that she could teach grades 5 and 6. Those were my favorites, too, what I had been teaching. But that's the way the cookie crumbles, as they say. say.

Partitions were built in two of the huge old downstairs rooms and I was quartered in the back section of the old primary room with my 3rd and 4th graders. We had no private entrance; we entered and left through Miss Frances's door--a situation which irritated her as much as it did me.

I had an added "fringe" benefit. My room was located practically on top of the outside privies. And, oh, my goodness gracious, when the wind blew, what a delightful aroma we received. But the Board practiced no discrimination in dispensing its favors; Clara received the same aromatic award on the other side of the building.

This arrangement allowed a free room for Mary Catherine to teach music--in my old room. Mary C. was a town girl from North Missouri and knew nothing of farm ways. She wasn't above learning, though. She married Martin Nilges and went to live on a small farm just outside the city limits (now the Louis Boes home). That first year she had a darling baby girl, Bonnie Sue. So now she had three jobs. She and Martin milked three cows and she delivered the milk on her way to school. She dressed Bonnie and took her to stay with Mrs. Ed Lock, who lived in the Hundepohl house. Her teaching job kept her busy from 8 a.m. to 4 p.m. Martin also had a fulltime job as a barber. Mary C. was always an early bird because she had to deliver milk from one end of town to the other.

Early one morning as I came up the front walk Mary C. was coming from the rear of the building with a perplexed look on her face. At the entrance, she blurted, "Grace, I've dropped my car keys down the toilet hole. I can see them, down there; they're lodged on a ledge, but they're too deep for me to reach. What shall I do?"

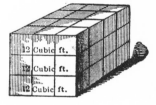

Naturally, I had to go inspect the exact location of the mishap--holding my nose as I did. It occurred to me that a hoe would do the job and I suggested that we go next door--to Buell Ferrier's house--and borrow one.

No, no. Mary C. was mortified at the thought of anyone knowing what had happened. But she had a hoe at home, she said, and Martin had the other set of car keys. So we hiked up the block to J.P.'s store and phoned Martin. He borrowed a car, came with his keys and drove home, got a garden hoe--and we rescued the keys from the ledge in the pit of the odiferous outhouse. And ever after Mary C. wore the keys to her car on a string around her neck.

Our faculty grew by two during those years. Young, blonde and blue-eyed Thomas Keller taught science and agriculture in a makeshift basement room partitioned off the furnace room. In my maturing tenure, I worried over such youthfulness being cast into such a dungeon. The windows were the typical, old-fashioned kind set at ground level. They were about 12 inches high and perhaps 24 inches long. Only murky light struggled through them because when it rained the mud spattered thickly on them. And beyond the mud were small iron bars to keep them from being broken. The only entrance was a small narrow door; then narrow steps led out of the main hallway at the entrance of the building...over the floors and steps, wooden, worn--and squeaky.

Still later, in the basement on the east side of the furnace, the powers-that-be fashioned an art room and employed Miss Louise Marr to teach art and music. Knowing Louise from my year at Warrensburg, I wondered how she would fit into Linn's less than affluent school system.

I'm positive that none of us expended much effort to help Louise like us or the town. Mrs. McMahan acted as chief art critic. Louise's first art display, she loudly announced, seemed "copied off scenic calendars." And indeed it did.

Louise also made musical mistakes. She tried to sing solos at the Methodist Church--a house of worship plentifully blessed with people who knew a good voice when they heard one. If they heard one. Then she chose a fancy operetta for the high school presentation rather than the good, old tried-and-true play.

The operetta required Dutch costumes by the score and hundreds of various-hued tulips--as well as the now-famous white picket fence. Mrs. Carroll came into her own again with her crepe paper and fine wire to help save the day. And at the last minute Louise decided that all first, second, third and fourth graders should be included in the musical section. So Frances and I had to spend all day, every day, for a week teaching the songs. Louise had guaranteed herself a low vote in any popularity contest.

She had ways, though, of getting even with us. She was quite attractive, had good clothes and she knew how to attract the best males available in town. She dated them all. And she dealt poor Frances untold misery by threatening to take Clarence away from her--before she finally settled on Don Huckstep. He was a very good catch because his mother, Oma, had so much money and property. Don was a few years younger than Louise, but he had desirable things going for him--like a car and a job. The Louise-ian invasion, however, only lasted one year. At the end of the term, she mysteriously melted away--like Ichabod Crane--at least out of our lives.

Perhaps it was her influence that caused Frances to choose that year to present "Rip Van Winkle" as the elementary operetta. Such a difficult production! The costumes were especially intricate. We had to have The Mercantile order bolts of special brown sateen for the dwarves and elves. The mothers had to buy the yardage, share one pattern cut from newspaper by Mrs. Carroll, and fashion the full knee-length, bloomer-like pantaloons and hip-length jackets. Frances and I made the large, high-crowned, wide-brimmed, buckled front hats out of black construction paper, working from the illustration on the front of the music book accompanying the operetta.

Most of the boys had a speaking part. The girls, all dressed in the typical Katrina Van Tassle Dutch dresses, did the chorus. The boys fought over the part of "Wolf," Rip's dog, because his costume didn't require "girl's bloomers." Corky Morton got the part because he was small and could bark quite convincingly!

Once more, we marched all of our groups down to St. George's Hall--to practice--day in, day out, in rain, sleet, hail or snow. The show must go on in Linn, too. The hall was freezing cold. The piano keys were like ice. We kept on our coats and galoshes while we sang, pranced, backed up and did it over, then backed up and repeated it all again, struck a few more sour notes and, finally, Miss Frances was satisfied with the production.

The big night came. The girls all looked properly Dutchy; the boys were all encased in their brown sateen pantaloons and jackets. A few hats were too big. When the boys tried them on, the crowns rested on their noses. But we soon remedied that by stuffing crushed newspapers in the upper crown.

Lillian was all set with her sound effects--thunder, lightning, let it come. Her main equipment behind the scenes was a piece of corrugated tin roofing and a small hammer with some padding tied around the head. For weeks she had kept this piece of roofing under her bed and had been practicing "thunder peals."

A flashlight was the best thing we could devise for lightning. But by standing on a tall stepladder behind the backdrop, I could run the beam of light quickly over the stage. We were on our way toward a huge success. Until the very end...

Outside the curtain, the rhythm band struck up the finale. In that cramped space, the children stood, some literally leaning against the curtain--which was also hand-operated, by a rope which rolled it up from the stage floor to the ceiling. The curtain opened, caught the red sateen capes of the children in the back row and rolled them up in it on its way to the ceiling.

Every child in the back row turned to watch their capes being lifted skyward, the rhythm band number ended and I reached over to turn off the record player. The curtain came down with a flourish, hitting me squarely on the head and flattening me on the stage. Of such were the rewards of staging a school operetta.

But by March such calamaties were forgotten and we looked for something new to do. In March Lillian and I planned a "progressive party," a popular pasttime in those years when the nation was recuperating from the Depression. Lillian borrowed the idea from her Aunt Ann Sawford, a speech teacher in Sedalia, Missouri. She had produced such a party on St. Patrick's Day the year before, and pronounced it a great success.

So we spread the menu around the town--appetizers at Sylvia Garstang's home, located on the steep hill going out toward the Flat; sandwiches and salad at Frances's apartment in the Jim Bryan home across from J.P.'s in East Linn--about a mile and a half from Sylvia's home; dessert at my apartment at Log's home directly behind the Courthouse. And as a final complement to this great endeavor, we planned an evening of bridge at Lillian's boarding abode, Oma Huckstep's house.

In honor of the Irish saint, we wanted everything in green. So we chose lime jello with chopped cabbage, celery and the like, cream cheese colored green with Easter egg dye, and--of all things--this was to be served on green bread cut into hearts, spades, clubs and diamonds.

Birdie heard this menu and gulped. "Well, I never," she finally said. "I just never! I believe I'll just ask Mama to bake you some homemade bread--just in case you run short."

We had "never," either. And how we laughed later about all of that green fodder. How right Birdie was!

The green bread raised quite a stir in Linn--more than we'd bargained for. We figured the people at The Mercantile would laugh at us if we ordered a loaf or two of green bread, so we took our order to Kuster's Grocery across from Jones and Ferrier's Drug Store.

Marie Boehm's eyes bugged at our request, and in her big, boisterous voice, she boomed out loud enough for everyone inside and outside the store to hear, "Hey, Pop, d'ya reckon we can git that there breadman to make up some green dough for St. Pat to have a green party?" Then she roared off into peals of laughter.

Lillian got mad. I got tickled. And we got out of there as quickly as possible. But Marie had a full week before the party to enjoy the fun. Every day at noon Marie would watch for me to walk past the store, so she could report in a loud, news-crier yell, "We ain't shore yit we can git that there green bread, but we're shore a'tryin'."

In desperation I started walking on the other side of the street, but Marie only yelled louder.

On the day before the party, she had a favorable report: "That there bread man said to tell you he'd have that there green bread on his truck tomorrow mornin' for shure."

I picked up my green bread the next morning and dropped it off at Lillian's house on my way to school, happily thinking the episode was ended. But not so. Every time I went in--or by--Kuster's front door, either Marie or Pop would ask, "How did that there green bread taste anyhow? Could you taste that there green in it? Shore did look funny..what I could see of it through the wrapper."

Telling about our experiences with the green bread enlivened the whole party. Lillian and I cut it into shapes and spread it with various green concoctions. We carried these, with the salad, to Frances's apartment, then home to bathe and dress. The members of the club, plus some special guests, gathered at my house (Birdie's living room), and from there we departed for Sylvia Garstang's for our first course.

Sylvia was a good cook, as well as lots of fun, so we spent more than our alloted time there. Then we walked the mile or more to Frances's apartment for the green sandwiches, along with green salad and green vegetables. Then we walked back down Main Street (Linn's one and only street at the time) to Birdie's for dessert.

Birdie had convinced me that by then people would not want any more green for dessert. But she and Log had made a green apple pie so we would have green on the menu. Lil Ferguson, Birdie's mother, had sent two loaves of homemade bread, and Mary Jones, Birdie's sister, had made a beautiful angel food cake with a delicately tinted green frosting. After all that walking, we were starved and made quite a dent in the assortment of stuff we called dessert. Log also had made a big pot of his special beef vegetable soup. By the time we plowed through all this, it was past 10 o'clock so the card playing was postponed until the following night. I'm not sure about the "progress" in our party of that name, but everybody in Linn and the surrounding community enjoyed hearing about our green bread-- probably more than we did eating it!

The Etc. Club members shared many more good times during those years. We often went to Log's and Birdie's cabin on the Gasconade River at Rollins Ferry; we took the usual picnic lunch and sometimes stayed overnight. Once we rented Dr. Gove's cabin to entertain Aunt Ann Sawford and a friend of Lillian from Sedalia.

It was early October and the weather turned cold. The wind blew heavy rains in through the cracks. The cabins were not built for winter; the only heat came from a wood cookstove. We simply froze for the whole weekend. The roof leaked in the room where I was bunking--on an army cot in the middle of the floor. With no mattress under me and precious little over me, I took such a cold as I had never had before. My whole face and nose ached. I coughed for two weeks afterward. I suspect that I had pneumonia, but I didn't miss any school. And, naturally, I didn't go to a doctor. Couldn't afford it.

LIke farmers for a barn raising, we teachers joined forces when one needed help. And during those years I came to know Mr. and Mrs. McMahon's furniture very well. They never lived in one place more than six months, and on their first move I felt sorry for them living so far out of town on Jim Bryan's farm, so I offered to help them move. Thereafter, every time they moved, I was duly notified.

I learned just how to take the beds apart and how to twist the baling wire which held the broken iron siderail to the iron headpiece and foot, just which legs were broken off the tables and the chifferobes and how to put them back on so they looked attached. Mrs. McMahan had to do most of the work herself because her husband had arthritis in his hands. They were stiff and straight. But he could always drive a car. Luckily for me, they had very little furniture. We learned just how to balance the load and get it all in the back of one stock truck.

Many evenings we motored to Jefferson City to see a movie. Ada Herndon could easily stuff six people in her Ford sedan. Sometimes we ate our evening meal at one of the several restaurants in the capital city. A movie, as I recall, cost 35 cents, and our entire dinner was about the same.

I liked this higher level of living. And I felt I should have better clothes to go with my improved status--even if it were mostly psychological. Bant should dress better, too...

The best bargains could be obtained from Sears & Roebuck. But always from the deep recesses of my mind I heard Mama's and Grandma's admonition: *"Wear it out. Use it up. Make it do. Don't buy new!"* I sat down and debated; did I dare spend money on clothes? Then my decision was made: On the reverse side of the order blank I read the instructions for ordering. I could buy everything--whatever I wanted--on a marvelous plan called "time payment." My mind was made up.

The sheer joy of purchasing and the anticipation of opening the mailed goods smothered any pangs of conscience. I ordered two pieces of 100 percent wool for skirts--one grey cashmere and one dark red basketweave--and two sweaters, one so-called twin set in white wool. This was a button front cardigan with a matching pullover; the other was a pretty green wool affair with a fancy belt. Then I added two pieces of pure silk for blouses--one grey, one beige.

For Bant, I got grey wool trousers, two grey cotton broadcloth shirts and a nice grey and blue wool sweater, some underwear--and at the bottom of the order blank I sneaked in a few "necessities" in the cosmetic line for myself. I got Maggie Ferguson--she previously had made a couple of dresses for me from the remnants I had found at Millsap's in Jefferson City--to make my skirts and blouses, so now I had a few changes in my wardrobe.

Clothes were bought carefully in those days. One looked at the wearing qualities and at the warmth of the wool for winter's chill winds. I had done that, I told myself; now I could "Wear it out. Use it up."

MAMA SAYS
On buying clothes, "Use it up. Wear it out. Make it do. Don't buy new."

12

Of babies and students

During the summer of 1937 I became a very knowledgeable babysitter. Yvonne was 18 months old when Anna Lo was born in July. Mom called me her hired girl. Only I wasn't "hired"--I worked for free.

Mae and Irvin had bought the Tim Nixon house, where they still live. Mae was to stay at home and again be attended by Dr. Leach so there was some organizing to do. I had been frequently helping Mae with the work and caring for Yvonne since school closing early in May. Now, as July approached, Irvin asked me to come and stay two or three weeks just to care for Yvonne. Mrs. Emma Busch was coming in to do the cooking and housecleaning from her home just across Goose Creek.

Mae and Irvin had no telephone. When they wanted to make a call, they went to Pete Langenberg's Store, threw a few switches on the proper call bells and reached us. How these telephone lines worked I'll never know, but they did most of the time. If people understood you when they called, they marveled, "My, you're just as plain as if'n you're right here in the room with me." If they couldn't hear you, they said, "My goodness, you're fur away. Where are ya'...down in the cellar? Ya must need new batteries in that thing..."

By such communication late one evening Doc was summoned. He had been ready since early spring. So had Mrs. Leach. All she ever had to do was "tie on" a big, freshly-ironed coverall apron and come. They telephoned for Bud to bring Mom and the long, hot, anxious night began.

I slept little. I heard Dad up and down at intervals, yawning and sighing, "Ho-hum, ho-hum, ho - hum..." Daybreak was beginning to light up the Weaver Hollow field when the long and two shorts sounded on the party line. That was our signal. I ran downstairs and Mrs. Leach announced that we now had a new baby girl in the family, weighing almost ten pounds.

Mae had had a difficult time because Anna Lo had decided to be a breach case, but everything was okay now. But everyone was worn out with the stress of the night, Mrs. Leach said, and could I come down right away! Her tone meant pronto. So before I knew it, I took over the care and feeding of two babies and the general management of the kitchen.

Anna Lo was scratched and bruised on her bottom where Dr. Leach had used instruments to help her into the world. It was a world she didn't exactly like at first sight and she told us about it for most of the next two weeks. She cried so much that Irvin decided a safety pin was sticking her or her navel band was too tight. So he completely undressed the fat, square-bodied tike and bathed her, re-arranged the band and put clean clothes on her. She was as good as gold, she rolled her big dark blue eyes at us and gooed--until we put her back in bed. Then the howling began again. She wanted to be held.

But she was a big baby and she was hungry. So in spite of "the book," I made her formula a little richer and gave her orange juice for a little extra nourishment. In about two weeks she became more accustomed to this strange world and decided to give up trying to change it.

Yvonne had to adjust, too--to having this new, little creature in the house competing for attention. One morning as I was bathing Anna Lo, Yvonne was sitting in the middle of the bed watching me. She leaned over and kissed Lo and put her fat arms around her little sister and hugged her close. It was a sweet sight for a sucker aunt.

Yvonne was a good baby. She decided, however, that she'd outgrown any need for an afternoon nap; they were a waste of her precious time. But "the book" said she had to have one. So each afternoon we went through the same process-- undressing, bathing, a cool drink, putting to bed...Then she yelled, "Cha, Cha, Cha." That was the closest she could come to "Grace."

I was forbidden to answer her. A few afternoons she actually did settle down and nap for a while. Mostly she moved the bed. It had rollers on it and by standing up and grabbing the window sill, she could move the bed just about wherever she wanted it. One day she maneuvered the bed close to the sewing machine, pulled out the button drawer and emptied it onto her bed--mixing the buttons thoroughly with a B.M. she had about the same time. I thought she was strangely quiet so I slipped around the back of the house to peek in.

What a mess! But I was no patsy aunt, I tell you. That young lady received quite a stern lecture from Aunt Cha. And all the time I was cleaning up the mess, she lay laughing and giggling up at me and clutching my hair in her fat little fists, saying, "Cha, Cha, Cha..."

My career in teaching seemed far away, in another world. But learning, if one pays attention, is always with us and I was learning. Just what, I wasn't sure.

Mrs. Busch came about 6:30 every morning to prepare the meals and clean the house. She also took the laundry home with her and did all of it except the diapers. With both babies in diapers, I was thankful when Irvin took over this chore. I never could find a whole lot of learning experience in that duty.

I was also thankful for Mrs. Busch's cooking, although Irvin was somewhat critical of it. One evening he brought home two young squirrels from a hunting trip. We dressed them and put them in the refrigerator. When Mrs. Busch arrived Irvin told her she could fry them for breakfast if she wished. And so she did, announcing when we came to the table, "Irvin, I put both heads on your plate because I remembered how well you like the squirrel head."

Well, anyone who has eaten squirrel knows the head is nothing but skin and bone--no meat at all. And Irvin looked so funny that I had to excuse myself and get busy with Yvonne to keep from laughing. That ended the squirrel hunting, once and for all.

Irvin also regularly inspected the refrigerator to get rid of Mrs. Busch's "dabs."

She saved all leftovers but never re-heated them or used them. So in a few days the refrigerator was jammed with little dishes of unappetizing had-beens. Mrs. Busch didn't come on Sunday, so her day of rest was "dab day" for us. Irvin and I played two-handed dab--"I'll eat this; you can have that. No, I don't care for this; you can have it." We cooked for Mae and Yvonne, but we ate dabs.

A new baby, of course, was quite an event in Cooper Hill, so everyone came to see Lo. This meant keeping the house in order and two babies presentable all the time. Every visitor found a resemblance in Lo to some different member of the family. But to this day she doesn't conform to the usual pattern in our family. She has blue eyes and as a baby she had the most beautiful blonde curly hair I've ever seen. Yvonne fit the Leach look--exceptionally dark eyes and hair, both almost black.

Not only the neighbors came, but relatives galore arrived from afar. Frank and Mae Leach, visiting at Elsners, came over with their daughter, Mary Agnes. They didn't tarry long, however. After Yvonne bit Mary Agnes and left tooth marks on her, Frank and Mae decided to take their darling and go home.

From Oklahoma came the Benedicts--Irvin's Aunt Mina, Uncle George and cousin Gussie Benedict, and Uncle Ed "Buckshot" Leach and Aunt Eliza. Aunt Eliza never had any children but she was the world's greatest authority on the care and feeding and rearing of them. She watched me very critically as I carried Anna Lo out of her big bed into the living room for observation.

But she needn't have worried about Lo's care. Doc came in every morning to look after her and Mae. Most of the time Mrs. Leach came along, just to make sure her grandchildren were being well cared for. She always inspected the band Anna Lo was wearing--to see if I had it too tight, too loose or too something. Usually she removed it, re-powdered the navel area and re-did the band.

All the while Doc would sit and blink and chew on his cigar, clamped tightly between his one upper and one lower front tooth. ("Thank God," he always said, "they hit.") Doc was short and fat and very bald. His only hair was a rim of white on the back of his head which connected his ears. Mrs. Leach always cut down Irvin's castoff suits for Doc, and she was so immaculate about her own and Doc's clothes they were neatness personified.

My term of learning about babies was short. After three weeks Mae was able to take over the household chores. I went home to help Mom--can tomatoes, clean house, wash and iron and get our clothes in readiness for another year at Linn.

A few changes had taken place. Clara Holstein had married her boyfriend of 25 years, Jack Reinholz, whom she had met when she taught at Gasconade. Clara was the one with the white face powder. Clara must have figured if a little of something was good, a lot was better. She put powder on so thickly that it caked on her face, on the neck and lining of her dresses and on the black fur collar of her winter coat.

Since she had left our midst I was quartered on the east wing in the back of the old "Grammar Department." I was back on the girls' side of the outhouses, entering and leaving through the 8th grade room.

All I had really missed by teaching grades 3 and 4 was to see less of my friend, Henry Balkenbusch, Jr. Henry was now a seventh grader, grown into an enormous hulk of humanity. He still recited long selections of poetry for me at any opportunity and he still greeted me at the front door nearly every morning.

But there were other interesting characters besides Henry. There was Fern Sullens. Fern copied pages on pages of arithmetic problems over and over. She never learned to add or subtract or multiply--just copied figures in beautiful columns in her notebook pages.

There was Marie Hicks. From Lone Star she came, a queer, little dark girl who came up and whispered in my ear, "Please, may I leave the room? My mother gave me an elastic pill this morning."

Then there was the story of Tom Hicks, not a student, but the father of 16 children. One day in American History when I asked the inevitable question, "Who is considered the father of our country?", Harold Boyce was sure he knew. "I know, Teacher," he said. "I know. It's Tom Hicks."

And I can never forget Mary Tillman. Mary was a twin, a victim of epilepsy, always spoken of as "fits." The symptoms came on quickly and at first Mary would dash out of the room screaming and running so fast that not even the big, long-legged boys could catch her. The school sat within 20 feet of busy Highway 50, so we were under constant tension, afraid she would be struck by a vehicle.

After I experienced a few of her seizures, I recognized the onset of the symptoms. She would be playful and want to wander about the room; sometimes she laughed aloud when there was nothing amusing. Then I knew to stay close to her and hold onto her with all my might. And when the climax of the seizure came on her, I'd say, "Okay, kids, pile on."

They did, literally. Some sat on her, some held her shoulders and after several minutes of her trembling and straining, they knew what came next. Mary would urinate until the room seemed flooded. My appointed helpers knew their duties-- someone opened the windows to let in fresh air and let the horrible odor out, someone ran for Dee Owens to mop up the flood. By this time Mary would have fallen asleep, absolutely unaware of having caused any hub-bub at all. I usually had to shake her awake when Alice, her twin, came to take her home.

Mary couldn't learn much, but her mother wanted her to go to school to get the experience. And I'm convinced now that her mother was right. After all, it was a public school and anyone beyond the age of 6 could attend. Later when I visited Linn I inquired about Mary. She outgrew the attacks and still lives in the same house with her mother on the Will Weeks' property.

So many episodes come back to me so clearly. All of them were assimilated, mostly unconsciously, into my learning--about life and teaching. But I must move on. Bant graduated from high school in 1939 and wanted to go on to college. And I wanted to save some money and go to the University and finish my degree for a secondary certificate. But with Pete still in school, I knew that was just wishful thinking. Bant stayed home the next year and worked on the farm with Dad and Bud, hoping to go to school perhaps the next year.

I went back to Linn for a fifth year--and a few more changes. Siegel Holland had taken Mrs. Duncan's place as 7th and 8th grade teacher, so now he had the challenge of coping with Henry Balkenbusch.

Siegel talked in a whiney, nasal Ozarkian twang. He never punished anybody for anything and the children--most of all, Henry--soon discovered that fact. Siegel was forever twanging out, "Hen-ery...now Hen-ery...you jist better quieten down back there. You hear me, Henery?"

Henery would proceed right on, doing whatever he had been doing. Siegel would fret a little more and start all over, "Henery...Henery, I'm a-goin' to come back there pretty soon." Siegel never "came back there." But poor Henery had a short, miserable life. His mother died, his father paid scant attention to him and one day he was found lying almost unconscious outside a shed on the outskirts of

WHO CAN TELL ME?
Who's the father of our country?
"I know, Teacher, I know.
It's Tom Hicks."

town and he died almost immediately. Somehow, I felt, the world had lost a punctuation mark.

That November I attended my first state teachers' meeting. A group of us made the trip to Kansas City. Irvin Laughlin had married Sylvia Morton secretly (she was in school at Warrensburg), so there were Irvin and Sylvia, Tom Keller, Lillian Sawford, Frances Huffine and me. To handle those hard times, we chipped in to pay the driver for his gas and oil. On the way we stopped at a little town named Pittsfield to get gas and "rest." All of us were a little timid and we wouldn't think of asking to stop because we needed to "rest."

A small, wizened old man came out of the country store to fill our gas tank just as all of the females started to cross the highway where we could see the facility we needed so badly. He seemed to sense our need.

"Hey, girls," he called out, "no need to go across the road. Just go on in the store and keep straight ahead until you come to the vinegar barrel. Then turn right. You can't miss it."

We all laughed and "rested"--and added a new phrase to our permanent vocabulary.

Frances had arranged for the three girls to stay with her Uncle Seldon and Aunt Lennie. Aunt Lennie was short and fat, a fine woman, holding down a responsible job as a fulltime secretary. And she set for us the nicest dinner I'd ever had, linen cloth, crystal and silver, food beautifully served. Uncle Seldon had worked at one time in Washington, D.C., so he had much to tell. He then drove us down to the meetings and picked us up in the evenings. Our beds were gorgeous, with starched, ironed sheets. We lolled in luxury and I was much impressed with the life of the rich in the big city.

During the year our Etc. Club began to break apart. Sylvia had married and gone to Warrensburg. Ina, her younger sister, married Red Moore and went to live at Gasconade. Lillian had made plans to go to M.U. for a master's degree. I didn't want to continue teaching in Linn for $65 per month the rest of my life, so when school was finished that May I borrowed $100 from the Linn State Bank to go to M.U. for the summer. Pete would be there, too. He should have been finished, but with working for his meals, he hadn't always carried a full load.

In Columbia Pete had found a room for me on Matthews Street, gone now, absorbed by the expanding campus. The upstairs room faced west--with furnace--like heat all day and most of the night. It never cooled down all summer. I had to furnish my own bedclothes--two sheets, a bedspread and one pillowslip. That's all my roommate, Ada Mae Woodruff, had, too. We were both poor country farm girls, trying to "further our education," as the explanatory phrase put it.

We worked out a quite obnoxious schedule. We found it impossible to study in the evenings because the bugs swarmed in when we turned on the light. If we pulled the shades we had no air to breathe. So we went to bed early and got up every morning at 3:30 or 4:00 to study. It was cool and quiet then--or reasonably so.

Besides the summer heat, we bore another cross--our next door roommate from Grubville, Missouri. My mind has crossed out her name but I can still hear her. She was studying drama and speech and all summer long she practiced the same reading over and over, beginning, "One egg, now, remember, one egg. Not two eggs. One egg, one egg over lightly. I repeat, one egg, over lightly..."

And I remember other sounds of that summer. The rooming house was operated by a Mrs. Shepard whose daughters considered themselves musical. In their living room, directly beneath our bedroom, Lois pounded the piano while Mary Helen belted out, "The Holy City." They practiced incessantly on, "Jerusalem..Je---ru---se---lum, Je---ru----sa----lum" until I thought, between "One Egg" and "Jerusalem" I'd lose my mind.

Downstairs in a dark, closet-like room lived one Edith Gander Gordon. She was writing a book, so all day and all night she pounded an old rattlety-bang typewriter. And in a front downstairs bedroom lived Supt. and Mrs. Williamson, from some small Ozarkian town near the Bootheel. They were the only quiet ones in the house. We never saw much of them. They were newlyweds but not young; they must have been nearly forty. He did play the clarinet quite well--and he found Mary Helen's rendition of "Jerusalem" quite unenjoyable.

Ada Mae and I made a mistake, I think. Mr. Shepard, in addition to his agriculture office job, farmed a large truck patch outside the city limits. Every evening he went out there and lugged home bushels of fresh green beans, perfectly gorgeous roasting ears, tomatoes that made my mouth water and other garden products which I could see as I passed by the kitchen door.

To get away from "One Egg" and "Jerusalem," Ada Mae and I ate at a club a few blocks away where the food was, well, "standard." Each day the menu was the same: Cubed Steak, Pork Chop or Meat Loaf--with a small serving of green beans and a tiny dollop of mashed potatoes. And pie, if you could afford it. Apple or cherry. I think the man of the house did the cooking because his wife ran a business school. Two college students of Japanese descent from Poughkeepsie, N.Y. helped with the cooking and serving. And I often wondered what they thought about their "learning" of American cuisine.

The courses I partook of that summer were somewhat like our menu. They were by far the dullest and most uninteresting I had yet encountered. I had the idea I would like to teach Home Economics, so I signed up for General Economics and Sociology. A German professor from Greencastle, Indiana, taught Economics. None of us could understand a word he said, and when he wrote on the blackboard it was even more complicated. When some of the students remonstrated, he yelled at us in German. If I had understood it, I might have been angry.

There was only one recourse--to read the text and study and study. This I did, beginning at 3:30 or 4:00 each morning. From such diligence, I remember one principle--the point of diminishing returns. I don't think I really needed to study that. So far, I had been experiencing that all of my life!

The Sociology course was worse. The professor couldn't explain anything in a logical manner; he seemed to always go round and round. When someone in class asked him to be more definite, he would remove his pen from his shirt pocket and say, "Now, take this pen for example..." Every day he urged that pen on us as an example of each thing we were discussing.

Toward the end of the summer, someone upbraided him, "Professor, you surely can't hold us responsible for examples on exams since your pen has been an example of everything you've taught. And furthermore, I can't really put my finger on anything you have taught."

But the professor was not convinced--nor deterred. He kept right on using his pen as an example. And all I remember from that course are the names of Cro-Magnon and Neanderthal man--and the pictures of their horrible head structures in our textbook.

Pete was in this class, too, so I did double duty. He was forever "in a bind" and never had time to study. So I made notes as I read the text and the outside reading books, then he studied my notes. I wrote papers for both of us and had them typed. He never saw the papers he handed in. (And he never got to class on time. He had to serve breakfast at Gabler's, then run to class on the Red Campus. He arrived usually just as the professor finished taking attendance. Several mornings he popped in just in time to respond "Here" from the doorway. His behavior became a sort of joke for everyone but me. I was ashamed for anyone to know he was my brother!

Pete came in handy, though, for Ada May. She was very studious and was cataloging the chemistry formulas by girls' names: "H" was Helen, "O" was Olga, "Ca" was Candace. She changed "O" to Ovary Pidgeon, when I finally convinced her that I had really known a girl by that name at Rolla.

Pete had failed chemistry the previous semester but now he had his own as well as several friends' notebooks and sometimes he and Ada May studied together. They sounded like two idiots reciting, "Helen 2 Ovary, water," and their versions of other formulas.

But Ada May had another axe to grind with Pete. She was madly in love with one Norman Clough. They had been engaged some three years earlier and had broken up after an argument about where they would be married. They hadn't seen each other since. Norman was now teaching in the College of Agriculture and Ada May wanted to see if Pete could locate him for her.

When we walked the streets of Columbia and Ada May saw any beaten-up gray Ford sedan coming our way, she'd stop and gaze at it, saying, "Now that looks like Norman's old Ford. I wonder if it could be..." Later Pete found out that Norman wasn't at M.U. at all that summer, so we stopped using our radar stares on old, gray Ford sedans.

The romance had a fairy tale ending, however. Ada May returned to M.U. in the fall; so did Norman. They met and married without any further argument and Ada May's trousseau was only slightly yellowed in the interim. Norman is now Dr. Norman Clough, an optometrist at Richmond, Missouri.

"Ader Tomater," and I correspond regularly. They visited me last when I lived at Linn. I was in the back yard bathing the dogs one Sunday morning when around the corner of the house appeared Ada May and Norman. I smelled like dog flea powder and I had soap suds up to my elbows. I was soaked from head to foot in my raggedy-est clothes. Buell was asleep barefooted in the living room with his dirty socks scattered here and there. But that didn't keep us from laughing about our M.U. summer--"One Egg" and "Jerusalem," chemistry formulas and Ovary Pidgeon. True friends and a sense of humor are invaluable companions, I learned early.

PART FIVE

OLD WOOLLAM

13

"Vee t'ink you're da vun."

When I came home in August I intended to borrow money and return to M.U. for a degree in Home Economics. Mama, however, had other intentions. She had heard of an opening at Old Woollam. The teacher, Clarence Wildebrandt, had resigned to go to Beemont near Gerald. So on Monday morning following my homecoming on Friday, Mama had Bud and me on the road to Old Woollam. (Yes, there was a New Woollam, too...somewhere.)

Old Woollam was a wealthy German settlement in Gasconade County, not far from Owensville. The school was only a one-room affair, but it was considered a fine place to teach. The men served as board of directors in name only. Their wives ran the school--and everything else.

So Bud and I called on Mr. and Mrs. Julius Landwehr. Everything at their place was laid out in apple pie, typical "Churman" orderliness. The corn rows were so even they could have been measured with a slide ruler; the wheat shocks were exactly the same distance apart. The paint on the white house and the red barn glistened in the early morning sun. The whole house had been scrubbed and polished within an inch of its life. And Julius's overalls almost begged for some soil.

We made our business known and Mr. Landwehr seemed impressed. But he gave us directions for getting to Aug Aufderheide's farm "right up a little draw" from his farm. As we drove away, we heard some little pigs squeal. Bud looked at me and said in a droll voice, "I'm surprised those pigs dare to grunt and squeak here."

Aug Aufderheide, it turned out, lived in quite "a draw." Most of the time we were in a ditch; sometimes the road ran along one side of it, then along the other. But most of the time Bud and I were trying to figure out just where the road was. After several miles of this we were about ready to turn around when suddenly we came upon a neat, white, green-shuttered farmhouse. A white picket fence ran around it and at the side was a beautiful green grape arbor.

We parked the car in the ditch, climbed out and up the bank and found Mr. Aufderheide sitting in a large wicker rocker just inside the arbor. He held his right hand, heavily bandaged, carefully on a pillow on his lap. We told him who we were and what we wanted and he held up his good left hand to stop any further explanation: "Ulius ust called me up," he said in a thick German accent. "We t'ink you're the vun. Ust set down a little wile and wisit wit me."

Our "wisit" was a lesson in Old Woollam pronunciation, Aug Aufderheide style, and the treatment of "boyils."

"Oh," he said, "I got such a boyil on the little finger as you nefer yet seen. Ust let me show you vunce already."

I had been wondering what that dark green was around the edge of the bandage. He began unwrapping it and I saw it was Jimson weed leaves--and he had a huge pan full of them by the side of his chair.

"It's time to change the leafs, anyhow," he said. "Do you know yimson leafs been the best yet for boyils?"

He finished unwrapping the bandage and I agreed that his "boyil" was the worst yet. Never had I seen anything as red and swollen. He laid those green leaves directly on that red, infected flesh, re-wrapped his hand and was silent. Mrs. Aufderheide came out of the kitchen with a pitcher of cool lemonade and from that moment on, Aug only raised his left hand or nodded his head. In assent.

The day was terribly warm. We seemed to have the job sewed up and were ready to leave when Mrs. Aufderheide said, "Now, you can't see Mr. Charles Neese today because they've gone to the state fair, but I'll talk it over with Mrs. Neese and Mrs. Landwehr and we'll let you know right away." She talked fast and all the words sounded like a single long one. But she was as good as all of them.

The following Wednesday morning, soon after we had finished breakfast, the two men appeared at our front door. August's "boyil" was much better and Julius's overalls were a bluish white they were so clean. I could teach the school, they informed me, for $75 a month, plus $5 extra for doing the janitor work. The school had a small dark basement with a furnace, so there'd be no wood to carry. They had coal delivered for it. They spoke of these things with great pride and I signed the contract, under Mama's supervision.

They had already contacted Emma Suelthaus (Mrs. Ben) to see if I might board there. (Emma was Julius's sister.) All was arranged; there was no use to fight City Hall (Mom). But I was disappointed. I would be teaching again in a one-room school, with no further study toward a degree.

But we were too busy for disappointment to linger long, and August passed quickly. Bant was going away to Warrensburg State Teachers' College and his clothes had to be got in order. Pete was still at M.U. and he always came home in August to get his clothes and bedding renewed and in order. And always and eternally there were tomatoes to be canned. Sometimes now I wake up at night and I've been dreaming that school is about to begin and I haven't got the tomatoes canned!

There are reasons for country ways. These country schools began the last week in August so the children could get out early in the spring and help on the farm. And there is wisdom in many of the country "sayin's"--such as "Don't count your chickens before they hatch" or "Don't borrow trouble." I tried to remember that lesson after I moved into my new boarding place.

The Suelthaus home was a delightfully large, old, well-kept brick house on the south side of the country road leading into Owensville. Both Ben and Emma had a knack for neatness, a will for working and a devotion to an "extra dollar." The whole atmosphere was different from my Hollandworth experience. For one thing, Ben and Emma had only one teenage daughter, Talitha, a high school junior. Mrs. Suelthaus's mother, Mrs. Landwehr, lived there part of the time; so did an elderly cousin, Etta, so it seemed as if there was always one extra person at the table. But Emma's table was quite different from the one in Horse Shoe Bend.

I remember my first evening there. Emma was showing me through the house-- the great parlor with the new piano, lamps hanging from the ceiling, pretty paper on the walls, Brussels carpet on the floor, the front porch. When she finished, she led the way to the cellar beneath the kitchen and said, "I was shure glad to get you to board. Now maybe we'll eat up some of these green beans."

She had shelves, tables and benches covered with half-gallon jars of green string beans! I appreciated her generosity, but I was fairly certain I wasn't going to be much help in that department!

I had a large upstairs bedroom, furnished with a great wooden bed, loaded with mattresses, feather beds and quilts to make me cozy and comfortable. And there were a washstand with a china bowl and pitcher--and a slop jar to match. I even had a large wooden wardrobe in which to hang my clothes. And on the floor was a rag rug, the kind you weave in strips and sew together to fit your floor. Of course, there was the everlasting wood stove. But I was becoming an expert on stoves, wood, kindling and such necessary accompaniments to keeping warm.

The Rural Electric Administration was just beginning to fulfill Franklin Delano Roosevelt's promise to have electricity in every farm house and Old Woollam was taking advantage of it, despite being a died-in-the-wool Republican stronghold. About two weeks after school began, houses in the neighborhood were inspected and Ben and Emma turned on the lone light in the kitchen and stood admiring the bulb hanging from a wire over the supper table. Earlier they had bought a refrigerator--on sale--so they now complimented each other on how smart they had been. Often afterwards we were rewarded with a Jello salad for our evening meal. Emma made it in a stone or earthenware crock and we passed it around the table. At first, that amused me; I thought it should have been served on salad plates. But remembering its taste, I was wrong. And I joined the many other glad recipients of "Ol' FDR's electric."

When I walked to school that first Monday morning, I found the way was mostly through open fields. Just before I reached the school building, there was a wooded area--not as pretty as Horse Shoe Bend, but inviting on hot autumn mornings and evenings. As I left the Suelthaus home, I went out through a lane to the country road, crossed the road and--again--fought a barbed wire fence. Ben had warned me not to push the wire down when I "crawled tru, else the ol' cows might get notions." So I was as easy on the wire as possible--and hoped it might treat me likewise.

At the upper end of this field, I scrambled over another fence--or under or "tru" it. By this time I was usually covered with Spanish needles and stick-tights. But I had chosen to be a teacher and fences and stick-tights apparently came with the vocation. (Besides, I was saddled again with the responsibility of helping the boys through school.) So began another endurance test in new surroundings.

As I came out of the woods and trotted down a sloping hill, I could see the schoolhouse. It seemed ready to swallow me for another eight hours and regurgitate me somewhere between four and five o'clock--whenever it chose to finish digesting me. I think its location gave me this eerie feeling. All of the farm sounds echoed loudly in the cavity surrounding the school--especially early in the morning before the children arrived. The farmers would return their cows to pasture after milking and the cows would be missing their calves and their mournful bawls stretched over the entire valley and reverberated in my ears.

I could see only one farmhouse. Bill Mueller lived there with his maiden sister, Anna. Just beyond lived their widowed sister-in-law and her three daughters. Hilda, the eldest, was through elementary school so she helped her uncle operate the farm. Lydia, the middle daughter, had tuberculosis and was in bed most of the time. Sophia, the youngest, became my favorite friend and pupil.

Coming for schooling besides Sophia was Irvin Borrenpohl, who lived with his Grandmother Schalk in the little village of Old Woollam; and across the field with Sophia came Sonny and "Sissy" (Verna Marie) Buecker and a charming little boy by the name of Chester Farris. From farther up the road came Bobby Judemann and, from quite a distance, down the road came Audrey Neese, the

EARLY MORNING

The farmers would return the cows to pasture after milking and the cows would be missing their calves and their mournful bawls stretched over the entire valley..."

adopted son of Charles Neese, the State Fair goer of my job-seeking trip.

These seven comprised my entire group of charges. Audrey had already been labled by Ben and Emma as my "problem child." He had run away from home several times. He hated school and often played hookey unless his father delivered him safely into the hands of the teacher every morning. "It's 'ust real hard for Audrey to grasp book learnin', Aug Aufderheide had said. Aug was trying to be tackful; Audrey, I discovered, was mostly trying. Period.

Emma also had explained carefully that Sonny and Sissy were quite spoiled, being late arrivals in a family with much older children. And Irvin Borrenpohl had three strikes against him because his dad had failed in the grocery business. He had left the Woollam neighborhood in debt--and owing money to some of these hard working frugal Germans is no way to be remembered kindly. The remaining three children seemed to meet with the approval of Emma and the other women. But I was positive that the next eight months were going to be sheer drudgery. And with this idea in mind, I suppose I proceeded to make them so.

With only seven pupils it was a bit hard to keep something going all the time. There was one redeeming feature--a good piano. And, thankfully, everyone liked to sing. So we often spent 30 minutes or more gathered on the high platform in front of the room yelling our lungs out. We sang everything as boisterously as possible because that's the way Sonny liked it. Sonny and Sissy had guitars which they lugged to school every morning so they could "harmonize."

Sonny was so obese that he almost wore himself out by the time he had tried to pick out a few tunes by ear. I went ahead with my own music and the remaining five pupils, while Sonny and Sissy twanged away in the background--off key. One morning Audrey, tired of the dissonance, informed all of us in his sing-song tone, "Miss Bacon, my pop said why don't you tell them Bueckers to leave their damned 'gits' at home?"

I guess my face reddened, I don't remember my reply, but from that day forward I treated Audrey with more respect. So did Sonny and Sissy. They also left their "gits" at home.

The evenings at Suelthauses were relaxing. I often sat on the side porch reading a book, checking school papers or sewing a bit. Emma was a bustling housekeeper. She wore a dress for a whole week and Ben wore his blue overalls and blue chambray workshirt all week--and neither of them got dirty. Emma covered her everyday dress with a big coverall apron. A large, stout woman, she wore her gray hair in a high, twisted, beehive knot almost on top of her head. Ben was a rather small man, with dark brown skin, hair and eyes. (He was really a Brinkmann, not a Suelthaus. His aunt had taken him to rear when his mother died with his birth. Ben's father had had three wives, with five children by each. Ben was the youngest child of wife No. 2.)

Talitha was a joy to all of us. She was a tall, thin 16-year-old. She couldn't understand why she was an only child and kept wondering why so many people in the Old Woollam Community had only one child. It was not a prolific settlement. Emma told her one evening how she and Ben had gone to Emmanuel Lutheran Children's Home in St. Louis to look over the orphans there. Talitha listened intently then said, "But, Mama, why did you go there?" Emma smiled, looked wise and went on paring potatoes.

Ben had a bumper crop of potatoes that year. Since digging time they had been stored in the garage. Now winter was coming on and one evening when I came home from school, Ben and Emma were moving potatoes. Between them they carried a bushel basket full of Idahos, and in her left hand Emma held a large bucket full while Ben, with his left hand, pulled a little child's red wagon on which perched two more bushel baskets. That was "teamwork," as J.P. McDaniel would have put it.

We had potatoes many ways for many meals--potato pancakes for breakfast, boiled "shookdown" potatoes for supper. Emma would station Talitha at the kitchen window so she could see the big stone barn. "Talitha," she told her, "when Dad puts the calves out into the pen, you tell me. Then it's time to put the potatoes on."

Talitha was mostly faithful at her battle station, but once in a while she slipped up. Then Emma would scold her, "Talitha, I told you," she would say sternly.

But Ben wasn't that much of a schedule man. "Ack," he would say, with a grin, "this way I get to read a little more of 'Farm Journal'."

All fall Ben begged Emma to let him buy a "dollar pocket watch" so he would know when a meal was ready. But Emma held out steadfastly. Her answer was always the same: "No, Ben, you had a dollar watch once already and you lost it. Much better we buy a dinner bell."

Ben and Emma did get a daily paper, the St. Louis *Globe-Democrat.* In the evening Talitha and I read the comics together. And we noticed the rumblings of war. The front page had pictures of Hitler's "Goose Steppers," and German tanks with big guns. Small countries were being overrun and this was of great concern to Ben.

After supper when we gathered around the kitchen table to read, sew or help Talitha with her homework, Ben would say, "Dat Hitler, I don't like him, from wat it say in the paper. I'm gladder every day we got that Atlantic between us."

In the paper we also read articles about defense for the United States. Getting work in a defense plant was great--with "good money"--but the war was no good! There also was Daylight Saving Time and talk of food rationing, gas rationing, shoe rationing. Registering for all of these things was done at the schools, amid much talk about the whirlwind changes blowing in on us.

When Daylight Saving Time became a reality, Ben renewed his plea for a dollar watch. "Ack, Mom, come on. Ben Witte has two watches now, one for Daylight Saving and one for God's Time." But Emma stood her ground. "Ben, I still rather we have a good dinner bell."

In October all the young men between 18 and 38 had to register for the draft. Pete got a rather low number and was called up almost immediately and assigned to Jefferson Barracks near St. Louis as a guard at the north gate. This suited Pete just fine, I think. He was tired of college and Elaine Carmichael, his steady girlfriend, was working in St. Louis.

Bud was classified 4F; fallen arches and imbedded wisdom teeth were the official reasons. But I believe it was really because they tried to leave one boy on a farm.

Men of Dad's age qualified as only half a man. He and Tim Leach were the only men we knew in this category and we used to tease him about it taking two of them to make a real man. Bant drew a higher number, so he wasn't drafted until later. But the handwriting was on the wall--and every day in the newspaper--and war feeling ran high in this heavily German neighborhood. "Down with Hitler. Give him Hell. Load cannon with nails and get him first." Such were Ben's heartfelt comments as he read the *Globe Democrat* each evening.

Each Friday afternoon Bud came to the schoolhouse to pick me up so I could spend each weekend at home. I didn't carry many clothes back and forth. At the beginning of school I had tried to be pleasing to my little students by varying my scanty wardrobe as much as possible. Then one evening Ben took the wind out of my sails. "What you tryin' to do," he said, "win a beauty contest? Looks to me like one set of tugs a week oughta be plenty." I had noticed, of course, that he and Emma wore one "set of tugs" a week, so I lightened my wardrobe accordingly and took only one change per week.

At Christmas time Emma baked cookies--nothing fancy, just good plain butter cookies. To some she added hickory nuts, to others some coconut or oatmeal. Some she frosted a bit. Evidently she baked a goodly quantity. For weeks my lunch box contained two. (I could eat the lunch she prepared for me because she thoroughly scalded and sunned the cream separator every day. She also bought lunch meat for my and Talitha's lunches.)

But came one night and no cookies were on the supper table. "Mom, get some more cookies once," said Ben, who liked sweet things.

"I can't, Ben," replied Emma, "they is all."

That was Old Woollam German for "They're all gone." And apparently cookies were only a Christmas goodie. No more appeared the whole year.

When the dark, dull days of winter began, I became almost frantic with so little to do at school. Three of the seven pupils would graduate in the spring; they were my big concern. Audrey needed some special help but he was no real problem. I rather liked him--especially after he got the Bueckers to leave their "gits" at home. Sophia and Irvin were very bright, and they could carry on by themselves.

Bobby Judemann, being a first grader, could only "grasp" so much. And my favorite little boy, Chester Farris, was absent much of the time because of an operation.

The Bueckers, Sonny and Sissy, sat on their fat little butts and looked daggers at me most of the time. I found, though, that Sonny was very good at exaggeration. He could sit all day at school without saying anything worthwhile, but it seemed as if he could repeat everything at home with embellishments--not only what the children said, but what I said, too.

Ben and Emma had informed me about this quality. So had Charles Neese. And Carrie Neese had added, "Them two spoiled brats is enough to run any teacher plum crazy." But I didn't plan to let Sonny and Sissy drive me anywhere.

Audrey helped. One day at noon we were all huddled over the hot air vent, eating our lunches, when Sonny began his usual bragging. "You know," he said, "I've found a good way to save .22 shells. I can kill rabbits by throwing corn cobs at them. Killed six that way last night, just while I was shelling corn for the chickens."

Audrey had had enough. He didn't weigh as much as chubby Sonny, but he was taller. Reaching out with both hands, he clasped Sonny's fat little neck and began squeezing, yelling "You know that's a damn lie, now don't you? If you don't want me to choke you plum down, just raise your right hand and admit it, that's a lie."

Sissy, of course, was pounding on Audrey. But all the other kids laughed and cheered Audrey on. In a minute Sonny feebly raised his right hand in assent and all was peaceful again. After that Sonny only bragged on the days Audrey was absent.

Soon after the Christmas holidays I became aware of how much spare time I had. I thought it over, sent to M.U. for a bulletin describing their correspondence

MEMORIES OF DOC

*The summer Grandma Tyree died
every night, and other bedside
recollections.*

courses and was soon busy at work on a six-hour course in American Literature. The University mailed all the lessons, the necessary text envelopes for returning the work and all pertinent instructions. So at last I was occupied with something besides Lazy Daisy and cross stitch embroidery.

During the holidays, too, Irvin took his father, Dr. Leach, to Jefferson City to consult with Dr. Bedford. The diagnosis was pernicious anemia. I had never heard of the disease and at first thought nothing of it. But Doc soon became quite ill. His face became pale and one Sunday when I stopped by to visit him I was amazed to see that his stomach had completely disappeared. Neighbors began going in to "sit up" with him at night, a common practice in those days before hospitalization. Bud became one of Mrs. Leach's favorites. He went night after night so Mrs. Leach could get some rest.

I sat up, too, when I could, and one of the last times I saw Doc we were reminiscing about some of the funny things that had happened to him and we recalled from a few years earlier "the summer that Grandma Tyree died every night." Grandma lived with her son-in-law and daughter, Mr. and Mrs. Tom Tyree, at the Feuresville Store site. Grandma was nearly 100 years old but not the least bit senile or childish. But she did stay in bed most of the time and when darkness came on, she got lonesome.

About every other night all summer long, just as Mom and I would be finishing our evening chores, the phone would ring. It would be Aunt Sal Tyree. Aunt Sal was a wee wisp of a woman, but--like her mother--she had a great sense of wit and humor. Even hers, though, was strained that summer.

"Grace," she would ask on the phone, "could you and your mother come right away? I think Ma's a-dyin'. You know she's nigh on to a hundred and she caint' go on forever."

Sometimes she offered to send Tommy, Jr. after us, especially if we had just been there the night before. They always sent for Doc, too. And, of course, Mrs. Leach. When we all gathered around her bed, Grandma began to feel better. She would prop herself up on the white pillows and begin to tell us how "Civilization is a-goin' to kill us all. Civ-i-li-za-tion (all five syllables accented) ain't no good for humans. No, sir-ree, no good a-tall. People ain't made to be civilized. Cars a-runnin' on air (airplanes), people a-talkin' through little wires a-runnin' along nailed on posts and trees, and these here lights civilized people got a-hangin' around now on strings right in their houses! Just don't make no sense. You know how them lights is made--somebody hitched up a whole mess of lightnin' bugs and tied 'em by their tails. Cain't be no other way."

She made "sitting up" real entertainment.

One night we got the "Grandma is dying" call and Mom and I put on clean dresses and walked quickly up the hill. Doc was ahead of us, listening to Grandma's heart through his stethoscope. We thought tonight--surely--Grandma would go to her reward. But, in a minute she opened one eye. She fixed it on Doc and with her usual twinkle she said, "Now, Doc, don't you pinch me on the tit--because if you do, I'll tell Kort." (Kort was an elderly widower who lived down in the woods near Tyrees.)

Doc shook his head, grinning, knowing that he'd be here another night. She didn't die that summer. Nor the next. But Doc and I enjoyed "the summer that Grandma died every night."

One evening when I came down the lane toward the house, Ben was digging post holes to set a new fence. As I came near him, he called out, "Hey, Teacher, look at this. I finally got mom to buy me my dollar watch." He pulled it out of the pocket on the bib of his overalls, where he had it attached securely with a braided leather piece string. Ben held it up and let it glisten in the sun. As I moved on, he said, almost under his breath, "Now, I'll bet I won't have to hear that stuff about rather having a dinner bell no more."

When I reached the house and had drunk the mug of hot milk--which Emma always had waiting for Talitha and me--I remarked, "Mr. Suelthaus is really proud of that new watch."

I saw Emma's face cloud over. She turned her head somewhat to the side before she replied, "Ach, ach, you know I didn't really want Ben to have that watch, but it really did bother me for Ben Witte to have two watches--one for Daylight Saving and one for Standard. I still rather we should have a good dinner bell. Any time. Ben will lose that watch. Just wait and see. You can't lose a dinner bell." And she turned back to peeling her Kar-to-ffle. (Or "Ca-Ta-fle," as they said.)

I--and all the rest of us--was well fed and waited on that winter by Emma. Quite a change for me from Horse Shoe Bend. In the early half-dark, half-light before dawn Emma would be up starting fires--first downstairs in the kitchen where she kept the big black iron range going full blast all winter, then upstairs she came to fire up. She had a large split hickory basket in which she carried finely split kindling, corn cobs and a small can of kerosene. In another large basket she carried split wood.

I would hear her go first into Ben and say, "Now, wait until the room warms good before you get out. It's below zero on the side porch."

Talitha sometimes dressed in her mother's bedroom as she was instructed to do--after Ben went downstairs. More often, she knocked on my door and asked if she might dress in my room. It didn't take us long; toilet preparations were scanty--especially in the winter.

Emma always brought me a huge pitcher of scalding hot water every morning for my bathing. Often she found Talitha propped up on my bed reading my thick copy of Poe or some other book from American Literature. Her child's liking to read pleased her, I think. Her face never showed much, but she would smile a little and say, "Ach, now bring the good books down by the fire where it's warm in the kitchen. It goes better down there." I was never sure whether she meant the fire or the reading. Maybe both.

Her breakfasts were a sight to behold and a feast to eat. She almost always had good, hot pancakes, a little thicker and heaver than I was accustomed to but very tasty. And to eat on them there was dark, spicy slightly juicy apple butter and lots of rich homemade butter. In addition to the cakes, she served homemade sausages of various kinds, a large pan of oatmeal and jelly. Always jelly. However, jelly on pancakes was not considered appropriate; we simply must eat apple butter on them.

There were large mugs of hot chocolate for Talitha and me. Ben and Emma and Grandma drank huge mugs of delicious looking coffee. All of the elders used rich cream in their coffee. They were one of the few German families I've ever known which used cream in coffee.

If we were going to have potato pancakes in the morning, Emma prepared everything the night before, peeling and grating the potatoes, setting out all of the ingredients so they could be "stirred up" quickly in the morning.

Small wonder that Ben was so patient about the watch. Where could he find a woman like his Emma? I certainly never found many like her. We all had so

EMMA'S PRESCRIPTION:

*"It's better to eat than take
medicine. You have to pay for
that."*

much; she watched over all of us so carefully. "It is much better to eat," she said, "than to take medicine. You have to pay for that--especially if you get sick and have to call a doctor."

I never boarded with a family that I came to think more of. They were fine, outstanding "salt-of-the-earth" citizens. I could give them little, but I do recall giving them a box of candied fruit for Christmas, something I thought they all would enjoy. One evening Talitha was eating a rather large piece of the fruit when Emma caught her. "Talitha," she admonished her, "that fruit's too rich for you. You'd better eat a piece of bread with it."

In their lives anything "too rich"--edible, material or spiritual--had to be leavened with the commonplace, the simple, the hard-earned.

During the spring I had a lesson in truth not always getting its just due. Emma and Ben had gone to Owensville and Emma had worn her Canada pin--her pride and joy because someone had brought it to her from Canada. It was in yellow gold, shaped like a maple leaf, with green veins in it and Canada written diagonally across it on a wavy banner. She had lost it but it was bound to be in the house, she said, because she remembered taking it off when she came home.

We finally gave up looking for it but we heard about it at every meal. Ben even had the audacity to twit her about it, "Mom, you could have bought a good dinner bell with what that pin would have brought on the market."

Several days passed and the incident was almost forgotten. Then one afternoon after school I was sitting in my favorite split bottom chair by the kitchen window. As the sun poured in the window I saw a golden gleam from the corner of the seat where the splits join around the leg. I looked closely, and it was Emma's Canada pin. I scratched it out from between the splits and announced proudly, "Emma, here's your Canada pin."

She came over to me quickly and grabbed it, almost roughly, out of my hand. "Ach, ach, child," she said, "where in God's name was it?"

I explained how the sun had shown in it and caught my eye. But I always felt that she didn't really believe me; she thought I had "planted" it there to return to her, rather than confessing to taking it.

An earlier event, I think, had given rise to this suspicion. Ben had shipped some calves to St. Louis and the returns usually arrived in a day or two. I usually brought the mail as I came by the box on my way home from school. But several days passed and no check came, and I began to feel a chill run up my spine each day when I appeared at the kitchen door with the paper and other mail but no calf returns.

One afternoon as I crossed the meadow, I saw an envelope caught on some tall dead weeds, not more than 20 feet from the county road where the mailbox stood. I stooped over and picked it up. It was Ben's calf check; I recognized the return address of the packing house in the upper left corner of the envelope.

Along with the check, I found a personal letter from Emma's brother in Oklahoma. I hurried happily to the house, anticipating the relief they would feel. But when I told how I had found the envelope clinging to a clump of dead weeds, Ben shook his head and said, "I was all over that damn meadow forty times and I never found nothin'. For the life of me I can't see how it is you found it."

I stopped bringing the mail; I could see they didn't trust me. That hurt, but it also taught me a valuable lesson, an adjunct to the knowledge that truth won't necessarily "out." And that is Don't ever offer to handle anyone's mail.

With the first warm days of spring I was basking in the glow of a little "extra" money. I wanted to spend it on the house at home. So I ordered Sears & Roebuck's cheapest linoleum. It took a large roll--and a sizeable chunk of my money, depsite the low price--to cover two 20- by 20-foot rooms plus the small hallway. But I wallowed deliciously in my unaccustomed wealth. I also ordered new curtains for the entire house, some bedspreads, bath towels and other household items. I even bought Dad a new "Sunday hat." He always liked a soft felt one. He couldn't wear a straw one because it irritated a small spot behind his right ear, a leftover from a mastoid operation.

Slowly but surely the last day of school came around at Old Woollam. The women insisted on bringing in the dinner and I had planned a short, simple entertainment--mostly singing, in which the adults could participate. I had asked the Rev. Stock, the Evangelical and Reformed minister from Bland, to deliver the graduation address.

The whole neighborhood, as usual, turned out for the exercises and crowded into the schoolroom. Everything was in order and I was going along just fine until it came time for the main address and no Rev. Stock. I waited a while. No speaker. Finally, in desperation, I extemporized on what I hoped were a few appropriate remarks and presented the diplomas. Then as soon as I could, I put my belongings in the car so Bud and I could get away quickly.

As customary at these school closings, the board of directors held a meeting. With three pupils having graduated, only four would be coming back. So the directors decided to close the school and make arrangements for these four children to attend other districts. I had applied for and been accepted as a teacher in the Owensville Elementary School but somehow I felt that the permanent closing of Old Woollam reflected on me.

But the saddest part of my leaving came on the last evening I spent with Ben, Emma and Talitha. Ben was late turning the calves into the calf pasture and late coming in for supper. Emma accosted him at the door.

"Why were you so long in the field," she demanded, "and why you walking up and down so long hunting for something?"

She never stopped for his answer or her breath. "You don't need to tell me," she said. "I just want to say one more time, I much rather that we should have a good dinner bell. You can't lose a dinner bell."

Poor Ben. And Ben Witte, I'll wager, still has his two watches.

But I forgot about Ben and his watch the next week when I was home. Doc died--Doc, who had been an everyday part of our lives for so long. I couldn't imagine not being able to go to the phone and call Dr. Leach. He had always been available--when Dad came down with kidney stones, when Bud cut his foot with an axe, when Pete fell out of the hayloft, when Bant broke his arm...

The day before the funeral I went to Mae's to care for Yvonne and Anna Lo while Mae and Irvin helped Mrs. Leach. The funeral director took the body to town for embalming; then most people had the body brought back home until time for the funeral. So Doc lay in state in the darkened front room. It was absolutely immaculate. People came from all parts of the county to pay their last respects. They would miss him. Day and night for almost 50 years he had answered calls--often without pay. Now Doc had answered His call.

It was also customary then for many people to gather at the home prior to the service. The minister held a short service before proceeding to the church. The funerals were timed--1 p.m. at the house and 2 p.m. at the church. This gave people a choice; they could attend one service, both--or neither.

Before the funeral Mae and I had to finish dotted swiss dresses for Yvonne and Lo--pink for Yvonne and blue for Anna Lo. Mae had almost finished them but the handwork still was to be done. Also, Mrs. Leach had bought a light pink Bomberg (Doc didn't like black.) which didn't fit her exactly right. She "pinned it' and sent it down for Mae to rip and re-sew. We worked late that night and I got up early the next morning to help Mrs. Leach scrub the porches and the room Doc was "laid out in."

It was a hectic day. I remember only a few details: Doc's face small and pasty against the soft white of the casket lining; the Rev. Stock losing the poem he was supposed to read, but determined to stop and look thoroughly through his papers and, finally, reading "The Touch of the Master's Hand; holding Anna Lo in my arms at the grave and Yvonne standing at my feet, holding my free hand; my arms aching from holding fat little Lo until the final "Amen" was said.

Doc's funeral seemed to set the pace for the whole busy summer. I had been in school so much that Mama allowed me to stay home if I promised to continue the correspondence courses. So along with cleaning house, doing the laundry, gardening and yardwork, I found time to read the books assigned for the American Novel. How dull most of them were! I'm glad "Wieland" was the only first American novel written like that! My professor in absentia leaned heavily toward Hawthorne's work, too. And after a hard day's work, I found it pleasant to sit in the yard and read about Hester wearing that scarlet "A".

I spent many evenings with Mrs. Leach. She disliked being alone and was afraid to stay alone at night, so she was grateful when I came to visit a while. She had always been one of my favorite people. I admired her ability to do her housework with such ease. The house always looked perfect; nothing was ever out of order. Her linoleum floors were always washed and waxed to a mirror-like shine.

She continued to keep a cow so she could have her own milk and cream and butter. Often I found her at the barn milking when I came up the road from our mailbox. I would hang over the barnyard fence and tell her about my day while she expertly whipped up a white froth in her milk pail with streams of milk. After she finished we carried the milk across the road, past Doc's office, up the front walk and over the porch to the kitchen where her scalded crocks and bowls awaited the warm milk. In them we carried the milk to the cellar where it would cool off for breakfast in the morning.

We often talked about the funny things that had happened to all of us. The summer before Mae and Irvin had remodeled their house, putting the kitchen where a bedroom had been and partitioning part of one bedroom for a bath. Mae had helped Irvin, so all of us had helped out with Yvonne and Anna Lo. Mom thought Mae and Irvin could finish the papering if we took the kids for a couple of days, so Doc offered to bring them out early. And when Doc said early, he meant early. About sun-up here came Doc, his usual cigar clenched between his two teeth, and grinning from ear to ear. It was August, but both girls had on felt winter hats and coats, and Lo's was on backwards. They had found them when Mae papered inside a closet the day before and insisted they wear them on their outing.

"Plum comical, ain't they?" said Doc admiringly.

That summer whizzed by and before I could turn around, the tomatoes had to be canned and day after tomorrow school would begin. Bant was off to Warrensburg for his second year; he seemed to be having his full share of fun living at Workmans on College Avenue and working in the kitchen for his meals. And I was off to Owensville to begin another year of teaching.

14

The principal "itched" his toes

I needed that year; it was hilarious from the beginning. Some administrative changes had been made and we were to be "departmentalized." I taught English, Spelling and other related subjects to the four upper grade groups. What this meant, simply, was the teachers changed rooms, the children stayed put. Thelma McWilliams taught Reading and Art. Waldo Landwehr taught Social Studies and some Math. Irvin Bartlemeyer was the coach and the elementary principal.

I had known all of the lower grade teachers for some time, mainly from summer sessions at Rolla. Lydia Roethemeyer taught first grade. (She cleaned everything--kids and furniture--with the same wet washcloth.) Mae Crowder (May the Lord bless her soul. She reared five orphaned nieces and nephews.) taught second grade. Nora Aufderheide (the wit and funster of the year) taught 3rd grade and Agnes Bagby (I boarded with her and her sister, Ollie.) had the 4th grade.

These comprised our little educating colony. (Later a music teacher shared our delightful groups with the high school, but the kids gave him such a rough time he resigned and Lorene Warner took his place.) But Principal Bartlemeyer provided our main hilarity. He was a dull, tedious, goodhearted fellow without the vaguest notion of how a school should be conducted. I remember that day after school when we were called into his office for our first meeting. We found him sitting in his swivel chair, barefooted, scratching between his bare toes.

He had to change from tennis shoes to "ledder shoes," he explained, because "dem tennis shoes all the time make me want to itch my feet."

The business of the meeting was to inform us that if at any time we needed help, just let him know. And that set the tone for a whole term of portentous callings-together.

Nora and I, together and singly, compared notes and the odds were that every time either of us approached his office door, he would have one foot up in the chair seat, "itching my toes," as he put it. At first all of us were well-mannered and acted as if all were in order. Then came the day when he called a teachers' meeting to make the momentous announcement that the flag which had been stored in his office didn't belong to us at all. It had been returned to the high school. A grievous wrong, apparently, had been redressed!

But the impetus for us to till this field ripe for fun came one day in early winter when Mrs. Bartlemeyer called the school: The furnace door was open, she said, and what should she do about it? I almost told her to shove her husband in and close it fast! But we would have missed him.

From then on we mustered up every item we could think of, enlarged upon it, compiled our collection into long lists and sent them to Principal Bartlemeyer daily, with the notation, "We need help on these problems immediately." We sent all items to Nora, our secretary, who confounded them into wordy statements which often didn't even make a sentence.

Then Principal Bartlemeyer would call his meeting, and we would come up with serious sounding requests--mostly jumbles of words involving curriculum and how

PRIN. BARTLEMEYER

He changed to "ledder shoes," because "Dem tennis shoes all the time make me want to itch my feet."

we could make our teaching more effective. And all the while he sat and "itched" his toes.

Several of us teachers ate with Ollie Bagby, an excellent cook with a doomsday turn of mind. In the fall we sat in the yard or on the porch after supper. Ollie would take her "sas-parill-ee" with her for the mosquitoes, then she would tell me all about her latest illness--terribly sick, she was, a serious liver ailment. Then, always, she diagnosed it, "I still believe it was the bottle of orange soda pop that did the dirt."

If we managed to turn Ollie's mind away from the soda pop, she told us about that old man at Leslie, Missouri. Someone had tried to get her to "go out with him." But she "had no notion whatever of draggin' that ol' bag of bones around with me anywhere."

But Ollie's exceptionally good cooking made up for her tales of woe. She never let one bit of anything go to waste! If we had cooked cabbage at noon, we drank the heated stock for supper. If the cake went stale, she dressed it up with a lemon sauce. Every morning she planned her menu for the day, walked to the grocery store, made her purchases and came home to cook it.

I particularly liked her pot roast for a winter dinner. She put it in a heavy cooking stewer and "seared in the juices." Then she put in some water and vegetables, carrots, celery and potatoes and served it with its own rich, brown gravy. Simply delicious!

Down by her woodshed in the back yard, Ollie had a small garden. She grew more stuff on that small plot than we did in our big garden. She had rhubarb, asparagus, strawberries, tomatoes, cabbage, celery and chinese cabbage--all in season, of course. Even spinach in the winter. She could make anything grow. Her brother, Mart, was a gardener for Shaw's Garden and a caretaker for its Gray Summit acreage, so evidently a green thumb gene ran in the family.

In October Pete, scheduled for overseas duty, made a short visit home. He came amid much talk of war. The daily papers ran big headlines about blitzkreig warfare in Europe. FDR came on the radio, saying "We will not enta the wah unless we arh attacked." I had no idea we would be attacked, so I felt secure, insulated. Almost.

Pete rode back to Owensville with me and Bud on Monday morning. The main highway passed in front of the Bagby house. And as I left for school, I waved at Pete, looking boyish and handsome in his khaki uniform, trying to hitch a ride back to Jefferson Barracks.

That was in 1941. It was my last glimpse of him for five years because in December we were attacked at Pearl Harbor. We were at war. Strong dissent dominated the conversations in Gasconade County. It was a traditional Republican stronghold and the people had little respect for FDR. And when the first bodies of our soldiers--I especially remember Wilbur Bledsoe--were returned for burial, the citizens were irate.

Those long war years which followed surprised us, confused us. Was this what we had labored so hard for--to send our sons and brothers to school for? Was this what I was teaching kids for? To have them be cannon fodder? We all felt so helpless--sure that we could ration ourselves back home, but few felt that would help much.

Pete and Elaine were married January 18. Pete didn't tell us; Pearl Langenberg saw the marriage license notice in the *Globe Democrat*. Again, it was time for Mom to "throw a fit." Mom opposed marriage for any of her children and

UNCLE SAM CALLS

Pete was boyish and handsome, and he was going to war. And all our lives were changing.

although Pete was her favorite, he was no exception in this respect. Elaine was working at the Scruggs cosmetic counter and Pete only had weekends free. *And it will never work out, you'll see.*

There were many war marriages in Owensville, too. But I was not so touched by them. I didn't know these people as well and they weren't relatives as so many were at Linn. In fact, I should have been content at Owensville. The children were easily managed. Most of them came from strict German upbringings, from hard-working families who still believed school was a privilege, not a right. They were a joy to work with, and there were no discipline problems--a good thing for our ever-alert principal with the "itchy" toes. (He must have had athlete's foot.)

But more and more I thought about going back to school at Warrensburg for a degree. Pete's finances, of course, were no problem, but I was helping Bant so he wouldn't have to borrow money. So looking ahead to college again, I bought a few clothes--not from Sears & Roebuck this time, but from a nice dress shop in Owensville which carried only women's dresses and suits. I bought a beige and blue herringbone weave wool suit which practically became my uniform for several years. I paid $15 for it, as I recall. I also bought a black crepe dress with a finely pleated skirt, and a dark red crepe dress. During the winter I even had Nilla Ebert at Linn make me a couple of dresses for school. I was coming up in the world!

Just before I left Linn I had been elected associate conductress in the O.E.S. But during my year at Woollam I had not attended "Chapta," as J.P. called it. Now I wanted to finish the offices and be Worthy Matron. I offered to pay Bud five dollars a trip and buy the gas if he would take me to the meetings. Faithfully, every second and fourth Thursday, he pulled up in front of the Bagby house and away we went.

Here I renewed my former acquaintance with cousin J.P. and his new wife--No. 3. She was an old friend from some small town in western Missouri, so he had had to hire some of the young men to drive him to court her, usually Bob Campbell. Bob enjoyed taking J.P. on these "love jaunts," as he called them. Bob said J.P. proposed to his lady on their first date, telling her how "ha'd" it was for him to "get away from the sto-ah" and since he had a fine, comfortable house, they might as well "just git married right away." She must have agreed; it was settled in no time.

At the "Chapta's" I found J.P. and his bride delightful. Also Miss Reika (Mrs. Pete Gove). She was still crippling around the "inner sanctum" performing the duties of the chaplain--on knees so stiff she could hardly get out of her chair. Angie McDaniel was still secretary, still reading her minutes ever so distinctly and peering at us over her spectacles and asking for "any corrections or additions." Of which there were few and the minutes "stood as read."

I remember corrections being voiced only once, when Miss Rieka and Angie played a prank on Mary Carnes. They wrote in the minutes that Mrs. Carnes had served as Organist Protem--and Mrs. C. had to protest such a title and service. And these women--as well as J.P.--were all well up in their 70s and 80s, carrying on like that!

Mrs. Carroll had made the ripple into O.E.S. after many failures. And there were many new faces. But I missed Ina and Sylvia Morton, Mary Bradley and others who had attended with me in the earlier years. I made it through, however, and was elected Worthy Matron for the following year.

Early in March Pete was dispatched to Camp Barkley in Texas. Elaine planned to close her apartment and join him later. But much to my surprise one Friday afternoon when Bud came after me, Elaine was with him. I was very taken with her. She was tall, slender and pretty. Almost black hair and beautiful skin.

She had surprised Mom, too, calling from Mt. Sterling. Mom was doing the wash--and knowing Mom's method of handling that chore, I could visualize what followed. First, Mom waited until every stitch of bedding, clothing, table linen, everything was soiled. Then she procrastinated: "I'll catch a pretty day." Then, "I've waited this long; there's bound to be a pretty day coming along about next week."

I can't remember if Elaine appeared on a "pretty day" but I know Mom was shaken when her new daughter-in-law was a few miles away and coming to visit her. Mom started figuring fast. She was in no shape for company--dirty clothes all over the kitchen and dining room, tubs of soapy water...and nothing special cooked.

She came up with one of her patented brainstorms: Bud would get Elaine and drop her off at Mae's for the first night until Mom could get organized. The next day, Friday, Bud could take her on a tour of the "sights" in and around Belle, Bland and Owensville--after bringing Mae up to help Mom. And by the time Bud, Elaine and I arrived Friday afternoon, all would be in readiness.

Great was the "moving out of Egypt." Mom's method of housecleaning was to carry everything to the wash house, the smokehouse or upstairs. And when we arrived things looked tidy and orderly--downstairs. She dared any of us to even open the washhouse door. I didn't really want to; I had been through these ordeals before!

We had a happy weekend. The weather was mild and Elaine and I walked over our hills and pastures. We went along with Bud to the cow barn when he milked and we rode the wagon to the far corner of Eaton House Hollow to get some wood which had been sawed into stove lengths earlier in the fall.

On Sunday morning I sneaked Elaine upstairs to see the big bedrooms. She picked up a volume of Gilbert and Sullivan Operas I had carried up out of Mom's way downstairs. She turned to the "S.S. Pinafore" and sang through the whole thing; she had had a leading part in a Stephens College production of it two years before. She had a lovely soprano voice! After Sunday dinner Bud and I took Elaine to Mt. Sterling where she boarded the bus to return to St. Louis. She soon joined Pete at Camp Barkley. And I never saw her again.

With the war everywhere now, all the young men felt uncertain about their future. They didn't know how much time they had--if any. So all the young people tried to do as much living as possible now. Viola Aufderheide was dating James Pollard. James was teaching Physical Education at the high school and Viola was substituting in all courses. Teachers were scarce. Waldo Landwehr and I double-dated with them occasionally. Wilbur Beck (now "Buffalo Bill" of Beck Motor Company of Freeburg) was dating an attractive high school teacher, Estelle Ballew.

This "live for now" feeling even caught Lena Sassmann and Charles Tappmeyer. They were in their 60s. They were both practically deaf and had "gone together" for years. Home Ec teachers were hard to find, so the school board offered Lena the job--on the condition that she buy a hearing aid. She did--and liked it so much she tried to talk Charles into buying one. But he never did. Sad to report, they never married, either.

The war would change much, including manners and relationships between men and women. But not yet in Owensville. One Saturday morning the "faculty" was busily engaged in plastering the gym walls with Thelma McWilliams art work--mostly posters--for an academic fair of some kind. I noticed Mr. Sindon and Waldo laughing almost to knee-slapping and they blushed rosy red when Thelma and I asked what was so funny. Soon we saw Waldo climb up a ladder, take down a poster and replace it, and slip the first one on the bottom of his stack.

After all that effort to remove it, Thelma and I had to find out what it was. Nonchalantly, we pretended to hunt through the stack for some suitable ones to hang. Then we were embarrassed. It advertised milk: "Health in every glassful." But the "g" and "l" had fallen off.

That same morning Lena Sassman was putting up her Home Ec display and grumbling about having so much to do. "And after I finish here," she said, "Mrs. Carpenter has to have a coffee cake yet." Mrs. Carpenter, the druggist's wife, was a sweet little woman, always impeccably dressed, and I remembered how Agnes Bagby and I used to laugh about a Brandhorst girl who always wanted to "get to Jefferson City once" so she could buy a hat "wit a wail" on it like Mrs. Carpenter wore.

Owensville had other characters. Like Mrs. Riecke, Lydia Roethemeyer's aunt. She lived next door to Ollie and Agnes and nothing Ollie, Agnes or I did went unobserved by Aunt Flora. When we sat on the porch in the late fall evenings, Aunt Flora came out to sit and listen to our conversation. When several other teachers came to eat lunch with Ollie, Aunt Flora counted them. Then she said to Ollie, "My, you girls must be raking in the dough--all that cookin' and boardin' goin' on."

There was a lot of trying to keep warm going on, too. It was a cold winter and we had to bundle up warmly. We tied our heads up in turban-type wrappers--the things were "all the rage" that year. Ollie had a brown velvet one she never took off; I had a bright red one, two strips of velvet sewed together across the crown of the head with the ends long enough to wrap around and tuck into the folds above the forehead. Ollie draped hers rather artistically, but mine flapped in the breeze like elephant ears. We also pulled our woolen mittens out of the moth balls; even so we nearly froze walking to and from school.

Ollie's beds were comfortable, but I never had enough cover to stay warm at night. I would wake up with my hip points aching from curled-up sleeping. I didn't have the nerve to tell her I was cold and Ollie never believed in having any fire in the stoves at night. She always reminded Agnes and me of the time "that flue caught on fire" when she lived at Leslie. So we froze it out and let Ollie manage the stoves.

She did all of her cooking on an oldfashioned kerosene stove. At the end of the day she put a few chips and a small piece of wood in the kitchen heater, then practically closed the damper. The outside of the stove never got warm all winter, I'll wager. But Ollie sat and stared at the stove as if it were going to set the house on fire any minute. Bud brought Ollie a load of wood, thinking that would help, but to no avail. She remained sure that flue was "goin' to catch."

Ollie didn't like living in Owensville; she longed to be back in Leslie, her home town. So if any mention was made about improving Owensville, Ollie said, "Won't do no good. Ain't nothin' goin' to help this town. I'd rather rot in Leslie than live like a queen in Owensville."

I was never so glad to see spring! I could finally thaw out. The whole winter seemed miserable. The war was growing in intensity and our nerves seemed to be on edge. It was a good time, Nora and I thought, to have a fire drill.

The fire escape opened out of my 6th grade homeroom on the second floor into one of those huge metal tunnels. We had had a nice shower a few days earlier so there was a dandy water-and-mud puddle at the bottom where the kids shot out. They thought it was great fun to "shoot the chute."

That day at noon when our august principal, Professor Bartlemeyer, returned from lunch, Nora and I suggested it had been a long time since we'd had a fire drill. That was enough for him to think it was his idea and in a few minutes we had sounded the alarm and were leading the kids up the wooden stairs to the "chute." We loosened the padlock and Nora and I began swinging the kids into the chute; they loved a push so they could zoom down faster.

Everyone had gone down and some rushed back upstairs for another ride. No, we told them seriously, "Mr. Bartlemeyer wants to go next." He looked funny, unsure. But in front of all the kids and teachers, he couldn't say no. Nora and I grabbed him by his hands and gave him our mightiest push. Down the chute he went and landed flat in the mud puddle at the bottom. It was a good thing he had to go home and change his clothes; it took us that long to stop laughing.

As the spring days became warmer and brighter, I received long letters from Elaine. They had found a small kitchenette apartment in Sweetwater, Texas. I got the impression she and Pete were having a hard time living on his private's pay, so I started sending them as much money as I could afford out of my $75 a month. I also sent her material for dresses.

During the winter I had taken an extension course at Linn in International Relations, taught by Professor Rolla F. Wood from Warrensburg. But I mostly remember John Peters. The sessions were held in the Circuit Courtroom at the Courthouse and Mr. Peters, an elderly lawyer, often came in to listen--and to take over for Professor Wood and explain about the Spanish-American War or some point of law.

"Judge" Peters was a tall, red-haired Irishman who had somehow acquired the status of a City Father. He was quite fond of the bottle and often in a dubious condition to plead a case, so he was not prosperous. He carried his dentures in his pocket, wrapped in a red bandana handkerchief, and in the courtroom or "lecturing" he attracted much attention by removing his dentures and wrapping them in that bandana. Then he'd reverse the process.

One famous tale about the "Judge" involved the most famous member of the Wright Brothers Clan, Charles. The four Wright brothers all looked exactly alike--small, with faces so bony the skin seemed stretched past its capacity, and clothes, skin and hair never touched by soap or water. But they all had an unlimited repertoire of stories, literature, poetry and general knowledge under their unkempt outer surfaces.

Like his brothers, Charles spoke in a high, whiney Ozarkian brogue. He had been arrested and jailed for being inebriated on the streets of Linn and he was being questioned by Judge Peters.

"What did you have to drink, Charles?"

"A glass of wine, Judge, a bottle of beer and a shot of Hadacol."

"Is this absolutely all?"

"Absolutely, Judge. Absolutely."

"How much does it take to make you drunk, Charles?"

"Well, Judge, ya oughter know."

By April I knew I had to make the Big Break: Go summer and fall and get that thing called a degree. Three of us returned our contracts to the Owensville school board unsigned--the music teacher, Professor Bartlemeyer and me. Prof. B. had decided that teaching wasn't for him; he was going to work for a St. Louis brewery. Nora and I wondered it he'd have time there to "itch" his toes.

The summer session at Warrensburg started the last Monday in May. So I barely had time to get Mom's house in order, can fresh garden peas and spinach and rhubarb, wash my clothes, iron, pack a small suitcase and take off. Dad's original fine Gladstone had been stolen by one of Pete's illustrious roommates at M.U. It had served its time, I suppose, but I still feel a deep attachment for that piece of luggage.

That summer was one of the most pleasant I've ever spent. I shared a spacious bedroom-dressing room on the second floor of a huge, white framehouse on College Avenue managed by Mrs. Burlingame. Our room faced the campus so the journey to class was short.

My roommate was Lois Kardell from St. Louis County. The former wife of Jack Kardell, the band leader, she was then a 7th grade teacher at Bayless School and later the principal. We shared some of the same professors, and after all our years of teaching, guess what we were both doing in summer school. Right. Practice teaching!

I had two courses--one in English with Miss Ruth Fitzgerald and Social Studies with Professor Cloyd Anderson, plus Methods of Teaching English under Miss Fitzgerald. I had pure fun in all of them. Miss Fitzgerald required nothing from us but learning to recite the various Newberry medal winners and the same for Cadmus Books. I often filled in for her when she had correspondence to catch up on in her office.

Most of our students were the offspring of summer school professors or failures from Warrensburg High School. All of the students doing practice teaching were girls. Few men and boys attended that summer. A few old men had returned to teaching because of the war.

Professor Anderson was an agile, quick-spoken small man who believed the way to teach historical facts was with human interest stories. I still remember his description--at length--of the inaugural of Andrew Jackson, "the people's candidate"--how they came in farm wagons and on horseback to camp on the White House lawn and cook in huge iron kettles, how they stayed for days and ate the big cheese which made the grease spot on the red carpet in the Red Room...which Eleanor Roosevelt finally had removed...and which now hangs in the Smithsonian Institute in Washington, D.C....

This same professor immortalized Thomas Jefferson for me by describing his many attributes--violinist, inventor, scribe and farmer, as well as a statesman. Even the early explorers--Chouteau, Laclede, DeSoto, Coronado, Father Marquette and Louis Joliet came alive in his lectures. If not a great teacher of fact, this man was certainly a fascinating storyteller.

Lois Kardell was a great favorite of mine throughout the summer. She was capable and amusing. She had two legitimate ways of earning a living, she said: Teaching school and teaching music. A third, she added, she would leave unnamed.

"Send Me One Dozen Roses" was popular that year and Lois could play it--and almost anything else--with or without music. In the evening we gathered around Mrs. Burlingame's battered old grand piano in the living room and sang many an hour away. Few of us dated; the war had taken our "raw material." So when the phone rang, Lois would say, "If that's my boyfriend, tell him I've gone to prayer meeting." We used the phrase for many occasions, especially when we didn't want the entire house to know our business. Or lack thereof.

Upstairs with me and Lois were two other girls in single rooms--Mildred Miller and Beatrice Long. Beatrice was recovering from the shock of her mother's death. She had no other relatives and she put on a brave front--worked her head off--but she never joined in the fun with me and Mildred and Lois.

One of the few boys around was Clifford, Mildred's cute 19-year-old brother. Or "Tiff," as we called him. He was too young to be a romantic interest but we spent a lot of time studying up pranks to play on him. Lunch at the Student Union cafeteria became a ritual for the four of us, and it so happened that Betty White, a Linn High School graduate, worked there in the food service department.

I always spoke to her and, accustomed to seeing her since her childhood, I saw nothing strange about her. But to Mildred, Tiff and Lois she was the ultimate "undesirable." She did have, I could see through their eyes, a protruding overbite and large eye teeth which the terrible trio called her "tusks." Her hair, standing up from her head in a mass of curls, was a shade of orange red. Almost like her skin, except it was spotted with freckles. And, poor thing, she walked sideways rather than forward, lumbering from side to side in an ungainly fashion.

Mildred teased Tiff unmercifully about Betty all summer and I continued to tell him what a really nice girl she was. Mildred was determined to make Tiff think Betty was hankering for a date with him and we all told him how Betty had called us and begged us to get her a date with him.

One day we paused at the pie counter and I introduced Tiff to Betty. That evening, Mildred decided, we had waited long enough. She called Betty and told her how taken Tiff was with her and how eager he was for a date. Betty, willing to accept, suspected nothing. And she agreed, at Mildred's urging, to stay close to the phone because Prince Charming might call at any time. And if Betty didn't hear from Tiff, it might be wise for her to call him. (And all of this without her name or relationship to Tiff.)

Fie, and shame on us!

Tiff didn't meet us for lunch the next day. Nor the next. Nor for any of the days that followed. Mildred, Lois and I pretended to know nothing, and when we met him on the campus we insisted he was being sadly missed. This went on for several days--until we could keep the secret any longer and blurted out the whole story. After that Tiff started eating lunch with us again at the Student Union and Betty continued friendly--so I was never sure just who played a trick on whom.

Soon after I arrived in Warrensburg, we were notified that Pete had been dispatched to San Francisco, and from there to Hawaii. His letters now became notes--most of them written on the wartime "Victory" letter forms. The letters were photostatic copies. I suppose this facilitated censoring. But he was permitted to tell us that he was in the Hospital Corps in a valley between two mountains, caring for the natives who couldn't prove legal citizenship to any country. He was an assistant to the medical doctor.

Often, sitting in class--what was it, four thousand miles away?--I thought of Pete in that faraway world, and of all the other boys being trained in camps to take the places of those killed and wounded. They were trying, troubled times.

Every day seemed full of decisions. I had planned to stay in school until I finished, but several times a week I received an offer to teach somewhere. The demand for teachers was great...and times were changing.

I remember two girls in my English class were going one afternoon to Slater and Sweet Springs to apply for teaching positions and Miss Fitzgerald warned them to be sure and "wear hose and hats" if they expected to be hired. They didn't wear either--and came back with signed contracts. Miss Fitzgerald shook her head. "War," she observed sadly, "brings on peculiar changes."

One of those changes was nylon hose. They were in their infancy and we thought they were a Godsend. You could rinse them out at night and they would be dry in the morning. You couldn't do that with any of the silk or rayon varieties.

In preparation for my seige of schooling, I invested in two pairs of these wonderfully airy, coal-and-water hosiery. They were as stiff as boards. When I rinsed and hung them on a hanger, they retained the shape of the foot, peculiar looking, I thought, sticking out from the leg.

One morning I awoke to the downpour of a genuine thunderstorm and I waited longer than I should have to start to class. At the last minute I grabbed my books, spread a newspaper over my head and dashed for the campus. At the slick concrete step by the Industrial Arts Building, I slipped and down I went--books and papers scattering to the four winds. Worse, when I looked down I saw blood streaming from a wide cut below the knee cap. But absolutely devastating was the wide gash in my beautiful new nylon stocking.

It was ruined. I was soaked. And embarrassed. I got up quickly, wondering how many people had seen me, and limped back across the street to my room. I stopped the bleeding, bandaged my knee, changed hose and dressed and arrived in class about the time it was over. I declined to answer any questions until Lois said, "Gracie, you might as well confess. I saw you go down."

I thought that gash would never heal. It kept popping open because it was in the same spot I had opened up on the Linn Mercantile Store front during the winter of the "big ice storm." But the real catastrophe was that now I had only three nylons for two legs!

School was easy that summer. I learned that it was just a matter of repeating Dr. Anderson's stories back to him on tests and memorizing the Newberry Medal winners for Miss Fitzgerald.

In August Lois and Beatrice graduated. The exercise was held outside on the lawn south of the Administration Building. The Commencement speaker was an emotional minister who wound up with a sad deathbed scene. Lois, Mildred, Beatrice, Tiff and I had planned to celebrate with a farewell party afterward but Beatrice was nowhere to be found.

We found her at Mrs. Burlingame's, crying in the bathroom, locked in. We waited a while, then with much cold water on her face and some good-natured cajoling, she was able to join us. Our source of amusement was to ride around town and stop in Buente Town for a coke. We came back to Burlingame's where Lois played "Send Me One Dozen Roses" and the session was over.

Lois was leaving for the Wisconsin Dells--a whole month. Mildred, Tiff and Beatrice left for her home the following morning and I was left alone. Yes, poor me. I had signed up for something called "Intersession"--with which I could obtain five hours of credit in four weeks. I really had the bug now. I was getting nearer and nearer. But...

Yes, but. August was perspiration month. And I had chosen a course called "Contemporary Lit," taught by Miss Anna Marie Todd, and one standard, English Grammar, taught by Professor Elijah Jacobs.

The Lit class was huge--nearly a hundred people jammed into the Little Theatre on the south end of the Administration Building. To earn five hours' credit meant that we did double time in class. Classes began at 7 a.m. (Daylight Saving Time, too. I needed Ben's watch!) Miss Todd lectured for two and a half hours every morning on the various authors and briefed us on their best works. And from a long list of books, we were to read 20 and report on them. I didn't see how I could possibly read 20 novels in four weeks--not to mention keep them all straight.

And that English Grammar...! I had taken a course earlier under Professor Jacobs and I knew his critical way of dealing with people who didn't have a strong background in the subject. I dreaded class every day. He never taught us grammar; we conjugated verbs in German, in French, in Spanish--languages none of us understood. He assigned long sentences to diagram and when we handed them in, he asked "What's that?" We would see them the next day in the wastebasket.

I never knew what he wanted. I don't think he knew, either...although at that time I never suspected a college professor of not having a full and complete knowledge of his subject matter. Many years later I ran across a small poem of his in *Farm Journal*. It had to do with how peculiar he found his relatives and it ended with a question, "Did they think me peculiar, too?" Well, I certainly did. I didn't expect to make a good grade in his class; neither did anyone else. So I figured I had better concentrate on Miss Todd.

She was fun but she worked our tails off, to put it indelicately. She admired Russian authors and she'd rattle off their names--Tolstoy, Dostoyevsky, Turgenev and all those other "oys" and "ois" and "Evs"--and admonish us, "Now, remember, you must spell them correctly." Then came the Germans and the Swedes and the English and the French authors--and her final regrets that the "United States never really had a 'Great American Novel'."

There were only two of us now at Mrs. Burlingame's; Hope Michener from Marshall had moved into Mildred's room. And in spite of our busy schedule (where there is a will, there is a way!), we found time to date a little. I had met George Hoagland, a pharmacist in a downtown drug store, and his friend, John, dated Hope.

George and I enjoyed each other a great deal, and I suppose I passed up another good chance to marry a fine fellow. By the end of Intersession, however, he was on his way to Ft. Benning, Georgia, for overseas training in the Medical Corps. I heard from him frequently; he wrote beautiful letters. But I never saw him again. I hope he found someone nice to marry.

June and July in Warrensburg were bad enough, but August was terrible. The heat didn't seem to bother Miss Todd one whit. She always looked cool as a cucumber, reading and reminiscing from her notes taken while she was a student at Oxford University.

I worked like a country dog in that class--memorizing book titles and authors, details of those 20 novels I had to read, plus skits from "best" novels of the literary world. Often late at night when I was reading and taking notes, I would hear a great trumpeting and snorting upstairs on the third floor. At first it scared me half to death; finally I worked up enough nerve to ask Mrs. Burlingame about it. She looked embarrassed and her face fell. "Oh, that's just Papa Burlingame (her husband)," she said. "He's having one of his spells."

I didn't press the matter further. I just hoped he wouldn't have too many "spells" until I got through Intercession.

15

My "major" at home

I had a brief vacation at home--during which I continued work on that household "major": Canning jars and jars of tomatoes. Mom always waited for that chore until I came home. Carrying bushel baskets, we headed for Step 1. "Cleaning up the patch," Mom called it. That meant we picked "everything that would do to can."

We washed and sorted and laid out on paper in the sun all of the tomatoes which were not quite ripe--but which might go to waste if we didn't pick them now. Then we cut the ripe and near over-ripe ones in pieces to cook and strain for juice. We poured some of this juice over the tomatoes in the jars as we cold-packed and pressure-cooked them; some juice we canned to drink in the winter.

Tomatoes don't need much cooking. Just bring them to a boil. Over-cooking ruins the flavor and the appearance of such a hard-earned product. Some of our neighbor women didn't cook them at all; they set the filled jars in a wash tub, poured in boiling water until the jars were almost covered, then threw a blanket or heavy canvas over them until the water cooled. But I was never brave enough to try that method.

Mom should have majored in psychology. She tactfully told me how great I was at all of these tasks, and her praise got lots of back-breaking work accomplished.

We teased her about sitting in her rocking chair so much. But she didn't just sit. She rocked. And rocked and rocked--and sang the oldtime religious songs:

"I shall sing you a song of a beautiful land,

"a land where sweet flowers bloom,

"where no storms ever beat on that beautiful shore,

"and the years of eternity roll..."

Mom placed great stress on "e--ter--nit--tee." And I waited each time for her emphatic syllabication. But one never corrected her. In our household Mom was the possessor of power--and "Don't you ever forget it" were her final words if

MOM'S HYMN TIME

Mom wakes up the day with "The Old Time Religion" and keeps it going "In the Sweet By and By."

anyone doubted it.

Her favorite singing time was early in the morning. Building the fire in the iron cookstove, she rattled the ashes down into the pan below the grates, scooted the stove lid hook noisily along the grates to push all the ashes down--all accompaniment to *"'Tis the old time religion, 'tis the old time religion, 'tis the old time religion, and it's good enough for me."*

Then she made her regular morning pilgrimage to the spring for fresh water, milk, butter and cream. On her path, directly beneath my upstairs bedroom window, she would be singing, *"It was good for Paul and Silas, it was good for Paul and Silas, it was good for Paul and Silas, and it's good enough for me."*

Her voice became fainter and muffled as she went on down the hill and entered the spring house. But as she picked up the water bucket and loaded her other items into another bucket, her voice took on renewed energy. She started the climb back to the house with *"It will do when I am dying, It will do when I am dying, It will do when I am dying, it's good enough for me."*

By the time she had rendered "In the Sweet By and By"--in its entirety--the biscuits were ready for the oven. Then came more poking of wood into the cookstove and more slamming the oven door hard two or three times. When she began "What a Friend We Have in Jesus," we could get up and be at the table just as she took the light, flaky, buttermilk biscuits out of the oven.

Breakfast was a mammoth meal. Along with those biscuits, we usually had eggs, bacon, oatmeal, fresh fruit in season, coffee, milk, cold cereal and I can't remember what all. But our favorite breakfast menu was biscuits, bacon and fried apples.

We could identify the menu by the aroma that drifted upstairs, or by Mom's tone as she sang. When she fried apples, Mom jazzed up "The Old Time Religion" a bit. If times were hard and she was worried about payments on the mortgage or taxes, "The Years of Eternity" (EE-tur-nuh-tee) were likely to be more drawn out than usual.

As soon as breakfast was finished, Mom started her daily hunt for her sunbonnet. She never ventured out to feed the chickens without this head covering. And if she came back with it, she seldom put it in the same place twice--although she vowed and declared that she "hung it on the kitchen door knob" when she came in from the garden yesterday.

When all the usual places had been searched and still no sunbonnet, I learned to dash for the garden. There, at the end of a tomato row, would be Mom's bonnet, slightly wet with dew, but in good shape after resting on the damp earth overnight. When I appeared at the door, bonnet in hand, Mom would exclaim, "Well, I declare. Did I leave my bonnet in the garden? I wonder what in the world made me do that. I never did that before in all my life." Never in all her life did Mom ever admit a mistake!

Now it was time to shell corn for the chickens...after Mom counted out the ears. If we were going to "take off" baby chickens, I accompanied her. Then we each shelled the corn, pressing one ear hard against the fleshy heel of the hand and raking the other ear against it to loosen the kernels.

After the chickens were fed, the cows were milked and we carried the milk to the spring to be strained into large, sterilized vessels. The house was between the cowbarn and the springhouse, so I detoured through the kitchen to grab the teakettle of boiling water and take it to the springhouse for washing crocks and jars.

Milk was "big" in our life--the daily equivalent in importance to seasonal tomatoes. And we put it to many uses. In the springhouse we skimmed off the sweet cream for table use or to sell. The sour cream was for churning. The clabbered and sour milk was poured into a big bucket to feed to the pigs or chickens. We set the fresh milk in the deepest part of the cool spring water to chill it for noon dinner and evening supper.

Nearly every other day we churned, quite a process in those pre-margarine days. Churning--what a nice, descriptive word!--meant lugging a huge bucket of cool cream to the house, scalding the big, wooden churn--which had been Grandma Bacon's--and pouring in the cream. Then came the technical part: You attached a wooden, stern-type dasher to a metal peg in the back of the churn, fitted the handle through the front, clamped on a lid and you were all set to crank and crank until the "butter comes."

Sometimes the buttermilk splashed up around the lid if you cranked too fast. Or it spilled out around the crank handle if the churn were too full. When the butter gathered, you lifted the lid, removed the dasher, took out the crank--and lifted out huge, still-cool globs of butter. They reminded me of small, yellow glaciers swimming about in an ocean of buttermilk.

After this came the rinsing out of the chunks with cool, spring water; then we turned and squeezed the butter with a wooden paddle Dad had carved himself. When all buttermilk had been squeezed out, we added salt and mixed it in thoroughly and started molding the butter.

Out mold had a sheaf of grain on its head, a distinct and impressive design, I thought proudly. Mom never thought it necessary to dress up butter we used on our own table; we only molded our sold butter. She pressed ours into a large blue crock, then we carried it and the molded rounds back to the springhouse to be sunk in the clear, cold water until we went to the store.

By now the sun would be well up and Dad and the boys would be harnessing Old Jim and Odie, the big black mules, out behind the horse barn, getting ready to plow corn, cut wheat, or mow hay. That was men's work. Mom's and mine included the hens.

Usually our hens preferred to "set" under the feed boxes in the mangers at the horse barn or in a deep hole in the loose hay up in the loft. Mom maintained that a hen wouldn't "set" anywhere except where she had made her own first choice. So 15 eggs were placed under each brown Leghorn biddie--after we had marked each egg with an "X" with a piece of charcoal from the ash bucket. This "X" was necessary in case another hen laid an egg in the nest.

Every evening when I gathered eggs, my most dreaded chore was reaching under a mad, ruffled setting hen to see if any fresh eggs had been "laid in" during the day. If so, I had to remove them and leave only eggs marked "X."

This was an exceedingly ugly task for me. All afternoon I dreaded for five o'clock to show on the beehive clock on the mantle shelf. When it did, I knew I had to get it over with. The task wasn't bad in the hen houses; I could easily slip a hand under the bald-breasted biddies and see quickly if any eggs looked fresh and unmarked. But in the barns it was another matter entirely.

First of all, it was dark in there. (Remember, we had no electricity on the farm in those days.) Second, the mangers were high and I was too short for the job. I had to hunt for something like a homemade, discarded bee super to stand on so I could divide myself somewhat evenly over the top board of the manger. With my feet barely touching the bee super and my arm extended beyond its natural

CHURNING

It was a ritual of careful cranking that produced small yellow glaciers swimming on an ocean of buttermilk.

limitation--and the uppermost board on the manger cutting your lower rib section in half--the fight began.

That old hen would recede to the farthest possible corner under the feed box. But this never interfered with her ability to pick at you--again and again. *Pick, pick, cluck, cluck*--and a flurry of words (from Gracie). About this time the support would slip out from under my feet and I'd be hanging headfirst in the deep, dark manger. All I could do was grab hold of the opposite side of the manger and scoot myself off by inches--usually taking some skin in the scooting.

But when the chickens began to hatch...ah, me...that was the ultimate in the glories of diversified farming. Brown Leghorns are small at any age, and the chicks can fall through a crack not wide enough for your little finger.

Usually Dad reported them at breakfast; "Jennie, I think you've got a new crop out about the barn." (Dad never liked this arrangement but he had learned better than to argue with Mom.)

"All right, all right," Mom always replied. "Just as soon as I get my last bite down, I'll tend to them."

Well, Mom never hurried about anything--hens, chickens or anything else. But all in good time we rounded up old buckets, usually leaky ones (Mom was a great friend of buckets; she used them for everything.), put a handful of hay in the bottoms, tore up some old cloth for strings and set out for the barn.

First, we dislodged the mean, pecking old biddie, amidst much flopping of wings and clawing with spurs. With a length of our cloth string, we tied her by one leg to the hay loft ladder. Then we began gathering up the baby chicks--counting them, hovering over the sleek, downy black ones, glowing over the perfectly dark, brown-striped ones that Mama took such pride in. Mama knew that black meant that her strain wasn't "full stock" so she just glanced at the black ones and said optimistically, "He'll probably be more brown than black in a little while. If he isn't, we'll use him for a fryer."

We usually had a "crop" hatching in the loft, too. So we went through the same procedure there except I didn't have to crawl under the manger. I had to reach 'way down in a deep hole--so deep I sometimes had to shove my shoulder into the matted hay. And sometimes I found that silly old hen sitting on a black snake and no baby chicks at all.

But the most fun was finding an old hen which had stolen her nest out. She always acted as if she had really played a prank on Mama, showing her she could do all the necessary work alone. But Mom never let any hen have a moment of glory. She addressed the hen as if she'd disgraced the whole family: "Why, you old codger you," she scolded, "I knew what you were up to. Missed you for a while when I was countin'."

Mom always counted her chickens when she fed them. By sex, too. So many roosters, so many hens, so many fryers (young roosters), so many pullets. Mom considered herself something of an expert with chickens and eggs. She taught Mae and me to read "Poultry, Butter and Eggs," on the *Globe Democrat* market page almost as soon as we could talk. We would get the paper as soon as it came, lie flat on our stomachs with the paper spread on the floor and quote Mama the prices of each item.

But at this time she kept her poultry record on a large sheet of cardboard, tacked to the inside of the granary door. When we killed two fryers, Mom subtracted from her "Fryer" column; at the end of the fryer season, she had an exact count:

"We managed to get away with 200 fryers. But they sure tasted good."

After a week at home with Mom and her "Poultry, Butter, Egg and Tomato" campaign, I was excited about getting back to Warrensburg. This was it. Finally. After so many years of summer terms, correspondence courses, extension courses, Intersession, I couldn't believe it.

Charles was there, too. He was rooming and working again in the kitchen at Workmans. I was still on College Avenue, but living with Mrs. Dow. Mrs. Burlingame took boys in winter. I ate my meals at Workmans so I saw Bant three times a day. I was so proud of him. He had grown up all of a sudden; he was six feet tall, with brown eyes and wavy golden hair. He was the blonde sheep of our family. He didn't resemble any of the rest of us. But if the war went on--and there appeared to be no end in sight--he'd be wearing the same clothes Pete was in now. I worried constantly about his draft status--and about how hard it would be on us to send the second son and brother of our family away to war.

My fall courses reflected no choices of my own; they were required for graduation. Most of them, however, became enjoyable--especially Entomology with Mrs. Nattinger and all of those field trips to collect beetles, moths, butter-flies, spiders...anything we could classify or identify.

I had Tests and Measurements with the dreaded Miss Humphrey and Public Finance with Professor Emmitt Ellis. And because I had never taken any P.E., I had to take two courses. One was a real dud. Because I was underweight, they for-ced me to rest one hour every day in the gym's "sick bay." For this I got one hour of P.E. credit!

The other one was pure fun. It consisted of activities which resembled things I had done on the farm all my life. After chasing squawking setting hens and run-ning down fryers-to-be for Mom, those body-builders were nothing.

The course was taught by Miss Louise Martin, an elderly near-deaf spinster. She looked...well, odd...when she entered the gym--wearing her blue bloomer gym suit, her white hair curling over her head and her hearing aid battery stuck in the middy-type pocket. But I admired her.

She lined us up in rows and put us through push-ups and bends, and bicycle races lying flat on our backs. And late in the course she decided that we were so good we would attempt rope climbing. Great--and serious--was the lecture she gave us...how dangerous it was, how we should not attempt it at all if we were afraid of heights and other dire warnings. And she asked for a volunteer.

I stepped out. (For once, I was a bit cocky. I was also the oldest!) I scampered up the rope like a monkey on a string. Miss Martin's eyes bugged, and when I was perhaps 15 feet or so off the floor, she begged me, "Miss Bacon, Miss Bacon, come down. Come down now. Don't go any higher. You'll fall."

But I easily shinnied on to the top of the rope--just to prove how great her initial instructions had been. She didn't know how many hours I had "practiced" this in the hayloft at home. And I never told her the secret of my success.

Miss Humphrey's Tests and Measurements was a four-week trek through Tedium. Boring, "busy work"--grading tests, finding averages and I.Q.'s. I remember one assignment she gave me which I'm sure was done for her own statistical use. I had to plow through the Missouri Teachers Directory and tally the times my major--English--was taught by itself and how many times it was taught in combination with one, two or three other subjects. Then I had to chart all this on a large wall hanging. This took several of my weekends--which I regarded jealously.

Another assignment was teaching two days for a 6th grade teacher-principal in the most distant elementary school in Warrensburg while the principal registered the people in the district for gasoline and kerosene. I got up an hour early, walked practically across town, taught 6th graders all day and walked back home. And I had to arrange to be absent from all my other classes. A real sweetie that Miss Humphrey was!

But out of all this I learned a powerful lesson from one overpowering experience. I had seen around town this tiny, crippled man. He had no use of his legs but he drove a Model T Ford by using his arms, dragging his legs and winding up in weird contortions. When I was teaching I chanced to see him from my window as he crawled up the sidewalk, up the stone steps and into the school building to register for gasoline. Often when I have become disgruntled with my physical abilities, I have remembered this disabled creature and how he did quite well, thank you, providing for and taking care of himself.

I fully enjoyed Public Finance. Prof. Ellis was a veteran of World War I and with World War II engulfing the globe, he spent much time regaling us with stories about himself and Harry S Truman--until some of the boys in class presented him with a full-page picture of himself, in full dress uniform, marching in a parade. Out of step. He seldom mentioned "us boys--me and Harry" after that.

I was finishing a correspondence course in High School Administration. It had to be completed and my grade recorded before I could graduate. But little by little I was getting closer to that B.S. in Education.

I interrupted my classes in October to go to St. Louis to be an honorary page in the Grand Chapter of the Eastern Star. But if I'd known Bant was to be stricken with acute appendicitis, I would have foregone the pleasure.

One morning when I went to Workmans for breakfast, Bant wasn't in the kitchen; he hadn't felt well in the night, his roommate, Wade Mumma, told me. At noon when I went to eat lunch Mrs. Workman met me at the door and led me upstairs to Bant's room. He was burning with fever and rolling with pain in his stomach region.

I called the student clinic and a young M.D. came over. He diagnosed it and wanted to move Bant to the clinic. I wasn't sure. I had heard too much unfavorable comment about the clinic. I called Morton's Funeral Service at Linn to take Bant to Kansas City and the doctor in charge arranged for him to go to Menorah Hospital.

It was late evening before Vernon arrived in the Morton ambulance. We loaded a silent but willing Bant in the back and I sat with him, feeding him ice from a large Thermos which Mrs. Workman had supplied. The night was black. I was worn out. I had to let Mom and Dad know what was going on, and I was near the bottom of my pocket book. Bant was dear to my heart. I couldn't let anything happen to him.

Things happened quickly when we arrived at Menorah. The orderlies hurried Bant out of the ambulance, into an elevator and up to the emergency room for the operation. I--of course--was escorted to the secretary's desk to give information concerning payment. This finished, she asked me where I was going to spend the night.

"Why, right here," I said, surprised. "With Bant, of course."

She smiled--probably figuring my surprise and indignation stemmed from lack of money--and opened the door to a small waiting room behind the office. It had a small cot and a blanket and a pillow and by the time she told me the surgery would take "a while" and that I could see him first thing when he came out from under the anesthesia, I fell asleep.

It was daylight when I awoke. I put on my dress and shoes and beat a beeline to the top floor. I found my patient able to smile and giggle a little. His pain was gone, the fever diminishing. All seemed well.

I caught a late evening bus back to Warrensburg. I offered to help in Workmans' kitchen in Bant's place, but Mrs. Workman declined my offer. Mr. Workman didn't mind helping with the dishes, she said. Later she told me the real reason: "You looked like you'd been drawn through a key hole, child."

On Saturday I went back to Kansas City to see Bant. He could sit up in bed and some of the college boys from Kansas City came to see him. Because Bant wasn't "of age," I had to sign his release papers, making me responsible for paying the hospital and doctors. I also had to round up some acquaintance to vouch for the facts I had given. For this I used Roscoe Cramer, a longtime family friend of Dad and an elementary principal in Kansas City for many years.

In the meantime I notified Mom and Dad. For once, they agreed that I did the right thing--if it had to be done. They always qualified any illness that way. As Mom told Bant later, when he went home to rest--and to prove, I guess, to Mom that he had had an operation: "If you had to get sick, then I guess this was as good a time as any to get it over with." Charles soon went back to school.

Then came one of those "little" happenings that often determine the course of a whole life. I had seen an advertisement in the Warrensburg newspaper for a secretary-clerk position with the Federal Bureau of Investigation. I was fascinated by the prospect and by the glamorous life in the nation's capital. I talked myself into going for an interview, was questioned, fingerprinted and practically promised a job. I didn't really think I'd get it, though.

Or if I did, would I have the backbone to go so far away from home? Would I really quit teaching...?

During the fall term I had been receiving bids from schools all over the central Missouri area. Come take this teaching job as soon as your degree is complete, was the message. Teachers were scarce, yes. But, after all, I did--or would--have my degree. Maybe, though, I wouldn't have to make the decision. Maybe I wouldn't get any offer from the FBI...

During my last week at Warrensburg the telegram arrived. I had been selected as a filing clerk in one of the special services, it said. Please proceed to Washington D.C. as soon as possible on my own. Oh, and bring enough money to provide yourself with living expenses for two months.

Heavens and Earth! I didn't have enough cash to live on for two days, much less two months. So money--or the scarceness thereof--made my decision for me. I took a high school job at Winfield, Missouri, for $125 a month. A princely, or should I say a queenly, sum. Of course, I've often wondered what my life would have been like if I had borrowed some "dough" and gone to work for J. Edgar Hoover instead of tacking another nail on my "Teacher" shingle. Well, J. Edgar will never know what he missed, either!

There were no graduation ceremonies for such fall quarter finishers. We simply dismantled "our tents and, like the Arabs, silently stole away." It was Thanksgiving weekend, but instead of giving thanks and resting a few days, I did the laundry for Bant and me. Bring in the wash tub and soap. Soak, scrub, rinse, hang out, bring in, iron and pack suitcases. Rest? Hah! I had to be in Winfield Monday morning to start teaching.

An Album

Notes and captions by the author

The land and the people
of the
Horse Shoe Bend country

These are the people of my people. Many of them are children and grandchildren of the original settlers, mostly German, who came to this land of Three Rivers* because it reminded them of their native country.

These river bottoms and timbered hills — so beautiful to the eye and dear to the heart — were often inhospitable to the plow. But from old ways and new needs these people made the land theirs. And on it they fashioned a way of life that still today marks the region. And me.

*The Missouri, the Osage and the Gasconade. And I like to add a fourth one — the smaller but lovely Maries.

A Gathering

This is a group of Cooper Hill residents. The picture was taken under the bluff at what is now the Norman Kuehn home. M.O. Reed, later county superintendent of schools (see page 35), is the young man in the middle of three in the left foreground.

An Album

 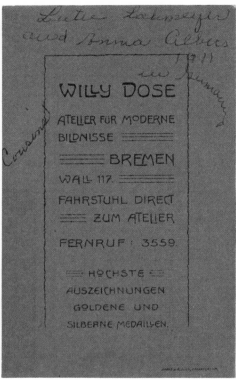

Visit in Germany

Cousins Lutie Lahmeyer and Anna Albers posed in their best finery for this studio photograph during a visit back to the "Old Country" in 1911.

Tie Rafting

Tie rafting on the Gasconade River provided extra income for area residents, including my grandfather Le Fevre. The ties were bought from the "hackers," bound or nailed into rafts, and floated downriver to Gasconade, on the Missouri River. It was a seven-day trip from Rollins Ferry — and the ties were sold at its end for about ten cents apiece. The man in the white shirt here is August Langenberg, Sr.

An Album

The Langenberg Boys

Bright-eyed Pete Langenberg posed for his picture in the studio of Charles F. Weeks, a popular photographer at Linn. His look-alike brother, Al (far left, front row), attended the summer session during his college days at Warrensburg in the mid-1920s. The state teacher's college's old Industrial Arts Building is in the background.

Gesman's Studio
WARRENSBURG, MO.

An Album

The Ladies' Aid

This Ladies' Aid group met at Mrs. Mary Carne's home, about 1916. That's as close a date as I can pin down — and, as you can see, I'm still trying to identify all of the members who attended that day!

Ladies Aid Group in Front
of Mrs. Mary Carnes Home

Seated on lowest step
1. Mrs. Mattie Peters
2. Child ~~Mildred Marie?~~ no
3. Child ~~Ruth Peters?~~
4. Mary Ellen Peters

on step above
1. Mrs. Nora Ferree
2. Mrs. Cora Vaughan
3. _____
4. Mrs. ~~Ruth~~ Angie McDaniel.
5. ~~Woman in front of~~ ~~Angie McD.~~ ~~unknown~~

Standing from L to R.
1. Harold Gove ?
2. Mrs. Carrie Maine with Juanita
   seated on bicycle.
3. Mrs. Anna Langenburg
4. _____
5. Mrs. May Vaughan
6. Mrs. Annie Baker no
7. ~~Mrs. Vashall sister~~ Mrs. Tom Dessieu (Jenny)
8. Mrs. Mary Carnes
9. ~~Mrs. Mrs. Peter Gove~~ Rika

(Annie)
10. Mrs. ~~Maggie~~ Charles Rahlfing
11. Mrs. Josephine McDaniel
    Jo Paris at the time picture
    was taken
12. ~~Mrs. Nora Jones~~ no
13. Mrs. Ida Zevely
14. Mrs. Berulia Fink

Standing on porch. Left.
1. Mrs. Belva Gove
2. Mrs. J.W. Vashall (Georgia)

I would like very much to
know who the two young
ladies are on right - daughters
_____ 1. Is this one of the Carnes?
Marila Carnes ~~Has no~~
~~Marila is Mildred Marie though~~
~~Carnes isn't in picture~~

Can you help identify
these persons? Write in
blanks, please.

An Album

Fording the River

Wagons crossing the river at the Cooper
Hill ford were everyday occurrences when the
Gasconade was low. The men are Hy Baker and
Ed "Buckshot" Leach, brother of "Doc" Leach.
Note the basket of eggs the woman is holding in
her lap. Farmers were always needing "egg
money" and where else could she protect those
fragile little money makers!

An Album

H. P. Huxoll,   Photographer

"Doc" Comes Home

Charles I. Leach — "Doc" — came back home to minister to Osage Countians for almost a half century after his graduation from medical school in Louisville, Kentucky. And he came to know, more than likely, all of the men congregated at the Cooper Hill store.

An Album

The Cooper Hill School

      Teacher Lulu Farrell was the teacher at the new Cooper Hill school built in 1904. I'm sure she knew all of her charges by name but I've been able to identify only eleven of them for sure. If you see your picture — or anyone you recognize — I'd like to know about it.

1. Rhua Reed
2. Myrtle Rhoades
3. Myra Reeds
4. Mollie Reed
5. Ben Enke
6. Henry Englebrecht
7. Nora Jett Rogers
8. Farida
9. Fred Schneider

   new school in 1904

Teacher Lulu Farrell
Englebrecht, Schultes
Enke — Pauline
10. Monda
11. Alfred

An Album

The Graduates

Mabel Holstein taught school in the area for years — and dated Alfred Langenberg for years and years. This was one of her eighth grade graduating classes at Gasconade in the early Twenties.

It's Still Used

The Cooper Hill school still looks much like this, some eighty years later. Today it serves the town and roundabout as the Community Center.

An Album

At the Institute

The annual Teachers' Institute was held in Linn for three weeks every August for county teachers to renew their certificates. That's Dad — George Bacon, Sr. — on the front row, second from left. Mama — Jennie Le Fevre Bacon — is in the third row, the tenth from left, with a bow in her hair. Adam Ferrier, Buell's father, is third from right in the fourth row.

An Album

Home

This is our house when the Hy Bueckers lived there, before Dad and Mama bought it in 1920. That's Mr. Buecker feeding the hogs, and Mrs. Buecker and Mrs. John Lahmeyer standing on the steps. I can't be sure but I think the man standing on the upstairs porch is Dad. He boarded here and taught school at Post Oak, just up the hill, in 1905-1906.

The Wedding
(See the next page)

Augusta Lahmeyer was raised by the Bueckers and she and John Langenberg were married in the south front room here at the Buecker farm in either 1902 or 1903. Mama was teaching the Post Oak School then and she told me that Mrs. Lena Berger came to the farm and stayed three weeks to help sew the wedding trousseau and to cook the evening meal.

When she came down the hill from school, she said, they had butchered a beef and had been cooking it all day long here in the side yard. They had made fifty pounds of cabbage into cole slaw, cooked scads of potatoes and baked she couldn't remember how many fruit pies. After eating, the young people danced upstairs in the north room. Some say the floor sagged that night. It was the area's social event of the times!

A few months after the Langenberg-Lahmeyer wedding, its seamstress married Charles Berger and came to Cooper Hill to live. Her husband operated the General Store, along with Buckshot Leach.

An Album

**The
Brides
and
Grooms**

Mr. and Mrs. John Langenberg

Mr. and Mrs. Charles Berger

An Album

A Basketball Town

Only ten boys could play on the team but everybody in Bland talked basketball — including me. The players' names were household words — and the basis of pep squad cheers: "Righty, Righty, Lefty, Lefty. If Right can't do it, Lefty can . . ."

This was one of their many excellent teams in the war years of 1943-1946.

Front row, left to right:	Back row:
Roger Ling	Stanley Stubblefield
Herbert Jett	Gordon Koenig
Junior Smith	Don Campbell
Norman "Lefty" Peth	Armin "Righty" Peth
Richard Howard Terrill	Raymond Steiner
	Coach Richard Terrill

PART SIX

WINFIELD

16

My Life on the Mississippi

On Sunday afternoon I rode into the Maplewood Loop with Irvin. From there I took a street car down to Union Station. From there I took the Burlington train to Winfield. I had signed a contract thankful for a job that would pay me enough to reinstate myself in the world. But I wasn't prepared for Winfield.

It was a Mississippi River town--a dirty, small river town. The railroad track zipped up its eastern side. Its one street ran along the west edge. On the second story of a weatherbeaten store front, the largest and most impressive building, in big, black letters, said "A.L. Ricks--Groceries-Clothing-Undertaking." The other buildings along the two blocks of sidewalks looked just alike--oldfashioned board fronts as wide as the building. Some sported signs, like "Alta's Beauty Shop." (I discovered later that Alta had no running water; she heated some in a tea kettle on a gas burner and rinsed your hair with icy water. From the river.)

I lugged my suitcase up the street, reading the signs and hoping to see someone I could ask about a rooming house. At the end of the sidewalk I saw several houses hanging on a steep incline leading up the river bluff. Turning the corner, I spied a place of business open on Sunday. Stumbling along, blindly intent on my main goal, I opened the door--and my nose immediately informed me I had discovered the town saloon.

I was already in so I decided to ask about a rooming house. Three men sat at the bar, waited on by a much-amused bartender. Where, I asked him, might I find lodging? All four answered in one breath, "Miz Shields' place, right on up the bluff yonder. She takes in all the boarders. And you don't know us but we'uns know you. You're the new school marm."

Arlie, the bartender, walked out on the sidewalk with me and pointed out the exact location of Miz Shields'. "That there white frame house acrost the road--settin' right squar' agin' the bluff. That's hit."

Everyone at the "Shields Hotel" (Winfield's term for it) was expecting me. I entered on the first floor. The basement. (I found out later the second and third floors opened out onto another street, higher up on the bluff.) Mr. and Mrs. Ernest Shields sat around an enormous wood heater in the basement dining room. Grouped around them were all the other boarders: Grace Pulliam, teacher and temporary superintendent of the school; Don Duey and Winifred Smith, both guards at the river Lock and Dam; Grandma Shields, Mr. Shields' 90-year-old mother; and Veva, the daughter-in-law. All of them were eating popcorn out of a big bread riser sitting in the middle of the dining table.

Veva got up to show me to my room--and inform me that we all shared the only bathroom. We had hooks on our bedroom doors, though, for our own towels and wash cloths--to carry into the bathroom. Veva was young and friendly and full of mischief and we got along famously. We went back downstairs where I was invited to partake of the popcorn. I plunged into the big bowl--partially in self defense, because of all the popcorn chewers I ever heard Ernest Shields was the loudest. So began the queerest six months in all my years of teaching--my own live-in version of "Life on the Mississippi."

In this river town--I always had the feeling the Mississippi had overflowed and left its mud caked on the streets and buildings, to then turn into dust--people came and went like the never-ending flow of its waters. For a week, two weeks, maybe a month--they fished for a living and vanished. School was a constant swinging-door change of faces. Of students and teachers.

Some of the transient teacher troopings resulted from the wartime teacher shortage--but not all.

I was the third replacement in the English Department since September. Miss Pulliam was the only permanent fixture at the school; she had been there seven years. The students feared her. They knew her step on the walk and on the stairs, and when they heard her coming, a great solemness descended upon the class.

Howard Ricks, a charming young man, was teaching science for a few weeks--until his call came from the Navy. After he left, we couldn't secure another science teacher so all the students had to finish the course by correspondence. As usual, I inherited the study hall where all the kids were working on the answers to those correspondence questions. I knew precious little about science, but these were rough, tough river kids and I figured I'd better try to help them; it was better to have them as friends than enemies, even though they might be gone tomorrow.

My morning roll call went something like this:

"John Jones?"

"Oh, Teach, knock him off. His old man ain't gonna let him go to school no more."

Strike John Jones.

"Jim Smith?"

"Nope, him and his old man shipped out; he won't be here no more either."

The class was dwindling fast.

"Joe Brown?"

"Oh, Joe? Yeah, him and his old lady had a fight. Joe got a job on a boat. Says he ain't comin' back."

But new faces took their places each Monday morning--people stopping off in Winfield to fish and work a few days before moving on down river. South. I approved of that direction. Never had I seen--or felt--such a cold place. The wind swept the earth clean as it bore down the Mississippi River channel. The snow swirled down the broad valley in whirlwinds until it was knee-high. And it stayed that way. Ice froze in layers on the streets and waited for the spring thaw.

Mr. Shields worked at Troy, tearing down a 1930s C.C.C. (Civilian Conservation Corps) building, and because he had to get up about 4 o'clock, he roused everyone else. "If'n me and Mame have to git up early, ever'one else can git their breakfast down at one and the same time. Mame ain't makin' no money on you'ns; only place in town you'ns can find what'll take you'ns in. So git up and git downstairs if'n you want anythin' to eat."

So breakfast was served at 5 a.m. all winter. While Ernest was reciting his favorite admonition, he would go to the dining room door, hold it wide open and, tilting his gold-rimmed glasses on his nose, he would hold up his lantern and read the thermometer. "Tain't so very cold this mornin'. Only 16 below."

I thought 16 below was plenty cold--especially when I had to climb straight up the bluff to get to school. There was sidewalk only part of the way. Then one had to get out in the street and take a chance on falling. If you did, you could easily slide the entire height of the bluff and land on the railroad tracks. There was nothing to stop you. When there were yard fences, one could pull oneself along and hold on tightly until one reached the peak of the bluff...

There sat the horrible old red brick thing--tall and skinny, even to the pitifully tiny belfry decorating the tiptop of this august institution.

Miss Pulliam conducted her "commercial subjects" in the basement, along with the shop teacher, Wilfred "Wilf" Byram.

George held forth down there, too. George, the custodian, was considered queer. He had "committed a great sin" years ago. Now he was making atonement with custodial work at the school and the Baptist Church basement. He would never enter the church sanctuary itself; he wasn't "fittin' to go upstairs," he said. Just downstairs. But George did anything at school he was asked to do--or died trying. The boys teased him for their almost-daily pastime, but he ignored them and went on firing the furnace, mumbling something to them about being "sinful young ninnies."

The elementary rooms were on the second floor. Four of them--two grades to a room. And on the third floor was my outpost--the English Department, encased in arctic cold; a small library, physically and numerically--with some 200 books, if all were turned in simultaneously, (I remember one book. It was new so it attracted my attention. "Planning Your Funeral" was the title. Inside it said, "Donated by A.L. Ricks, Winfield, Mo.''); and the study hall. Opposite my English Department was the Science Room, now empty and teacher-less.

This was one of those experiences you read about in books, I thought--except no author I'd ever read had explained how to deal with these rough river rats. I decided to be polite and ladylike. That would keep them off-balance, I reckoned, because they knew next to nothing about polite manners. But I set myself a hard task.

I was determined to make friends of two of the hardest characters, Rosalie Grisby and Kenneth Caple. Rosalie, I soon discovered, was simply fighting her own fear. Her mother ran a roughhouse, short order beer joint and had a reputation to match her place of business. Rosalie feared that the kids would tease her so she beat them to the draw by being mean and loud-mouthed and unmannerly. I started my efforts at softening Rosalie by asking her to help me down the bluff at noon when I went home for lunch.

Kenneth's "cure" was more dangerous. He was a senior and had a car, a bright green coupe which he drove in from the country every day. I won his friendship by riding down the bluff several days when he was showing off his driving prowess. I'm sure I risked my life, but those hair-raising rides nurtured a mutual respect between me and Kenneth. And if the rides were rough, they helped smooth out my life somewhat.

I was five-feet, two inches tall and weighed in at about 105 pounds, so I knew I had to cope with the situation in some manner other than brawn--even though I would have dearly loved to use muscle sometimes. I had been assigned to teach girls' P.E. but when Miss Pulliam saw me, she decided immediately to have me teach 8th grade Social Studies. A much larger woman, the regular 8th grade teacher, coached the girls in P.E., but I was on a par now with them. They liked me, so they made things rough for Vivian. Consequently, she deferred to me in P.E.--a perpetual puzzlement to Miss Pulliam. She couldn't understand how I got that gang of ruffians to organize. It was simple. I told them that, at the slightest sign of dissatisfaction, I'd turn them back to Miss Vivian! We even fielded a track team that won first place!

But in Winfield, I must admit (wholly unprofessional though it may sound), school was secondary in my mind. The rough town, the hard-living people, the strange food all added up to a lesson in raw living for me.

Cornbread for breakfast at Horse Shoe Bend had amazed me; but at Shields' community table it was biscuits. "Ernest likes biscuits," Mame said simply. So we had baked biscuits three times a day during the week and fried biscuits on the weekend. Ernest's mother, Mame explained, had "spoiled him" with weekend fried biscuits.

Ernest's tastes dictated several other specialties. He had a standing order at the Winfield butcher shop for a beef heart. Once a week, one beef heart would be available. Mame stuffed it and served it to the ten of us sitting down to an evening meal. Now, a beef heart--even stuffed--embodies a minimum amount of meat, and often after Enest had helped himself the rest of us were left with scarcely a bite.

Another frequently served food was fish. Living on the river, everybody went to the dam and bought "de-boned" fish. This meant the fish had been run through a large machine which cracked the bones. The fish from the river were so large they had to be "cracked" to cut them into serving-size pieces.

By spring I felt as if I had become part fish. Ordinarily, I like fish, but these big Mississippi varieties were extremely oily, making them quite impossible to fry crisp and brown. So Mame's fish was always white, tough and watery inside when it came to the table. And its taste reminded me of mud.

Other than the beef heart and fish, we usually had small boiled potatoes and "biled" cabbage. Mame informed us, "what with the war and all," there was no sugar and she just couldn't "bake nothin' for us." Miss Pulliam, from the safety of her seniority, frequently went to the kitchen and made cookies, however; she knew, with the rest of us, that Mame was either hoarding the sugar stamps for next summer's canning or selling them to her neighbors.

But these were war days and all of us were willing to sacrifice anything if it would end the war and bring our boys home. Winfield, like all small towns, had organized a "bomb alert." Each person had a guard duty station--just in case of an attack. And regularly every Wednesday evening a trial run was made. Every Winfield resident ate supper early so lights could be turned off. The goal of the entire endeavor, it seemed, was to immerse the town in total darkness. Anyone having a light on during the drill was fined heavily.

The stations in town and on the street corners weren't bad. But Veva drew a post far up the river bluff on a solid ledge or rock. She could see for miles--even in the dark--but it took careful climbing to get up there safely--much less to get down.

On one miserably cold, wet winter night a drill was in progress and everyone was at their station. It was unlikely the town guards would see an enemy bomb drop so they watched for any light spoiling the desired total darkness. Everything was in apple pie order, we thought. Mame and I had put Grandma to bed and explained carefully that we would be in the upstairs sitting room and if she needed anything all she had to do was call us.

Grandma was 90 years old and she didn't quite understand about the no-light decree. So, without making a sound, she got out of bed, went to the bathroom and turned on the light. Ipso facto, Ernest's house was liable for a fine. High up on the bluff, Veva saw the light and started sliding and running down toward the house. Down in town, Ernest saw it and stumbled pell mell up the bluff. As he turned the corner from town, Veva, propelled by gravity down the precipitous

ERNEST

His mother had "spoiled" him with fried biscuits on the weekend... and we paid the price thereafter.

bluff, plunged headlong into him. They both fell down, puffing and yelling.

Or rather Vera puffed. Ernest yelled. "Mame, get that damn light off!"

The whole household was in a tizzy. Except Grandma. "How do you expect an old lady to go pee in the dark?" she asked.

Forty years later that makes sense to me.

Grandma and I got along famously. She was a sweet old lady. But she did complain a great deal about her "pain." Whatever it was, it always hurt her. Mame wouldn't let her have aspirin; she might get addicted to it. The truth was, now that I think of it, Mame was stingy.

I hadn't been in Winfield long when Mame awoke one morning with the "flu." That was one morning Ernest didn't have his biscuits. Miss Pulliam and I made some toast, got some oatmeal and coffee on the table--and the eternal black molasses which served as dessert every day. At noon we ate cold leftover fish and potatoes.

By evening we were all starved for a good, warm meal--all eight of us. After school Miss Pulliam said, "Miss Bacon, if you'll make the biscuits, I think I can manage to cook us a pretty good supper." So we pitched in. Mrs. Shields was piled up in bed in a small side room just off the kitchen. From there she gave orders, but we paid little attention to them.

I helped Miss Pulliam with the vegetables, but I was confident I could handle the biscuits by myself. After all, I had made the things dozens of times at home. I gathered up my ingredients and mixed them, and rolled out the dough, cut it and stuck the raw results in the oven to bake.

They looked fine, other than not being quite as risen as I had hoped. But when I put them on a plate to serve, they fell to pieces; I had overdone the shortening. But everything else was ready and there was nothing to do but carry in my plate of biscuit crumbs--and look mortified.

Bless the men. They laughed and grabbed at them, loudly assuring me, "That's just the way we like 'em, by golly."

Grandma began to criticize everything: "No salt in the potatoes. No salt in the gravy, either. Meat's too salty. Guess it'll all balance out."

Then came my biscuits. She took a few bites and turned to me with a twinkle in her eye. "Well," she said, "they air a mite crumbly...but they shore do eat good." I drew a long breath of relief.

Finally, there wasn't a bite left. And poor Ernest still had a dab of molasses left on his plate. He looked around the table and laughed, loud, in a lefthanded compliment, "Does look like you'uns woulda' left me the last crumb to sop up with."

For several days Mame lay in bed and bossed and Miss Pulliam and I did the cooking, the dishwashing and laundry. With fish and beef heart the standard fare, we didn't have to wonder about the daily menu. And our suppers were never "a little late" because of Alvin.

Alvin was Mame's only child and Veva's husband, and many were the tales about him. He was in "Northafrica," as Mame pronounced it, and often when I came home from school I found her sitting at the big table in the basement dining room laboriously writing a letter to Alvin. And that was real labor for her. Years before she had cut her right index finger and it had healed into a stiff, straight stick, useless with a pencil. Yet there she sat, hunched over a writing tablet, her overly plump form hanging over the sides of the chair, her elbows on the table, frowning as if it were doomsday. But the light of mother love lit her eyes.

"Supper'll be a little late t'night," she would say. "I'm writin' to Alvin."

That saying explained many a delay in our schedule. Miss Pulliam, Don, Smitty and I used "Supper'll be a little late t'night; I'm writin' to Alvin" to cover a multitude of sins--from honest-to-goodness, unavoidable delays to plain procrastination and pure laziness.

I had scarcely got to know my way around school when the Christmas season arrived--with Winfield wind, snow, ice and sleet. Miss Pulliam and I took the task of producing a Christmas Cantata--whatever that was. Some girls could really sing; Dorothy Powell could play the piano. They would be our cantata "core."

The school had no auditorium so we had to scoot down the bluff each afternoon to practice at the Baptist Church. George Sears had to spend more penitential hours in the church basement, stoking the furnace--because angels and shepherds and virgins weren't accustomed to ice cold church interiors of a Winfield December. Miss Pulliam and I took turns going up and down the bluff and putting the girls through the Cantata. No wonder I never had a weight problem. I walked it all off on that bluff!

The program was set for 2 p.m. the Sunday before Christmas. Even as I approached, I could smell smoke much too plainly. When I arrived the cast--most of the pupils in school--was fleeing the church, choking, coughing, holding handkerchiefs to their noses. I inquired innocently if the church were on fire. "No, no, just the flue and the furnace pipes," they answered. With George refusing to enter the church proper, the soot had built up and now it was on fire. And such a mighty mess you never saw!

When we finally could see the sanctuary where we had set up our stage, all of the white, filmy cheesecloth angel wings and costumes were covered with smudgy, black soot. Our lovely homemade creche looked like the last days of Pompeii. Even the camels looked more like Black Angus cattle than creatures of the Biblical desert. The benches looked as if they had been painted with a black flat paint--mixed with dust.

But Rosalie Grigsby and Kenneth Caple, my rehabilitated friends, got things moving. Rosie ran around the corner to her mother's beer joint and came back in a flash with not only a big bucket of streaming hot soapy water, but mop and rags. Right behind her was her mama with a still larger tub-shaped bucket and mop.

Rosie's mama was large of body, red of face and Irish all over. She had a bad reputation but a big heart. Her big, red thick hands made quick work of cleaning the benches and floor while Kenneth helped me carry the angel wings and costumes outside where we could shake off most of the soot.

All the while George Sears was in the basement, crying and wailing, "I've ruined the cantata, I've ruined the play. I've ruined Christmas for everybody. Now that's what happens when you let sin ruin you." With each phrase, tears ran down his cheeks.

After I got the soot somewhat controlled--or at least subdued--and the girls assured that we could go on with the show, Kenneth and I went to the basement to quiet George. I told him we had the mess all cleaned up and we weren't hurt much. But George still had some penitence to get out of his soul--and his eyes.

Kenneth knew George better than I did--and how to handle him. After more of his caterwauling, Kenneth grabbed George by his necktie and said roughly, "Now, George, look here. Miss Bacon asked you to shut up and if you don't, I'm going to beat the tar out of you." George believed that. He stopped bawling and I went on with the cantata.

It was dark when we finally got everything put away. The angels had folded their sooty wings for the last time, the well-worn cantata pamphlets had been folded and stacked on the green brocade piano scarf atop the weary piano. A strong suspicion of smoke still hung in the church and, if you looked up there, definitely fuzzy black creatures clung to the light fixtures. We just hadn't had time to wash all of the soot away.

I thought of Rosie's mama. I had to thank her again for what she had done. I probably would never see her again. I took up my coat, stepped out into the bitterly cold night, slipped around the corner and knocked rather timidly on the back door of the bar room.

"Who is it?" a rough voice inquired.

I was scared now, because I thought Mama had a visitor. "It's me," I said. "Miss Bacon. I just came to thank you again."

The big gray door opened wide. I stepped up on the dry goods box to enter the door and warmth and good food odors rushed out to greet me. Rosalie and Mama were "just havin' a bite." Wouldn't I have a bite with them?

I was happy to. The "bite" was a feast. Ham, sweet potatoes, fried Irish potatoes, homemade bread, pickles--all of it good and hot right off the wood cookstove which grinned at us through red-hot teeth. We ate and visited.

"Mama," Rosie kept saying, "I told you she was the nicest teacher I've ever had."

And Mama kept saying, "You're all Rosie talks about. I never seen no woman like you. You ain't my kind. I wish't I ain't what I am. I yusta go to church ever' Sunday. But today when I packed that water over there and hepped scrub up...that's the first time I been in church since I married Rosie's pa."

For a short while in that Winfield winter Rosie and her mother and I were bosom pals. We talked and ate and we drank hefty cups of golden brown coffee. Suddenly Rosie's mama jumped up. "Miss Bacon," she said, "you best go on now. It ain't goin' to be good for you if folks find out you been in Ol' Grigsby's kitchen."

I didn't argue with her. Rosie and Mama held onto my hand as I eased out the door onto the dry goods box, and I waved as I rounded the corner of the Baptist Church and climbed the bluff to the Shields Hotel. After that I wanted to cry when the townspeople and children in high school called Rosie's mama "Old Grigsby." She wasn't "that kind of woman." She was a victim of circumstances which were rough and hard to manage. Even for Winfield.

WARTIME CHRISTMAS

"He's been surrendered nine times — and he ain't gone yet."

I went home for a wartime Christmas. I rode a small Golden Crown Coach into St. Louis, took the city limits street car to the Maplewood loop where Irvin was waiting for me, then we drove the 100 miles home.

The talk of war was everywhere. Pete was still in Hawaii, he and that doctor still in charge of six thousand inmates of a concentration camp who couldn't prove their U.S. citizenship. He was now, he said, a section of the "pineapple army." Each day there, he knew, was a blessing. Sooner or later he would be moving on to the South Pacific.

Bant, too, was anxious. His days at Warrensburg were fast coming to an end. Try as we might to be jolly, to make the holidays bright and cheerful, our thoughts always came back to the fellows who were away from home--some already "killed in action," some missing in action, some prisoners of war. And some who had found ways and means of escaping the service.

This was a touchy subject with our neighbors. Some of them were just as eligible for the draft as our boys. Yet they married and produced a child quickly--sometimes too quickly. Or they bought a small farm, invested in a few old cows and set up business in a "vital industry." Mama referred to it as "rock pile farming."

But there is nothing fair about war or its conduct. If you are eligible, your number comes up and you go. Sometimes you don't come back. And sometimes others with the same qualifications and eligibility stay home.

Mrs. Kraenow, our neighbor to the north, summed it up, unknowingly adding the saving touch of humor. "I just don't understand," she said. "Harold Ahrens has been surrendered nine times--and he ain't gone yet." (She meant "deferred.")

Christmas wasn't very exciting or happy. In addition to the war, Bant's operation had set us back financially. I was repaying the Linn State Bank for my education, and many things like sugar and gasoline were rationed. No sugar meant no homemade cookies, no candies, no cakes and the like. No gasoline meant no traveling--not even a short trip. Sometimes it was "nip and tuck" to decide if the old Chevrolet had enough gas to get to church and back. Soon I was back in Winfield, wondering what had happened to Christmas...and what would happen to Bant when he entered the service.

Miss Pulliam took the occasion to assign a few more teaching duties to her two helpers, Mr. Byrum and me. I was told:

1. You will take over the Science classes. And they will meet in the study hall during your free period.

2. You will take over Vivian's 7th and 8th grade room at least two times per week while she coaches the girls' P.E.

I didn't mind, No. 1, except it was a correspondence course and I had no textbook. All I could do was depend on my own brain--and ingenuity. Some of the better students had good ideas so we filled in the blanks with identical sentences which I wrote on the blackboard for them. I've often wondered who graded those papers and why they didn't object to the sameness of the responses!

One question I'll never forget was, "How is the human eye like a camera lens? List at least 10 similarities." Now that took some studying! And some research in our pitifully inadequate library.

It was a tiny enclosure at the end of the hallway at the head of the staircase. Shelves--perhaps five feet long--ran along one side. An old desk, used for the filing system, was pushed against the opposite wall. Near the floor on the bottom shelves were a few odds and ends of dictionaries and a few hit and miss volumes of encyclopedias. There were no complete sets of anything. And here, inside its picket gate, I spent many weary hours digging out information about the human eye, a camera lens and various other bits of scientific fact for these poor, bedraggled river rats.

There was another kind of pupil, too. There were a few truly fine sons and daughters of well-to-do owners of the Mississippi River farm land which lay beyond the town of Winfield. All winter the land was covered with snow and/or ice and I didn't realize until spring came what productive--and rich--soil this was. We also had some students from smaller towns around Winfield--Old Monroe, Foley and Peruque.

Taking over Vivian's 7th and 8th grade bearcats was more than I could bear. Or wanted to. But the girls in the class again came to my rescue. Rosalie and Iva Mae kept after me: "You don't really want to neglect us, do you? We want you for P.E. We'll work for you."

I TACKLE SCIENCE
How is the human eye like a camera lens?

And they meant it. Talk about organized labor! These girls organized the entire class so tightly that the AFL or CIO professionals would've been proud of them. And on Monday they sat down and informed Vivian they weren't performing one iota of anything until she returned to her classroom and I was released from supervising the 7th and 8th grades. It worked. We went into basketball, volleyball, shot-put--and great were the physical feats accomplished. Vivian wasn't very friendly after this, but it worried me little. And the kids not at all.

In the long evenings I found plenty of time to do my fancywork. Having been so busy for two years getting a degree, I was starved for needlework. I started all sorts of projects--a quilt to finish, a French boutinierre, fancy dishtowels to embroider, pillowcase edges to finish with crochet...I reveled in it all, especially on the weekends.

And I thoroughly enjoyed my fellow boarders--or at least liked getting to know them. Don Duey was a plain "good guy." He worked as a guard at the dam eight hours a day, but had little else to do. So we all used him for an errand boy. Mrs. Shields would send him down the bluff to A.L. Ricks' store to bring her a can of "baking powders"--for biscuits, of course--or a "cartoon" of pop. And it was Don who always seemed to be handy to go to the butcher shop for the eternal beef heart, or bring home the fish for supper--after it was run through the "de-boner." And when there was an errand out of town, Ernest always inveigled Don into going "because I just don't have the time."

Don also "saw to" the furnace and fuel oil, and the pump which furnished us with water in the one bathroom. For all this, he occupied a third-story bedroom, bragged on the biscuits and spread goodnatured conversation when Miss Pulliam or Mame was "out of sorts."

Smitty was another guard at the dam. But, unlike Don, he was quiet, almost to total silence, and he ran no errands. He roomed in a tiny, unheated cubicle just off the coal cellar. Smitty drank--anything he could get his hands on. Frequently he didn't appear at meals, so Mame would dispatch Ernest or Don to "see about Smitty." They would return and duly report that Smitty "didn't want anything to eat."

It took me quite a while to catch on to the simple fact that Smitty would rather drink than eat.

When he was sober, however, I liked to converse with him. He had been in the Army several years and had become angry because he could never get an overseas assignment, so he put in for a discharge. He was still angrier because the war was on and now he figured he would have been sent overseas if he had been patient a short while.

Smitty would come to the second floor to take a bath and often stand at my door and talk for an hour. In him during these talks I found a great love for good books and poetry. By the hour he could quote Shakespeare, Browning, Burns, Dickens, Chaucer and dozens of other writers.

I started lending him my English and American Literature books, although I suspect he took them only to please me. He had volumes of Shakespeare and other writers of classics which were well worn. When he had committed a passage to memory, he would bring the book upstairs and say, "Now, you watch the words and correct me if I make an error."

I never had to correct him. He always knew it letter perfect. I always wondered what he might have been if someone had discovered him when he was young. Isn't it preposterous what talent goes to waste in this world! And in Winfields all over the world.

In March Mame was beside herself with joy. Alvin was back in the states from North Africa; he had written her a letter. Veva sat behind the coal stove in the dining room and looked bewildered when Mame made the announcement. Like thousands of wives of returning servicemen, I'm sure, she wasn't sure what would happen now.

On one of Winfield's black, blizzard-y evenings the basement dining room door flew open and there stood Alvin--duffle bags, uniform, stiff leg and all. Mame's big mannish form shot past Ernest and Viva, then they all kissed and hugged him. A footstool was brought down from the parlor above for "poor Alvin's crippled leg" and every comfort was showered upon him.

For a few days the food improved markedly. We had baked chicken and dressing, stewed chicken and dumplings, and pie and cake and fruit. Determined to "fatten him up some," Mame kept saying, "Poor boy, poor boy, he shore does look bad. Now don't you'uns think he looks bad?" I'd never seen Alvin before so I could give no sensible answer but Mame's motherly mind was made up anyway, and we all reaped the benefits thereof for a while.

After a two-week furlough, Alvin left to report to Camp Pendleton, California, for discharge later. Veva followed him a couple of weeks later. I was lost without her for a while, but apparently things had been smoothed out for her and Alvin, and Mame and I were delighted for her.

I was crossing off the days on my calendar, making big red X's each morning and wondering how many thousands of teachers in this land "from sea to shining sea" were doing the same. And how many felt the futility of their "calling" in these times when many of their charges knew not if this day might be their last. Teaching, after all, was meant to prepare students for life--not death.

In Winfield that wondering became even more pronounced as the Monday morning roll call became all too familiar: "Oh, he ain't here no more. His old man got fired off the job." Or "Mark her off, Teach. She went down." (This mean down river, usually to St. Louis.)

When spring finally came I felt like a bird out of a cage. I could walk in the sunshine after school and on the weekends. On one of these warm, sunshiny Saturdays, Dorothy Byrum, Wilf's wife, and I planned a small party, asking a few couples in for dinner and cards on the following Saturday. One of them was Katherine and O'Garland Ricks. O'Garland had just completed a course in funeral directing, following in one-third of the footsteps of his father, choosing to sidestep the "Groceries" and "Dry Goods" on the sign which was my first sight of Winfield.

Saturday came. Dorothy and I cooked and baked all day. O'Garland was just bringing the spirits and we were just getting ready to tip a merry little drink. *Rrinnggg*. It was the telephone; a bad accident. No help available.

Away sped O'Garland, Wilfred and the other men in the ambulance, leaving all the women to get home as best we could. We knew there would be no party that night because O'Garland would have to take the injured people either to Louisiana, Missouri, north up Highway 79, or south to St. Louis.

Katherine Ricks and I were walking carefully down the bluff when "Bang!" Katherine and I thought we were shot, but when we recovered sufficiently to see what had happened we burst out laughing. The bottom of the paper sack in which Katherine was carefully carrying home the remains of the party bourbon had fallen out, the bottle had shattered and the bourbon had splashed all over our feet.

Katherine was in hysterics; she had to go by way of her in-laws' house and pick up baby Katherine. And the Ricks didn't approve of liquor in any shape or form--even the smell. And smell it they would and she would be in the dog house. We sat down on the curb and thought. I'd also be in the dog house--the Shields's--if I went in the hotel smelling like liquor.

So back up the bluff we trudged to Dorothy Byrum's house. We washed our hose and shoes, put them all back on--still wet--and shivered back out into the chilly spring night. It must be true, as the old saying goes, that God takes care of drunks and fools. We didn't even get a sniffle.

In fact, despite its miserableness, I wasn't sick that whole winter in Winfield. Maybe it was Mame's fried biscuits...they did "stick to your bones," as Mame said. On Saturday and Sunday mornings they were standard fare and often appeared unscheduled. I was beginning to hope I would never see another biscuit. But they had intriguing aspects. When Mame would lap up five or six of them at a meal, dribbling thick molasses around the edges as she lifted a loaded half to her mouth--with that right forefinger sticking straight out from the goo--I became so entranced that I forgot to eat.

In between bites, she would remind us, "Ernest likes biscuits. His mother spoiled him to biscuits. Ever'one in Ernest's family likes biscuits."

One Friday evening I decided to find out how she made them. I went down to the basement kitchen early. Mame was kneading the biscuit dough in her big wooden dough bowl. I plopped myself on the high stool by the cook table. Trying to be diplomatic, I sounded more like timid when I asked her, "Are we having baked or fried biscuits tonight?"

"Well, darlin'," Mame replied, "which would you druther have?" Her straight forefinger pointed directly at me, never touching the biscuit dough.

I thought I had been the shrewd one until she went on, "I intended to fry them, anyway, because Ernest likes a special treat once in a while."

That took the wind out of my sails. I couldn't figure out what was so special about fried biscuits when we had them every week. But I found out how they were fried.

Mame put a huge cast iron griddle on the front burner of the electric stove. She greased it lightly and heated it to smoking. Then she laid the biscuits on it carefully, so no two biscuits touched. When they became brown on the bottom side, she turned them with a spatula and stood by patiently until each one was perfectly golden brown. Mame's beef heart and fish were never brown and crisp, but her fried biscuits were always perfect. And to this day making them ranks high among the good things I learned at Winfield.

17

They have to be tough

And, although the experience could hardly be called good, I learned about the raw, awesome power of a mighty river on a rampage--and why the people in a river town like Winfield have to be tough.

When I think of my six months there, I grow cold. I see snow and water...flood water. At Horse Shoe Bend I had spent hours hoping the Gasconade River never severed my connections with mainland: Home. Now I was rapidly crossing off the days on my small desk calendar--15 left, then 14, now 13. Suddenly, as it sometimes does in late April and early May, the rain began to fall. It fell in sheets and buckets, in torrents. It ran down the bluff in small rivers. It met you at the door. It pushed against you with cold, wet fingers as you stepped out into it to scale the cold, clammy face of the bluff to get to school. At supper rain blew into the dining room with each late comer. Dripping McIntoshes, galoshes and umbrellas crowded into the dining room and kitchen and the smell of wet rubber permeated the entire house. Upstairs at night I lay awake and listened to the steady downpour and wondered when--if--it would ever stop.

On one of these nights another bomb watch was held. Ernest volunteered to take Veva's place high on the bluff. Three times he started out with his lighted lantern (he would extinguish the light when he reached the designated watch); three times the wind and rain drowned the light. The third time Ernest slammed the door shut. "Damn watch can go to Hell," he said. "Ain't no man nor beast goin' to git out and hunt bombs on a night like this!"

For once I agreed with Ernest. Mame popped corn and poured it into the big bread riser before we had to turn out the lights. Then we laughed as we sat in the dark and ate the corn. It was too dark to see who was reaching for the next bowl or handful--Don or Smitty always seemed to be reaching when I did--so the result was a sort of "hand holding contest" in the deep bread riser. When bedtime came we groped our way up to the second floor bedrooms for another night of the heavy downpour drumming its steady beat on the roof.

I had never seen so much heavy rainfall. And the town's conversation centered around the rising river. When Don came in from guard duty, Mame would meet him at the door. "How many feet is there now?" she would ask.

"Not too much, Mame," Don would reply calmly. "She's still not out of the banks."

But the day soon came when "she" went out of her banks. The wide, whirling Mississippi came a-rolling. Great waves of brown, silt-laden water had to spill over onto the Missouri side because the Illinois side was a sheer wall of white rock cliff.

Dike by dike, it edged closer. Each dike had a name, none of which meant anything to me, except that each one they mentioned was nearer to Winfield.

They were named for the owner of the farm land and "runnin' over Old Jones' dike" was no cause for alarm. Neither was runnin' over "Old Bockemeyer's." Even Brown's Dike going under wasn't too spectacular. But when Don announced one morning at breakfast that the water was fast approaching Bell's Dike, everyone but me gasped in astonishment. That meant a flood for sure. A real flood.

I had only 24 hours left in Winfield. The Missouri River was backing up at St. Charles. There was talk of closing the bridge--definitely if water became 12 to 15 inches deep on the bridge. At Old Monroe, the Cuivre River was already 12 inches over the railroad bridge...

Mame, Don and I drove down to see this unstoppable phenomenon after school on Thursday. I was anxious to get away before the river made it difficult--maybe impossible--to leave. But life had to go on--and school had to close. The seniors had a banquet at the Odd Fellows' Hall (Mame cooked it), and from there we marched in a steady, cold downpour to the Baptist Church where caps and gowns

THE RIVER

"It's runnin' over Ol' Jones's."

were donned for the Commencement program.

A little ray of amusing coincidence shone on the dark night. All winter at school the big boys had used the phrase, "Let George do it," a good-natured poke at George Sears, the custodian. Incredibly, the Commencement speaker chose that theme for his evening address, how wrong it was for people to stand by and say, "Let George do it."

Kenneth Caple started the rippling response. He got tickled and, knowing I knew the reason, he glanced across the aisle at me. I glared back and frowned. The effect on Kenneth and his henchmen was the exact opposite to what I desired. I could see their shoulders shaking under their oxford gray gowns. The tassles on their caps jiggled and some of the girls clapped their hands over their mouths.

I must confess that I might have joined them, enjoying the respite from worrying about a flood and getting home and last-minute duties, if I had not been a Teacher and supposed to set an example. But I was most relieved when that address was finally over. Perhaps I should have joined in the fun, because according to my future plans, I would leave Winfield the following day. Never, never, never to return.

That night Don and Smitty helped other skillful river men bring in people whose homes had been inundated. The Shields Hotel, as well as several homes on the bluff, overflowed with people escaping from the flood. These people were frantic. Their livestock was gone; their houses floating away or filled with muddy, never-ending Mississippi water. Some couldn't believe the water had breached Bell's Dike. It never had before.

I had mailed my boxes and big suitcases home so I had only one small bag with the simple necessities in it. I bunked in with Miss Pulliam for the rest of the night to make room for the refugees. With each motorboat load of people, Don and Smitty came in soaked to the skin, their tiredness showing on their faces more each trip.

Toward morning they were called to rescue the owners of a night club on a small island. None of the men liked this assignment. The island was out too far in the river; it was dangerous out there tonight. Miss Pulliam and I heard Don and Smitty muttering ugly words under their breaths as they came upstairs to get dry shoes and socks before setting out again.

Anxious for them, no one returned to bed. We went downstairs. Mame was making a fresh pot of coffee and starting the biscuits for breakfast. There would be several extra people this morning so she made an extra batch. Daybreak came, bleak and wet, and with it came Don and Smitty. Their shoes squished water with every step. And with them straggled in the tavern owners--their dog, cat and all. The wife was in tears. She was only adding to the water problem, I thought, but her sobs were pitiful. Don explained to us that they had not been able to rescue her pet billy goat...and when they left Billy was walking up and down the keyboard on the piano.

Don went to bed for some much needed rest. He was to take me to St. Charles soon after noon--if the bridge over the Missouri hadn't been closed by then. I went to school for the last time. The flood was far from the seniors minds; they were all still laughing about the Commencement theme. They answered every question, "Let George do it." Poor George just looked puzzled. Hewing to his self-imposed punishment of never entering the church sanctuary, he hadn't heard the address.

My darling sophomores, grateful for my pulling them through General Science and its human eye-camera lens problems, had taken up a collection and bought me a "boudoir lamp." Now, how was I going to get that lamp home! I hardly needed anything less in my flight from the flood. They thought I should be overjoyed--and I was. With the sentiment. Enjoying the lamp came later.

Miss Pulliam thought I should leave by 11 a.m. It was definite now. The bridge would close at noon. The Missouri National Guard was stacking sand bags now at the water's edge. I practically ran down the bluff, my heart thumping as I stumbled and slid. Finally, I was on my way.

But through it all, I remember, I kept thinking Poor Rosie, poor Kenneth. Poor Rosie, poor Kenneth. They were only two of the many young people I've known who needed a friend more than they needed a teacher...

Mame had a bite of lunch ready for me. "You're mor'n likely to have a long, torin' (tiring) trip," she said. I sat down and ate quickly. Fried biscuits, with something else. I forget what.

Don came downstairs, looking a little rested. He was clean shaven, wearing a clean khaki shirt and slacks. He looked quite handsome as he sipped coffee while I swallowed a few bites to please Mame.

Hurriedly, I ran upstairs to get my small bag. I'd put in my toothbrush and be ready. On top of the bag was a brown paper sack. I recognized Smitty's neat backhand writing on the outside: "To my favorite school ma'rm. Please read this little volume frequently in memory of a merry, miserable winter." Inside was a copy of Robert Service's complete poems. Now I had to find a larger paper bag and put the lamp and the book in it. I had been so sure that it would be so simple to sever that winter's ties to Winfield. I was certain that I had been less than happy in this queer little town. Why, then, were my neat plans for leaving with no regrets unraveling? The flood. That was it. The flood...

Don and I set off for St. Charles. There I would board a county bus for Wellston--if I was lucky. According to the news broadcasts, buses were still crossing the bridge, but not on any schedule--just when there were enough passengers to make up a load. I reasoned that they didn't want just a small catastrophe if the bridge collapsed; they wanted enough people to make a worthwhile disaster.

Don and I laughed. He turned off the car radio and drove on through the rain. I sensed something was bothering him. He talked more than usual, mostly about his family. One of his sons had been killed in Europe. Now another, his favorite--David--was missing in action. One daughter, Elizabeth, was married to a colonel...he was very fond of her...she had just had a new baby...

All these bits of information came rushing from him as if he had only a limited amount of time to utter them.

I'm not good at comforting. I hardly knew what to say when he spoke of David. There was great apprehension connected with the "Missing in Action" phrase. He knew it, and so did I.

Finally, Don blurted out, "Oh, I'm just messing things up good and proper. Would you be interested in marrying me? We could go live in Arizona close by Elizabeth, get away from everything."

I almost dropped the paper bag--lamp, book and all. I can't even remember what I said, so I must have been "shook." But I could understand why he had been acting so strangely of late...and reaching for popcorn in the bread riser at the same time I did.

I was relieved to arrive at the St. Charles County Bus Terminal. I insisted on boarding the bus sitting there. I was anxious to get away from Don. I guess I'm

DON

"We could go live in Arizona... get away from everything."

strange. I had never thought of him as anything but a good friend--someone to bring Mame a "cartoon of Coke" from Ricks' grocery store, someone to rescue stranded Mississippi islanders, someone to bring home the fish from the "deboner."

These thoughts raced through my mind as I sat on a dripping, gray, asthmatic bus wheezing as it waited for enough passengers to make its trip worthwhile. The gray-clad driver had come aboard and started the motor, got off again, returned to the coffee stand in the terminal, sat down and had drunk still another cup of coffee. Don was still hanging around, sitting in his car. In case the bus didn't run, he had told me, he could take me around by way of Weldon Springs. Heavens to Betsy, of all things I couldn't bear the thought of right this minute was another hour with Don. What would we talk about? What would I say?...

Finally the driver came back out. This time he actually sat down in the seat, actually placed his hand on the big black knob atop the gear shift, and with a monumental roar we ground out of the bus station. I could stop thinking about Don and his proposal, about his waiting...

In minutes we were plowing through the water--deep water, over the floor of the Missouri River bridge. I looked beneath the seat and brown water was seeping in. As I looked out the bus windows, I saw men on the river banks passing sand bags from one to another in a human chain. I don't remember being afraid of all this water. I guess I was too eager to get headed homeward. I would have "swum" if necessary. All the way.

For a while it appeared that I might have to do that, part of the way. Irvin met me at the Maplewood Loop as usual, but as we started out of town, he said, "You know, it might be days before you can get home from Cooper Hill."

That was a new--and unwelcome--thought. The rain had been falling at home, too. The Gasconade, a tributary of the swollen Missouri, was backed up all over creation. When we reached Cooper Hill, we had to leave the car on high ground and walk around the edge of the hill to get to Mae's and Irvin's house. Everyone had set out stakes with yard sticks attached to them or measurements marked on boards so they could determine how fast the water was "comin' up."

All night we could see flash lights and lanterns streaking across the blackness. We could hear Pete Langenberg answer Basil's question: "Come up another inch and a half in the last hour." And on into the night. People knew the consequences: If you had to move things out of the basement, better start early.

Harold Enke and Frank Tschappler always measured the water on the Goose Creek side; Pete measured the store side where the rising water backed up on the river side of the road. There were always at least two distinct measuring groups and their measurements never exactly agreed. This gave the men at the two Cooper Hill stores a subject for discussions lasting days after the water had receded.

A mathematician and practical problem solver, Irvin always figured out a way to get a thing done. When morning came he had the solution to my last leg home. The water stood several feet deep over the road leading home, so he would take me in the skiff--to which he had attached a motor. He had anchored the skiff at the foot of the hill below the house. So far, fine.

Mae, Yvonne, Anna Lo and I climbed in. Then Irvin had another idea. Why not take the bees he had been intending to take over to the farm? Up and down the hill he went four times, a hive of bees at a time. They were completely safe, he assured us. He had stuffed cloths in the openings so no bees could escape. With all of us and the bees properly balanced, Brownie, their pet dog, took his place, poised with front feet on the motor, and we put-putted into the floodwaters.

Crossing the flooded Missouri the day before, with its water seeping through the bus floorboards, was "duck soup" compared to this. I was petrified now, with all those bees, the kids, the dog, and no life jackets. No nothing. And you never knew what would come sweeping downstream in a flood like this.

Irvin, of course, steered for the main stream; it was too dangerous along the shallow edges which ordinarily was farm land. We skirted the north end of the bridge and were somewhere in the middle of what in dry times was Millard Hassler's fertile corn field when we saw a gigantic straw stack floating swiftly toward us. It was grown together with vines and mold into a solid mass. As it floated, it dipped and turned and rolled, with the current steering it directly toward us.

Irvin, his eyes widening more than I cared to see, speeded up the motor--as much as he could. And we all calculated the angle, wondering if our skiff could beat the stack. In a minute or so--it seemed like an eternity--the skiff crossed the current and we pulled safely away from the soggy monster which could have upset us and perhaps drowned us all.

We actually motored all the way to the line fence between our farm and Irvin's. I would never have believed it had I not been one of the "crew." Irvin set the bee hives on the bank under a massive sycamore tree, then deposited me on a high spot from where I could work my way around the hillside to the house.

I had come home in farm wagons, buggies, spring wagons, on foot, on horseback and in cars, but this was the first time I'd arrived via motorboat. With bees yet! When I opened the kitchen door, Mom threw up her hands in surprise and demanded to know how I got there.

"By boat," I told her, light and airy, as if it were nothing.

"Well," she said, "I knew you'd get here some way if you had to charter a plane." (That was one of Mom's favorite phrases; she was always thinking of "chartering a plane" as the epitome of accomplishment, whatever it took.)

For night after long night following this homecoming, I was haunted by water. My dreams ran full of rundown buses that just wouldn't start, bridges under water too deep to cross, boats with underpowered motors, straw piles and bee hives. It all began to flow together and carry school along with it, and I caught myself thinking I'd never teach school again. Surely, there must be something else to do. A better place to live than the one I'd just evacuated.

I got little peace from Mom on this score. She couldn't see why I hadn't wanted to go back to Winfield. Mom never considered feelings or emotions--or whatever happens that causes unhappiness--important. You do what has to be done at the time and ignore the surroundings. I'm not sure that Mom was capable of doing this herself, but she felt it expedient upon her to make me feel iron clad.

Winfield wasn't the kind of town that you can erase from your mind the way you press blotting paper with a warm iron. It had taught me some lessons just as valuable as the ones I had learned at Horse Shoe Bend several years earlier. One of these was understanding the ways people live. There are people who live in the same house, with the same furniture and the same neighbors, for 50 years or more. There are people who have never known what it's like to stay even five weeks or five months in the same place. They're always "movin' down river."

I belonged, I thought, to that first group. Put down roots and stay where they are all my life. But I never have. I'm like those Winfield river rats. I just get settled in one place and it's time to move on "down"...somewhere. For the first 25 years of my career I lived out of a suitcase, and that kind of near-transient living became associated in my mind with teaching. But I had chosen it. Why? It wasn't just Mom's pushing; I was sure I'd have wanted to teach, anyway, because...At Winfield, I wondered. And I wondered at times about turning down J. Edgar Hoover.

The windup then was that I couldn't bear the thought of returning to that dull little river town. Once, many years later, I chanced to pass through it on the railroad. Only one thing caught my eye as the train whizzed alongside Winfield's now-dusty main street. I was staring hard for anything that looked familiar and there it was. That store sign. It still read in big black letters: "A.L. Ricks-- Groceries, Dry Goods and Undertaking."

PART SEVEN

BLAND

18

A gift on "Black Saturday"

After my return to Osage County the rain continued to fall, soaking the countryside. And Mom dampened my spirits inside. Every morning began with, "What do you intend to do? Are you going to become a one-year teacher? (This was a barely oblique reference to my one-year tenures at Old Woollam, Owensville and Winfield.) Don't you intend to get a job? Have you applied for any? If you aren't going to teach, you'll have to find something to do. Maybe in the shoe factory."

That final thrust always irked me. After all, during all of those previous teaching years I had given Mom my "profits" to send the boys to school. She also pried unmercifully at my status with the Linn State Bank. Had I paid off my loan? Did I have any money left in my account? That was really what she wanted to find out.

But there were many comforting aspects about coming home. The house was my pride and joy--cleaning it and buying small, inexpensive furnishings or new curtains and wallpaper gave me such pleasure. In this respect I must be like my father. He was always so glad to see me. His eyes would shine when I told him some funny little detail about Winfield--especially the fried biscuits.

Dad liked a clean, neat, well-kept house; he like music and fun and laughter. He enjoyed young folks. But he was always so busy making a living from farming that he never had time to enjoy reading or playing the violin. Nor much even to hear my stories, funny or otherwise. Mom wouldn't question me when Dad was around. She waited until he went outside. Then the fur would fly!

But the nights were peaceful. I enjoyed reading in bed after everyone was asleep. I'd lie in my own world, propped up on pillows in the heavy cast iron bed upstairs close by the kerosene lamp on the table--so close I could feel the heat of the flame through the glass globe. June bugs joined me--thick, squatty beetles attracted by the light. They buzzed around the globe in a frantic circle, their shadows flitting across the pages like tiny eclipses. Usually they burned their inner gauzy wings and fell on the table, and there, on their backs, they buzzed away their final moments on earth.

And among the June bugs were the tiny night insects lured by light. If I read a long time, they would be piled in a dark circle on the table scarf...reminding me of the circular funeral pyres of India. And making me wonder if my career, like funeral fires, was going up in smoke.

I had cleaned house, helped Mae with some sewing, washed and ironed and had been patient with Mom's questions until mid-summer. I began to wonder if perhaps I should join the WACS or the WAVES. I wasn't interested in teaching at that point, and Mom wasn't going to be happy with me around the house. Then from the blue came the "gift": A job--teaching--came to me and I didn't have to move a muscle.

It happened on "Black Saturday." The house was a mess. Dad was sick and Mom was mad. Dad had worked too hard pulling some stumps out of a patch of new ground. He'd also foolishly worn some leftover shoes which didn't fit and had worn a huge blister on his heel. Bud and I spoke in guarded tones that day. I didn't dare clean house much because Dad was sleeping--or yelling a series of orders at me:

"Bring a drink."

"Call Doc."

"I'm hungry. Bring me something to eat."

"Bring me the chamber pot."

I was on my way through the front hall with the latter--the big white Alfred Meakin china one--when I glanced up and saw a strange man at the door. I managed a weak "Hello" and a wave, then ran to the rear of the house where I disposed of my burden and returned to greet the stranger properly.

He had been joined by two other nice-looking, youngish gentlemen. They introduced themselves as George Essman, Ferd Lahmeyer and Henry Steiner. Among them, they were the Bland School Board. Board members, they called themselves then as I guided them into the living room.

They soon got around to the reason for their calling. They badly needed a teacher at Bland High School, they said. And they wanted a lady. Girls in high school needed lady teachers--at least one.

"Would I be the only lady teacher?" I asked.

They all hesitated. Finally Mr. Essman said, "No..ooo. Not really. We have Miss Smith." And he ended his sentence.

Talk about events bringing families together! In our house it was not so much playing together or praying together; it was school-boarding together. One minute I was alone in our cavernous, damp, even chilly (for August) living room being interviewed for a teaching job. The next minute Mom and Dad were both there.

Dad looked surprisingly well in a clean shirt, trousers and bedroom slippers. Mom came in from the side porch all chipper, with water streaks still shining in her gray hair from interrupted grooming, but wearing a clean, starched dress and apron. I knew Mom's ears. They had heard two words--School Board--and that was all she needed for instant transformation. You would never have known she was the same person who, only a few moments earlier, had been raising the roof with all of us.

Both Mom and Dad became talkative. They had known these Bland families for years...George Essman's uncle, Henry, was one of Mom's first teachers; Ferd Lahmeyer's aunt was Mrs. Hy Buecker, who had lived in our house for half a century.

The reminiscing dragged on and on. I wanted them to get to the question at hand and after a time they did. But what they wanted, I thought as they reeled off subjects, would have to be some kind of wizard. The things I would be expected to teach ranged from English to World History and on to American History, World Geography, Missouri History, Hygiene, Girls' Physical Education and--last but not least--Music.

The list scared me. I kept listening for them to say Science. And that would have sent me straight up the wall; going through the human eye and camera lens again would be more than I could abide. Or maybe even survive.

Mom got up to excuse herself. And I knew why. It gave her an opportunity to give me that look which meant: You'd better get this nailed down. And quick!

The Bland board trio offered me only $115 per month--$10 less than I had received at Winfield. But I balked at letting Mom sign me up to another contract without thinking about all those subjects I had to teach. Dad agreed with me; I should be paid more. I'd think it over, I told the Board, and let them know in a few days. The music was the final straw. I had never taught it. About all I knew was middle C on the keyboard, and I hadn't touched a piano or organ since we sang "Just like a tree that's planted by the wa---ter, I shall not be moved" back in Horse Shoe Bend.

The front door closed behind the august school board and Mom turned on me with the opening overture to a brief dialogue: "Well," she said, "I guess we finally got you a job for one more year. If it hadn't been for Dad and me, you'd 'a let that one slip right through your fingers. Think it over! I'll let you think it over until tomorrow morning, young lady. That's how long you can think it over!"

"But, Mom, I can't teach music. I just can't. I don't know anything about music!"

"Huh. Make them think you can. Anybody can teach music. Besides, you can sing louder than anybody I ever heard. Now, I don't want to hear anymore about it. Subject closed."

That final sentence was one of Mom's favorites. And it ended the "discussion."

In a day or so I notified the Board that I would accept the position. And Mom continued to remind me how great it was that she and Dad had practically got the job for me.

This latest skirmish with Mom quickly evaporated amidst the widening war. It more and more occupied the minds of everybody. The daily papers ran headlines about Tobruk, Guadalcanal, Saipan, Moscow, Berlin, London. People were leaving England for Canada to escape the bombing. Would anyone ever get home safely?

Pete was somewhere out in the Pacific now. We didn't know where. We tried to figure it out from the little information he was allowed to write on a Victory letter and fill in the rest from the newspapers. We knew his general location but never the exact island. Bant was still at Washington University; he came home on leave occasionally. But every week when the *Unterrified Democrat* was delivered, we read unwanted news--sometimes an obituary, more frequently words about the wounded servicemen, where they were stationed, the names of their relatives...

And if the heartaches and worries marked our daily lives on the "Home Front," coupons were our badges. You guarded coupons for everything considered necessary for the war effort--gasoline for the car, kerosene for lamps, shoes, sugar, meat. The ration books were issued at long intervals and with the greatest of care. And woe be unto anyone who lost his book of gas stamps--as Bud and I soon did!

My boarding places, it seemed, were always arranged for me--by Mom or a friend of the family or some relative. But this one at Bland was a God-sent blessing. Mrs. Ella Steiner was looking for someone to occupy a spare bed and keep her company. Her husband, Gus, had just died. Dorothy, her young daughter, was in the 6th grade and Gus, Jr. was planning to attend the University of Missouri. At the last minute, Beda House, the first grade teacher, also came to board and share a small bedroom off the kitchen with me. And the one bathroom.

School Board President Henry and Mrs. Henry Steiner lived next door. At the back was John Lahmeyer's Feed Store, and towering above it was the Bland Water Tower. It said so--almost proudly--in big black letters on the side. But from underneath, it sneakily leaked water constantly for three years, rotting the roofs of Mrs. Steiner's house and chicken shed, John Lahmeyer's Feed Store and Gertha and Bertha Lickleider's General Merchandise. In winter it looked like a mammoth Eskimo Pie with icicles hanging from it.

Three years? Yes, three fast years. I decided to disprove Mom's theory that I'd be a one-year teacher all my life. The teaching was pleasant. Bland's residents and the surrounding farm families were from principally Germanic ancestry. The children were quiet, well-behaved, well-groomed young people--offsprings of a way of life completely foreign to Winfield's transient river people.

We had barely 100 pupils in high school so our class load wasn't very heavy. The burden was seeing that all the subject matter was taught.

Out of all of it, nothing bothered me but the music--that eternal, infernal music. It actually consisted only of Chorus--on Mondays and Wednesdays, Girls' Chorus; on Tuesday and Thursdays, Boys' Chorus. Ah, but on Friday--dear, good T.G.I.F. Day--the administrative "They" put them all together. Every student in high school gathered in the gym. There on the stage I took my throne-- the piano bench--and "taught" Combined Chorus. While everyone else had an extra free period. And teachers scream today when class sizes exceed 25!

But, thank Heaven, these were mostly good kids, so far as behavior was concerned. Musically...? While I twanged out songs from The Golden and The Silver and The Brown versions of "The ———————— Book of Favorite Songs," they sang with all their might, adopting the old adage, "If you can't be good, be loud."

The town of Bland was small, its population, I reckon, no more than 400 people. It had three business blocks. A half block south from Mrs. Steiner's brought us to the corner where Gertha and Bertha's General Store held forth. There we turned east one block past the Post Office... to Edna's Beauty Shoppe and Chris Schaepperkoetter's General Merchandise.

In the next block was John Homfeldt's General Merchandise and Bernard Homfeldt's Drug Store, Lahmeyer's Drugs & Sundries and the Krause Hardware.

The Bland International Shoe Factory was the third block. It kept Bland from disappearing from the face of the earth. At least one member--often two or three-- of almost every family worked in this enterprise. With the war in full sway, the product was Navy gloves. I couldn't imagine why the Navy needed so many gloves--but I guess I just don't know that much about naval supplies and wars. Many students, I soon found out, worked there on the extra shift--from 4 to 8 p.m. Everyone, I remember, was doing his bit for the cause of freedom. And the pay wasn't bad, either.

Next to my music stint, I despised Girls' P.E. the most. Our equipment was one softball and one bat. In the fall the boys, of course, played on the "good diamond." The girls and I were assigned a weed patch on the hillside south of the old, patched-up, red brick school building.

The girls were mostly farm girls--pretty, intelligent, eager to learn. And they made a colorful picture romping around the baseball diamond, with each one in a patterned cotton percale dress. Some of the dresses were made from printed feed sacks, a fad at the time. Three of these sacks--when emptied of the ground cattle and hog feed--would make a dress. If your dealer had only two bags of a particular pattern, you traded a sack of another print you didn't want to a neighbor and you had a new dress.

But in my mind, those bright dresses and a weed patch diamond didn't go well together. Our superintendent was a Mr. Thadeus Ellis (T.E.) McIntosh and our principal was Mr. Richard Terrill. They, with Miss Smith and me, completed our faculty. So with the full weight of one-fourth of the faculty, I soon went to Mr. McIntosh and asked if the weeds could be cut--some way. I meant with a tractor and a mower.

"Yes," he told me cordially, "you and the girls are perfectly welcome to cut them anyway you can."

I saw right then that he and I were going to become fast friends!

I reported back to the girls. They were furious. "I'll tell Dad what he said," said Gladys Michel, one of my favorites. "Dad"--Henry Michel--arrived early the next morning, mowed the weeds, skinned off the rough spots and we were in good shape. So good, in fact, that the boys wanted to trade diamonds with us!

I knew about as much about P.E. as I did music. But the girls knew. So for three years I "coached" ball games of all varieties--in the autumn it was softball; in the winter, basketball and volleyball.

A few years earlier the Bland boys had won second place in the state basketball tournament and they were always trying to do it again. The entire town ate, slept and played basketball. The men on the street argued about which boy was the best player. Farmers often came early to pick up their children and watch the team "practice a little." There was almost an overabundance of school spirit.

Worse, they considered Owensville their mortal enemy. I teetered on the fence: The boys on the Owensville team had been my students two years before. But the girls "helped" keep me in line and rooting--at least in public--for Bland.

Because I taught Music, most of my classes were assigned to the "Music Room." This was a large, cold enclosure on the northeast corner of the building, from whence the winter winds blew. In it was a piano, four large homemade tables and 30 to 35 folding chairs. During music classes I sat at the piano. During academic classes I stood at the front of the class and faced those four tables of boys and girls.

From this eminence I guided them through Hammurabi, Hannibal, Alexander the Great, the myriad bones of the body, the circulation of its blood, pylorus and "Pygmalion", Missouri statehood, John Brown's Raid, Jesse James, all of the Who's Who in Missouri...

Then I'd walk the length of the hall to the "English Room." Here we defined, parsed, diagrammed and tested for the rudiments of decent grammar.

But the climax of my day came during the last period with World Geography. It was required for graduation and offered only on alternating years. So all Juniors and Seniors had to take it. This made a sizeable class so we met in the Study Hall. This was a long room connecting my music room and the English room. It also was the library.

To complicate matters further, we had no geography books. I don't know what the previous teacher had used and it was weeks before the books I ordered arrived. So I improvised. From my own high school copy of "World Geography" I wrote notations on the blackboard for them to copy into a notebook. We located loads of places--cities and towns and countries found in the war news. And we learned to spell most of them. I drew heavily, too, from my college course--that one with the list of 300 "well-known physical features."

There's only one thing wrong with a class like this; the teacher is responsible for all the lecturing--and any teacher who does that is a fool. But I did. Finally, our books arrived--large and blue and typically geographic in appearance. And, oh, so disappointing on the inside. I had to agree with Wes Wittrock, the custodian, who always sat in my class because "It's so downright interestin'."

"Let's just throw the book away," he said, "and go on with that stuff you wuz teachin' before."

But teachers are so book conscious. And we read it and I re-read it because it required concentration.

The hour-long classes stretched into lengthy days...made longer with the chore of "waiting for the second run." This meant staying after school until the bus driver delivered his first load of students and came back for the remainder. Mr. McIntosh drove the "Red Bird Bus" (or the "Red Bird Express," as the students called it) so he never pulled this late-day assignment. Usually either Miss Smith or I stayed with the high school youngsters, along with one of the elementary teachers.

While we waited there was only one acceptable thing to do: Go to the gym and play ball. Even the tiny first graders would be there, scurrying around in their tennis shoes and sometimes heavy jackets. But in their own estimation they were six feet tall. "Watch me, Teacher," they'd shout. "Watch me! See, I can get the ball in...almost."

While I watched and nodded at their prowess, I could hear the pep squad from the balcony shouting at the top of its collective lungs, "We want Lefty - We want Lefty - If Lefty can't do it, Righty can. Righty - Righty - Lefty - Lefty. If Righty can't do it, Lefty can."

Lefty and Righty were twins--Norman and Armin Peth. Both were good basketball players. Lefty was right-handed and Righty was left-handed and--naturally--some town wit had long ago dubbed them the opposite. And in the process he had given rise to a rhythmic chant for the basketball team.

I often thought that my days must be as regulated as Pete's over there somewhere in the Pacific. The factory whistle blew at seven a.m.--sharp--and its blast seemed to ramrod every man, woman and child in Bland and the surrounding countryside into action. The people who worked there had to punch in for duty. The ones who didn't work inside the steamy, smoky, smelly structure sold goods or services to those who did.

Mrs. Steiner always rose early, moving swiftly about the kitchen, preparing her delicious coffee, toast, eggs, cereal, bacon or sausage, and sometimes waffles. Never--bless her--no, never biscuits! After she put the coffee on, she went to the basement and shook down the furnace. This rumpus usually rousted me and Beda, a goodhumored sleepy head, out of bed. We took turns in the bathroom, dressed, made the bed and laid out our coats, scarves, gloves and such--at the ready after breakfast to take off for school.

While we ate breakfast, Mrs. Steiner would go to the stair door and call to Dorothy, "Honey, get up now. It's time to get up." After two or three calls, Dorothy tromped grumpily down the steps and plopped into a chair, glaring critically at the table. If none of the food appealed to her, she glared at us some more and stalked into the living room, where she would take a nap on the divan. I suspect Dorothy resented what had happened to her, to her mother. Certainly, her father's death left an impact. Also, now she was sharing her home and her mother with Beda and me. Sometimes she walked to school with us, but usually she took a longer route so she could meet Betty Ann Phelps and Paris Ruth Jett.

At school the buses often were late--especially Mr. McIntosh's Red Bird Express. He never learned to drive the thing and the students' report came to be almost routine: "He got off in the ditch--again." When the much-battered bus arrived, the children would scurry to their classrooms, ashamed at being late. But

Mr. Mc took his own sweet time getting into the building, sauntering up the steps and meandering toward his office, munching on the remains of a juicy red apple.

Occasionally he got around to visiting the classes he was supposed to be teaching, but his visits were...well, short of enlightening. He had stock answers for any questions his students might ask: "It's in the book" and "What does the book say?"

Always a step or two behind her husband came Mrs. McIntosh. I've heard it said that when two people live together a long time, they begin to look alike. That had happened to the McIntoshes. They both had gray hair, they both had red faces. They both wore gray clothes. Always. They were both of medium height, and both walked at a loping, no-hurry gait.

And all of us--Mr. Terrill and I and all the students--soon noticed how often during the day the McIntoshes eyed the one and only big, round clock face on the wall just above the study hall door. And during the last hour of the day their eyes fastened on it as they waited impatiently for the welcome sound of that four o'clock bell.

Suddenly, they came alive. Mr. Mc dashed out of the tiny office cubicle above the stairway. Mrs. Mc rushed down the stairs, a step or two behind him, and out the front door they flew. Once aboard the Red Bird Express, Mr. Mc would lean on the horn to warn late passengers he was taking off...right now. Then came his turning around process--shifting gears, gunning the motor, backing up, twisting the steering wheel. Then it would happen. *Ker-plop*, off he would go into a ditch. Trained by now, the boys would jump off and push, then run for dear life to catch the bus in motion, because when Mr. Mc got it going, he never stopped.

Of such were the contributions of Mr. Mc to my days. In retrospect, he enlivened many of them. Or lived in them, perhaps, is a better phrase.

So did Miss Virginia Smith, the English teacher. She had taught the third grade for many years without marked success; now she was trying to teach high school. Poor Miss Smith. She had, in my estimation, the least qualification of any person I've ever known in the teaching profession. She had no idea of how to discipline, tease, cajole--or force--an assignment out of a student.

She looked like yesteryear's teacher--medium height, broad of beam, her red nose set squarely in the middle of a broad, serious face, around which her mouse-colored hair strung in a dozen wisps. One wisp was always working its way toward her mouth--and only at the last moment did she brush it away. She wore this mass of hair long and combed back into an untidy knot on the back of her head. Her clothes were brown or gray or black. She had long lived in Bland and many of the youngsters' parents had gone to school to her--and many were the tales about escapades aimed at her, often ending with her crying and begging the students to be good. But the teaching profession--like any other, I suppose--was not immune to misfits, wartime or no wartime.

Mr. Terrill was the Science teacher and the basketball coach. He knew about as much about basketball as I did music--but we both put on a brave front and did the best we could. Like Mr. Mc., Mr. Terrill owned a farm out on the Dry Fork, so he was always in a hurry to get away and do his farm chores.

My "second day," like theirs, started after four o'clock. Usually there was music to work on for the next day. War songs were popular and I worked out my own system for playing them--mostly by ear. The boys loved "Johnny Got a Zero," "The White Cliffs of Dover," "Anchors Aweigh," "The Marines' Hymn" and "Rosie the Riveter." The girls sang those plus "Don't Sit Under the

Apple Tree," "Chattanooga ChooChoo," "Stage Door Canteen," "Marsey Doats and Dozey Doats," "I Never Knew Any Girl (Boy) Like You" and "They're Either Too Young or Too Old."

The town girls stayed at school to practice their pep routines. The first and second basketball teams stayed on to work out winning strategies. Wes and Mrs. Wittrock came in to sweep and dust. They were a fine, jolly couple. And so clean. Her dresses were always starched and ironed perfectly. They were friendly and kind to me--as were all the parents of the students. It was a warm, friendly family feeling I was privileged to share during those years at Bland.

After all of these extra curricular activities were finished, I could rush home to Mrs. Steiner's clean, comfortable home and there eat a well-prepared meal and spend a few hours on my needlework, grading those unending test papers or writing letters to the boys in service. Our light came from one bulb hanging from a cord in the center of the room, so Beda and I put a pillow against the foot of the bed to be underneath it.

We usually reserved Sunday and Monday nights for letter writing. Beda was engaged to Emmett Dillon, who was in the Pacific area. Pete had been sent to Eniwetok, 10 days before completing two years in Hawaii. But his stay there was short; he landed on Saipan on June 15th and was there 35 days. I wrote long letters to him, telling him what was going on in quiet little Bland. Bant, too, was moving around; from Washington University he was sent to Amarillo, Texas to try out for officer's training. But his eyes failed to hold the target in testing and he was sent to Sioux Falls, South Dakota, to communications school. A few weeks later he was sent to England.

The war was growing in intensity in both theatres and when Bant told us about his overseas assignment he thought he would have no chance to see us before he was shipped out. So we were pleasantly surprised one Friday evening in late February when he called. He would be at Scott Air Force Base for the weekend and wouldn't some of us, please, come to see him?

The family council began. I wanted so much to go, but I wanted Mom to go more. Besides, I couldn't bear to go and think it could be the last time I'd see him. So it was decided: Mom and Bud would go. Dad and I would stay home. We all agreed, too, that they should leave about 2 a.m. to arrive at the air base early in the morning.

All was made ready the previous evening. The weather was bitterly cold. As Mom and I prepared hot coffee and the usual bacon and eggs, we noticed large flakes of snow floating lazily to the ground. But the chosen two soon donned their best clothes and were ready to start. Dad carried the big Rochester kerosene lamp to the front door to light the way down the front steps and out to the dependable, old blue Chevrolet waiting at the gate. Snow came down swiftly and Mom and Bud disappeared into the car.

We heard the thud of the car door, then they were on their way. Dad and I returned to the dining room where a wood fire crackled and spit in the old heater. When Dad put the lamp down on the table, I spotted Mom's glasses. Too late. I couldn't hope to catch them by doing what we so often did--dashing out the smokehouse gate and running pell mell across the point of the hill. Mom depended heavily on those glasses. I remember thinking she might not be able to see how Bant looked!

I wondered later how many other families all over the country had been doing the same thing, sending some members off to Scott Field to see a son or brother, perhaps for the last time, while some stayed behind at home. And I wondered what they did while they waited...

Dad and I washed the dishes, then sat down to await daybreak. Early light seemed a good time to begin a peculiar chore. A day or so before Bud had brought home from Tom Miller's a filthy, flea-bitten puppy. He needed a thorough cleaning up. So, together, Dad and I spent the morning, heating water in the oval porcelain wash kettle, bathing the puppy, combing the snarls out of his long black hair and dosing him with kerosene to kill the fleas and lice. When we finished he was a darling, friendly--and clean--pup.

Bozo grew into one of our all-time favorite dogs--principally, I think, because he was so stupid. He would never learn anything--not even when it concerned his own welfare. His great fun, for instance, was to bark and nip the farm mules on the hocks. The mules, however, didn't think it funny at all. They would be patient to a degree, then they would haul off and kick Bozo halfway across the barn lot. There he would lie in an unconscious heap for 15 or 20 minutes. Then he'd get up, shake his head to clear the cobwebs and go right back to his barking and nipping.

He did learn one helpful chore. He could catch any chicken you pointed out to him and hold it with his forepaws until Mom or I took it from him. He acted so important when he accomplished this, as if to say, "I can do one thing well."

While Dad and I worked on the beautification of Bozo, Mom and Bud were battling the elements. The snow continued to fall, making the highways almost impassable. On the way, they realized the possibility of a large crowd assembling at Scott Air Force Base that day--that they were probably among hundreds of people on the same mission. So Bud thought it wise to leave the car in Maplewood and take a bus into St. Louis. From downtown terminals buses ran regularly to the Air Base.

It was God's blessing sent to simple people that he and Mom actually got to see Bant for a few hours because he didn't know anybody was coming to see him and Mom and Bud were among hundreds of other families sent to the Visitors' Center to look for "their boy." Mom liked to tell later, "I never saw so many people in all my born days, and everybody trying to see their boys all at once."

Happy at seeing Mom and Bud, Bant returned to his barracks to face "only" his shipping out Monday to England. But the two travelers spent the entire night getting home--amid frequent wondering if they'd make it at all.

Between Scott and St. Louis the bus slid off the road and all the men jumped off and pushed it back on track. At the St. Louis terminal Bud met Bill Lahmeyer from Bland and a slight acquaintance of Bill's, also from Bland. They wanted a ride home. But the slight acquaintance was bringing home a trunk and it wouldn't fit in our car. The men solved that problem, however; they lashed the trunk on top of the car. This, of course, necessitated driving with the car windows down a couple of inches--enough room for the ropes. And snow.

The men, however, came in handy. The road by this time was covered with ice and snow, and when Bud saw he wasn't going to make it up a slick hill, Bill and friend would jump out before the car stalled completely and push. Aided by several such efforts, Mom and Bud slid in home at 6 a.m. on Monday--just in time for me to load my suitcase and start for Bland.

The week promised to be a long one. I was tired from being up nearly all night for two consecutive nights. The snow was heavy and deep. We waded through it twice a day on the days we went home for lunch--which I did if possible because lunch at Mrs. Steiner's was a pleasant occasion.

We had an hour off, unless it was your week to supervise the kids who brought their lunch. On those days I carried my sandwich and Thermos bottle in a paper bag and ate at my English room desk--grading papers while I munched.

Lunch at Mrs. Steiner's had two attractions: One, she was an excellent cook and, second, usually some International Shoe inspectors were there. Some were "regulars"; others came only once or twice and we never saw them again.

At noon Mrs. Steiner set the table in the dining room because Florence Jannick had come to board. She occupied the large, front bedroom. And Arthur Harring, a fine young man who worked at a machine job in the factory, became a noontime regular.

Earl Crites and his wife, Katherine, always spiced up the conversation when they came to dinner. They had a room at N.B. Stockton's and ate their three meals at Mrs. Steiner's. Both were extremely short and fat; both always ran late. They would come in for breakfast, panting, and Earl would announce, "Katherine, we'll have saucer and blow." And Katherine would cool her coffee by quickly pouring it into the saucer and blowing hard on it, pursing her fat lips together. But "saucer and blow" became useful to me and Beda to describe hurried mornings thereafter.

For the three years I taught at Bland I didn't need a watch to keep track of time. At a quarter till seven--sharp--all the car motors in Bland (or so it seemed) sputtered, chugged and clattered off in the direction of that green-eyed monster, "Inter National." From its rooftop, promptly at 7 o'clock each morning, that whistle sounded. Again, at 12:00 p.m., the cars sputtered and chugged and clattered--headed somewhere for lunch. And at 4 p.m. the factory's "You can go now" whistle blew--but with an ominous trailing sound as it died, as if to say, "But you'll be back at seven." At changing of shifts, people walking home from work hustled along the sidewalks as if the go-to-work whistle was Chrybdis and would suck them back inside Inter National for another eight-hour shift.

Some men and women spent most of their lives inside that building. The women worked alongside their husbands, sometimes earning more. They worked by the case, sewing those gloves. Those high school boys and girls worked the four-hour shift from 4 to 8 p.m., sewing straps and buckles. They had to be excused from their last hour class, usually P.E.

But this was war time. Everybody sacrificed. We had a common bond: Nearly everyone had a son, a husband, a brother, a grandson in the service. Some returned only for burial. Some never came back home.

THE NEW WORLD

Bant heads overseas and the
Steiners mourn the death of Charles.

I was at home for the weekend when I heard that Mr. and Mrs. Henry Steiner had been notified of the death of their oldest son, Charles, in Europe. He was their pride and joy and had been the Bland boys' favorite basketball coach when he was inducted. I dreaded the return to Bland, but dread doesn't postpone the inevitable.

On Sunday evening as I deposited my suitcase inside my bedroom door, Mrs. Steiner came in from the back porch. "Come with me," she said. "Aunt Clara wants you." Without speaking, we walked next door. Aunt Clara was lying on a couch in her living room. The shades were pulled; only a table lamp burned dimly on the far side of the room. Erline, Charles' widow, was there. Everyone had been crying; all eyes were swimming in tears. I sat and held Aunt Clara's hand. Words choked us.

War had come to Bland in full force. More and more I thought about Pete and Bant. Would this happen to them? Would I be mourning as Aunt Clara and Uncle Henry were mourning now? And how could I face Raymond, Charles's younger brother and one of my favorite pupils?

At the memorial service a picture of Charles was placed on a small table at one side of the M.E. Church. Raymond sat quietly in the front pew with his father and mother. Beda and I sat directly behind them with Mrs. Steiner and Dorothy. The service was short, interrupted by deep sighs and quiet sobs from Aunt Clara and Erline.

At home later, Ella made coffee and we carried it and cookies across the back yard to Aunt Clara and Uncle Henry, Raymond and Erline and the others next door. We sat in the kitchen, huddled, speaking in low tones, all of us wishing we could wave a magic wand and bring back the cheer and sunshine of last year, last week, yesterday--days unappreciated for their absence of grief.

But life goes on. The whole world doesn't go dark because one candle has suddenly been extinguished. Each of us took up his own day again and went bungling through. Some of us bungle more than others; I seem to have a special talent for doing and saying the wrong things.

But I needn't have worried about Raymond. Young people, it seems to me, have a strength and resiliency to bear these things. After a few days he was his usual cheerful self, going about his business--and his basketball practice--as always. He had a basketball backboard and hoop affixed to the gable of his father's garage, and for hours on end he crouched, poised, with the ball on his fingertips, leaped into the air, sighted and shot the ball through the hoop.

The team nicknamed him "Stinky," and it stuck, even when he became a professional player with the Phillips 66 Oilers. I guessed that the name was one of those opposites; he was immaculately clean, every hair in place and creases razor sharp in his trousers.

I'm sure Stinky became more and more precious to his father and mother. Their middle son, Weldon, was also in the service then, still stationed in the states.

But there were good times, too, with home made fun, I call it. I became friends with several young women who worked in the office or on the machines at International. Maxine Scheel, Margaret Branthorst, Lora and Hilda Drewel and others often came by after work or to spend an evening stitching on fancy work, writing letters, sitting around the dining room table, comparing notes and picking out bits and pieces of interesting conservation to quote to faraway servicemen.

Some evenings we played pinochle or bridge. And many an evening I was prevailed upon to open up the school so we could play volley ball. I didn't really like this, but they took on the responsibility of helping me clean up the gym floor and lock up the building afterward. At Bland you had to be sports-minded!

About this time the pep squad girls began to feel neglected and unappreciated. They wanted a bigger role in the basketball season. What could they do? I was stumped. How could you inject young ladies into a definitely boys' game? In those days of gas rationing, they weren't always even able to go to the "away" games.

After much thought, I asked what they would think of crowning a basketball queen and letting each member of the team escort one of the pep squad members to the stage. They'd be the queen's court. The Queen, of course, would be escorted by the team captain.

They jumped on the idea. The boys chose the Queen by secret vote--counted in secret by me and Mr. Terrill. The first choice was Maurine Koenig--frail, blonde, sweet Maurine. She was a lovely Queen.

All of the girls of the "Court" rounded up formal gowns. If they didn't own one, they borrowed one and stitched up the hems and pinned in the seams or let them out, whichever their figures demanded. And we ordered sweet pea corsages from Jefferson City. In those years we were forever ordering sweet pea corsages. And carnations for the boys. Those extras, mind you, cost 75 cents and were paid for out of hard-earned money.

The whole business was no small task. First, we had to compile a list of those who wanted the added decoration; then we had to collect the money and leave the order at Bernard Homfeldt's Drug Store at least two days before our special event. Bernard or Gladys handed the order to the driver of the ice cream truck who carried it to Busch's Florists in Jefferson City. If he weren't coming back through Bland on the day of the big affair, he would phone the driver for Fashion Cleaners, who also stopped at Homfeldt's to leave and pick up cleaning. So by some hook or crook (My goodness, that phrase shouldn't reflect on those drivers!), our flowers were always delivered, although there were times when I shared some anxious moments with the girls.

Flowers were so important to them, and I must admit they made a bright spot on each gown. These kids never forgot, either, to "chip in" an extra nickel to buy a special corsage for me. These basketball crownings--conceived out of my desperate flounderings to involve girls more fully in a boys sport--have become an annual event in these central Missouri towns where basketball is still big. And that still includes Bland.

19

I take up hitchhiking

It was in early winter of my second year at Bland when Bud lost our gas ration book. Or, rather, the book disappeared. We never thought of locking anything and I think someone "filched" it out of the glove compartment of our old blue Chevrolet. The stamps in that book were all-important. No stamps, no gas. No gas, no travel by auto. No auto travel, no weekends at home. And it would take months of red tape to get a duplicate.

I would have to hitch hike, a recourse not to my liking. It has always been hard for me to ask someone to do something for me. So when I spotted a neighbor in town I'd blush and timidly ask if I could get a ride home. Most of them, I'm sure, were glad to accommodate me, but I was uncomfortable in the role. And sometimes in the outcome of a ride...

One evening I rode home with Mr. Kraenow and Bernard, our neighbors on the south. After I left them, I had a mile and a half of woods pasture to walk through and a creek to cross. Asking for a ride had been bad enough and I hadn't given the creek a second thought until I reached it. Fall rains had washed it out along the far bank and it was running several feet deep with swift water.

I walked up and down a gravel bar, carrying my suitcase full of soiled clothes. Finally I spied a fallen tree further down the creek. It made a natural bridge, sort of--if I could climb up the roots and hold on to the small trunk...and not think about falling six feet or so into the swift stream rushing below me. I was positive I could balance myself. But the suitcase...I had to carry it, too.

I had to try. I climbed up the root wad, stood up, took a deep breath, balanced the suitcase in front of me--like a tightrope walker, I thought, in a last-minute whiff of confidence--and started the perilous journey. Carefully, slowly I placed each foot on the slippery tree trunk. I remember being glad it wasn't a sycamore. I wanted to close my eyes, but couldn't. I don't think they even blinked. I did survive. I reached the opposite bank, struggled through the limbs and landed on solid ground. From there I could see our house and I began to feel the security of home.

Enough, though, of hitching rides at random. I finally fell on the idea of riding with Grace Hayes and a group of neighborhood women who worked in the factory. Grace drove a panel truck and picked up passengers all along the String Town Road leading into Belle, then down Highway 28 to Bland. So I began a wholly new experience, marked by enlightening encounters and assorted adventures.

Grace was a natural born wit with a gift for colorful conversation and a fear of nothing. Her large family would have been more than enough to keep most women well occupied at home, but that factory money could buy many articles that she and these other women had never known. Grace and her family I knew quite well, but I had to learn to know the others.

Laura Hassler, Grace's niece by marriage, was a stout little woman of Russian extraction. She was the wife of First Hassler but she called him Frank. "First, dat sounds like a number," she explained. "I call him Frank, which is his name, too."

Opal Tyree, Grace's sister-in-law, must have been one of the Seven Wonders of the World. She had to be to live with Joe and be the mother of numerous children. They lived in a tiny, three-room shack--with a pack of hound dogs occupying equal space with the family. Opal bore the brunt of Grace's wit but never seemed to mind it.

Sis Tyree was the daughter of some of Grace's brothers or sisters. Their family tree was a tangle which I never got completely straightened out in my mind. Sis lived with her grandmother--Aunt Suzan Tyree, we called her--in a small shack up the road from Joe and Opal.

Grace picked up other various and sundry passengers, but these were the regulars.

As the winter wore on, I became accustomed to our loose arrangement. If I wanted to ride, I'd wait for Grace where our road left the main county road. But, of course, on the worst night of the year the telephone line broke under a heavy coating of ice and sleet and there was no way of letting Grace know I was to be one of her passengers on Monday morning.

Grace always left home promptly at five o'clock so Dad and I agreed we'd leave our house by 2 a.m. and walk the two miles or so to the Hays home. Dad dozed on the couch in the dining room and kept the wood fire going. I went to bed but not to sleep. Rising time came quickly. At 1 a.m. Dad and I had bowls of hot oatmeal with hot steamed bread--made by placing a colander over a boiling teakettle and melting gobs of butter on slabs of home made bread.

As soon as we swallowed our last bite, Dad lighted the kerosene lantern. I closed my suitcase and we donned our warmest outside coats, caps, head scarves, overshoes and gloves in preparation for the hike ahead. We stepped out into a perfectly gorgeous, snow-covered, brightly-moonlit world. We didn't need the lantern.

The road up our steep hill was almost impassable. Ice had formed a thick crust, then snow had fallen on top of it. You could hardly stand up, not to mention walk on it. We could save some distance, anyway, by way of the "school path." We all knew it well. It led up a steep knoll back of the granary and over a ledge of giant limestone rocks. Then we followed the wide V's of the sagging rail fence which separated the pasture around the house from the hog pasture. This morning the pansy patch was a mound of white snow and the rail fence was only a faint, gray zigzag in the deep white.

Here we began to drop into a hollow. The cedar trees cast dark shadows against the oaks and hickorys. We needed the lantern until we climbed another rail fence and picked up our way around a cluster of large slick rocks, always slippery, even without ice. This was the worst. Then we came out on the county road and turned northeasterly up a hill, steep, with no vehicle tracks marring its virgin whiteness. We floundered and fell and proceeded slowly past the Post Oak School. Beyond that, several hundred yards, lay the private road to the Hays farm.

Again we were aware of the beauty of the night. Snow on the ground heals the scars made by man. Once or twice a cottontail scurried out of a fallen log, headed for another shelter only he knew about.

Soon we could see the yellow, lamp-lighted windows of the Hays house. Grace and Roy were up. Dad and I literally slid down the last steep hill--"We could've made good time if it had been down hill all the way," Dad remarked on the way down--and we entered the kitchen where an almost unbelievable array of tasks were underway.

Grace and Roy had just finished their breakfasts. As they rushed around, both gulped mouthsful of black coffee. Grace was making things fly around six lunch buckets lined up on one end of the oval kitchen table. She sliced thick slabs of home made bread and laid one on the bottom of each bucket. Then, hefting a heavy iron skillet from the stove, she slapped two pieces of fried rabbit on each piece of bread, and topped them with more bread. Then she laid an apple beside each fried rabbit sandwich--with instructions to Roy not to put on the bucket lids until the rabbit cooled off enough "so's steam won't get on the lids."

Roy paid her no mind. He was busy, putting on his heavy coat to go outside and pour a teakettle of boiling water on the manifold and another one in the radiator of the panel truck.

"That ol' wreck jist might not start," he said matter of factly.

"That ol' wreck wouldn't dare," Grace retorted.

It didn't dare. It turned over. Roy gunned the motor a few times and Grace and

I climbed in, then Dad. He'd ride up to the county road--lighted lantern and all. Roy went back into the warm kitchen to get the kids up and off to school. (I decided on the spot he was the smartest one in the bunch.) We let Dad out at the county road to re-slide and re-slip his way home.

For about a mile all went well with Grace and me. Then steam boiled out of the radiator like a small Mt. Vesuvius erupting. Better uncap the radiator, Grace said. So out we jumped in the snow and, somehow, loosened the cap--enough for it to blow up in the air and bury itself in the snow. I started looking for it but Grace was impatient. "Wasn't doin' us no good no how," she said. "We'll find it when the snow melts."

Minus the radiator cap, we ran smoothly...until we came to Connard Hill. There we began to puff and steam again and the motor knocked and pounded with its last ounce of strength. We struggled up to the flat top of String Town Road and as we rounded the last curve and pulled up in front of Joe and Opal's low log cabin, the motor sputtered and gave a final groan.

Grace was not disturbed. She climbed out with a cheery invitation, "Come on in. Let's jolt Opal for a cup of coffee, because if anyone can fix this ol' wreck, Joe can."

Opal was glad to pour us a cup of the blackest, heaviest brew I had ever seen. Her children were all up and running around in various stages of dress and un-dress. Nellie Mae, perhaps fourteen, was mothering the little boys and helping them turn socks, get their overalls on, and their shoes on the right feet. Like Grace, Opal had an arrangement of dinner buckets on the kitchen table. I couldn't see what these contained, but Opal reminded Nellie to put some more coffee in the pot and "give the boys a jarful" to take to school. Children often brought coffee with cream in a glas jar and placed it near the stove to keep it warm until noon.

Joe was bundling up to "go attend to that wreck Grace was herdin' betwixt the ditches." He reckoned "Hit cain't be nothin' much if yuh pulled Connard Hill and got this fur." Opal had tied up her box containing her clean cotton print dress and a flannelette nightie--she stayed in town from Monday to Friday. She grabbed an empty coal oil can by the door and we were all ready to take off again--if Joe's mechanical ability matched Grace's faith in him.

He made a comical figure as he led the procession out the door and through the snow drifts--no cap, no jacket, no boots, his long, mouse-colored hair blowing out ahead of him as he carried a kerosene lamp in one hand for examining the motor. Joe was acutely cross-eyed and he had to turn his head far to the right as he looked for the source of our trouble.

"Git in," he told Grace, "and tromp on that thar starter."

Grace obeyed. The motor snorted. Joe leaned his long form over the motor and squinted his bad eye as he sighted his good one into the open radiator. "Danged thang ain't got no water in it," he yelled above the clanking. "Done bin drivin' it bone dry."

Grace yelled back that Roy had filled it before we left home.

"If'n he did, the dang fool didn't plug the petcock," said Joe. "Roy never though of nothin' important yit." He loped off to the kitchen for a teakettle of boiling water and filled the radiator while Opal held the lamp.

It worked. All went well as we headed again for town. We stopped for Sis and Laura, and in Belle the panel truck became loaded to capacity for its final run for Bland. We made it--at exactly 7:00, by the final whistle. Inter National's big wooden doors opened and sucked Grace, Opal, Laura and Sis into the realm of

Navy gloves, straps and buckles. And I wended my way to Mrs. Steiner's where I ate another breakfast, changed my snow clothes for school clothes and started another week.

The weather remained cold, snowy and blowy. The study hall where I spent two hours of each day was especially cold. Its entire south side was windows and when I went near them I could feel the good, cold fresh air squeezing in around the frames. And somewhere out there in the cold a sheet of tin roofing flapped in the wind, almost keeping time with the clock, *Tick, tock. Flap, flap.* Then *FLOP*, as the wind died down for a few minutes.

Evidently it bothered no one but me. I heard it in the music room, in the study hall and in the English room. I suppose I was more tired than usual from the strain of the strenuous weekend. But come Friday evening and I was ready to repeat the performance all over again with Grace, Sis, Opal, Laura, Sophia and the others.

As I climbed into the back of the panel truck a variety of odors greeted me. I could identify the coal oil. Opal's can was full and sporting a small potato on the spout to prevent spillage. And the onion--overpowering--was easy. Sis was in the process of making an onion sandwich for everybody. All hungry, the women eagerly accepted Sis's thick slices of onion between bread. I declined. Sis's hands were not overly clean. And she had just finished describing a small boil on her face by announcing, "Hit wuz botherin' me sumthin' terrible 'till I took it and squizzed it real good."

There also was the smell of new paint on metal. Laura had bought two bright red Express Flyer wagons, one for each of her two little girls. They were for Christmas. Laura's joy filled the panel truck.

She would have Frank hide them in the barn and the girls would be so surprised. Her broad, brown face beamed when she touched the treasures. If anyone shifted feet or moved, however slightly, Laura put out her small, square hand to protect the wagons.

Opal was guarding her coal oil, too. Grace knew Opal's intelligence was not great, but her capacity for goodnatured teasing was, so every few minutes Grace would inquire, "Opal, did you get your coal oil?"

Dutifully, Opal would reply, "Yep, I got it."

In a few minutes Grace would repeat the queston and Opal's answer never varied. Nor did her patience. But she never caught on that Grace was teasing. And I never caught on until years later that it was Grace's way of paying attention to Opal. With the Christmas spirit upon us, she was giving a little extra.

In Belle we added some new crew members and accompanying new odors. Buell Pointer joined us and I could smell new leather. He had a gunny sack tied in the middle for easy carrying over his shoulder. In one end, he told us proudly, were new leather shoes for his children; in the other, groceries.

On the farm-to-market road heading out of Belle, Opal began to giggle and point to a man walking along the road. "Looky yonder," she said, "what's Joe a-doin' up here?"

We stopped to let Joe join our jolly tour, but he'd beat us to the punch with jollity. His breath left no doubt as to what Joe had "been a-doin' up here." With whiskey-loosened tongue, he began to relate his trials of housekeeping:

"I ain't no woman, but that's what I bin ever since Opal went citified. Just one good thing about hit; ain't nobody to give me no back talkin'. No, sir, Opal. Ain't no back talkin'. Ain't I allus made ye a good livin'? Now, ain't I?"

He warmed up now and turned around to all of us. "But I'll tell youn's

JOE

Opal hadn't come home. "It was Ol' Plunger, asleep in the rockin' cheer."

somethin'. I woke up t'other night and heered the awfulest snorin' and I re'ched over t'other side of the bed. I though shore Opal had come home. Then I knowed she ain't. It was Old Plunger, asleep in the rockin' cheer."

Joe kept up his line of chatter all the way home. I tuned him in and out, lost mostly in my own thoughts of the coming Christmas and the strange warmth that filled this truckload of varied characters.

It was completely dark when we left Belle and all the houses along the way looked bright and cozy. Many had Christmas trees and decorations in the windows. Laura would turn to look wistfully, "Ain't the lights purty?" she'd say. "Makes me think of home." Then she would touch--ever so tenderly--the two little red wagons she was guarding so carefully.

We turned onto the String Town Road and one by one deposited our passengers. First was Buell--loaded with his shoes and coffee and salt bacon and other "vittles" in his gunny sack. He had a long walk across the snow-covered fields before he arrived home.

Then Laura. Frank came out to help her with her bundles. The yellow lamp light streamed from the house across the snow and we could see Frank (First) and Laura heading for the barn to hide the wagons.

Before Sophia Kwiatowski left us, she had to unwrap a cheap oval glass dish for all of us to admire. "It's for Laura," she said proudly. "That sister of mine always wanted purty things."

As we came to each little gray log house, it seemed that someone was anxiously awaiting a loved one. Aunt Suz stood in the doorway beckoning all of us in to "get a bite of hot soder biscuit." But we were all eager to be home, too.

The last stop--at Joe and Opal's--was simply joyous. All six youngsters, still in various stages of dress and undress, came tumbling out into the snow--along with Old Plunger--to greet their parents. Poor Nellie Mae looked serious and bedraggled. I wondered if she had ever got all the kids dressed at one time during the week.

All the while Joe, his liquor wearing off, was whining, "Now, Opal, you know I allus did make ya a good livin'. But you want to go 'n get citified. Cain't no man live with ya till ya git that citified notion out'n your haid." Wordlessly, Opal picked up her coal oil can and trudged toward the house.

Only Grace and I were left as we headed down Connard Hill and onto the Mistaken Creek concrete slab--and met our Waterloo. The truck stopped dead. Grace coaxed and fussed at it, all to no avail. Finally, we left it sitting and walked into Cooper Hill and called Roy from Frank Tschappler's Store.

It would take Roy a while to come on the tractor so Grace and I decided to give the stalled truck another try. We looked at each other in astonishment when it started. Not trusting it to keep going and to get a run at the steep incline, Grace gunned the motor. But she had it in reverse. We shot backward off the slab as the motor roared and the truck banged and scraped the edge of the concrete slab.

We climbed out the driver's side and over the radiator--the only part of the truck still on the slab--and stood back to survey the scene. I almost giggled, the poor little yellow bus looked so comical, its nose up in the air and its rear buried in ice and snow and water halfway up the side. But Grace was less than amused. I rescued my suitcase, clambering over the protruding radiator, and Grace hurriedly dispatched me on my way, knowing, I suspected, that Roy would not be overjoyed with the situation when he arrived.

I walked the remaining two miles from Mistaken Creek. Mom usually waited supper for me on Friday night, but I was long overdue and they were worried. When I appeared in the kitchen door faces lit up, the lamps were brought out from the dining room, the potato soup was ladled all around and all was well in my weekend world. Like the others in Grace's yellow panel truck, I had come home.

Those war time Christmas seasons brought a peculiar problem: Mailing packages to our boys overseas--then wondering if they were delivered in time. Or at all. A host of regulations governed the shape and sizes of boxes, and even what you could send to certain areas of the world. The daily papers carried this information, as well as long lists of acceptable gifts for the servicemen. Many mothers and girl friends sent cakes, cookies, home made candies and the like--even angel food cake packed in popped corn! Some seemed to arrive in good shape in Europe, the only "hazard" being voracious fellow soldiers or sailors. But Southeast Asia was a different story: Boys told of hanging the container from the ceiling on a wire to prevent ants and other vermin from getting it.

Except for ten days on Tinian in July, Pete had been on Saipan since June 15th. He had come in contact with that fearful Dengue Fever, better known to servicemen as break-bone fever. He wrote only occasionally, usually a Victory letter, but he did write that he had been very ill, so I wanted to send him something especially nice for Christmas. He liked Wildroot Hair Creme, so I searched everywhere for a bottle of that and some Quinsana, a preparation for treating athlete's foot, which he also had asked for. These two items, together with a package of hard candy (on the government's "recommended" list) was all I could squeeze into the little government-approved rectangular wooden box.

Then came facing Mr. Edgar Stone, the postmaster. Everyone in Bland, it seemed, was hurrying to mail these little boxes--and get them past Edgar Stone. He was cranky about any piece of mail but he gloried in rigid adherence to all of the fine-print details of wartime overseas packages. My heart would turn over and land in my throat when I had any kind of package to mail.

"What's inside, young lady?"

"How have you packed it?"

"How, now, is it tied?"

No matter. It was always wrong.

Both Beda and I had to carry our little wooden boxes back to Mrs. Steiner's and unwrap them, re-pack and re-wrap and re-tie them several times...until our annoyance overcame our timidity. Finally, we sent our packages to Owensville by Henry Steiner for mailing there.

Months later, in a Victory letter, Pete acknowledged receipt of the little box. The powder for his athlete's foot had come open and spilled all over his candy. He would just spread a thin layer of candy between his toes, he wrote, and he was sure it would have curative value. I was so disappointed--and plain mad. I was sure Edgar Stone was to blame--although I couldn't quite figure out how.

Then came the bright spot in my Christmas vacation. Dad and I always put up a tree and decorated it, principally for Yvonne and Anna Lo. Their eyes would sparkle with delight, especially when the packages were handed out. Mae always made hand-embroidered dish towels or a housecoat or something nice for me. When the girls came to this package, they would bring it to me and say, "Us made iss for you." And they'd stand by to bask in my praise of them.

Wartime rationing put a crimp in my usual fruit cake making. It was hard to get the fruit. But I substituted raisins and home made candied orange peel for the traditional dates, cherries and store-bought candied fruit. Mae made fruit cake,

OVERSEAS GIFTS

Pete figures that hard candy sprinkled with Quinsana will surely cure athlete's foot.

too, aided on the sly by Yvonne and Lo. They were enamored with the ripening process, when Mae sprinkled the cake with wine to keep it moist. One day she checked the cake and found it soaked, reeking of wine. "I told you," said Yvonne, when questioned, "Lo and I already took care of it!"

Christmas was scarcely past when Mom made her usual announcement: "Won't be long now until we can make garden. I think we'll just butcher while you're home this week." She always acted as if the thought just struck her. The next day the big kettle was put on and the water heated. And from that moment until the last bit of head cheese and stuffed sausage was fried down, there was no "peace in our valley." I was thankful to start back to Bland and breathe fresh air untainted by the odor of rendering lard and frying sausage. But I must admit that those home-cured hams, shoulders and sides of bacon and that home-canned sausage would be quite appetizing the following summer.

20

Two-wiener sticks and other fun

With nine-month terms of school, we considered the term half finished at Christmas time. Then everyone began to look forward to spring. The days lengthened, the sunshine returned and flocks of redbirds began to inspect the rose bushes and cedar trees for new housekeeping facilities. And with the first semblance of a warm day, someone voiced the eternal cry, "Let's go on a weiner roast." Upon me was always bestowed the privilege of "walking to the Dry Fork" with the kids--a high honor preceded by a sudden onslaught of leg ache. Dry Fork must have been four miles or so out of town. And I knew every gravel in the road, every tree and every shrub along the ditches and fencerows.

Come 4 o'clock on the appointed day, and a good crowd would have gathered. The hot dogs would have been purchased, the buns and marshmallows, the pickles and the mustard divided into "fair share" bags for the big boys to carry. I'd hurry to Mrs. Steiner's and change into low heels, a slack suit and head scarf. All the girls did the same, and in a half hour we were all hiking out the highway to the Dry Fork road.

Here we turned south on a gravel road. The pace was fast because the kids were hungry. Getting there, building a big bonfire and letting it die down to wiener-roasting, hot-coals size was the Big Thought. While the fire blazed high the boys took off to the woods to cut forked sticks to roast the wieners. These were usually date affairs, so each boy wanted a two-wiener stick.

Despite the best laid plans and intentions--made with full stomachs--everyone usually was so hungry that we started roasting before the fire had burned low enough. In which case, the wieners caught fire and burned black. We ate them anyway. Our burned-wiener recipe was, "Pour on lots of mustard and you'll never know the difference."

Later came the marshmallows, toasted on the same sticks. By this time we'd all be in a better mood, warm and with full bellies.

For the climax of our "big" evening we sat around the fire and sang--war songs like "The White Cliffs of Dover," "Johnny Got a Zero" and perennial campfire favorites like "Home on the Range" and "Let the Rest of the World Go By."

After a couple of hours around the campfire--sometimes even before full darkness fell--we headed back toward town. Some took a byroad or a path through the woods, a shortcut to home and, perhaps, a short stint of neckin'. These forms of recreation were so simple and so inexpensvie by today's standards. These rural teenagers were taught respect for economy and work. And I learned that enjoyment was an effective antidote to anticipatory leg aches.

For even less formal entertainment we had a small town's usual cast of characters. Would that I were a gifted writer to fully portray them. I can only sketch them in broad outline, but if you've lived in a small town, you'll recognize them.

I should thank Albert Phelps for many moments of amusement. Albert drove the feed truck for John Lahmeyer. He was seldom ever sober. But he was a hardy soul. Every morning he walked from his home six miles or so into town to drive the delivery truck.

Driving that truck was a feat in itself. It was a mere skeleton--mindful of a shell-struck World War I model--no doors, no rack to hold sacks of feed. A motor, a fender or two and a battered chassis--that was it. It had no brakes so Albert parked it against the curb. He had to crank it to start it, so with one hand holding back the truck, he would crank and crank and crank. When it finally gave a chug, Albert would run quickly to the driver's side and adjust the necessary gadgets to keep it going. All of this would have been taxing for a sober fellow. With Albert, it was hilarious. And nobody in our section of town tried to talk until Albert safely guided his truck out on the road.

And Henry Koening. Henry always wanted Mrs. Steiner to bake him a cake. He was a harmless, gentle soul and wanted to do the right thing. Always he asked Mrs. Steiner how much sugar the recipe called for; after all, it was rationed. And always he brought it in a small brown paper bag, all weighed out exactly. But he never realized that the frosting required sugar, too. So Mrs. Steiner always used her own sugar for it, because Henry always admonished her to make "that there icin' good 'n thick."

And I won't forget the Rev. Allen, the M.E. minister. He also taught the 7th and 8th grades. He was a tall, slender man, built rather like a pulpit. Any word ending in "a" with his back-East pronunciation, came out "er." In church he was often calling on "Alpher and Omeger" to help him out. And when any all-school activity was planned, he never failed to volunteer: "I'll look after the 'soder pop'."

Then there was Lowell Terrill. Lowell was a strapping, six-foot hulk who had been an amateur wrestler in his younger days. Usually he came to town to pick up his girls after school--and to stop at Gross's Tavern. Then the incongruous sight wouldn't be long in coming--small, pale, white-haired Bob Gross ushering an inebriated Lowell out to his truck. But the comic aspect for me was sobered by the sight of four little, cold girls waiting patiently for their daddy, shivering under a dirty quilt on the truck seat.

Ezra Koenig was something of a curiosity; he knew all...well, a little...about everything. Or almost everything. Ezra managed the bookkeeping department for his brother, George, the superintendent of the factory. He also was the "vent" for George's anger. But Ezra was so bent on holding his job that he never returned the bad treatment bestowed upon him so lavishly.

Ezra also filled in for any town emergency. If you needed a check cashed, Ezra performed the service--for a small remuneration, of course. If Bernard Homfeldt needed to be away from the drug store over the weekend, Ezra sold the patent medicine and manned the "soder fountain." If cranky Mr. Stone at the post office was indisposed, Ezra sorted the mail. And if the Evangelical and Reformed minister was late returning from his rural charge on Sunday morning, Ezra took over and opened services.

I was there one Sunday morning when Ezra started a sermon on "Jeremiah and the wall of Jericho," only to be cut short by the appearance of the regular minister. I've never known what Ezra was building up to, but I'm positive it would have had a fine moral at the end, like "Cast thy bread upon the water and your chickens will come home to roost." That was one of his favorite quotes. I never figured out if he were that mixed up metaphorically or if he meant to be funny.

A different kind of "amusement" for me in my years at Bland was shopping. Mr. and Mrs. Chris Schaeperkoetter and their daughters, Fern and Violet, ran a fine, clean General Merchandise store on Main Street and it became my principal stopping place to and from school. If an item was hard to get, Schaeperkoetter's was my best hope.

With the war, many kinds of groceries were hard to get. Sometimes grocers would have no sugar or no meat. Bolts of yard goods were doled out like precious commodities. Yardage was limited--no more than four yards of one piece to a customer. When a new supply of yard goods, embroidery thread, hose, handkerchiefs and such came in, Beda and I were usually among the first to be notified. Today I still feel the thrill of inspecting those delicious shades of lavender, coral, pink and green skeins of thread as Fern exclaimed over each one:

"Just look. This is a new one. We've never had this shade before."

I made a good customer. I was enamored with pretty embroidered pillow slips, table cloths, crocheted doilies--even difficult sheets. Nobody could get sheets. Everybody was pleased to get unbleached domestic and hem their own. But one day white cotton percale sheets arrived in Bland. These were "under the counter" merchandise--soon gone if put on display.

When I went home at noon, Fern was waiting for me in front of the store. Those sheets had arrived, she whispered. Would I like some?

Lordy, yes. I had ordered some stamping patterns in hopes of just such a stroke of good luck. Now I proceeded to stamp and stitch like silly. Scarcity, indeed, enhances desire.

The Schaeperkoetters had one son, Alvin, in service; that was another bond between us. I didn't know Alvin, but from his parents' and sisters' descriptions, he was one of the world's seven or eight wonders. They kept us up to date on Alvin's location, his hardships--starting with how he never should have gone to war because he was their only son.

The end of the war seemed to be in sight. The European theatre was becoming much more quiet. Bant wrote of being billeted in the Mouser Mansion on the Rhine River--and of a young German woman housekeeper, Maria, who darned the troops' socks and did their laundry. He was glad to leave England with its fish and chips wrapped up on newspapers--and its mist and fog.

He wrote, too, of seeing pretty peasant girls hoeing potatoes in France. But he didn't relish the odor of garlic when he rode the street cars over there. Once he drove in a convoy of Army trucks loaded with Jeeps across the Bavarian Alps to Germany. Little ol' Bant Bacon of Cooper Hill, Missouri, was seeing the world! Multiply Bant by millions and you knew the world had changed and would change even more when they all came back home. But how...? In what shape?

Battles still raged in the Pacific. Pete had arrived on Saipan on August 1, 1944, his birthday, and was there until November 9. In his brief letters he told of the Army feeding the troops on canned fish of various kinds--principally salmon--and fruit cocktail in heavy syrup. Not too bad, I thought, out of an upbringing in which salmon was a delicacy. But flies and other insects abounded "by the millions," giving each bite of food a hazardous trip on its way to his mouth. And his stories of the sacred frog on those island left something to be desired in the matter of drinking water.

Pete landed on Leyte on November 16, after six days aboard an LST. He was a member of the Medical Corps and went in with the Marines assigned to soften up the new line of attack. His was a "bastard outfit," usually attached to the Seventh Army Division, but it could be sent anywhere, anytime.

The fighting was heavy. Pete's duty was to attend to the wounded, giving what first aid he could, then attaching a card listing medication given to the victim's dogtag before moving on to the next casualty. As soon as possible, the wounded were moved to a hospital tent or hospital ship where surgery or proper medication was administered. Some members of this medical detail became mentally deranged by the sights and sounds of almost constant combat. One of the doctors, Pete wrote later, drank all of the liquor ration, then drank everything containing alcohol in his supply of medicines. He finally went berserk and was returned to the states. General Sherman was right. War is hell.

Those war years seemed so long. Sometimes it was hard to remember life before it. The days seemed even more endless and the people became even more anxious for peace as the eventual victory looked assured--eventually. Then one cold, rainy evening Dorothy Steiner burst through the back door after running all the way home from Schaepperkoetters' Store. "President Roosevelt is dead," she practically shouted. "President Roosevelt is dead."

Beda and I, embroidery in hand, rushed from our bedroom and stared at each other and stood with our mouths open. Mrs. Steiner looked at her in disbelief. Finally, we recovered enough to turn on the radio and hear the announcement for ourselves. It was true. We huddled around the massive Atwater Kent and listened to the details of his death at the Little White House in Warm Springs, Georgia, and the swearing in of the new president, Harry S Truman, a Missouri boy.

We looked at each other, wondering, What now? FDR had been president for so long many people couldn't remember another one. And for years we had listened to his oratory, "Mah de---ar Aa--mer--i--can friends." It was unbelievable

FDR DIES

The man from Missouri takes over the country and "baby brother" comes home to Mt. Sterling.

that he was dead in such a critical period of bringing the fighting to an end. And what did Harry Truman know about being president?

But in a few months the war in Europe ended and the boys from Osage, Gasconade and Maries Counties began arriving home almost daily.

Bant came home in December. I was at home when the box telephone on the wall rang--weakly, as always on its battery power. I picked up the receiver.

"Hello."

"Hullo, yourself. Guess who...!"

Often the most momentous occasions come simply garbed.

Bant was calling from Mt. Sterling and could we come get him. I could hardly wait to see my "baby" brother, who now weighed in at about 200 pounds. Bud and I headed for Mt. Sterling to fetch him home. We didn't cry on the way back, but all of us fought tears of happiness.

The word spread rapidly in the neighborhood when any of the boys arrived home and almost before supper was finished the neighbors began to knock on the door: "We just stopped by to see Bant." Some of the young men were veterans, also newly discharged from the service. One, I remember, was Adolph Kraenow, Jr., home from the Pacific. He had been with a demolition squad and told of sleeping on dynamite stacks. Others regaled us with stories of narrow escapes and near misses, of service drudgery and tedium--stories funny now that the tellers were all home safe and sound. It was one of those rare evenings of undiluted gaity, when the moment's joy shuts out worries of yesterday or tomorrow.

Pete, still in the Pacific, was one of tomorrow's worries; Mom, thankfully, became one of yesterday's. With Bant home, she began to recover quickly from the summer's two-month-long treatment and surgery for an overactive thyroid gland at Missouri Baptist Hospital in St. Louis. From August 1 to October 1, I felt as if I were waging my own three-front battle.

Mom was sick--and the garden poured out produce to can and pickle and preserve. There was an enormous crop of apples and peaches to can. And in September I had to go back to teaching at Bland. I tried to be three places at once. But most of my time was spent with Mom.

She wouldn't eat anything when I wasn't there. They were feeding her through a tube in her nose and she did begin to gain a little weight, but nothing satisfied her. She was as cross as a bear. She wanted to come home, especially when the doctors started talking surgery. No one was going to cut on her neck. Nosirree, no one was going to "chop on me."

Her brother, Uncle Harry LeFevre, a doctor, came down from Shelbyville to encourage her to have the surgery. To no avail. Aunt May Hancks came from Wamego, Kansas, to stay a week and try to persuade Mom to let them operate. She told about numerous operations by her husband, Uncle John Hancks, also an M.D. But Mom was adamant.

"No - sir - ree! I don't care how many people John Hancks and Harry LeFevre have chopped up. I'm not one of them. And nobody is going to change my mind."

She gained some strength and Dr. Andrews let her come home. One week showed her how sick she really was. When I came home on Friday evening she announced that "we" were returning to St. Louis on Sunday and she was going to have her "neck cut off."

Her switch to humor was a welcome relief. "Might as well go to the guillotine first as last," she would say.

I made a quick trip to Bland with lesson plans, washed and ironed and cleaned the house--and looked helplessly at all the good apples and peaches going to waste. (Later, Bud asked Mrs. L. Czeschin to can some for us.)

Mom parted with her thyroid gracefully and responded beautifully. All she wanted "was to get home and have a good boiled potato with a good brown biscuit." The hospital food was "awful." Once she smelled lamb chops cooking. She wasn't too sick to know the aroma of "mutton," she said. She gave me a knowing look. "They may think I'm going to eat that old sheep leg," she said, "but I'm not."

When the nurse appeared at the door, Mom was prepared. "You just take that old sheep leg right back where you got it--and don't you ever think I can't detect the odor of old mutton cooking."

I knew right then Mom was on the road to recovery. Her spunk was back--full force. I picked up my purse and went to a restaurant to get a hamburger. For both of us. With everything on it.

A week later we went home. I had phoned Morton's (Funeral Home, they called it then. An awful term). But please don't bring the ambulance, I told them. Mom had made it explicit: She wouldn't ride in "no funeral car." She wasn't dead yet and had no intention of being so. Morton's misinterpreted my instructions and dispatched an ambulance. Mom almost refused to get in "that old thing." But she wanted badly to go home.

Finally, she condescended to go--if she could ride up front with the driver. I rode in the back on the bed--gladly. I had had almost no sleep for more than six weeks. Periodically, on the way home Mom would look back at me and ask, "How are you feeling? Feel better? Shall we stop and see if you're breathing? You look sick. I doubt if you live to get home."

With her "neck cut off," and rapidly regaining her strength, Mom was witty and funny. And I went to sleep.

We arrived home in the early afternoon. And came a whirlwind--of cleaning house, cooking, gathering in things that Mom and Dad could cook later in the week...and cleaning up the cooking messes that Dad and Bud had made. The bread drawer was full of hard, dry, dark round knobs--evidence of Dad's love for biscuits. On a platter was some strange looking meat--Bud's attempt, I found out later, to fry a wild duck. And Dad and Bud had collaborated on a trial run of making cottage cheese. Neither of them knew the clabbered milk had to be heated. They had just tied the milk in a bag and squeezed--and sour milk quirted through a hole in the bag and hit Dad full in the face. So much for cottage cheese.

Late that evening, I returned to Bland.

Now I was more settled. I was thankful for two big happenings--Bant was home safely and Mom was getting well. I still worried about Pete. Elaine had grown tired of waiting for him to come home and was getting a divorce. I knew how much this must be hurting him. What would he have now to come home to?

The remainder of the year passed quickly. And it was class picnic time, time for the annual sojourn to Meramec Cavern or the St. Louis Zoo. Time for another joyful ride in Rainey Devault's or Henry Michel's stock truck. I wish I had counted the times I accompanied a group of young people to Meramec Caverns. In dreams I still am constantly riding in a truck between Bland and Sullivan.

Our destination depended upon how much money the class had earned; Meramec charged admission; the Zoo was free. Destination determined, we called the trucker, either Rainey or Henry. Well ahead of the scheduled departure time,

THE STOCK TRUCKS

On the road to Meramec Cavern with boxes of fried chicken and kids, kids, kids.

they would appear, their stock beds still dripping from the scrubbing they'd given the floors (but not the slats forming the sides and ends of the rack). The pig perfume especially was...well, memorable. And pungent. But the wet bed would be covered with a thick layer of straw, and if we were lucky, a tarpaulin over the straw.

In we would climb and off we would rattle. Our teeth chattered sometimes from the cold, but mostly from the bouncing of the truck over rough roads. Our heads at times felt as if they were being detached from our bodies, a shake at a time. Slowly, impatiently but inexorably, we ground up the long hills in "grandma gear." Then we flew downhill, with the big boys yelling, "Pour it on 'er, Henry. At this rate we'll be there by the middle of next week."

Everybody was in a gay mood. The girls and boys "going steady" sat next to each other, holding hands underneath the yellow straw. The others teased: "Don, where's your right hand? Something happen to it? Wilma June, where's your left hand? We can't see it. Are you sure you brought it with you? Maybe you left it at home!"

At the front of the truck bed was our "commissary"--a big basket loaded with several baskets or boxes of our combined lunches. Everyone was assigned a dish to prepare for this great day, and in they poured--deviled eggs, potato salad, sliced ham, fried chicken, pie, cake, Thermoses of coffee and iced tea. Everybody contributed more than his share--and we began to "lunch" as soon as we were well on our way.

Armin Peth or Stinky Steiner would open his supply of deviled eggs and around the container would go. Next would come the big boxes of fried chicken. I learned early that kids are more easily managed when "stuffed." So I always insisted on lots of food. And we always had a surplus.

When we arrived at Meramec, the earth swallowed everybody. And deep underground we were conducted through the "Grape Room" and the "Organ Room" and all the other damp, drippy rooms--and the natural staircase. When we came out once again into the fresh air, I'd be tinged with the green mold of envy of Miss Smith. She was never elected class sponsor. She never got to ride in a truck over bouncy roads and get dripped on in a cavern. No wonder she always looked like the cat the caught the proverbial canary when she said Goodbye to us on the mornings of our leavings!

After lunch some young people rowed on the lake, some took another excursion through the cave "because So-and-So saw something I didn't see" and some of the "steadies" wandered off, hand in hand, into sun-dappled woods. Or somewhere romantic. But by early afternoon we all had to pile back into the stock truck and snuggle down into the straw and tarp, because the "Red Bird Express" would be "pulling out with Casey Jones (Mr McIntosh) at the throttle" on the dot of four.

On the way back we passed around the luncheon leftovers, with the girls as hostesses: "Here, clean up the crumbs of this cake. Mom won't like it if I bring even one piece home. Let's clean up this chicken before it gets any colder. It won't be any good tomorrow."

By the time we pulled up in front of the school, every bite would have been devoured, the proper containers distributed to proper owners. Then came the scramble off the truck and onto the Red Bird Express. The boys jumped out and ran; the girls sat down sedately on the edge of the bed and propelled themselves more gently to the ground.

My chore was to "settle up" with Henry or Rainey and see to it that all those who had "missed their ride" home were taken care of. Usually Henry volunteered to "see to 'em." Then I'd brush off the last few blades of straw from my slack suit and wobble home to Mrs. Steiner's.

21

When the boys came home

My third and final year at Bland was to be one of change--the kind of change that steers your life in another direction. Teaching was easier. I felt I was a part of the community. I knew all the young people and their parents. I had become acquainted with the habits of the faculty:

Mr. McIntosh eating apples any time of the day and watching the clock at all times of the day;

Mr. Terrill saying, "I seen him go down the hall just a minute ago," or "I think we're goin' to have a shar'." (A shower.);

And, of course, Miss Smith continually smiling, picking the wisps of hair out of her mouth and still failing to get the students to do a lick of work.

This year Miss Maggie Michel taught music, because I had insisted I wasn't accredited for it. Miss Maggie was Henry's old maid sister, but unlike him, she had never been young. She hadn't taught school for several years and had only a vague idea of how to do it. She wore only black--as if we weren't mournful enough. And while my musical ability was limited, I never heard her or saw her even touch a piano. But you may be sure I made no inquiry about the music department. I was relieved to be free of that.

In school and around town there seemed to be a constant flurry of activity. Gasoline was easier to get, so travel to nearby towns became a matter of less serious consideration. The boys were coming home from the service in increasing numbers and they brought--and caused--change, too.

Beda and Emmett had married as soon as he came home from the Pacific. She had been teaching in St. Louis County, but was asked to resign when she married.

Now they were living in St. James, Missouri, where Emmett had gone into the fire clay business with his brother, Floyd.

Demand for Navy gloves decreased that year, too; that meant a changeover at "Inter National Charybdis." New faces appeared almost daily at Mrs. Steiner's dining table, faces of men--and sometimes women--who were overseeing the installation of new machinery to make shoes instead of gloves.

Often George Koenig would call Mrs. Steiner about 11 o'clock to inform her he was sending "six or eight people to feed"--energizing news, to say the least, with only an hour before eating. Added to her eight regulars, these "extras" sometimes resulted in small servings, but her food was so good that no one complained.

But over all of these changes floated the happiness of looking forward to Pete's homecoming. He landed on Okinawa on the Saturday before Easter. After the atom bombs were dropped on Japan, Pete and his unit drifted for 16 days toward Luzon, then sat aboard ship until they landed August 28. He was moved from one camp to another three or four times, but always toward Ft. McKinley near Manila. In Manila Bay he boarded the "Yarmouth," an old pleasure craft, bound for the States. On board his duty was caring for P.O.W.'s and the wounded, and later he told of having to go above deck to grab breaths of air away from the stench in the hold area.

After 23 days they arrived in San Francisco. And on October 17, 1945, he was discharged at Jefferson Barracks after four years and seven months and one day in the war business. He hardly looked like the same fellow. His dark, curly hair was gone; he was almost bald. His sparkly blue eyes didn't sparkle. He looked tired and old.

We were so glad to see him and have him home again, so it was a shock when he informed us he had a job at Solvay, New York, in a chemical plant. We had hoped he would go back to the University of Missouri where he only needed a few hours to graduate with his degree.

The return of one of Bland's war heroes set in motion a series of events that would culminate in an equally happy occasion some 20 years later. Jim Peth had been badly wounded during the southern European campaign but had recovered enough to come home before the war ended. He laughs about arriving in Bland on the Rock Island train one day at noon. No one knew exactly when he was expected, but the Schaeperkoetters, who watched all things, great and small, saw a uniformed figure alight from the coach. Thinking it was Alvin, they all ran to the depot--only to find it was Jim.

Jim's wife, Erna, had lived during the war years with her parents, Mr. and Mrs. Benjamin Drewel, across the street from the school. She and Erline Steiner, Charles's widow, worked in the factory so we were all happy to see Jim and Erna together again. In January of that year, a son was born to them: Steven Drewel Peth. Steve was only ten days old when I stopped by to see the new baby and to pick up the maternity dresses Erna had worn. They had belonged to Rev. Anderson's wife, who now wanted Mae to have them because she was expecting again. Little did I suspect that, some 20 years later, Steven Drewel Peth would become the husband of Jennie Mae Leach. Life, indeed, is strange--and unpredictable.

The whole country was happy. That spring there was more excitement in our small school activities. We sang more exultantly as we tramped out to the Dry Fork on our weiner roasts. We teased more at school. Finally, the hideous war was behind us. And the students wanted to add something extra to our basketball carnival--now in its third year and the event of the year. What could be different? Much study and deliberation brought forth the answer: A dinner. We would serve a dinner to the members of the basketball team and the pep squad--plus the teachers, the coaches and the board members. This meant, mind you, planning a menu which would be served without a stove, without a refrigerator and without much expense.

I think our feet and our backs were stronger than our minds to even harbor such a thought. But with the help of the two Mrs. Steiners, Mrs. George Essmann and others, it became a reality.

So did something else. All that last week a hot pain burned in my right side, like a triangular branding iron. Arrows of pain--one twanging right after the other-- would begin in my side, zip across my abdomen to the navel region, then straight down, and back to the side. I felt feverish.

But I had to teach. I had to attend to the dinner, pin up and stitch a fat formal for a thin girl and let out and let down a thin formal for a tall, fat girl. I had to order the sweet pea corsages and the carnation boutonnieres for the boys, and I had to be sure that no important personage was omitted from the guest list. I had no time to be ill. But ill I was. Each day at noon I went home to bed, without eating. My hands shook so much I couldn't bear for the people at the table to see me.

I looked "peaked" the kids informed me. And I informed them in no uncertain terms, "I am all right."

They all pitched in. The stage was decorated with the usual red crepe paper roses, green leaves, a white picket fence and a gate through which each young man guided his lady. They all knew their places and their lines. I saw and heard nothing. I wished I could feel nothing. The pain by now was excruciating.

At the dinner I served plates and carried trays from the elementary section to the gymnasium where the tables were set up for dining. Everything seemed to be going smoothly. I was too sick to know. I remember Aunt Clara and Uncle Henry later telling me to "go on home now and get to bed."

Bud was waiting for me and we jostled home to the farm. I fell into bed and I suppose I slept some. I was awakened by Mom calling, "Grace, get up. You've got to teach for Mae today. She's sick."

It was a Saturday! But Mae evidently was "making up" a day so I crawled out of bed, pulled on some clothes and went to Cooper Hill to teach all grades in a one-room school (including Yvonne and Anna Lo.) The day, I thought, would never end. When it did, I went directly to bed.

By Sunday I knew something had to be done about the pain. We called Dr. Bunge who sent me to the hospital at Washington, Missouri. I had a kidney and bladder infection--also an ovarian cyst and a tumor and infected appendix, which had to be removed immediately.

For three days after the surgery I felt or heard nothing. Then I began to recover. Cards and letters from the kids and the patrons at Bland poured in. And so many people came to see me! I was surprised and, at first, I couldn't figure out why all

BEYOND THE CURRICULUM
Days and more days of sweet pea corsages.

the outpouring of friendly concern for me. But I felt appreciated. And a Teacher seemed a worthy thing to be.

Mom came and stayed with friends, Amy and Dewey Jett, in Washington. She had double reason for coming; Mae had checked in, also with a kidney infection. She and Mae went home in a few days, and after three weeks, on Easter Sunday, I followed them.

Anyone able to stand up can teach school, Mom thought. So on Tuesday I went back to Bland. I remember being so weak I had to hold the bannister along the stairway to get up to my rooms. And I remember holding to the corner of Schaeperkoetters' store when the wind blew against me. Only a few weeks later, thank Heaven, school was out.

I again was surprised. The schoolboard was making some changes. Mr. Logan Steen, my former high school teacher, was to be superintendent and I was invited to attend the board meeting and recommend the things "women wanted" and "girls needed" around the school. I felt important! Then the suggestion was made that I prepare myself for principal.

But a little matter of "comparable worth" had been stuck in my craw all spring and I had to spit it out. (The phrase hadn't even been coined yet; I just thought of it as "Fair's fair.") A Mr. Fred Brandenburger had been teaching math that year, with only a few hours of college work and experience--and making more money than I. The board acknowledged those facts when I confronted them, but, they explained, teachers were hard to get...etc. And if I would consider returning, they'd certainly be willing to pay me the same as Mr. B....

That hardly cleansed my craw. I was teaching six subjects--not one--and I was doing all of those extra curricular activities. Plus I was qualified.

The more I thought about staying in Bland, the less appealing it became. As usual, Mom had an opinion and vocalized it, strongly and often: I should stay. She couldn't bear the thought of me unemployed--even if I weren't exactly a "one-year teacher" any longer.

I was still in that frame of mind that spring when Mrs. Leach became ill. I remember spending a Saturday with her. She had me call Dr. Bunge. His first order for me was to break a fresh egg in a teacup and have Mrs. Leach swallow it--to "get something on her stomach."

She looked at that egg and made a face. "Don't look at it," Doc said. His voice was trembly. "Swallow it." Somehow she managed, but she didn't feel any better. Basil and Selma came in later in the evening and I went home. When I went to school on Friday Dr. Bunge met me at his office and told me Mrs. Leach had died. I and many other people had lost our best friend--and a reasonably good doctor.

When a home remedy was required, Mrs. Leach could prescribe: Coal oil for cuts and bruises, flax seed poultices for inflammation of the joints, hot salt bags for a toothache, a few drops of kerosene on sugar for a croupy cough, a bread and milk poultice for a boil....

The funeral day dawned dismal and rainy. She lay in state in the front room of her small, neat home. But the body in the casket didn't look like Mrs. Leach. I sought in vain for one familiar feature. I found it in her hands. Those hands. Not beautiful by modeling standards, but, oh, so capable. Broad across the palm, long, thin fingers. Heavy veins across the backs. And those long, flat thumbs--the most memorable of all--now rested peacefully.

How many times had I watched her wring her dish cloth dry and carefully wipe her cook tables as she finished her meticulous process of dish washing. I can still see her spread those wide, flat hands and wash all of the table tops spotlessly clean--as well as the big, black iron cook stove.

And I can remember that day's mud. The road leading into the Leach family cemetery was impassable for cars, so the casket was unloaded into a farm wagon and pulled from the John Volk house to the final resting place. I couldn't help feeling angry: Mrs. Leach had always wanted everything perfectly clean and organized; this shouldn't happen to her.

Someone reminded me of an old adage, "Happy is the corpse that the rain falls on." That helped some. Later in the evening we had a torrential downpour with thunder, lightning and hail. Such a night! So often I've noticed this same weather pattern after a much-loved one is laid to rest.

It seemed like the right time to move on. Early that summer I applied for positions in Kirkwood, Webster Groves and a couple of other St. Louis County schools. Then I plunged into housecleaning. I was glad for a change. Soap and water fascinated me; I could find complete happiness in a bucket of warm, soft, soapy water.

I always started upstairs, airing bedclothes, cleaning walls, washing windows, turning the little storage room inside out. Putting everything neatly back in place gave me great pleasure. Washing and ironing, too, I enjoyed.

Mom never could understand. "It'll just get dirty again," she'd say. "Why don't you just let it alone? Sweep up the dirt and make the beds. That's all we need to do." What she wanted me to do was pull weeds and hoe the garden.

That was during the day. Nights, too, were busy. We raised quantities of chickens and this meant getting up at least twice nightly, staggering downstairs, stumbling through the dining room, across the porch, down the porch steps, over the foot bridge and into the so-called brooder house where one poked up the fire and put several sticks of fresh wood on the coals to keep the baby chicks warm.

Mom and I took turns doing this. Sometimes I used to stay a little while, just looking at those tiny, fluffy forms stretched out, resting, with their heads propped on each other so peacefully. The new wood would catch fire and blaze cheerfully, crackling and sputtering in Grandpa's old box heater, and I felt peaceful, too - like the chicks.

In about three weeks I'd have the house completely clean--curtains crisply starched, floors shining with varnish and fresh wax. And, sometimes, a room or two re-papered. Then the garden stuff would be ready to can.

One August I went to Sedalia to work at the State Fair--and wound up with a week I'll never forget. I was assigned to the Home Ec Building where I was surrounded by displays of cakes, pies, canned goods, home made soap, handwork and the like. I wrote out entry sheets and noted the class and case display number. During the judging I kept records of the prize winners in the departments. And later I made out the checks to the winners.

I stayed in the Womens' Building on the grounds, along with the judge, Charity Bye Shank, and Mrs. William Wombles, both M.U. graduates. Our instruction sheet had said, "Bedding Furnished." That was one sheet per bed, ordinarily sufficient in a Missouri August, but not this one. It was cool and rainy--and full of the sights and sounds of Fair time. And we slept fitfully.

Our building was near the stall of "The World's Smallest Mule--On Display Night and Day." And all night the high, whiney voice of a "barker" called out, "Come and see. Come one, come all. See the sight of your life, the world's smallest mule. Come one, come all. See the world's smallest mu-ele."

Then above his sing-song pitch would come the ice cream vendor's chant: "It'll cool your tongue and curl your hair and make you feel like a millionaire." It did cool my tongue but I didn't feel like a millionaire, and I was glad when it was over and I could go home.

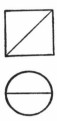

PART EIGHT

KIRKWOOD

22

Life at W.W. Keysor

By the second week of August, I had decided I would return to Bland to teach a fourth term. One warm day I walked up to the mailbox and, lo and behold, there was a letter from Mr. Frank Tillman, the Kirkwood superintendent, asking me to come to his office for an interview. My "definite" decision faltered: Should I be content with teaching at Bland or should I try the big schools of the St. Louis suburban area?

Kirkwood was a far cry from Bland--an even further one from Horse Shoe Bend. I knew country ways and small town living. I knew the people. I was one of them. I knew a few of the Bessies and a smattering of Rosies and Karls--kids who needed a friend as much as a teacher. Would there be any Bessies in the big city suburbs?

Dad encouraged me to go, at least, for the interview. Mr. Tillman was an Osage County product, a friend of Dad's and a cousin of Uncle Vic Pinet. So I girded my loins and rode the bus to Kirkwood on the appointed day. It was my first glimpse of the area where I would spend most of my teaching years.

Mr. Tillman was moving about in a walker when I met him in the High School building (now Nipher Junior High). He questioned me more about Osage County and people who lived there than about my qualifications as a teacher. After a half hour or so he said he would "see what I can do."

That wasn't exactly an encouraging ending. I waited on the street corner for a bus back to Maplewood, and I found myself thinking better of Bland. Maybe its name fit, in comparison to this bustling metropolitan suburb. But there were advantages. At least, if I waited on a street corner in Bland, I'd see someone I knew.

Besides, I thought more about it on the long bus ride back home, the pay wouldn't be a great improvement over Bland. I'd be teaching sixth grade--back in elementary school. There would be an art supervisor as well as a music supervisor. I'd have to supervise playground and cafeteria for my students.

And those students...Were kids really kids, wherever you taught? Or would I be trading an occasional Henry Balkenbusch with his bizarre tastes in behavior and poetry for a steady diet of incorrigibles? After all, what was wrong with teaching in small rural towns the rest of my life instead of transferring to a big suburban school? Besides, Mr. Tillman didn't really sound too encouraging...

A letter and contract from Mr. Tillman came a few days later and I knew the answer. I would try the St. Louis job.

Dad was glad. "You never get anywhere by being afraid of changes," he kept saying. "Try it. You never know about a job until you try it."

Mom tackled the first practical problem--finding me a place to live. She remembered that Dora Schulte lived in Kirkwood; maybe she would know of someone who would like a "boarder." Off went Mom's letter and back came the news. Dora had found me a place just two doors down the street--at 322 Central Place, with Mr. and Mrs. Albert Ruhl.

I had enjoyed working with high school students and I wasn't sure I'd like returning to elementary teaching. I'd have Arithmetic, English, Science, Social Studies (History and Geography), Spelling and P.E., plus art and music. That was worse than Bland!

There was one teacher per grade at W.W. Keysor School--Kindergarten through Grade 6--and one principal. That was Mrs. Lillian Denny, a scrawny little woman who sat in her office on the first floor and wrote notes to teachers advising them of their duties.

Mary Elaine Presley taught Kindergarten. She was newly married and educating her husband, Bill, at the Missouri School of Mines at Rolla.

Presiding over the first grade was Mrs. Agnes "Cinny" Bear. She kept a running account of all teachers, all custodians, all cooks, all neighbors. She never missed school; she might miss a tidbit of gossip. Her room, so she said, was a model of efficiency. She couldn't be improved upon so, therefore, she argued rhetorically, why should she go to school to further her education. "Young teachers don't know anything."

Carolyn Blankenbaker taught second grade. She was a beauty. Tall, slender and dark. She was engaged to a fellow with a funny sounding name--Farquar Bridge. And all we heard was Farquar - Farquar - Farquar. Say it three times and your tongue gets all rolled up.

Marie Hall was not young and not exactly old. But she had taught third grade for ages and she knew then what many teachers never learn: Some children don't care to learn. Marie put them in a "listening group" and there they stayed until they indicated some desire to participate.

Marie's sister, Rose Compton, was principal at Pitman, another elementary school in Kirkwood. And Marie's mother became one of my favorite people of those Kirkwood years. A native of Germany, she had come to the United States as a young girl. She loved to crochet; such artistic work I've never seen. She cooked, too, almost as beautifully as she crocheted. Such lemon pie you never put in your mouth!

Fifth grade was the domain of Ora D. Hayes. She was a great help to me, especially in briefing me on the traits and abilities of my sixth grade students while we supervised playground together. Ora D. was an art teacher and had been originally employed as such. She could concoct anything out of empty cardboard boxes or egg cartons with the help of water base paint and clay.

Emily Winter taught Grade 4. She was my nearest neighbor across the hall--and a better one I never had. She knew the answers to all my questions. She also knew practically everyone in Kirkwood. Her father, Dr. Wirth, practiced medicine there for more than half a century and lived to be almost a centenarian.

Emily stood out in another way; she was the only teacher in the building who owned a car. And anyone was welcome to ride into Kirkwood with her after school. She endeared herself to me, though, with her propensity for changing first letters or syllables in names or words. She would write a note, "Let's Kirk to go wood after school." Or "Would you send Oe Jedelbeck to me?", meaning Joe Edelbeck. Mrs. Denny became Mrs. Dillian Lenny, Marie Hall was Harie Mall, and so on. In a slight departure from that form, I became "Pork Chop"--for all of my 11 years at Keysor School.

As the new sixth grade teacher, I found myself confronted with a large group-- 38 boys and girls of many sizes, most shapes and divers degrees of intelligence. As usual, one or two posed special--sometimes urgent--problems.

One was William Hopkins. "He can't sit still a minute," was Ora D.'s thumbnail sketch of him. "He just wanders around the room bothering the people who are working." Mrs. Lenny--er, Denny--also warned me "not to expect anything at all of William."

Roger Kiburz's reputation for unruliness ran a close second to William's. He'd been known to throw books at the teacher--or whatever was handy when a temper tantrum struck him.

When Ora D. and Mrs. Denny fed me these "inside goodies," I half wished I were back in Bland--ordering sweet pea corsages and riding to see caves and eating cold fried chicken in damp stock trucks. But Roger and I got along famously. He was extremely bright and all he wanted was some peace and quiet so he could concentrate on his work. That was easy to fix.

William, I soon found out, was simply a spoiled, soft, white woolly worm type who figured he could intimidate--or wear out--all teachers. In a few days he and I came to grips with his wandering, disturbing ways and for a whole year William sat still. And if his work wasn't the best in the room, it certainly wasn't the worst. Several others laid strong claim to that distinction.

Several weeks later Mrs. Denny walked into the room and looked around, surprised at the unusual sight of a quiescent William. "How do you manage to keep William in his seat?" she asked, surprised. "I never thought anyone could do that!"

I'm not an affectionate person, but I wanted to hug her. I'd "made it" from one-room Horse Shoe Bend and small town Bland to The City. Kids were the same wherever...I wanted to whisper loudly, like Bessie, "I done it, I done it!"

More difficult to contend with, but out of my direct jurisdiction, was a first grade boy named Francis Telle. His sister, Carolyn, was in my room. Every morning soon after classes began I would hear this ungodly screaming arising from somewhere downstairs and hanging in the stairwell just outside my door. The first time we heard it everyone looked stunned, but we tried to go on with our recitations.

After an eternity of 45 minutes or so, Mrs. Denny would appear and ask for Carolyn. It seemed the only way to stop Francis's howling: Carolyn would start home with him, then somewhere between home and school, Mrs. Telle would take over. I was told by Carolyn that a "regular battle" took place between Mama and Francis. But after a few weeks, Francis was declared the victor. He was allowed to return to St. Peter's--at which I wondered about the continuance of the renowned patience of the nuns.

W.W. Keysor School, a beautiful, large red brick building, sat on the advancing edge of northwest Kirkwood's residential district. Beyond was farm land, and that fall--right there in Kirkwood, St. Louis County--while I did playground duty I watched corn being cut and shelled. Just like home! That was the land's last corn crop, however. In early spring the land was sold to an "area developer" and the first houses of what is now a mass of subdivisions began to take shape.

The houses also marked the genesis of post-war modern home construction versus the solidly built pre-war houses. I remember the criticism well: "Those houses won't stand up. The ground was still frozen when they poured the concrete footing." And "The lumber is too green" and "The basement walls are too thin. They'll fall in."

The houses are still there and as building standards go today, I'm sure they are quite substantial.

That autumn was quite eventful. I walked to school, a distance of some six long blocks. I loved Kirkwood's tree-shaded streets and I often took a side street--Cleveland, Simmons or Essex--to fully savor the pretty houses, well-kept lawns and abundant flowers.

The Ruhls were Germanic. Linda was a tall, thin woman with a somewhat larger than average bosom. Al was a short, stocky fellow, perhaps in his sixties, but growing stooped. He worked for Mr. and Mrs. Andy Burger as an all-around man; in the summer he tended their garden; in the winter he cleaned the house. And whatever the season he gave the Burgers a full measure of loyalty. Andy Burger of Burger Chevrolet was under investigation at the time for embezzlement of funds--a process that went on and on. But Albert Ruhl never would believe that Mr. Burger wasn't "always 100 percent honest because that's the way he treats me. 100 percent honest."

Al and Linda were childless, a situation that Lnda resented. It was all Al's fault. She knew so, because all her brothers and sisters had families. She dwelt on the subject by the hour, counting up all her nieces and nephews as we sat in the evenings on the immaculate, screened-in front porch.

One thing, maybe, irritated her more. That was neighbors walking their dogs and permitting them to use Linda's and Al's hedge for "lifting their leg." That made her tight-lipped. "Here comes that dog again," she'd spit out. "I guess he'll lift his leg again when he gets to my hedge."

When not so riled, Linda was actively religious. I guess I wondered at times about her motivation. She always said, "If you don't go to c'urch, you don't know anything what's going on." Her entire life was "c'urch." She never missed guild meetings or services during Lent or any funerals because, she said, she wanted "a nice crowd on my last trip to c'urch."

I used to wonder if Al would be among that "nice crowd" on her last trip. He never went with her otherwise. He always had to work on his "machine"--his 1936 Ford. No machine ever got better care. Every Sunday morning he backed it out of the garage. Then he removed the spark plugs and polished them, measured the distance between the coils with a dime, removed the generator, sanded the armature with emery paper...All removable parts were disassembled and reassembled. Finally, the weekly bucket with rich soap suds appeared and all exterior parts were washed and polished--including the tires and hub caps. After proudly surveying his efforts, he drove the blue Ford "machine" back into the garage.

Then Al washed out his cleaning rags and hung them on the clothes line and went into the house. There he spent the rest of the day scrubbing himself--taking a bath, shampooing his hair, trimming his toe nails, massaging his feet and legs. Between keeping himself and his "machine" in good shape, he had busy Sundays.

For most of my forty-plus years in teaching, "room and board" was an integral part of teaching. And looking back now--or remembering with my stomach--I marvel at the ability of the human body to adjust to circumstances. Linda was an immaculate housekeeper. She cleaned, washed, ironed and dusted constantly. But her cooking...well, it was a far cry from Mrs. Steiner's.

With the wisdom of 40-year hindsight, I'm convinced that Al controlled the menu by always accompanying her on grocery shopping jaunts. Linda's menus never varied two iotas in five years. Mornings featured breakfast bacon, one egg, toast and blackberry jelly. (Al liked only blackberry jelly.) In the evening we had either roast beef or roast pork with potatoes or Creamettes. Linda thought these store-bought noodles were a true delicacy.

Her much-touted dish was creamed spinach--and I was never overly fond of cooked spinach, to start with. She enhanced it not one whit with her skimpy creaming process--only flour and water mixed and poured on the spinach. No butter. No rich milk. She also chopped away at the mixture as it cooked until the finished product came to the table looking like brownish green sea weed swimming in greenish brown gravy. The smell of it cooking was fair warning: It would last at least a week and be warmed over every evening.

I say "We" because after I had been at the Ruhls about a month, Claribel "Pat" Rafferty moved in to be my roommate. She was one of the first grade teachers at Pitman, an elementary school in Kirkwood's business district. The two of us were rather cramped in the small back bedroom. We shared one small closet for clothes, shoes, rain gear and so on. Pat jammed in much more than I; I still had barely enough to get along with in those days.

Pat also had a car, a Plymouth, the cause of much concern to Al and Linda for a while. The driveway was wide enough for only one car. Linda brooked no car parking on her "lawn" and Al didn't like this "Plymut" parked on his "chat yard" in the back. And Pat didn't like to park on the street.

Impasse. Pat finally rented an old dilapidated garage a block away. But she never adjusted to the strain of walking a block and a half in the opposite direction from Pitman to pick up her car.

I was accustomed to walking to school. It was a part of my day as again my life assumed a definite pattern: Getting up, trotting to the kitchen, eating one slice of bacon, one egg, two slices of toast, blackberry jelly, and two cups of coffee. Pat had the same, except she drank tea. And on Friday no bacon: "I'm not going to eat a little old bit of bacon and call it meat." Then off to school.

At Keysor I was more or less an outcast that first year. All the teachers had been there for years and had formed a rather tightly knit social group. Besides, I was only a replacement for Ruth Engler, who was taking a year's leave of absence. Mrs. Denny didn't especially like me, either; I was too strict in my discipline to suit her--even though it had worked on Will-yum. She seemed to think that any first-year teacher at Keysor should have "lots of trouble" disciplining that sixth grade.

The only truly difficult thing for me was all of the preparations. And standing for P.E. That's what it consisted of--watching while the class played some game. We had to go outside unless the "weather was falling," as the handbook stated. In such cases, we had "class" in a small concrete stall in the basement where we could play games not requiring running. Running, you see, encouraged falling, and falling encouraged concrete burns, skinned heads and elbows and associated problems. This itty-bitty stall was directly beneath the kindergarten room, so on days of "falling weather" Mary Elaine Presley nearly lost her mind. (This concrete rectangle also did duty as our audio-visual room, our P.T.A. Hall and housed any other impromptu gatherings.)

HOT LUNCH
The only warm thing about it was its name.

Across the concrete hallway was another concrete box. That was our cafeteria. The food was served by volunteer mothers--after it was prepared at the high school kitchen and trucked over about 11 a.m. in something which resembled huge garbage containers. Pure coincidence, I'm sure.

The wide choice of sandwiches was staggering! Cheese, Peanut Butter or Bologna. All cold, of course. You were fortunate if you ate on the first shift. The beans would be somewhat warm. But if you hit the last shift--as I always did--the beans were barely shy of icy cold.

The only suggestion of warmth was the name of the thing: "Hot Lunch

Program." I almost envied the kids who brought their sack lunches and ate at a separate table in the rear. They had Thermos bottles of hot soup or chocolate--and good looking roast beef or roast pork sandwiches. Many a day I strongly considered launching a new program of teacher-student fraternization.

After lunch came my session of standing on the playground. Then the bell rang and we lined up and marched into the building--up three flights of stairs and into our brown-tiled cubicle called The Sixth Grade Room. The afternoons were long. I tried squeezing all the leftover subjects into three hours--minus a half-hour recess when we all again donned our wraps (in cold weather), formed lines and marched down the steps, out the corridor and onto the dirt playground. With 38 kids going through that rigmarole, you can imagine how much playing time was left!

At an early teachers' meeting Mrs. Denny had quickly disposed of the recess scheduling problem: Each teacher could choose her times--starting with Mary Elaine Presley, Kindergarten, and going on up the ladder. Since I taught grade 6, you can imagine my "choice." My recesses fell just before and after lunch. I thought this was hilarious; so did Emily. We would write notes back and forth asking, "When do we have Pl.G today? I've forgotten."

The afternoons dragged on interminably. (Yes, students, they're that way for teachers, too!) And at times the recitations and the lectures and the questions all blurred into a continuous, monotonous drone. Then followed the longest 20 minutes of the day--the time we were required to stay in the building after classes were dismissed. Most teachers congregated in the lower hall just inside the door nearest the parking lot. Marie Hall and I and a few other "walkers" waited for the 4:20 bell inside the front door. That way we covered the entrances and exits--and prevented Mrs. Denny from leaving, too.

Poor old soul, she was on her last legs and we should have been ashamed of ourselves. But we weren't. She took great pride in her authority to "release" us. "Okay, girls," she would say, "you may go now." And we'd practically take the doors with us as we burst through them.

Pat and I usually arrived at 322 Central Place at about the same time. After washing off chalk dust and pencil graphite and paper ink, I was quite willing to sit down to do a bit of embroidery or quilt piecing. I was still tired, too; the surgery of early spring had left me lacking my usual strength and energy. But Pat was always ready to go. "When I hear the word," she'd laugh say, laughing at herself, "I'm half way there."

One of her favorite after-school excursions was to drive around Kirkwood and locate the homes of her first grade pupils. (R.B.'s she called them--Rich Bitches.) I was usually prodded into going with her, resenting my own weakness in not saying, "No, Pat, I'm not going." Now I think this came from my early home training where I was taught to do what other people ask and to always put your own wishes last. (Boy, have I changed!)

After Al came home and splashed in the tub for an hour or so we ate dinner, with Al amusing us with stories from the Burgers. I remember one argument with Mrs. Burger over rose plantings:

"Mrs. Burger says 'Roses should have no wet feet.' And I say, How they going to get a drink? Roses, I say, drink t'rough dere feet, don't dey?

"She just say, 'Roses should have no wet feet.'

"I get so mad. I say, 'Dig a trench and trow dem in. Let dem figure out what to do wit dere feet.' Dat's just about what I say--and dat's just about what I do.

"She goes back in the house saying, 'All I say is roses should have no wet feet.'

And I say it one more time already, 'Let dem figure out what to do wit dere feet.' She didn't say no more.''

Then Al would laugh heartily until his upper teeth fell down. Linda would look at him and tighten her lips. But she never said anything. I guess she knew better.

Each Tuesday evening after dinner it was written in stone: Al and Linda went to the grocery store. The grocery list, like the weekly ritual itself, never varied, because Al liked only certain things. Those Creamettes were a great treat, a dish Linda always brought to our attention. Another luxury we were permitted on special occasions was "cream bread," and every meal we were reminded that this was Cream bread--emphasis on Cream.

During Lenten season, Linda would splurge and buy some Hot Cross Buns, extra special because she bought them from the "bread man" who delivered from door to door. Al liked to dunk his Hot Cross Buns in his coffee and would tell how his mother used to make the buns before Easter and "store them in a big crock." But by the time Easter came they would be "all"--meaning all gone.

That would be Linda's cue. "I don't remember your mother ever making Hot Cross Buns. I did--and my mother did. But not your mother."

No matter how many times this argument was re-hashed, both Al and Linda retained their own firm convictions as to whose mother made Hot Cross Buns. I used to shudder whenever I spotted these items on the table. Now I wonder why Linda bought them. I think she must have enjoyed the crossfire.

For five years Al and Linda furnished us the near comic relief that almost any life situation needs. For instance, there was Linda, R.N. I would come home some evenings to find her decked out in the full dress uniform of a registered nurse: Starched, immaculate white shirt waist, cap, white silk hose and regulation nurse's oxfords. She even substituted her large E & R "C'urch" pin on her bosom for an R.N. insignia. She had purchased these uniforms a few years before when her mother was ill and Linda had taken on the full responsibility of giving her hospital care. Now she wanted to "get the good out of the uniforms."

In her dream world Utopia was a hospital. She was head of the "Sanitation Squad." Everything in her house had to pass a "sanitation test." Their clothes, bed clothes, their rugs were sprayed regularly with Lysol and Slay, and when you entered the house your nostrils and eyes began to smart with the piercing mixtures of deodorizers and chemical sprays.

These products had to be purchased from Famous-Barr--often, to be fresh. So every few weeks Linda would arise early, leave our breakfast on the stove and betake herself downtown to purchase the new supply of "Mott and Bug Killer."

"Motts" (moths) she couldn't understand. "How did they get into the house? I don't want no motts around."

Often when Pat and I went home over the weekend Linda would spray and wash everything in our rooms to give it that "hospital look"--as well as smell. In such times, our only recourse was to open the window. But, of course, Linda didn't sanction that. We were wasting heat.

The second of Linda's great ambitions was to be associated with the "c'urch." Every Wednesday evening she went to Prayer Meeting. Dinner would be a little early so she had time to dress--after she asked Al for the car. Always--and first-- she had to ask Al for the car. This I could never understand. After 35 or 40 years of marriage, didn't Al know she was going to Prayer Meeting?

I'd seen many marriages, none of which had loomed as a temptation for me to change my status. And this one must have had many things buried--or certainly submerged--in it. Al and Linda never seemed to really enjoy each other or enjoy doing things together. They occupied the same house and shared the same bedroom and the same car. Never any more. A strictly business sort of a deal, I thought.

The only places I remember them going together was the grocery store and the doctor's office. The latter was a must; they had a standing appointment to get their "pill prescriptions" refilled and those pills held a high priority in Linda's life. Her first report of the day usually was how many "gray pills" she had already taken.

"That pain in the top of my head," she would say the minute Pat and I appeared in the kitchen door. And she would straighten all five fingers of her right hand and press hard on her forehead.

Sometimes she'd dote on those "feel better" pills. "I don't know what's in them," she'd say, "but Dr. Barnett always says, 'Take these. They'll make you feel better'."

At the very top of her scale of Important Events was having "The Reverend" to dinner. She rarely addressed or spoke of Mr. Polster or even The Reverend Polster; always he was "The Reverend." In preparation for his coming, the entire house had to be sanitized. She washed the walls and ceilings with Lysol. She hung fresh curtains. She hung the rugs on the clothes line and beat them within an inch of their jute-backed lives. She scrubbed the floors and polished all the beds, and she vacuumed the upholstered furniture and sprayed it with Slay. She removed all dishes from the cabinets and washed and sprayed the shelves before she sterilized the china and put it back. Even the basement got a thorough renovating. After all, she couldn't take a chance on having a "mott" around when The Reverend came to dinner.

For The Reverend on these special occasions she always prepared a special dish. Creamed spinach. The Reverend was very fond of creamed spinach. These dinners were always planned for Sunday evenings and for five years I tried to figure out some way to arrive too late for them. But I knew Linda would be hurt. I must partake of this special feast. So I learned to sit down and enjoy it.

Besides, an evening with The Reverend was worth even creamed spinach. He had a gift for story telling which, along with his strong German accent, made for good entertainment. He and Al matched storytelling prowess--tale for tale--all evening. After dinner we always played a few hands of pinochle--always with a double deck. The only real disadvantage of The Reverend dinners was having to eat leftover creamed spinach for a week--and listening to Linda's constant string of "The Reverend said"'s. She seemed to come to life and blossom in the presence of the man.

Perhaps this was the reason for her great attachment to "c'urch." Now, there's the cynic in me.

Pat and I found other ways to spend spare moments. Mary Beth Bealke and Frances Lee Key, previous acquaintances, were teaching at Lockwood Elementary in Webster Groves. They shared a bedroom in Tom and Cora McFarland's home on Greeley Avenue and we often drove over to spend an evening with them. We had fun talking shop and swapping humorous happenings. Sometimes we went to the Opera, or to a movie.

St. Louis was like a sun with a whole galaxy of suburbs around it and life twinkled like a brand new universe for me, but I never felt a part of it the way I was a part of Bland and Owensville. Even Winfield. And our social life was somewhat restricted. Most of all, we were still teachers, still struggling to teach what we thought was important for our young charges to store up in their brains. That assignment stayed the same, wherever you were.

I have put a great deal about my life before and after school into this book and very little at times about the children, so some readers may decide I cared little about the students or what I taught them. But to me that is a "given"--an accepted, assumed reason--of teaching, and a discussion of the subject, if not reined in tightly, would lead me off into pedantic ravings, enough to fill another book. Maybe more. Here let it suffice to assure you that I was always more than busy.

TEACHING GROUPS

The Blue Birds, the Red Birds and the Black Birds...or the Dum-dum Crows.

In those days, for instance, arithmetic was considered basic and necessary and I taught it religiously. We--my pupils and I--spent many hours per week on it. We also had to teach reading--effective reading, supposedly. And I intend to imply that the teaching of it today is less that effective. Our methods then were not perfect, either. We had to teach reading in groups--Group One usually being The Blue Birds, group two The Red Birds and the bottom group The Black Birds or Crows, or some such dum-dum grouping. Poor kids. Small wonder if they felt left out!

As I sit here writing these memories of some 40 years, Alan, Yvonne's husband, is lying on the family room floor, helping their daughter, Nancy, with her spelling lesson. He is saying...But listen:

Alan: Easter...This is cursive writing? East-er.
Nancy: E-a-s-t-e-r. Easter. E-a-s-t-e-r.
Alan: April.
Nancy: April. A-p...
Alan: Ap-ril.
Nancy: April. A-p-r-i-l...?
Alan: Spring.
Nancy: Sp-ring. S-p-r-i-...
Alan: What did you do in school? How many times have you written these?
Nancy: Three times...but, Daddy, I may have forgotten some of them.
Alan: Sick. Make that a "K" and I won't correct you. Now, doctor.
Nancy: D-o-c-t-o-r? That one has a check mark; I'm not sure.
Alan: Hospital. How do you spell hospital? H-o-s-p-i-t-a-l. Hospital. Angel?
Nancy: Angel. A-n-g-l-e.
Alan: What were you doing when you wrote these?
Nancy: Writing them.
Alan: Audience.
Nancy: Audience. A-...
Alan: Now, you write these three times and I'll check on Mark.
Nancy: THREE times?
Alan: Yes. Three times. It's good for you.

Some two hours and 11 spelling words later, we were well on our way to getting 100--even with the super-duper word, "audience." Alan was still away somewhere, perhaps with Mark. Yvonne was getting ready to go to "The Barn" with some friends. I had wiped dirt, several times, off her squirmy knees and elbows and Nancy kept asking, with long sighs, "How much more do you have to write?"

And so I see a new, smarter generation growing up, learning the same words, studying by much the same method we used 40 years ago. And to my way of thinking much needs to be improved upon. Ah, but see, there I go, lecturing about Teaching when I just intended to tell a few stories about the life of a teacher.

That first year at Kirkwood was a busy one, much of it fraught with anxiety over Anna Lo. She had run a temperature for months and was taking all sorts of medicine--for something no one seemed to have an answer for. When dysentery struck her in early autumn she was brought to St. Mary's Hospital in St. Louis for a thorough examination. Jennie Mae was only a few weeks old and Mae was breast feeding her, so I took it upon myself to go see Anna Lo every evening after school.

I caught a county bus into the Maplewood Loop, then took a City Limits bus up to Clayton Road. From there I walked the short block to the hospital. And after visiting with Lo, I returned by the same route. I soon knew every bus schedule of both the county and city buses. I may not have helped Anna Lo, but I made myself feel better to see her.

She was always waiting in her little white bed, looking quite proper, her big blue eyse wide open and staring at the ceiling. She was only six, so she needed JoJo. JoJo was a large brown teddy bear she had received for Christmas. He sported a bounteous bow of red ribbon around his neck, but his large, yellow-brown, shoe button eyes seemed to shine for Anna alone and in the crook of her elbow he was always relaxed and at home.

On one visit I waited outside in the corridor while a nurse finished changing sheets. I opened the door to see fire in Lo's eyes. "That silly nurse," Lo told me tightlipped, "hung my JoJo on the door knob."

I looked on the inside of the door. Sure enough. There hung JoJo by his bright red neck ribbon. And I ingratiated myself with both Lo and JoJo by restoring him to his place of honor in Lo's loving arms.

JoJo approved of me one other time. One evening I risked missing the bus to stop at a florist's shop and choose some bright autumn mums for Lo. I thought they were simply gorgeous, but Lo's chubby little face fell when she saw them. Aunt-like anxious, I quickly inquired what the trouble was. Her words tumbled out in a sweet, low voice: "Aunt Cha, if you gonna bring me flowers, bring me woses, please."

The next afternoon I could hardly wait to get away from school, catch the bus, stop at the same florist's and make my purchase and deliver the "woses." Her face lit up and I think I saw JoJo wink at Lo, as if to say, "Well, we brought her around in a hurry."

Often I reached Central Place late, but whatever the time Linda would have left my dinner on the low burner. I protested the bother of her thoughtfulness, but I did appreciate it.

Anna Lo's illness was never definitely diagnosed but she got better and the day came for her to go home. She and JoJo were all dressed and waiting when Irvin came to sign her out. Her big blue eyes were shining. She sat up front in the car with her daddy and held JoJo tightly in her arms. She was eager to see "new" Jennie Mae and every so often she would spread out her arms and say, "I'll bet Jennie Mae be iss big." And I'll swear that bear smiled. I know Daddy did...and Aunt Cha.

I continued to spend most of my weekends at home. Irvin was now teaching in University City, after having taught in Webster Groves for almost 20 years. Every Friday evening he came by 322 Central Place to pick me up and we'd start our 100-mile journey comparing teacher notes and family news.

I remember one Saturday in particular. Jean Herkert had a sale of her household articles and I had great fun buying some pieces of furniture we were to enjoy for many years. The most prized one was a fine, golden oak dining table.

Second, perhaps, was a sofa-bed combination.

The table was a thing of beauty once in place in the kitchen (later in the dining room). It had three large leaves which extended it 12 feet or more. I repaired it and re-upholstered the sofa bed for the next 20 years as it was in constant use as a napping place for Mom, Dad or Pete--or Nancy, the dog.

Soon after the Christmas holidays we knew Mrs. Denny wouldn't be returning to Keysor. Teachers now had retirement benefits. Besides, she had had pneumonia in the spring so retirement seemed wise for her. Mr. Woodson Smith, director of testing for the elementary schools, would become our new principal.

I regretted another change. My good friend Emily Winter had carried on lengthy correspondence with the school board about her credits for teaching. But Emily lost the battle and stepped aside. This involved a change for me. Ruth Engler was returning to teach Grade 6 so I would take Grade 5 because Ora D. Hayes wanted Grade 4. And Pat Raffery was being placed at Keysor because Pitman no longer needed a third First Grade teacher.

This final twist of fate concerned me the most. Seeing Pat in the morning and evening was fine, but 24 hours a day under her eagle eye was another matter. I liked Pat as a friend. She was fun at times to be with, but our tastes and likings ran in different paths. I wanted to find solace in a quiet evening at home. Pat wanted to go--some place, even if just to locate where some teacher-friend lived, or one of her "R.B." kids.

Pat always wanted me to help her check the first grade work books in the evening. My sixth and fifth graders exchanged books and we did our own checking. I preferred to walk home; she wanted to ride in her "Plymut." And she wanted me to ride with her--to open the garage door for her.

But these were small differences and for five years our pattern changed little. Pat and I shared the tiny, ultra-sanitary bedroom, which was regularly "demotted" and sprayed with Slay. Mr. Ruhl spent his evenings defending Mr. Burger's honesty, regardless of newspaper items to the contrary. Linda continued to feed us on Creamettes, now even more since she had found a new way to serve them: Sprinkle the top with little cubes of bread, toasted and fried in butter over a few stewed prunes.

The only dessert Linda ever produced from scratch was a cherry pie--a pie unlike any I'd experienced before. It had a custard base, make with egg and milk and such, but with very little sugar. She used the cherries sparingly--allotting one red globe to about every six square inches of custard. The crust was thick and doughy. But Linda ranked the pie in the "special treat" category and always made several--as many as six. The pies did have an advantage: Once they were made, dessert was no worry for days. They held up well!

So did Keysor School, and I vowed to try to remember the faultiness--and the futileness--of preconceived notions. The music supervisor and the art supervisor turned out to be good friends--not the ogres I had anticipated all supervisors to be. Laura Triplett taught me to like art, although I knew nothing about it. Under her guidance I slopped around fairly well with water color, pastellos, crayon, charcoal and even some oil paint and India ink. Also Ora D. was an artistic person, always involved in silk screening and stenciling and the like. And whenever I got "hung up" on art, Ora D. helped me out.

When I got "hung up" on music, Ruth Engler helped me. She was a truly grand person. She lived with her elderly mother on about 50 acres of land on Sulphur Springs Road a few miles west of Kirkwood. I enjoyed visiting with them a great deal. Lively and alert for all of her 85 to 90 years, Mrs. Engler delighted in telling funny stories about her young grandson getting stuck in the doghouse. And strawberries. She loved to grow strawberries--and even enjoyed picking them. From many an aching back, I could swear to that being the acid test of a strawberry lover.

"I don't get too tired," Mrs. Engler would say, "because it's so much fun to wallow in the strawberry bed."

Mom felt much the same way. They were lovers of the soil and Mother Nature had a way with them. Or perhaps let them have their way with her.

Along with the personnel changes at Keysor School came growth by leaps and bounds, almost literally. With the GIs back home, marrying and starting families--or adding to old ones--new houses were springing up in many places, in desirable neighborhoods. There was much talk of a new high school building on Essex and Daugherty Ferry Road. Consequently, new additons had to be built onto Keysor.

Soon we had expanded to two grades of everything. Then three. We couldn't keep up with room additions and furniture. Some years we had 35 to 40 pupils in our small classrooms. Some years we taught with a tarpaulin hanging over an empty wall where a new addition was being constructed. Also, finally, we had a new and decent cafeteria--with a large, all-purpose room. And on the first floor! This gave us a place to play on rainy and cold days...and a decent place wherein to hold those momentous meetings of the P.T.A.

Presiding over these unprecedented growing pains was our new principal, Mr. Woodson Smith. He was a tiny man but quite handsome, with blue-black, curly hair, dark eyes and a pleasing personality. He was quiet but demanding. Every Tuesday afternoon we had a faculty meeting, regardless of any other committments and regardless of any topics for discussion.

Once at the beginning of a new term of school Zelpha Hogan was determined to get some school policies "down in writing." She unwisely prefaced her remarks with "Before I become known as an old teacher, let's get some rules and regulations down in writing which will help new or young incoming teachers to know what's expected of them."

Woodson's face flushed. He began to back away from any such rash proposal. So long as no rules were laid down, we didn't have to abide by any. And he could make his own.

He began to stammer in his quiet, spaced way of speech: "I---know what---you're trying to do---. You're---you're trying to back me into a corner. And---I---I---just won't be---backed into a corner."

And he never was. We continued to operate according to the dictates of each of the separate principals in each of the elementary schools. No rhyme. No reason. Each teacher was granted power over his own specialty--Ora D. Hayes, art; Ruth Engler, music; Mrs. Bear, discipline. And in a way, I suppose, it all balanced out in the course of six years. Or perhaps I became accustomed to it, as is the case with so much in our lives.

In addition to being Chief of Discipline, Cinny Bear was by far the most inquisitive person I've ever known. "Secrets" was not in her dictionary--although she thrived on them. If she couldn't pry information out of you personally, she tried to pump it out of your best friends. There was only one way to escape Cinny Bear's probing questions: Don't tell anybody anything.

Cinny also was the official "Scrap Eater" at lunch time. She existed on other teachers' luncheon discards. On occasion she did go to the cafeteria and buy a bowl of navy beans or turnips. They cost three cents. She supplemented this by reaching out and taking things from our plates or sacks. She prefaced her reaches by saying, "Bakey, you don't need two hot biscuits and all that honey butter. I don't mind helping you out with it." By the time she had informed me of her helpful intention, the biscuit and honey butter would be "down the hatch." Cinny's.

Or, eyeing a particularly tempting piece of fried chicken I had brought from home, she would say, "Bakey, you don't want all that fried chicken. I never get any good country fried chicken. Why don't you share with me?" And before you could blink an eye the drumstick or pulley bone would disappear.

To us "old" teachers it was all amusing for awhile. Until the faculty began to grow. Then the new teachers would warn her: "Now, Mrs. Bear, you don't know until I finish how much I'm going to eat. So you just wait until I declare my plate free for grabs."

Confidentially, Cinny told me, she considered such an attitude quite greedy. And she truly did! She had a big heart and, away from eating places, she did nice things for all of us.

Her husband was a house furnishings buyer for Scruggs, Vandervoort and Barney, the old-line St. Louis department store frequented by "blue bloods." He made a fine salary and both were well off financially. But "Teddy Bear" as we called him, was...well, eccentric. He mowed the lawn clad only in his shorts (the underwear kind). He would not have a car. He handled all of the arranging of furniture, draperies and bric-a-brac in the Bears' beautiful home on the corner of Peeke and Clay Streets, and only certain appliances were permitted in the kitchen.

When a new refrigerator became a must--he returned the first one delivered because it had a light blue interior--Mrs. Bear wasn't allowed a mixer because there was no place to store it artistically. However, he brought beautiful pieces when he came home from New York market buying--once a grandfather clock, once a French door knob. His favorite saying was, "Every house should have at least one French door knob." And he enjoyed my paraphrasing him to say, If he lived where I did, he would say, "Every door should have a knob."

However peculiar we thought them, this tiny couple (both were less than five feet tall) were fine people. Residents along Peeke and Geyer vowed they could "set their clocks" by Cinny Bear going to school. Or if they missed her, by Teddy Bear as he trudged to the street car line in downtown Kirkwood on his way to his job in the city.

Our modern society could well emulate their loyalty to routine, although Cinny was sometimes overly zealous in this respect. I've seen her come to school so ill with colds, fevers, and various viruses that she could, I'm sure, infect all of the students in her room--and maybe some out in the hallway. But she'd brook no substitute. "A substitute can ruin the kids. You just have to begin all over again."

But there came that day for Cinny, as it comes to all of us, and she had to give way to a sub. She suffered a severe heart attack one warm Saturday morning when she was making catsup. After weeks of bed rest, she came back to school, but never again was she the same Cinny Bear--grabbing food off our plates and throwing advice to all of us. She was quite subdued, her body movements slow and studied. And we all missed one of her earlier traits of running to the "john," pulling up her skirt as she trotted, prepared for action by the time she reached the door. She was so afraid she might miss something while she was away from the hall. Cinny tried to teach another year but she had another attack and she gave up the ghost gracefully after more than 40 years of primary instruction.

After five years of living in the Albert Ruhl home--stacked on top of the other years at Horse Shoe Bend, Owensville, Winfield and Bland--I chafed more and more under the Room and Board Syndrome, that occupational hazard of single teachers. I was positive I could no longer endure the tension of constantly being with other people, nor deny the ever-growing desire to be alone more. I liked the quiet life, the feeling of freedom to do as I pleased after school and on weekends.

My patience and forbearance were worn threadbare by the constant abrasion of Pat's remonstrances and advices: I should wear "Blue Swan" nylon panties and only Life Stride shoes, use the iron only after she ironed, use only Colgate toothpaste and snuff salt water up my nose every morning so I'd "be antiseptic" all day. I was requested to stay in town on the weekends she stayed and only go home when she went. I was a queer little "country bumpkin from the sticks" because I was fond of stitching a pretty pair of pillow cases or quilt blocks.

I'm certain--now--that Pat meant no offense. This was her way of helping me become more sophisticated. But simple Gracie didn't want the country taken out of the girl. So during the summer I arranged for new living quarters.

Earlier that spring Dorothy Warriner, a teacher at Pitman, had talked about my taking a room in her home; we could cook in her kitchen and share the grocer bill. I was desperate--and without much consideration I jumped directly out of the frying pan into the fire.

Her home was nearer Keysor School and, true, I didn't have to snuff salt water up my nose every morning. But I shivered at night with little bedding and almost no heat in my room. Dorothy occupied a back bedroom off the dining room and "Mac," a gentleman roomer, occupied a back bedroom off the kitchen. We scarcely saw "Mac." He seemed to work various shifts at the McDonnell-Douglas plant. As I look back on this arrangement, it must have appeared rather queer. Unknowingly, I probably served as a "buffer zone."

But the bad part was the food deal. I had paid Mrs. Ruhl a flat monthly rate. Now I might be paying any amount. I was to itemize anything I brought from home--eggs, cream, dressed chickens, etc.--then deduct it at the end of the month. Dorothy shopped for groceries and I paid half of the bill. For the first time in my life I realized how many household necessities can be purchased at a grocery store--soap and detergents for the laundry and bath, toothpaste and toiletries in general, kitchen tools and shelfpaper. I soon found my living expense had doubled.

When we unpacked those big brown paper bags, I wondered where did all that good stuff go? We seldom ate any of it. Our most frequently prepared evening meal was a piece of boiling beef cooked in the pressure cooker with a potato and carrot or cabbage added. This worked well, too, with the fat stewing hens I brought from home. But I found myself doing more and more cooking and housework because Dorothy was always tired or having to work on government forms to collect benefits for her sons after her estranged husband's death.

The year was not without its bright spots, however. I had charge of my own decisions. I could buy a suit or dress without Pat telling me it was a "poor choice" and I could choose suits with "mileage in them." I could even walk home by myself and not feel guilty--especially in a snowstorm.

The first one of the year hit hard. We awoke one morning in early November to find almost two feet of the white fluffy stuff on the ground, and the air was so full of flakes I drew them into my mouth and nostrils as I waded to school. No automobiles could navigate; people who tried it were stuck in their driveways. Only a few of us tramped our way to school--where the telephone in Mr. Smith's

MOVING TIME AGAIN
And I find out how many household necessities can be bought at the grocery store.

office was ringing off the desk.

We answered the inevitable question: "Will there be school today?" In Kirkwood the response--always--was "yes." A few parents walked to school with their children, and the teachers who'd mushed through the storm took the children from teacherless rooms and tried to go about business as usual.

Around noon the word came down from Central Office: "Dismiss." However, Mr. Smith decreed that no child could leave until his parent came for him. They had to appear at the classroom door and account for each child. Sometime after four o'clock I turned my last scholar over to his St. Bernard father and stepped out into my brave new world. I felt that I needed a flask around my neck to sustain me for my few blocks' walk to Evans Avenue.

The yearly state teachers' meeting was held that week, too. But it was poorly attended with traveling being almost completely stymied. From what I read in the newspapers and heard when I went back home, the only creatures which profited from the big storm were the deer. It was open season but few hunters ventured out.

This whole experience, I knew, was costing me dearly. But I think I grew a great deal. I was becoming myself again. I didn't carry around a constant resentment inside me for allowing Pat to lead me around. What I had done, I had done on my own volition. So I would look around carefully before renewing any further contract. But my new location came to be without my looking.

When Dorothy's father died, her family came to town for the services. She needed my bedroom, so I was shuttled out to Dell Duncan's home on West Washington in downtown Kirkwood. Dell taught the third grade at Pitman. She was unmarried, owned her own home, was "deaf as a doornail" and needed someone in the house with her, especially at night. She also was an exceptionally good cook and loads of fun. I still remember how she would twist her mouth as she recounted one of her blunders or repeated something a pupil had misunderstood. We "hit it off" famously and made our arrangements, but agreed that I would continue to live at Dorothy's for the rest of that school year.

My weekends and summers at home served to cushion the impact of this teaching, worrying and struggling to find my own little niche in the world. And that summer I particularly looked forward to the great riches of canning and preserving of food, and of doing some necessary renovating around the house. When I came home our laundry was always huge because I tried to be Mrs. Leach-clean. But we now had electricity, so washing and ironing wasn't quite as burdensome as it had once been.

But carrying peaches from the orchard in big buckets and bushel baskets hadn't changed any. Neither had the canning process. It still involved carrying baskets of glass jars from the smokehouse to the kitchen and forming the assembly line--wash jars, scald jars, drain jars, fill jars with cold, peeled peaches, tomatoes, beans or whatever was in season. Then you covered the goodies with liquid, and transported the sealed jars to the wash house where "Old Murphy," its belly full of finely split wood, was roaring with fire.

TOMATOES

They're lovely things to work with — and to look at in the cellar.

Some things, like green beans, required a three-hour boiling water bath. Soft fruits took only a half hour or so; tomatoes required only a thorough heating. If they boiled, they shrank into juice, unappetizing to look at in the jar. And I wanted my final rows of jars in the cellar to look pretty. Tomatoes are lovely things to work with--and we always had more than plenty. Mom's quota was four rows, all the way across our big garden. She never liked canning a few jars at a time. "Get a few big batches," she said, "and then you have a good start."

The "really big" canning started with washing and sorting the tomatoes. We laid out the firm, unblemished fruits on newspapers in a sunny corner of the south porch to get a final taste of the sun. The small ones and those with rotten spots were cored and put on to cook for juice. This usually was a day's work--hard work--because the cooked tomatoes had to be pressed through a sieve to remove the useable part--juice and pulp--from the skin and seeds. I often processed as many as 200 quarts of this juice alone for the winter's drinking and in cooking. We reserved some of it until the following day to be used as the liquid pack over the whole tomatoes.

But when the summer was gone we had hundreds of jars down in the cellar, jars filled with green beans, peas, cucumbers, okra and peppers. And those red tomatoes shown like rubies next to the yellow corn and golden peaches. Blackberries and various shades of plums were interspersed on the unevenly spaced shelves with jams, jellies, relishes, sauerkraut, sweet potatoes, beet pickles, pickled pears, peaches and watermelon rind preserves. As these summer fruits and vegetables were eaten, the jars were refilled with meats and fried-down sausages from the winter butcherings. No wonder the most famous of farm women's slogans is "Let's run to the cellar and get a jar." What a secure feeling!

Now I wonder how profitable all that canning was. We burned cords of wood which Dad split by hand. We spent hours and hours planting, weeding and hoeing before the stuff could be harvested. We spent most of our summer days slaving over two fiery furnaces, jumping in and out of the wash house to keep the boilers going full blast. Mom and Dad thought any other way of living was wasteful and extravagant. This way, we were sure of having enough to eat--something we were never certain of during the years of drought and depression. Could this memory be the compensation for all that hard work?

About this time I became intrigued by "new" vegetables--hybrid Big Boy tomatoes, cauliflower, broccoli, brussel sprouts, asparagus. I raised the Big Boys and the asparagus successfully; the others I could produce but only with great effort and poor quality. Mom and Dad knew I was wasting my time, work and money on this "newfangled stuff." And they never hesitated to tell me.

But one summer I inveigled Dad into helping me put the "spring patch" in new crops--acorn squash, egg plant, sugar lump cantaloupes. We even put in some new kinds of pie pumpkin, along with yellow pear tomatoes and some others I can't recall right now. The summer was dry, and Dad and I dipped water from the spring and carried to those precious vegetables and melons. They were just beginning to produce when school began and I had to forsake my "Walden Pond" garden and return to the "salt mines of Kirkwood."

I've often wondered myself why I chose to do what I did in my "sensuous summers." I saw Bud and Dad and Mom working out their very souls to keep things going--summers are golden, yes, but also short to the farmer who must make a living--and I couldn't even pull myself away for even a short vacation. I should have gone to school but I didn't. Money was always too scarce.

So the summers flashed by, somewhere out there, just beyond my grasp. By the time I had cleaned house, canned the "garden sass," baked a few dozen pies and loaves of bread, the whole "beautiful blob" was gone. And I'd be packing a couple of new cotton gingham, shirt waist dresses in my battered black leather weekender with a few older, faded checks and prints to take off for Kirkwood and another term of kids and counting milk money. Two cents for white milk, three cents for chocolate. Twenty cents for a plate lunch...

For the next five years Dell and I lived together in peace and harmony. We disagreed about a few things, as any two people will, and each of us adjusted to the other's quirks. Dell wanted, for instance, her room rent in cash every week. No check. And not $28 once every four weeks. She wanted $7 in cash every Monday morning when I came down for breakfast. That was to be her grocery money for the week; we had to get by on it. My room rent was extra. I paid that by the month. By check!

GRACIE AND DELL

Watch out, Famous-Barr. Watch out, Stix, Baer & Fuller. Here we come!

Dell's one great pleasure was "going downtown" on Monday and Thursday evenings when the big stores were open. And I joined right with her. We would hurry home from school, change into our "downtown uniform" (hats and white gloves) and away we'd go--walk one block south to Adams Street and catch the "56-Kirkwood-Manchester" bus and ride to the heart of the city. The ride was restful after a day of chalk dust and playground dust--or mud. And it readied us for inspecting every bargain in Famous-Barr's and Stix-Baer & Fuller's basements. And maybe Woolworth's.

Both of us were fond of the housewares department--bargain sheets, towels, table linens, yard goods, stamped pillow cases, dresser scarves. Everything! Sometimes we bought nothing. Or I might buy a quantity of remnants, bright prints for chair cushions and Mom's aprons. Usually I could find bargains in men's clothing, too, socks and everyday cotton shirts and trousers for Dad and Pete. Or winter overshoes and heavy underwear. Longjohns or longhandles, we called them back home. There was always something to look for--perhaps just a skein of embroidery thread.

But for Dell the primary downtown lure was to eat flounder, that famous white fish with a delightfully delicate flavor. She garnished it with a little game. If it wasn't on the menu, she upbraided the waitress: "Why haven't you got any flounder tonight? That's why I rode the bus all the way in from Kirkwood, just to eat flounder with you." Then loudly so half the restaurant could hear, "At your store!"

Convinced, finally, that no flounder was to be had tonight, she would assume a hurt, petulant attitude and condescend to eat there, anyway. Reluctantly. When the waitress named the choices of salad dressings, Dell was ready. In a tiny, quavering voice, she would say, "I'll have a dab of each, please, since you don't have any flounder tonight." With the poor girl out of hearing, Dell would laugh, gleefully anticipating her "dab of each," and she'd say, "Well, it worked again, didn't it?"

At first when we ate out Dell paid for my dinner. In the second or third year inflation became more noticeable and Dell informed me that she would pay half of my bill--as long as the cost didn't exceed the amount she spent. Toward the end of my stay with her bus fare became much more expensive and waiting for buses on Fourth and Chestnut in downtown St. Louis became less and less appealing. And Famous-Barr opened a branch in Clayton, so most of us switched our bargain-looking patronage. Besides, they served flounder there every Friday night.

About the third year with Dell, Ordith Harris brought a whiff of fresh March breezes into our orderly lives. Ordith was the P.E. teacher at Pitman, fresh out of college by way of Callaway County, Dell's home territory. She was a typical P.E. major--well-built girlish frame (tennis type), brown skin, dark brown eyes. I'll bet she had a wicked backhand. She had her strong likes and dislikes and was even stronger willed than Dell, with no temerity in voicing her opinions. When Dell served oatmeal for breakfast, for instance, Ordith refused to eat it. She stormed out of the kitchen, muttering something that sounded like, "I like bacon and eggs for my breakfast--food that'll stick to your ribs."

Dell couldn't believe her ears, even with her hearing aid turned on. She turned to me. "What did she say?"

After that Ordith didn't eat her meals with Dell and me. She could get a better breakfast cheaper, she said later, at the Katz Drug Store around the corner.

Ordith moved into the upstairs bedroom on the southwest corner. Mine was a larger, lighter front room, facing north. "The Pink Room," Dell called it. She had painted the wall paper pink when she bought the house a few years before. She had white dotted swiss curtains at the windows. There were three pieces of furniture in the room--a twin bed, a marble topped dresser and a wicker rocking chair. No rugs, no pictures. A small closet in the corner was half filled with boxes of Dell's things.

The room's most noticeable feature--and its noisiest--was the old, popping steam radiator. Such popping and cracking you never heard. *Hiss - hiss - hiss - crack - pop - pop - roil - roil - hiss - hiss.*

Some evenings when Dell was away from home she wouldn't leave the thermostat turned on, so I would simply freeze until she came back. Seems to me I've spent half my life waiting on heat. I was afraid to touch that monstrosity in the basement. Once or twice I threatened to go down and fire it up, but when I saw the apparatus I backed off. An augur arrangement carried the coal from the bin to the furnace and the furnace had cracks in it you could stick all four fingers into.

Ordith suffered no such physical fears nor mental qualms. She told Dell that she expected to be comfortably warm or she would deduct from the room rent. After that Dell would turn the thermostat up...to the lowest level on the scale.

Dell seemed impervious to weather changes. No matter how low the temperature fell--inside or outside--she wore her sleeveless house dresses. As soon as she arrived home in the evening she changed into one of her many bright-colored sleeveless aprons, then sang or whistled as she went about preparing our evening meal.

She was never quiet. Perhaps because she was so deaf, she like to have noise around her. Her deafness also served as a reason to go downtown. When her hearing aid became silent she would be out of business until she got new batteries. She wore them inside an unbleached muslin pocket stitched inside her brassiere. A most unhandy and uncomfortable business, I'm sure.

But it deterred Dell hardly at all in her enjoyment of life. We had much in common. She was a farm girl, too, almost a generation older than I. She owned a farm of her own, in addition to a share in her home place where her unmarried sister, Marian, and brother, Ted, lived. She had a keen eye for business. "I know a bargain when I see one," she often remarked.

She had another favorite quote: "When I sells my pigs, I wants my money." That was always good for Monday morning breakfast--especially if I didn't have that $7 for her in exact bills.

DELL'S MOTTO
"When I sells my pigs, I wants my money."

But Dell appreciated the beautiful Big Boy tomatoes, sweet potatoes, strawberries, rhubarb and other fresh vegetables and meats which I brought from home. She was an excellent cook and knew how to serve a meal beautifully. We ate breakfast in the kitchen but the evening meal was served in the west end of the living room on a bridge table covered with a pink linen cloth and accompanied by real linen napkins.

From here we could see the scenery and watch the passersby on Washington Avenue. In the autumn the tree-lined street glowed with color; in winter the car lights gleamed on the snow and ice; in spring the whole street was alive with birds and squirrels.

Along with Dell and Ordith adding "color" to my Kirkwood years were the students. One year I had an exceedingly difficult one, Dick Prince. Dick's mother bordered on genius, people said, but her children had to shift for themselves. Poor Margaret and Dick always looked unkempt and unhappy. Both bordered on yellowish-red skin and hair, accented by deep, dark circles under their eyes. Both had deep emotional problems and would fly into a rage over nothing. And Dick sucked his thumb, despite desperate attempts by teachers to stop him. The remainder of his arm and hand were practically crusted with dirt, but that thumb was angelic white.

PARENTAL HELP

"...let my mother sth-strh-gle with it. She knowth everythingth."

But he said funny things. Long division wasn't Dick's favorite subject and one morning he tried all the usual wrong ways to solve the problem I'd assigned. Finally, he removed that woolly-worn white thumb from his mouth and announced, "Well, I'll just take this stuff home and let my mother sth - str - rgle with it. She knowth everythingth."

Suzanne Lawler was unusual because of her size. A fifth grader, she was so large and well-endowed she looked like an adult female. Poor Suzanne. She could never sit in an ordinary desk. Her clothes were bought from women's racks and altered to fit her large, ungainly form.

Suzanne's younger brother, Tommy, was a rather small fifth grader. Tommy evidently trained his large brown and black-spotted hound to follow him to school. About three times each week, Tommy would come to the door by the playground and call out, "Miss Bacon, I'm leavin' now. Gotta take Old Drum home."

For a while Mr. Smith thought this was funny. Then Tom began staying home with Old Drum. That wasn't so funny. But Tom reminded Mr. Smith that he had permission to take Old Drum home.

"Yes, yes, Tom," Mr. Smith would say. "But I didn't give you permission to stay home with Old Drum."

There were other interesting characters in my room...twins I can't identify. Their names, it seems, were always Karen and Sharon, although I did once have a Karen and Camille. I learned to identify them by their shoes: one wore red and white saddle oxfords and one wore blue and white. Because Camille had larger feet, the mother advised me, the girls couldn't exchange shoes. She had trouble telling them apart sometimes, too, she admitted, if they were barefooted.

I had some exceptionally bright children; some exceptionally dull, too. But, all in all, they were mostly good kids from good families. As I look back on this section of my life, it seems I taught the same year 12 times. But from my years of experience I could feel--with a strange degree of assuredness for me--that I was a good teacher.

At Horse Shoe Bend and at Winfield and Bland and all the other schools, I had learned the whats and hows of teaching. With the Bessies and the Ruths and the Karls and the Henrys, I had learned some of the whos and whys. I hoped I had taught them something and, more important, I felt I had helped them find themselves. And I was happy with my own niche at Kirkwood, happy enough for anyone, anywhere...

Then, it seemed, the stars, the sun and the moon all became dazzling in all their beauty. And it was all right here on earth.

PART NINE

THE CLAY DOG

23

A few simple words

The summer at home had gone smoothly. I'd plunged into the usual cleaning and canning, then we took aim at the first week in August. This was Mom's time to have the Women's Guild, the first Wednesday in the month. And so we did. Such cleaning and baking and putting on the dog! It was a huge success...

The next day, Thursday, I put the laundry to soak in the big wash tubs, after building a fire in Old Murphy to heat the water. Then in the afternoon Mom and I attended the final rites for an old friend in Belle. As we were headed back home, the car sputtered and choked and had to be nursed along. We made it to Owensville and finally to Rosebud to be fixed. While we were waiting, we decided we'd get a bite to eat in Wehmeyer's Cafe. It was a roadside plate lunch and sandwich kind of place--an unlikely abode for romance.

Then in came Buell Ferrier. A clay dog, he frequently called himself. That was a person connected in some way with the fire brick industry, a big business in central Missouri, centered around the A.P. Green Company, the world's largest refractory, in Mexico. Buell's family and mine were old friends. His father had taught school, as did my Mom and Dad, and he had been county collector of Osage County when my father was a deputy collector.

Buell recognized Mom and me when he entered the restaurant and came over. He asked to join us in our booth and we passed bits of family information back and forth. His wife, Georgia, had died the previous winter. (I was sure he was quite lonely.) He and his 16-year-old son, Dan, were living with his daughter, Fern, and her husband, Sam Manley, in Linn. And they were all engaged in farming and cattle raising at the farm near the city limits. Buell's biggest interest seemed to be in restoring the small log cabin just north of the old farmhouse for his office.

Mom and I enjoyed the visit, but I thought nothing of this chance meeting. I was much more interested in getting home so I could get on with the laundry and tomato canning, because when August arrives, school is always beginning day after tomorrow.

The following evening I was sitting on the front porch resting a few minutes when I saw Buell rounding the curve at the foot of the hill. When I went down the steps to greet him he explained that he had picked tomatoes that morning. Some special ones, Purple Kings, had an extraordinary flavor, he thought. So he had brought us some. Of all things I needed, it surely was more tomatoes! I still didn't recognize this trumped up excuse for his visit. I thought he just enjoyed our family fun.

Dad and Pete had gone to town. And after explaining the tomatoes, Buell said he'd like to see our cattle. We visited a while, then I took him out to the lot to see the calves we were fattening. One, I remember, was a blue roan we called "Ike." He was quite playful, racing around the enclosure with his tail over his back, showing off like all young creatures do occasionally. Buell, standing by the fence and watching the calf cavort, seemed quite impressed.

We strolled then toward the car. Suddenly Buell stopped and drew a long breath. I turned to see whey he was so quiet and he asked me point blank, "Grace, if I asked you--sometime--would you consider going out with me?"

I was so astounded that I didn't answer quickly. I can't remember what I said, probably, "I don't know."

"Well, think about it," he went on. "I'll wait for an answer."

He didn't wait long. The next day I got a short letter, saying how much he had enjoyed visiting with Mom and me. Also, he'd like to come back over when Dad and Pete were home to see the whole herd of cattle. He didn't forget Ike either; he sent him "Best Wishes."

I never got a chance to answer the polite note, because on Saturday evening Buell appeared. He wanted me to go to Hermann with him. He had some business to attend to there and, besides, the Gasconade County Fair was going on...

I had nothing decent to wear--a typically female lament, I suppose, especially under the circumstances. All I had was a light blue cotton dress, very simple, but I pressed it quickly, got dressed and we went to Hermann to the fair.

From that day on, Buell talked in terms of "we" and "marriage." He never did propose to me; he just spoke of me as his "near future wife." He chose the rings; he took me to see the little office-house because he was planning for us to live there. But I had to approve everything, organize the kitchen, of course--and continue to teach in Kirkwood.

This last item bothered Buell. His work was classified as field superintendent for the Mexico refractory and he wanted to be responsible for me, for our living. That meant he wanted me to stop teaching. Stop teaching? But I was just getting good at it...and Keysor was a good school...and Kirkwood wasn't a bad place to live...and...

I had been independent too long. I simply couldn't feature having a husband provide for me. Besides, it wasn't just me. What would become of Mom and Dad and Pete? At first, I just knew I couldn't leave them...and the house. What would become of everything I had held dear all these years?

But Buell was not to be daunted. "You can do as you please," he insisted. "Stop that school teaching. Do the things you always wanted to do but never had time for." That sounded fantastic to me--but not realistic!

Come September and Buell was busier than his phrase, "a cranberry merchant in July," trying to keep up with the clay mines. Making the payroll for truckers and miners and paying royalties to pit owners was done semi-monthly. Then every Thursday he came to Kirkwood and on Friday we went home.

The weekends were busy. I still carried my laundry home to wash. And we had an enormous tomato crop--also butternut squash. Buell teased me constantly about canning "too much of these vegetables." I valued them more than his company, he'd say and grin. But that was my countrified way of living: Never waste food.

That summer I set up a schedule with him in mind. Monday I did the family laundry; Tuesday, the ironing; Wednesday, mending; Thursday, canning squash and other vegetables. That left the weekend for him. He treated this like a big joke and laughed at me for my rigidity.

Buell was not conservative. He had become a successful businessman because he had no fear of "splurging": One had to take chances if one ever expected to become financially independent. So he had bought three farms lying along Linn Creek and had gone into the white-faced cattle business, with a fine herd now of registered Polled Herefords.

The farms and cattle were cared for by his son-in-law, Sam Manley, and a neighbor, Dennis Schroeder. Dennis lived on one of the farms, the one his father had sold us. These two "boys," as Buell referred to them, were good workers. They took turns working on the farm one week and uptown in the "Blue Goose" one week.

The "Goose" was off limits to the fairer sex. But the men--the "men about town"--couldn't exist without it. Nothing really untoward occurred there. Just card games, a bit of imbibing, some sexy stories and exchanges of town gossip. It was the healthiest place in town, Buell always said, because "no self-respecting germ would live there." It was also know for its wonderful hamburgers. And the "Bony Burger," instigated by Buell. Ah, but enough of the "Goose." It deserves a book by itself.

The settled pattern of my life was in tatters. I was torn between choices. I could continue teaching school in Kirkwood all of my working life. Or I could marry Buell and be a wife, cook, housekeeper, bookkeeper...many things. Many of the things I knew I could do well, I had done them growing up on the farm; others would be completely new to me. But leave teaching? I knew that, too, now. But I had been at it for 25 years. And it seemed too good to be true, perhaps, to leave it. For a while, though, maybe...

Buell continued to press for a wedding date and I continued to try to postpone it. I wanted a little more time. But Buell was insistent. He could get away from the business the latter part of October. That would also be deer season. Oh, yes, deer season. Buell was an ardent sportsman. Guns, dogs, horses, hunting, skeet shooting, trap shooting--he loved it all. And he was Missouri's rifle champion for a time.

So it was only fitting and proper. We'd pay homage to deer season by getting married!

The rush began. I hadn't intended to buy any new clothes but all the girls at school were right: This was a once-in-a-lifetime affair. So I hurriedly rushed downtown to Stix, Baer & Fuller. I purchased a soft, dusty blue wool, two-piece suit, a pale pink, lacy, embroidered blouse and--of all things--a black velvet hat. A skull cap type, with octagonal points and a veil. Plumb wild. I also got a pair of black suede shoes and the filmiest of hose. Nylons.

Buell insisted on a fine, red leather jacket--for long walks in the deer woods. That he purchased for me. And I began to think maybe he was eager to get the marriage behind him so he could enjoy the hunt. He had a deer cabin in Gasconade County where for many years he had entertained friends lavishly during the season. He could hardly wait for this year. So my suitcase was hurriedly packed.

We left Kirkwood that Friday evening bound for Hernando, Mississippi. That was one of the places Buell had found which required no waiting period for marriages. We arrived in Hernando on Saturday morning, checked in at the Cote House and went to stand in line--with both blacks and whites (mostly the former)--to get a license permit. Then we repeated the process to get a license.

By now the happy expression on Buell's face had vanished. He hadn't counted on this. The day was sultry, sticky. My wool suit was uncomfortable and Buell was perspiring as we stood in line surrounded by perhaps two dozen black couples. I couldn't help wondering where the musical "Hernando's Hideaway" was--and wanted to be there.

After about an hour, we were granted a license and asked if we preferred a judge or a minister. Buell's inquiry was firm: "Is there a white minister in town?"

Yes, there was, a Presbyterian. We secured directions and phoned to be sure he was home. Upon our arrival, the Rev. Green found all to be in order and he performed the simple ceremony, pronouncing all the words of the old ritual in a typically slow, southern drawl. Buell Ferrier and Grace Bacon were man and wife. My name was Grace Ferrier.

It's still strange to me how a few simple words read out of a little insignificant looking black book can change one's name, life and work so drastically. I had embarked upon a new voyage. Some of it would be my happiest years. Some would be the greatest grief I had ever experienced.

24

To Tupelo and back for a deer honeymoon

Cliff English had the cabin open when we arrived about noon on Sunday. After the ceremony Buell and I had driven to Tupelo, Mississippi, to look at some fine herds of Herefords, then headed home for "the season."

A dozen cars, campers and pickups were parked between the cabin and the road. The usual crowd was there: Cliff and Eva Mae, Fern, Sam and Dan, Jack and Marceline Karsch, Earl and Virginia Ferrier, Roy and Elva McDaniel, and Ike and Helen Williams. Others came later.

Cliff always opened up the cabin, stayed the entire week and closed up when all was over. He never went hunting. He was always "going" but by the time he cleaned his gun, cooked, washed dishes, hauled in drinking water and shopped for the necessaries, Cliff never got around to any hunting.

Killing a deer wasn't the real motive for all this. The men liked the sportsmanship, the camaraderie, hiking through the rough timber, sometime checking out possible clay mining areas. But mostly they reminisced: "Do you remember the time when..." and "That first year Joe went, remember he..." On and on they recalled old memories and added new ones.

In the evening neighbors dropped in to visit. Several of our crowd played an instrument. But we always had Cliff on guitar and Paul Jones on violin, and you could count on a banjo picker showing up. We sat around the fireplace and sang the old songs--really old songs. None of us knew much about music, but that probably helped. To our untrained ears, we sounded like the Mormon Tabernacle Choir--with a Grand Ol' Opry flavor. For a time we forgot all worldly cares out there in the depths of the woods. I've often wondered since what the woods creatures thought when once a year their domain was so cruelly disturbed by this foolish form of life called man.

For the duration of the season we held open house, with Cliff always as host. Almost everybody went home at night--late. Most of us lived in Linn. That year Buell wanted to be in the woods early the following morning--Monday--so we made a quick trip to our new home in Linn, which was also Buell's office.

We were back at the clubhouse by 4:30. Cliff was already up. He had a fire roaring in the cook stove and the gray speckled granite coffee pot was steaming up the whole kitchen. We gulped down a mug of the smoking brew and rushed out to be on stand by five o'clock. "On stand" meant having an assigned position on a well-known deer trail. Others "drove" the deer, meaning they kept the deer moving--with the hope one would move past your stand.

Usually somebody in our crowd was successful in bagging a deer. So herewith a few precautions I learned if a truly wild deer is to be at all edible. First, it must be dressed out quickly. The digestive system must be removed almost at once--the sooner the better, especially if the deer have been feeding on acorns. Then the carcass must be skinned, loaded into a pickup or car trunk and taken to the locker to cool.

This coming and going continued for the entire season. It was a brand new experience for me and I thoroughly enjoyed it. Everyone took turns at the housekeeping and everyone brought his share of food. The amount of food that passed over that table was astronomical and its quality was quite "gastronomical," if I'm any judge. To these deer hunters, food was an important part of their "ritual"--indeed, their lives.

Buell especially loved good, hearty food--the staples, "stick-to-your-ribs" kind of food. Bread, meat, potatoes, gravy and vegetables. Not just ordinary meat, though. Steaks, so thick and tender. Roasts, cooked all day in the woodstove oven. Mashed potatoes with real cream whipped in. Gravy, with cream. Vegetables, crisp and tender, with cream or butter. And coffee--always coffee, with cream. Real cow cream.

Cliff was an expert in the corn bread and biscuit department. Nearly every evening he made a pone of cornbread; every morning he made biscuits. Usually, no lunch was served. But anyone feeling hunger pangs in the middle of the day was welcome to anything left over--or left out in the middle of the table.

At least two boilers of coffee were always going full blast. And there was always a line of coffee mugs on the sink top--waiting to be filled and sipped as you carried them to the big L-shaped porch to sit in the afternoon sunshine. As each foot-weary hunter straggled into camp, his first words were, "Gimme a cup."

As the week waned, so did the funny stories. And the wood pile. "When the last stick goes in the stove," Cliff would say, "we'll all pack up." He meant what he said. On Friday evening Cliff, Buell and I were all alone. We swept the floors, disposed of the leftover food, waited until all the fires were burned out, locked the doors and headed for another year of routine. Our deer season honeymoon was over. It was the first of many such beautiful weeks for me, weeks of being close to Mother Nature in a way I'd never been before, weeks of getting to know a side of Buell unlike any man I'd known, weeks that I stored away with loving nostalgia.

On Sunday I had to return to Kirkwood. Buell had to be back on his clay job--visiting each mine under his supervision at least once each week, collecting truck weights (tonnage hauled to Mexico). He was also continually buying clay, either by royalty or in the ground, whichever the owner preferred. We saw each other on weekends. This was a bit of my stubbornness; I didn't see how I could stop teaching so suddenly and Buell kept telling me he couldn't live in Kirkwood.

In the middle of the year the decision was made for me. I developed a series of benign tumors. I was sicker from worry than I was from them, so I went home to Linn and actually became a housewife. For a short time. But in the spring the Linn High School had an opening for an English teacher and I accepted it--not realizing how many duties were attached to that word "teaching."

That summer was beautiful, if a little hectic. I still had dreams of providing for Mom, Dad and Pete. Mom continually reminded me, "You've got to go on helping Pete." I always believed I had to do everything people thought I should do, so I was making myself miserable trying to be Buell's wife, housekeeper, cook, chauffeur, gardener. And I was determined to help Mom and Pete financially.

That Linn job--like many small town teaching positions--was practically a 24-hour deal. I was elected Senior Class sponsor. It was not one of those empty titles; it meant going to everything. Every time the doors were open, as the board of directors phrased it. Every week seemed to bring some money-making event.

I began in the fall with chicken barbecues. I not only split the chickens--200 of them--I helped set up the broiler pit, make potato salad and slaw, cut pie, set out plates and silver and coffee cups, serve plates, collect money, receive compliments if the food was good. And I took the criticism if some was left over. How was I to know the exact number of people who would show up to eat?

In late October we held the school carnival. This was the big event for everyone in Linn School--old and young, big and little, thin and fat. Each senior class chose a motto. "Here Today, Gone Tomorrow" was ours. I thought it sounded like an epitaph on a tombstone--or perhaps a description of my early teaching career--but I kept my amusement to myself. The class was pleased and the kids might resent my two-cents' worth.

CLASS MOTTO

"Here Today, Gone Tomorrow" sounds too much like my epitaph.

Next came building our float on a hay wagon. Locating available hay wagons and tractors to draw them in the parade was an annual major problem. After a wagon was located it was moored at the corner of the cattle barn on the Osage County Fair Grounds a short distance from school. Then we began stuffing toilet paper into the chicken wire forms. This year we used red crepe paper and white toilet tissue to outline the motto.

Every evening was spent in the barn with the kids, teachers and parents vying with each other for the best prize. (Mr. Vanderberg usually decorated a wagon all by himself for his daughter Margaret's class. He roped off a space and forbade any child to come near. On the big day his wagon usually won.) Our high school band led the parade down Main Street, playing "When the Saints Go Marching In"--the only piece the kids could play.

We moved regally out onto Highway 50 where the State Patrol held up traffic for a couple of hours so we could display our toilet tissue sculpture. On windy days, the tissue began to blow away, tuft by tuft, as soon as the floats emerged from the barn. This meant that the real handiwork never got to the parade at all; it was in the tree tops, blowing over the grounds and dangling from rooftops all over town.

After the parade the evening was filled with activities--dinner in the cafeteria, games in every room, plays in the gym, bingo in the study hall, cake walk in the music room. And bedlam in the halls. All this might sound like fun--and it was, for participants. In addition to overseeing building the float, I had to coach a play; line up the Kings and Queens--one pair from each grade; round up the robes and crowns--and see they got on the royalty; see to the money in the senior concession stand; see that more hot dogs and buns were always cooking...

I spent the evening pushing my way through the narrow halls, up and down. My room--the Control Center--was at the extreme north end, the worst possible location for management. The whole evening was one big rush with hard work, nervous excitement and scant thanks. I still remember--with anger--the criticism from Supt. Willett when he thought we didn't make enough profit!

But the students were appreciative and cooperative and I enjoyed doing it for them. Many times that first year I was hurt by critical remarks. I was teaching nearly 200 students from Grade 7 through Seniors--English and Social Studies. Through no fault of their own, most of them were lower achievers and there was so much teaching to do for them. I needed 24 hours a day to teach.

But I must tell you about my reunion with an old friend, an old, crippled friend. On the first day of school I was assigned that queer little end room at the north entrance. I marched down the hall, turned the key in the lock, and there patiently waiting for me was my old lame desk from McDaniel--the one Lou Kenney had put together on that zero-degree morning way back in the Thirties.

I could hardly keep from crying. Instead, I laughed. I stuck my head underneath to see how Lou's carpentry had held up all these years. It looked just fine-- the same eight penny nails, the same little cross pieces nailed across the corners to support the legs. So I had one friend I could always depend on for the next five years. Whenever I felt completely overcome by class sizes, paper grading, extra curricular activities, illness, grief or harassing worries, I held onto my scarred, ink-stained, dusty smelling--but friendly--McDaniel.

I worked harder that year than ever before or since. I seemed to always be on my way to school, teaching, sponsoring a class function, P.T.A., coaching a play, having a barbecue, splitting chickens, cooking hot dogs for basketball games--or stuffing toilet tissue in chicken wire for a float.

There was little time for home. Fern and Sam and Dan helped all they could. Dan was a senior and had to attend most of the same functions. And just when we seemed to be coming to a free evening, Mr. Willett would plan a potluck faculty supper. Oh, all the "duties" that come under the heading of Teacher! Woe awaits those who go into the profession lured by the "easy hours." And a curse upon those who say, "It must be nice to be done with your day's work at 4 o'clock."

Life, however, had its lighter moments, like those enjoyable evenings when Buell would be waiting for me after school so we could go to the clay mines or collect the weights or perhaps visit an old friend. He had been in business for many years; he knew and liked everybody. We also had lots of company--people coming by to chat a minute, people passing through who hadn't a place to spend the night. Between the two of us, we knew almost everybody in the mid-Missouri area. And in our spare moments we went home to see about Mom and Dad.

For two years we lived in Buell's "office"--the small re-constructed log building at the west edge of Linn. Downstairs one large room ran the width of the cabin; back of that was a kitchen and bath. Upstairs over both was a large bedroom. Buell loved living there, but it was much too public for my out-in-the-country liking.

The rear of the house was much too close to the creek, too, we found out the first spring we lived there. We had three inches of rain in 45 minutes and all the creeks and branches poured down upon us in a turbulent flood. I had been ironing and baking bread all day. When I first spied the rising waters, I carried my ironing upstairs and warned Buell that the creek was rising dangerously. He was taking a nap and refused to be disturbed.

I carried boxes of important papers upstairs from the downstairs closet and I moved the cars to higher ground, away from the rapidly surging brown water. It was all around us now; we were an island in the middle of a small lake, growing bigger. The fence back of the kitchen was gone. And when the cattle crossing floated by I called one last time to Buell: I was leaving. He could go down with the

THE FLOOD

Buell naps, the waters rise. And there go Ray Weber's pigs.

ship if he pleased.

The wise Mr. Ferrier came bounding down the stairs, his eyes bugging. He had on his hat and his shorts, but no trousers. He began sentences and left them hanging in mid-air. I remember one especially: "Why didn't you tell me it was raining?" And "You didn't say it was flooding!"

In short order he pulled on his trousers and we waded our way to the car. We drove over the highway to Fern's--actually making a circle, because Fern and Sam lived on the creek bank just above us. Here we saw the water we had just escaped. It covered the floor boards of the bridge and completely surrounded our farm house and cabin. As we watched, stunned, several of Ray Weber's hogs washed out of his feedlot above us and floated downstream. One went under the bridge. I was sure his day would be done--but he surfaced nonchalantly, swam to shore and politely ambled over and sat on Fern's front porch! There he waited until the flood waters receded. Then he waddled away toward the hill--only to be rounded up a few minutes later and returned to a somewhat soggy sty.

A couple of years later we moved to the farm house. Fern and Sam had built a new house about a half mile distant down the Luystown Road on the Schroeder place, actually Hundepohl land then. Fern had selected the site, full of big oak and hickory trees, for her new house--which came when Sam's totally unknown aunt died and left him a goodly inheritance.

DAN

Can a hard-nosed school teacher succeed as a teenager's mother?

Dan moved with us, so I headed for a new experience--the care and feeding of a teenager. His mother had seen to it that Dan had wanted for nothing. He had been fed the richest of food, clothed in the best money could buy. He had been sheltered from life, period. Her death had left him distraught, trying to make some sense out of life. He was a lonely, lonely young man. Fern was 20 years older than Dan and Sam possessed a happy, goodnatured personality, so all together we tried to help Dan over the rough spots.

I didn't try to humor Dan. I cooked good wholesome food, the kind both Buell and I liked. If my menus failed to appeal to Dan's appetite, he would supplement his breakfast with hot dogs, which he fixed himself.

We disagreed heartily on money. Dan had been brought up thinking you wrote checks when you needed money or you simply said, "Charge it." One of Dan's first words as a toddler, Buell said, was "Let's charge a check." Dan was always working a Big Deal--a car, a truck, a tractor, a boat, or a herd of cattle. And like his father, he got them all--and more!

Now I look back and wonder how I did all the things I did. I did all my own housework, the laundry, cooking, mending, yardwork, tended flower beds and gardened in the summer. And I canned and preserved an enormous amount of food for our winters.

As always, one of the things I enjoyed most was the garden. On the east side of the house lay an acre of fine, rich sandy loam. There I grew tomatoes, cabbage, corn, carrots, beets, beans, lettuce, asparagus, onions and a few lesser known vegetables as experiments. In the center of the patch was a row of multiflora rose which Dan and Sam had "heeled in" to await spring planting. Their "spring" never came--except in my garden.

I put in a strawberry patch on the west side of the house. Some years it was almost too productive. One spring Jennie Mae, then in junior high school, helped me pick, stem, preserve and freeze the patch's crop. Every morning we picked six to eight gallons; every evening we preserved and froze. The first couple of days went well enough. By the third day Jen was tired. When she started to the patch, I said, "You go on and begin picking. I'll be along in a minute with the buckets."

She looked disgusted. "Buckets? Buckets?" she said. "You mean there'll be enough for several more buckets again today?" We filled a couple of buckets which I gave her to take home.

Buell was fond of those homegrown food products; he relished every bite of them. In addition to the garden stuff, we had giant wild gooseberry bushes and blackberry bushes. And there was a cherry orchard on the Schroeder place and plum thickets on the Gasconade County land. So I was always well supplied with fruit for jelly, preserves and for canning for pies in the winter.

Gooseberry jelly and pie were Buell's favorites, so he always found the finest berries when he was out looking about the cattle. Then he would drive me to the location and sit in the car and read "A Tale of Two Cities" or Sherlock Holmes while I picked berries. He always said I didn't need help. I could pick faster if he weren't around to "help me."

I thoroughly enjoyed the Hundepohl house; it was so homey. The living room and front bedroom were separated by a hallway and stairs which led up to two big bedrooms and a bath. Back of the living room was a large dining room; back of that the kitchen. Back of the downstairs bedroom was a bathroom and closet area, and filling one large corner between the bedroom and the dining room-kitchen was a beautiful utility room where I kept my canned fruit and such. It had an extra sink as well as my laundry equipment. It made a delightful eating area in summer, and in winter Buell "cured out" his pork there.

Oh, yes, and ah, me. That meat curing season! We went through it every January. As soon as Christmas was officially over, Buell called his meat packing friend, Barney Stegeman, and ordered hams, shoulders, sides and sausage meat. Then we laid layers of brown wrapping paper on the floor and counter space. When the "green" meat was delivered Buell went into complete ecstasy. He almost danced as he mixed up the salt, pepper and brown sugar concoction in my big brown crock. And he'd laugh like a schoolboy as he spread this mixture carefully and lovingly over each ham shoulder and "middlin'", as Missouri folks call the side meat.

His glee doubled when he began to mix the sausage. He had various flavored recipes; some were celery, some garlic and some sage, some heavy with white pepper. All were delicious. We mixed small amounts and fried a couple of patties. When our taste buds approved we fried it down, sealed it in a jar for summer use, then began a new batch.

My worst job was thoroughly cleaning the intestines. They would hold the finest of our sausages--some of each flavor to be given to Buell's company workers from Kaiser Aluminum, merged with Mexico Refractories.

When we finally stuffed all the sausages, we hauled them to Clem Franken at the locker plant to be smoked--ever so slightly--with fine corncob smoke.

Sometimes when the sausage season was over I breathed a sigh of relief--only to arrive home some Monday evening to be greeted with more sausage aromas from the kitchen. There'd be Buell wearing my best apron and grinning at me, up to his elbows in fresh sausage, brown sugar, black pepper, celery seed and garlic. I knew what was coming: "Honey, I gave away so much sausage I didn't have any left for myself." And so on and on. Sausage, sausage, sausage, hams and bacon...

Our life was certainly far from dull. We had no private life. People streamed constantly through our house--truckers, miners, drillers, pit owners, Buell's coworkers who drove down from Mexico, company executives and lawyers.

Once when we lived in the office we had to record testimony concerning mining of a pit which was involved in settling an estate. Two Philadelphia lawyers came to Linn to meet with Buell and Bob Branson and a few other men who remembered details of the pit in question. We had no fence around the yard and our cattle herd often partook of the shelter of the car port on the east side of the house. Of course, on the day of the recordings, they practically surrounded the house. Later we'd play back the recordings and hear Bob Branson saying something like this:

"Yas, yas. Wahl, hit ware, yas, hit ware in the sprang of the yare..."

Moo, moo. Softly, outside.

"I remember. Wahl, I recollect real clear now. Yas, it ware in the sprang of the yare. When we'uns got stuck plum to the gills buildin' that thar road in thar..."

Mooooooo!

It was a loud demanding bellow from Old Bullet who had found his way onto the "cow port."

Bob Weigle would intervene, trying to get definite details of some consequence for the record. But all Bob seemed to remember for sure that "hit ware in the sprang of the yare"--and "that thar mud mighty nigh" caused him to stop "minin' operations fer good." However, it was a good recording of Old Bullet's bellowing and Buell laughed himself into paroxyms every time we re-played it. I felt badly about those lawyers and the company having to depart minus the information they had come so far to get, but Buell said it was all on paper over at Mexico. All they had to do was dig it out. But I'm sure no information could have been as interesting as Bob and Bullet.

In the summer we had good times at the Ferrier family get togethers. Buell had three sisters and one brother, and with as many of their offspring as could be rounded up, we often went to Merle and Homer's clubhouse on the Gasconade River at Rollins Ferry or to our clubhouse in Gasconade County, to Fern's or to Earl and Virginia's house in town.

Once or twice, on very special invitation, we went to Paul and Verna Jones' house. Verna was next to Buell in age and they had a close relationship. But Verna was more a businesswoman than a housekeeper or cook. She never cooked when we visited. There'd be plastic over everything--the living room furniture tied up in plastic covers, the living room and bedroom rugs covered with plastic. Even her electric skillet was securely enclosed in a plastic bag and fastened as if it had never been used. I was fascinated! For these "company" occasions, Paul and Verna had a summer house built in the back yard. There she kept her supply of large white coffee cups and paper plates and there we ate. We never went to the house. (They "took" all their meals at "The Green Gables.")

That way, though, we didn't miss Paul's bouts with Old Teddy. Old Teddy had been Mr. and Mrs. Ferrier's dog and when they died Verna had a fancy house and pen built for him. It was Paul's job each evening to feed Old Teddy. And Paul hated Old Teddy. I guess the feeling was mutual. Even though Teddy was blind, he would growl and raise the hair on his back whenever Paul approached. Paul, an angelic man if one ever drew breath, would throw the food at Teddy and run for dear life, usually muttering, "I wish that damn dog would die."

If Verna heard him, she would almost cry and take Paul to task for "not caring for poor old Teddy...who is blind and Papa's last pet on this earth."

Merle was Verna's opposite. She was an excellent cook and constantly used her kitchen--one of the nicest and most conveniently planned I ever saw. Her family was her whole life. Homer Turner, her husband, and Paul Jones were also in the clay contracting business...with A.P. Green. And Paul and Verna shared the business and Homer did the supervising and the actual work. So while the women cooked and exchanged recipes and swapped gossip in the kitchen, the men re-hashed and re-mined every clay pit in central Missouri.

Added to the fullness of my life in Linn were a series of notably unnotable dogs. "Dumpy," the first, was Dan's doing. When we first moved to the Hundepohl farm house, Dan begged for a dog. Buell "sort of promised" him one but delayed carrying through. One day I noticed Dan was confiscating all the table scraps, wrapping them in his paper napkin and slippng out the back door to the barn. When I mentioned this to Buell he nodded. "All signs point to a dog in the manger," he said wisely. How true. He probably was party to the plot.

In a few days Dan brought forth his prize winner--if prizes are awarded for more fleas, more lice, more mange and less fat than any dog I had every seen. He was not to be classified in any book and Buell and I laughed and cried over the poor, miserable little creature. Buell, who had bred and trained dozens of fine dogs in this country and Canada, was appalled at the sight and we set to work on him with medicines, powders, sprays, bath preparations and cleansers.

In due time it came out that Dan had made the acquaintance of this newly-refurbished dog at the city dump when he and cousin Linda Turner had gone to feed a litter of kittens someone had dumped there. It only stood to reason: Dan's fine dog would be christened "Dumpy."

Dumpy was soon joined by another stray, a beautiful, long-haired black and white male. "Little Boy," we called him, for his gentle, sweet temper. We hauled him and Dumpy to Jefferson City for their appropriate rabies and distemper shots--so we could keep them in town. And within a few days both dogs disappeared, never to be seen again.

I was still mourning Dumpy and Little Boy when the dog of my life appeared--on the back steps. Every morning I went out to feed the cats and there would be this small orange and white female rat terrier. She was always starved. I didn't want another dog. And I certainly didn't want a female. But Buell reminded me how much we were all missing Dumpy...and I might as well go on feeding her until we could find a way to dispose of her.

She knew how to make use of her reprieve. She continued to sit and wait for me on the step. She jumped for joy when I spoke a kind word to her or reached down to stroke her hard little head. She seemed to have one idea: Win over Grace.

She brought me gifts. One morning she'd leave a dead mole on my back door step; the next morning a dead rabbit. So I was surprised one morning on my way to school to see her dragging across the highway a whole ham bone I had given her. That evening when I arrived home I was even more surprised: On the back step were two cute pups, one black, one brown. Failing to drag the ham bone to the pups, Nancy had brought the pups to the ham bone.

She had won. We fed all three and babied all three, and dear little Nancy became my constant companion. She helped me as much as any dog ever helped a human being on this earth. She possessed in her canine heart, so help me, a love that surpassed human understanding. We only disagreed on one thing: Every holiday Nancy had pups. I finally became a bit disgusted with having to dispose of her string of babies. In return she would treat me with utter disdain for a couple of weeks. Finally I could stand these gifts no longer, so I had her spayed.

Buell named her Nancy, after our old yellow cow--and out of his love for the name itself. Years later, when Yvonne and Alan Kouby named their daughter

DOGS OF MY LIFE

"Dumpy" and "Little Boy" get the works for town living — and disappear. But Nancy comes to stay.

Nancy, Mama said, "Grace, you've just got to change that dog's name. We can't have a dog and a baby girl with the same name." But Nancy dog remained Nancy dog.

Those were happy, busy and prosperous years for us. We built up a fine herd of registered Hereford cattle. Earlier Buell had sold the herd to Sam and Dennis but soon Buell and I re-bought them. I put my savings into my half interest. We had a full time farmer on the job now so he looked after most of the chores, but we liked feeding them in the evenings.

Dan also helped on the farm. We bought the George Voss farm to supplement the other two. I was particularly proud of this acquisition. Mom and Dad had begun their married life there and the first four of their children were born there. But that's another story.

While I lived in Linn my first real sadness and losses came to me. Dad became ill in July--with heart congestion--and his condition never improved. He died on my birthday--February 28, 1960--exactly 40 years to the day after we moved to the farm at Cooper Hill. At the time we were snowbound and icebound and the thermometer was stuck on zero. But on that Sunday morning after Dad died I paused on the back step and looked, almost blinded, at the dazzling sunlight on the snow. There, in a sheltered spot under the grape arbor, a pearly snowdrop bloomed bravely, trying to show me that life is everlasting if ye have the faith of a mustard seed!

I needed the snowdrop's message. Following Dad's death came Buell's fatal illness. First his hands and legs began to pain him severely, then came swelling and general deterioration. He would fall asleep sitting in a chair, at the table, driving a car. He stayed in bed, hardly moving at all until afternoon. I took care of the business--gathering truck weights, writing pay checks, doing the semi-monthly report for the company. With his help, of course.

Then came a series of hospitalizations. First at St. Mary's in Jefferson City. Buell's ailment was diagnosed as peri-arteritisnodosa. There is no recovery, the doctor said. I was stunned, felled at my roots. What would I do without Buell? He had become my rock. When things weren't going well for me, I had only to pour out my soul and he made all well again. We were just beginning to live. Now he was going to die.

Again and again, he made me see that one must be happy and optimistic even in the face of adversity--especially in the face of this adversity. He forced me to sit and take notes on what was yet to be done with each clay mine we were working.

Each farm had its unfinished chores. The cattle would have to be sold and perhaps one farm to pay our outstanding debts and lessen the burden of operation.

And there was farm machinery in partnership. This had been troublesome when Cecil Laughlin died unexpectedly the previous December.

All this time Buell admonished me to "be happy." *Don't feel sad when I'm gone. I've been richly blessed. I've had everything I ever wanted in this life.* Of course, what he wanted was dogs, cattle, farms, machinery, guns, good steaks and mashed potatoes, cars, riding horses, skeet shoots, trap shoots...And I was pleased I could say it: Me.

We spent Thanksgiving and Christmas at the hospital in Jefferson City, and most of the time in between. His room was like our house--running over with people all the time. In January Verna decided we ought to take him to Barnes Hospital in St. Louis. Dr. McBryde, whom I had known in Kirkwood, was our

BUELL

We were just beginning to live. Now the doctor says there's no recovery. What would I do without my rock?

friend there as well as physician.

Buell did get some better. He could walk, with some help. His mind improved. They took him off Cortisone and Orinaise and the other steroids. His appetite perked up and after three weeks I took him home. He was able to do the company reports. At last, I was able to feel a little of the way he told me: Be happy; be optimistic. I could manage part of one. At times. We found a man, John Gelvin, to stay with Buell and I went back to school.

In March of that year Mr. Willett deemed it necessary to curtail my services with the Linn Public School. He couched his reason in flimsy, porous words, like "You have a sick husband. Your services will not be required after this term." And so on.

His notice of my termination bothered me, of course. It intruded upon--perhaps lessened--my worry about Buell. After his improvement, for a while, I put those words "No recovery" in the back of my mind. He had improved, I told myself. Doctors had been wrong before. Maybe...

The night before he died he said, "Honey, I'm going to get almost well. We'll cut down the farming operation some and with Cloe to help us, we'll just live comfortably and have each other."

He always wanted me to say the Twenty-third Psalm with him before we slept. After we prayed together that night, he turned to me and said, "Darling, I feel better than I've felt for years. Like your dad said the night before he died, 'I feel good enough to go rabbit hunting'."

He giggled softly, went to sleep and never awakened. It was Easter Sunday, April 23, 1962.

PART TEN

BACK TO KIRKWOOD

25

And a decision made long ago

As soon as the word spread around town that I was out of a job, Cecil Kuster called me. He had done his practice teaching in Linn under my guidance in the Thirties. Now, he wondered, would I do him the honor of teaching at Westphalia the following term. In my sad state of mind I gladly said "Yes" and signed a contract for considerably more than I had been getting at Linn. At least I wouldn't starve while the estate was being settled.

There was one hitch. To teach speech I would have to go to summer school. That turned out, however, to be another Godsend for me. It required that I become completely involved. I had to get up early and be at Lincoln University in Jefferson City by 7 o'clock. Sometimes I rode with other teachers from Linn; most of the time I drove my own car.

I took three courses--a total of 10 hours of speech. The instructor, Mrs. Teabeau, was a master teacher. She was black, completely capable of teaching speech, rebuking an unmannerly young man, correcting the boom-booming of an Ozark preacher--all with the kindness which marked her as the true lady she was.

I had her for all three of my classes--two of them quite small--and we became good friends. She was in the same boat: Lincoln University had found it didn't require her services any longer, either. So she was preparing to make her residence in Wilberforce, Ohio, where she had secured another teaching position. I was glad I got her before Wilberforce!

That summer Mrs. Teabeau refreshed my memory and my mind with the proper reading of old ballads, with old and new poetry, by both black and white poets. We made speeches--sometimes three per day. We re-learned our vowel sounds--the fricatives and the plosives, the dipthongs and our N g's. All of it, with Mrs. Teabeau, was engrossing and fascinating.

Jennie Mae and Anna Lo were at the University of Missouri that same summer. They worried about just how Aunt Grace would come out grade-wise. I must admit I was a little concerned myself, with all the turmoil of my mind. So I was absolutely amazed when my transcript arrived in August: It had three As on it! I never did find out how Lo and Jen came out, but I let them know about mine.

In August between summer school and teaching, we had the machinery and farm equipment sale. All those pieces of various colors, makes and models...John Deere, Oliver, Case, New Idea, Ford, I.H., New Holland. All the Lundell machinery, which was practically new. Only a year before Buell and I had gone to Cherokee, Iowa, and bought several pieces. Now it had to be sold. There were scales, feed bunks, the pickup, shovels, scoops--big and little, old and new. It all had to be sold except what we needed to feed the cattle until I sold them.

I also sold Buell's office equipment--adding machine, check writer, desk, chair and filing cabinets. I couldn't go to see these things sell. I shut myself up in the farmhouse and cried. I wanted to run away. But we don't always do what we want to do.

Then it was over. The acreage around the cabin, the office, everything was bare.

GODSEND

I go to summer school at Lincoln University and Mrs. Teabeau, Teacher, becomes a friend.

Everything was hauled away. I was living alone. All alone. With Nancy.

Again Nancy was my constant companion. She guarded the house vigilantly when I left and she greeted me with great affection when I returned. Most nights, she slept in an easy chair out in the utility room. And if anyone came near she growled and bristled viciously. I needed her.

Almost as soon as school began at Westphalia, I saw that I had another one of those impossible jobs. I had four Junior and Senior English classes with an average of 50 pupils per class, plus two speech classes with about 25 per class. That was enough ordinarily, but now I was weary in body and soul. Buell's illness had sapped my strength. I had been up and down all night, administering to him. Now I was having to do some long-range planning. With the estate I was going to be better off than I had originally thought, but I had to decide: Either settle down in Linn for the rest of my life or relocate myself in short order. I knew myself; once I got set in a pattern, it would stick.

I could come up with only one sensible answer. I'd inquire about a job in Kirkwood--as soon as the New Year rolled around.

Meanwhile, I must do the best I could do at Fatima in Westphalia. The school district was composed of 13 small town areas stretching from Jefferson City to Linn--to Wellsville and St. Thomas, Freeburg, Meta, Koeltztown, St. Elizabeth, Taos, Rich Fountain, Loose Creek and Bonnots Mill, Schubert and large acres of farm land in between.

The entire student body was Catholic. They thought in true terms of the Church. Their speeches in speech class were on the Ecumenical Council being held in Rome at the time. In spite of my devious and numerous methods to pry them slightly away from Pope John and Cardinal Ritter, they insisted and persisted in their ways.

They were good kids; no discipline problems. And they had a great desire for learning. I felt inadequate. I could tell them the stories in books, but our library was devoid, so it seemed to me, of anything Protestants ever heard of. There were treaties of Pope Pius XV and Pope Gregory and Cardinal So and So, but not one volume of good English or American Literature.

I mentioned to Cecil one evening about the need to add a few good books each year so they could eventually assemble a good library. He hardly danced a jig, but a few days later he informed me that we could have $200 to spend on books. Then I danced a jig! With the help of some avid reader friends and the Junior and Senior classes, I spent it quickly. We bought paperbacks to stretch our funds and, my, what fun they had with those little books.

I enjoyed the Fatima cafeteria as much for its amusement as for its food. Both were good. Each class lined up and marched to the cafeteria. Not one word was spoken. It was almost regimental. The strict discipline outlined by Mr. Kuster, superintendent, was enforced in the halls and cafeteria by Mr. Kuster, principal, his brother.

Everywhere the kids turned one of the Mr. Kusters would remind them that if they departed from the beaten path, their parish priest would be notified. For verification Mr. Kuster, Supt., would look at Mr. Kuster, Prin., and say, "Isn't that the way it should be, Mr. Kuster?" To which Mr. Kuster, Prin., would reply, "True, true, Mr. Kuster. Very true."

This Mr. Kusters business went on in assembly, in the office, in the halls. Everywhere.

"Isn't that right, Mr. Kuster?"

FATIMA

At Westphalia it was heavy on the Pope and light on literature. But, oh, the fun we had spending Cecil Kuster's $200 on books!

"True, true, Mr. Kuster. Very true."

My sympathy was truly with the kids. So I tried to see that we had some fun. We read poems which were just plain fun. We read stories just for fun. They were reasonably well grounded in grammar; their Sisters of Notre Dame had seen to that!

I never found one Protestant student in the entire high school. But among some rooms over the shop in a building behind the main school house was a room for Protestant elementary children. One of them I remember for two good reasons: One, his mother was a Church of God minister. Two, his name. In a community full of Balkenbuschs, Berhorsts and Dudenhoeffers, Hilkemeyers, Kloeppels and Luebberts, Mengwassers and Mertensmeyers, Plassmeyers and Schwartzes, Stuckenschneiders and Winkelmans, his name was Sidebottom. Robert Sidebottom. We became good friends.

These kids were not far removed from nature. Their lives in many respects were almost primitive. Most came from extremely hardworking farm families of German ancestry. They talked in terms of chickens and turkeys, pigs and cattle, of church affairs (parish picnics were the big events of the year) and drinking beer (its status was somewhat like water at our house). While my Catholic knowledge was woefully weak, luckily, I knew a little about farming.

I knew nothing, however, about plumbing and I needed such knowledge after I severed my last link with Buell's farm and cattle operations. I sold our cattle herd in October. Sometime in the morning after the sale I awakened to hear water pounding in the utility room and Nancy barking loudly. I jumped out of bed, ran to the kitchen and opened the door. Water was running like a flash flood all over the place and Nancy, standing dry in her chair, was yelping wildly about it.

The water pressure had not been turned down at the end of the sale and the valve in our utility room closet had burst.

I couldn't budge the knob to close it. I ran to the phone and called our plumber friend, Fred Nilges. Fred answered sleepily. "All right, Grace, just wait until I get my pants on." In a few minutes Fred was there and closed the valve. But I swept and mopped water for two hours until time to go to school.

That winter brought plumbing and heating problems for many people. Snow piled up--deep to a nine-foot Indian. All the water pipes on our hill froze. Sam brought me cans of water from the fire house in East Linn. Bathroom facilities resembled a commode; dishes were washed in a pan. And the furnace, true to form, went on the blink about 2 o'clock one morning.

Outside the temperature hung at zero--and it was beginning to feel that cold inside. Again good friends came to my rescue; this time Ed Lock came down and got the furnace started again. But all winter I had to jump out of bed and give the brush a spin to start it.

My life seemed out of control. Buell's death not only had taken away my anchor; it left me to handle affairs which I was at best only conversant with--and that only because Buell had insisted we go over things before he died. I had to teach. That much I was sure of. For the first time, I realized I needed to teach. The money, of course, would come in handy until the estate was settled--and after. But more than money I needed to be needed. There just might be another Bessie out there in some school, some class room...

I appreciated Cecil Kuster's asking me to teach at Westphalia, but I knew I would always feel like an outsider there. I felt buffeted, unsure of my bearings and uncertain about what to do, where to go.

Soon after the holidays I made my decision. I again contacted Mr. Alva Crow, the superintendent in Kirkwood, about an opening--any opening--in the schools there. I received his reply by mail in early February. It was encouraging: As soon as an inventory was made, he wrote, he was positive a place could be found for me.

That very evening the phone rang. It was Mr. Crow. Would I like to teach English and Social Studies at Nipher Junior High School?

Would I like it? I was afraid after I hung up the phone that I had been entirely too exuberant. I was in ecstasy. I went to bed and cried myself to sleep! At last, at last, things were looking up for me!

I began early to make plans for the change. There were so many household items to dispose of. Some I knew Fern or Dan wanted; others would want certain things. And sometimes it seemed every time I turned around someone was there to get something they said was theirs. For some items I knew better, but I didn't say so. So I began moving things. The Voss farm was mine so I moved some furniture there in the midst of having some work done on the house--papering, floors covered, painting.

In May I bade goodbye to Fatima and the two "True, True" Mr. Kusters, Superintendent and Principal. I think they thought I'd be dependent on them for the rest of my teaching life. That leaving turned out to be my farewell to country and small town schools. And in spite of all the hard work, unscrupulous superintendents and ill-informed school boards, I'm not sorry I experienced them. I would have been living under the misapprehension that rural schools are just as well managed and supervised as suburban and city schools--and supplied just as well. And though it may disturb traditional, nostalgic memories, I think seeing the fact clearly is important to teachers and administrators and parents.

I spent most of the summer with Mom and Pete on the farm. Or I and Nancy, I should say. Wherever we went she rode on the top of the back seat, so happy and satisfied. She had been a faithful and true friend all winter, meeting me every evening at the junction of the highway and our private road. Now she immediately crept into Mom's and Pete's hearts, too, as I often had to leave her with them when I had to be away on business errands.

My "setting sail" on a new life was marred that summer by several deaths, especially by that of Kim, Bant's and Waunita's four-year-old daughter. Buell, I could understand. Dad, I could understand. But Kim...only four years old, so sweet, so dainty, so beloved, so needed. One day she was alive and seemingly well; the next...I couldn't understand. I don't think I ever have. Life plays strange pranks on us.

That first year at Kirkwood was a sad one. I had looked forward with such pleasure to returning. But that return was tainted by my grief. I'm sure Anna Lo, who was teaching in Brentwood, must have frequently been distressed by my references to Buell, Kim, Dad and my financial burdens. But she was always cheerful and full of fun and gave me a much-needed lift.

I settled down in Kirkwood with great ease, finding staunch true friends--some old, some new, all much appreciated. Those next ten years were to be the happiest and most rewarding of my entire career. And they pointed the way toward the rest of my life.

Along the way, in addition to a passel of students for 10 years, I watched my own family take wings. Anna Lo accepted a fellowship in Science at the University of Virginia, where she met her husband, Dr. Wilbur Slawson. Yvonne and Alan

Skouby had a fast fling at life--with Esso at Baton Rouge, Louisiana, a fellowship at Leland Stanford University, a nice job with Monsanto in St. Louis--all leading to his position as controller with Atlas Crankshaft in Fostoria, Ohio. Jen and her husband, Steve Peth, taught in St. Louis County along with me.

And only yesterday, it seems, Yvonne was born.

Mama lived to be 90, never relenting one iota in her spartan mannerisms. She always worried about whether I had a job, would I keep it more than a year, would I get there on time. She was always a little amazed that I carried on under my own steam when she wasn't around. In my life I never heard her speak a word of praise, although she was quite proud of her family. If Mama said nothing derogatory, we judged she approved.

She was the mentholatum in her one medical remedy, prescribed with assuredness: "Anything mentholatum won't cure isn't worth having." But her most effective prescription for living--for my life--came not from that green bottle. She might not have approved of it but it had her hand writing on it...

For once in my life I didn't wonder Where next? after Kirkwood. Nancy, too, was gone and Pete lived alone in that big old farmhouse. And that's where I longed to be. I yearned to have an hour in the sun, a hoe in my hand, a song in my heart. I yearned for the feel of good, black loam breaking into bits in my hand and the feel of tiny seed dropping from my fingers into tiny furrows. I yearned for the feel of soft, furry calves just born, of puppies and kittens brushing against my leg.

I had had hundreds of rewarding experiences in my 40 years of teaching. I could remember the awed whispers of several Bessies, the grateful pourings of a few Ruths, the shared memorizings of a Henry or two, the excited discoveries of some Karls. But I remembered, too, my kinship with farms and farm animals.

When I went home for short periods Jack and Bob would greet me by lying down, rolling over on their backs and moaning, then crawling on their bellies toward me. Around the corner of the house would come Smokey, followed by an entire litter of blue- and white-spotted kittens. And old Funny Face cow would bring up her baby calf--with a face twice as funny as her own. Then I knew there was no choice to make.

I had made it long ago, when Dad and Mom chose to buy a farm and rear their family on the land and in its wide open spaces.

From a painting by Paton.   " YOU'RE NO CHICKEN "

A Sampler

To test your own schooling . . .
and to revive some memories,
some lessons and problems
from the pages of textbooks
used by the author
during her student days
at Post Oak School "up the hill"

Grace Virginia · Bacon

1925 ·   Post oak School,

A Sampler

68   PERCENTAGE

11. This load of hay weighs 2200 lb., the wagon 1200 lb., and the team 2600 lb. *a.* The weight of the hay is what per cent of the entire weight? *b.* The weight of the wagon is what per cent of the entire weight? *c.* The weight of the team is what per cent of the entire weight? *d.* How many tons must the bridge support?

12. *a.* In 1905 the Chicago baseball team won 92 games and lost 60. What per cent of all the games played did they win? *b.* The Boston team won 78 and lost 74. What per cent of all the games did they lose? *c.* The New York team played 149 games and won $47\frac{97}{149}$ % of them. How many games did they lose?

13. By selling paper at 150 % of its cost, a stationer receives 90 cents a package for it. What is the cost of a package of this paper?

14. Twelve pounds of seed for a lawn contained $2\frac{1}{2}$ lb. of white clover seed. What per cent of the mixture was white clover seed?

REVIEW AND PRACTICE

150. *Oral*

1. What number is composed of 5 units, 7 tens, and 3 thousands?

2. Read XLIV; CCLXII; DCXCI; MCMVIII; CDLIV.

3. *Give results rapidly, adding or subtracting the tens' figures first:* $36 + 45$; $29 + 32$; $57 + 76$; $93 + 28$; $93 - 27$; $84 - 45$; $72 + 39$.

4. *Give quickly the number of:*

a. Quarts in 98 pt.

b. Pecks in 28 bu.

c. Hours in a week.

d. Seconds in 1 hour.

e. Inches in 2 yd.

f. Square inches in 2 sq. ft.

g. Square yards in 450 sq. ft.

h. Inches in 2 yd.

i. Dimes in $15.

j. Feet in 2 rd.

k. Dollars in 36,000 cents.

l. Gills in a gallon.

m. Days in two common years.

n. Tons in 1600 lb.

o. Square rods in 10 A.

p. Yards in 10 rd.

q. Days in 14 wk.

r. Days in a summer.

s. Eggs in a crate containing 30 doz.

5. A half dollar, a quarter, 2 dimes, and a nickel are how many cents?

6. $\frac{1}{2} + \frac{1}{3} + \frac{5}{12} = ?$

7. $3 \times 8 \times ? = 48$

8. $8 \times 9 = 6 \times ?$

9. $88 \div ? = 8$

10. $15 - \frac{7}{8} = ?$

11. $18 - 1\frac{3}{5} = ?$

12. $5\frac{4}{9} + 13\frac{5}{9} = ?$

13. $7\frac{2}{3} - \frac{5}{6} = ?$

14. When 36 men can earn a sum of money in 15 da., how long will it take 12 men at the same wages to earn the same amount? 9 men? 6 men? 72 men?

A Sampler

88   ELEMENTS OF ARITHMETIC.

TABLE.

I = 1	XIII = 13	LX = 60
II = 2	XIV = 14	LXX = 70
III = 3	XV = 15	XC = 90
IV = 4	XVI = 16	C = 100
V = 5	XIX = 19	CC = 200
VI = 6	XX = 20	CCCC = 400
VII = 7	XXI = 21	CD = 400
VIII = 8	XXIX = 29	D = 500
IX = 9	XXX = 30	DCC = 700
X = 10	XXXIV = 34	M = 1000
XI = 11	XL = 40	MMM = 3000
XII = 12	L = 50	MDCCCXCII = 1892

EXERCISES.

Read the following:

XX	XIX	CDXX	XL	XCIV
LXX	XLIV	XXV	XC	$\overline{\text{XIX}}$
XCIX	XXXV	LXIV	$\overline{\text{VIII}}$	MDLIV
XXI	LXIX	CCXXIV	LX	MDCCC
XLIX	XXXVI	CCCLIX	DCXL	MMDC
MDCCCX	CCXXVI	DLXXI	MDXL	DCCL
CXCV	CCXLIV	MMMD	IVDXL	CCXCV

Express the following by Roman Notation:

23	61	84	35	312	517	1010	1900
34	19	59	47	419	493	1800	8000
15	36	62	86	226	499	1492·	9000
27	43	97	214	384	278	1607	1721

ADDITION.

67. **1.** How many blocks are 5 blocks, 3 blocks, and **7** blocks ?

2. How many splints are 3 splints, 2 splints, and 8 splints?

3. How many oranges are 7 oranges, 2 oranges, and **5** oranges?

4. How many are 5 and 6 and 7 ?

5. How many are 7 and 8 and 6?

6. How many are 5 and 9 and 2 and 6 ?

7. How many are 3 and 7 and 4 and 8 ?

8. How many are 4 and 8 and 5 and 9 ?

9. What have you been doing with the numbers **given** above ?

68. The process of finding a number that is equal to **two** or more given numbers is called **Addition**.

69. The result obtained by adding is the **Sum,** or **Amount**.

70. The **Sign of Addition** is a small upright cross $(+)$ It is read *plus,* and is placed between the numbers to be added.

Thus, $4 + 2$ is read 4 plus 2, and means that 4 and 2 are to be added.

71. The **Sign of Equality** is two short parallel horizontal lines $(=)$. It is read *equals,* or *is equal to.*

Thus, $3 + 2 = 5$ is read 3 plus 2 equals 5.

89

A Sampler

FACTORING.

118. 1. What is the product when 3 and 2 are multiplied together? What are 3 and 2 of their product? (Art. 86.)

2. What factors will produce 9?

3. What numbers when multiplied together will produce 12? What are 3 and 4, or 6 and 2 of their product?

4. What are the factors of 20? Of 36? Of 15?

5. What are the factors of 27? Of 25? Of 32?

6. What are the factors of 21? Of 33? Of 50?

7. What are the factors of 63? What else may 7 be called of 63 besides a factor?

8. If 9 is one of two factors of 18, what is the other factor? If 3 is one of the factors? If 6 is one of the factors?

9. What numbers will exactly divide 18? 25? 36?

10. Give the exact divisors of 42; 96; 35; 50; 27; 72.

11. Give the factors of 36; 40; 48; 70; 80.

12. Give the exact divisors of 44; 56; 64; 84; 96.

13. Name the exact divisors of 49; 88; 63; 24; 27.

14. What numbers between 0 and 10 cannot be exactly divided by any number except themselves and 1? What numbers between 10 and 20? Between 20 and 30?

15. What numbers between 0 and 10 can be exactly divided by other numbers besides themselves and 1? Between 10 and 20? Between 20 and 30?

16. Select from the following the numbers that have no exact divisors except themselves and 1: 35, 42, 63, 56, 61, 47, 49, 81, 37, 26, 18, 45.

138

FACTORING.   **139**

17. Select from the following the numbers that have exact divisors besides themselves and 1: 24, 36, 41, 39, 27, 45, 33, 37, 50, 44, 60, 71, 72.

119. A number that expresses whole units is called an **Integer**.

Thus, 5, 27, 35 are integers, or integral numbers.

120. The integers which, upon being multiplied together will produce the number, are called **Factors** of the number.

Thus, 5 and 3 are the factors of 15.

121. An integer which will divide a number without a remainder is called an **Exact Divisor** of the number.

Thus, 2, 3, 6, and 9 are exact divisors of 18. They are also *factors* of 18.

122. A number that has no exact divisors except itself and 1 is called a **Prime Number**.

Thus, 1, 3, 5, 7 are prime numbers.

123. A number that has exact divisors besides itself and 1 is called a **Composite Number**.

Thus, 24, 36, 40, 100 are composite numbers.

124. Factors that are prime numbers are **Prime Factors**.

Thus, 7 and 5 are the prime factors of 35.

125. A number that is exactly divisible by 2 is called an **Even Number**.

Thus, 8, 12, 20, 24 are even numbers.

126. A number that is not exactly divisible by 2 is called an **Odd Number**.

Thus, 15, 21, 35, 43 are odd numbers.

127. The process of separating a number into its factors is called **Factoring**.

A Sampler

Find:

2. $\frac{3}{4}$ of $\frac{4}{5}$.   6. $\frac{12}{17}$ of $\frac{5}{6}$.   10. $\frac{8}{11}$ of $\frac{4}{5}$.

3. $\frac{5}{7}$ of $\frac{7}{9}$.   7. $\frac{13}{14}$ of $\frac{28}{65}$.   11. $\frac{7}{12}$ of $\frac{7}{12}$.

4. $\frac{6}{7}$ of $\frac{14}{15}$.   8. $\frac{18}{27}$ of $\frac{54}{72}$.   12. $\frac{9}{14}$ of $\frac{17}{20}$.

5. $\frac{8}{9}$ of $\frac{36}{37}$.   9. $\frac{11}{25}$ of $\frac{35}{44}$.   13. $\frac{12}{17}$ of $\frac{10}{13}$.

Find: Multiply:

14. $\frac{2}{3}$ of $4\frac{1}{2}$.   18. $\frac{3}{4}$ of $\frac{1}{2}$ by $\frac{5}{7}$.

15. $\frac{5}{8}$ of $10\frac{2}{3}$.   19. $\frac{5}{9}$ of $\frac{7}{11}$ by $3\frac{3}{4}$.

16. $\frac{7}{10}$ of $8\frac{5}{18}$.   20. $5\frac{3}{5}$ by $\frac{2}{7}$ of $3\frac{1}{5}$.

17. $\frac{11}{12}$ of $7\frac{3}{8}$.   21. $6\frac{5}{6}$ by $\frac{4}{5}$ of $4\frac{4}{5}$.

Find the value of:

22. $\frac{2}{3} \times \frac{3}{4} \times \frac{4}{5} \times \frac{5}{6}$.   24. $\frac{5}{6} \times \frac{7}{8} \times \frac{9}{11} \times \frac{14}{15}$.

23. $\frac{3}{5} \times \frac{4}{9} \times \frac{10}{13} \times \frac{12}{21}$.   25. $2\frac{1}{2} \times \frac{3}{8} \times 1\frac{1}{3} \times \frac{3}{4}$.

26. There are $16\frac{1}{2}$ feet in a rod. How many feet are there in $\frac{7}{8}$ of a rod? In $3\frac{1}{2}$ rods?

27. When hay is worth $\$20\frac{3}{4}$ per ton, how much will $\frac{7}{12}$ of a ton cost?

28. At $\$6\frac{2}{3}$ a ton, what must I pay for $8\frac{3}{4}$ tons of coal?

29. A man purchased $\frac{2}{3}$ of $420\frac{3}{5}$ acres of land and then sold $\frac{3}{5}$ of what he had bought. How many acres did he sell?

30. At an auction sale a cow was sold for $\$39\frac{2}{3}$, and a horse for $3\frac{2}{3}$ times as much as the cow. For how much was the horse sold?

31. If a square foot of land is worth $16\frac{2}{3}\cancel{c}$, what is the value of $10\frac{7}{8}$ square feet?

32. The cloth of Ruth's dress cost $\$8\frac{3}{4}$. The making cost $\frac{4}{5}$ as much, the trimming cost $\frac{7}{10}$ as much as the making, and the linings cost $\frac{3}{7}$ as much as the trimmings. What did the linings cost? What was the whole cost of the dress?

FRACTIONS.   **169**

DIVISION OF FRACTIONS.

181. **To divide a fraction by an integer.**

1. If $\frac{4}{5}$ of an orange is divided equally between 2 girls, what part of the orange will each girl have? How much is $\frac{4}{5} \div 2$?

2. A man divided $\frac{3}{4}$ of an acre into 3 equal lots. How large was each? How much is $\frac{3}{4} \div 3$?

3. If a horse ate $\frac{8}{9}$ of a bushel of oats in 4 days, how much did he eat each day? How much is $\frac{8}{9} \div 4$?

4. In dividing a fraction by an integer, what part of the fraction is divided?

5. If $\$\frac{1}{2}$ is divided equally between 2 boys, what part of a dollar will each boy get? How much is $\frac{1}{2} \div 2$?

6. When 3 pounds of sugar can be bought for $\$\frac{1}{4}$, what is the price per pound? How much is $\frac{1}{4} \div 3$?

7. If $\frac{1}{2}$ of a ship is owned equally by 5 men, what part of the ship is owned by each? How much is $\frac{1}{2} \div 5$?

8. In what other way, besides dividing the numerator, can a fraction be divided by an integer? State both ways in which a fraction may be divided by an integer.

9. If 3 dozen oranges can be bought for $\$\frac{6}{7}$, what do they cost per dozen?

10. If $\frac{2}{3}$ of a pound of tea is divided equally among 3 persons, what part of a pound will each receive?

11. If $\frac{3}{4}$ of a bushel of walnuts fills 4 bags of equal size, what part of a bushel does each bag hold?

12. Mrs. Jay filled 5 tumblers with $\frac{10}{12}$ of a gallon of jelly. How much did each tumbler hold?

13. Divide $\frac{2}{3}$ by 2; $\frac{6}{7}$ by 2; $\frac{9}{10}$ by 3; $\frac{8}{11}$ by 4; $\frac{10}{13}$ by 5.

14. Divide $\frac{3}{5}$ by 2; $\frac{7}{8}$ by 3; $\frac{5}{6}$ by 4; $\frac{4}{7}$ by 5; $\frac{7}{9}$ by 6.

15. If 3 yards of cloth cost $\$1\frac{4}{5}$, what does 1 yard cost?

16. When 5 bushels of potatoes cost $\$4\frac{2}{5}$, what does a bushel cost?

A Sampler

202   ELEMENTS OF ARITHMETIC.

1.   *Brooklyn, N.Y., June 25, 1892.*

Mr. Horace E. Gray,

                              Bought of JONES & PURDY.

4 bags Coffee,	300 *lb.*	@	$.35½	$106	50
3 chests Tea,	260 "	"	.87½	227	50
8 boxes Raisins,	200 "	"	.12½	25	00
2 bbl. Coffee-sugar,	432 "	"	.06¼	27	00
2 bbl. Crackers,	150 "	"	.05½	8	25
Received payment,				$394	25

                    Jones & Purdy,
                         Per G.S.

Make out in proper form, find the footings of the following bills and accounts, and receipt them:

2. Miss Lucy Graham bought of Luckey, Platt & Co. 15 yards of calico @ 10 cents; 36 yards of sheeting @ 18¼ cents; 2 pairs of gloves @ $1.50; 1 sun-umbrella @ $3.75; 5 yards of Hamburg edging @ 25 cents; 6 handkerchiefs @ 37½ cents; and 7 pairs of hose @ 50 cents.

3. Messrs. Henry Davis & Co. bought of James Harkness 150 barrels of flour @ $5.90; 105 bushels of wheat @ $1.20; 325 bushels of corn @ $.68; 675 bushels of oats @ $.40; and 50 barrels of potatoes @ $1.25.

4. Mrs. Charles Reid in account with Roger Caldwell: August 7, 1892, 9 yards cashmere @ $.75; ½ yard velvet @ $1.50; 12 yards lawn @ .12½; 1½ yards silesia @ $.30; ¾ yards silk at $1.50.

5. Darwin Howard bought of Stone & Bacon 15 pounds nails @ 4½¢; 4 pairs of hinges @ 37½¢; 18 dozen screws @ 11¢; 5 dozen milk-pans @ $2.75; 7 locks @ 75¢; 2 saws @ $1.35; 3 hammers @ 85¢; and 2 planes @ $1.50.

REVIEW.

WRITTEN EXERCISES.

235. **1.** How much will 2 dozen pairs of kid gloves cost at $1.25 a pair?

2. A man·paid out the following sums: For a pair of horses, $375; for a carriage, $295; for harnesses, $115. How much did he pay for all?

3. A farmer sold 12.35 cords of wood at $4.75 per cord. How much did he receive for it?

4. A man purchased 8 tons of coal at $5.75 per ton, and 7 cords of hard wood at $5.50 per cord. How much did he pay for fuel?

5. If illuminating gas is sold at $2.50 per thousand cubic feet, for how much gas will $17.50 pay?

6. Find the sum of 15 dollars 9 cents 3 mills, 12 dollars 5 cents 4 mills, 18 dollars 14 cents 7 mills, and 16 dollars 10 cents.

7. If 5.5 yards of ribbon cost $2.75, what will 9.75 yards cost?

8. If a clerk earns $520 per year and spends $110 for clothes, $215 for board, and $75.50 for other expenses, how long will it take him to save $1000?

9. If 54,600 letters were mailed from a post-office in 30 days, what was the average number mailed per day?

10. How many pairs of curtains can be bought for $414, if 12 pairs are bought for $138?

11. A drover bought 280 head of cattle for $12,740, and sold them at a gain of $8.75 per head. How much did he receive for them per head?

12. A man paid $87.50 for materials to paint his house, and he paid 3 painters $2.50 per day for 4.5 days to do the work. How much was the entire expense of painting his house?

A Sampler

220   **ELEMENTS OF ARITHMETIC.**

2. Multiply 4 bu. 3 pk. 5 qt. by 7.
3. Multiply 5 gal. 1 qt. 3 pt. 2 gi. by 6.
4. Multiply 5 lb. 6 oz. 10 pwt. 8 gr. by 8.
5. Multiply 7 lb. 8 oz. 5 dr. 2 sc. 10 gr. by 7.
6. Multiply 3 hr. 20 min. 35 sec. by 5.
7. Multiply 2 T. 5 cwt. 48 lb. 15 oz. by 8.
8. Multiply 2 rd. 3 yd. 2 ft. 10 in. by 9.
9. Multiply 12 cu. yd. 15 cu. ft. 1115 cu. in. by 6.
10. Multiply 8 sq. yd. 2 sq. ft. 45 sq. in. by 5.
11. Multiply 5 da. 8 hr. 15 min. 25 sec. by 4.
12. Multiply 12 rd. 4 yd. 2 ft. 8 in. by 8.
13. Multiply 5 R. 8 qr. 16 sheets by 9.
14. Multiply 6 bar. 10 gal. 3 qt. 1 pt. by 7.

DIVISION OF DENOMINATE NUMBERS.

267. 1. Divide 14 gal. 3 qt. 1 pt. by 4.

gal.	qt.	pt.
4)14	3	1
3	2	$1\frac{3}{4}$

EXPLANATION.— One fourth of 14 gal. is 3 gal. and 2 gal. remainder. The 3 gal. are written in the quotient, and the 2 gal. remainder are united with the 3 qt., making 11 qt.

One fourth of 11 qt. is 2 qt. and 3 qt. remainder. The 2 qt. are written in the quotient, and the 3 qt. remainder united with the 1 pt., making 7 pt.

One fourth of 7 pt. is $1\frac{3}{4}$ pt.

Therefore, the quotient is 3 gal. 2 qt. $1\frac{3}{4}$ pt.

2. Divide 21 gal. 3 qt. 1 pt. 3 gi. by 6.
3. Divide 15 bu. 3 pk. 5 qt. 1 pt. by 4.
4. Divide 13 yd. 2 ft. 6 in. by 7.
5. Divide 23 cwt. 68 lb. 10 oz. by 5.
6. Divide 42 lb. 8 oz. 15 pwt. by 9.
7. Divide 22 lb. 7 oz. 5 dr. 2 sc. by 8.
8. Divide 19 hr. 10 min. 36 sec. by 6.
9. Divide 21 sq. yd. 7 sq. ft. 45 sq. in. by 4.
10. Divide 15 rd. 4 yd. 2 ft. 8 in. by 5.

DENOMINATE NUMBERS.   **221**

PRACTICAL MEASUREMENTS.

268. To compute the area of rectangular surfaces.

1. What is a square inch? Draw a figure 6 in. long and 1 in. wide with all its angles equal. How many sq. in. does it contain?

2. If the figure were 2 in. wide, how many sq. in. would it contain? How many if it were 3 in. wide? 4 in. wide? 5 in. wide? 6 in. wide?

3. What is a square foot? How many sq. ft. are there in a strip of ground 12 ft. long and 1 ft. wide, with all its angles equal? How many, if it is 2 ft. wide? 3 ft. wide? 4 ft. wide? 5 ft. wide? 6 ft. wide?

4. How many sq. yd. are there in a walk 15 yd. long and 5 yd. wide, having its angles all equal?

269. A figure that has four straight sides and four equal angles is called a **Rectangle**.

The angles of a rectangle are all right angles.

Rectangle.

270. The number of square units that a surface contains is called its **Area**.

Thus the area of a rectangle 4 in. long and 2 in. wide is 8 sq. in., for it may be divided into 2 rows, each containing 4 sq. in.

For additional instruction in measurements, consult the author's STANDARD ARITHMETIC.

WRITTEN EXERCISES.

271. **1.** What is the area of a rectangular walk 22 ft. long and 5 ft. 6 in. broad?

$$22 \times 5\tfrac{1}{2} = 121$$
or,
$$264 \times 66 = 17,424$$
$$17,424 \text{ sq. in.} = 121 \text{ sq. ft.}$$

EXPLANATION. — Since the walk is 22 ft. long and $5\tfrac{1}{2}$ ft. wide, its area in feet is 121 sq. ft.

The same result can be obtained by expressing the length and breadth in inches, and reducing the result obtained to square feet.

A Sampler

368   SIMILAR SURFACES

gons of the same number of sides are similar ; two rectangles are similar if the length and breadth of each have the same ratio.

565. It is proved by geometry that *if two figures are similar, any two lines of one figure have the same ratio as the corresponding two lines of the other figure;* and *a line of one figure has the same ratio to the corresponding line of the other figure that any other line of the first figure has to the corresponding line of the other figure.*

For example, in the figures shown in section **564,**

$$AB : AC = A'B' : A'C' \qquad EF : FG = E'F' : F'G'$$
$$AB : A'B' = BC : B'C' \qquad DG : D'G' = FG : F'G'$$

If the side AB equals 21 ft., the side AC 12 ft., and the side $A'B'$ **14 ft.,** we may find the length of the side $A'C'$ by the following proportion :

$$\text{21 ft. : 12 ft.} = \text{14 ft. : } x \text{ ft.}$$

Find the value of x.

566. *Written*

1. In Figs. 1, 2, 3, and 4 :

a. If $AB = 14$ ft., $A'B' = 28$ ft., and $BC = 11$ ft., what is the length of $B'C'$?

b. If $EF = 15$ rd., $FG = 10$ rd., and $E'F' = 18$ rd., what is the length of $F'G'$?

c. If $DG = 27$ mi., $D'G' = 33$ mi., and $FG = 18$ mi., what is the value of $F'G'$?

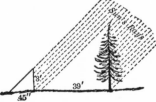

2. A man, desiring to know the height of a tree which stood on level ground, drove a stick into the earth in a vertical position, and it measured 3 ft. above ground. Its shadow measured 45 in. At the same moment the tree cast a shadow 39 ft. long. How tall was the tree ?

SIMILAR SURFACES   369

3. A rectangular field is 70 rd. long and 50 rd. wide; what is the length of a similar field whose width is 12½ rd. ?

4. One side and the diagonal of a quadrilateral are respectively 18 ft. and 44 ft. Find the corresponding side of a similar quadrilateral whose diagonal is 110 ft.

5. A boy found the height of a flagstaff as follows :

He found that he could hold a cane upright just 30 in. away from his eye. He placed his thumb 22½ in. from the top of the cane, pinned a card on the flagstaff just as high as his eye, and walked backward until he could just see the paper by looking across the top of his thumb where he held the cane, and see the top of the flagstaff by looking across the top of the cane. He then found by measurement that he stood 72 ft. from the flagstaff while taking the observation, and that the card was 5 ft. from the ground. How high was the flagstaff?

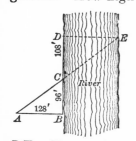

6. Two boys, wishing to know the width of a river and having no boat, constructed the right triangle *ABC* by driving three stakes. They sighted from *A*, across *C*, to the opposite bank, at *E*, and drove a stake at *D*, so as to make the right triangle *CDE*. They then measured *AB*, *BC*, and *CD*, and found *DE*. How wide was the river?

567. It is proved by geometry that *the areas of similar surfaces are to each other as the squares of any two corresponding lines.*

Thus, on page 367, if the side *AB* of Fig. 1 is 21 ft., the side *A'B'* of Fig. 2, 14 ft., and the area of Fig. 1, 96 sq. ft., we may find the area of

An Index

A guide to the main characters
in this true chronicle,
the events of their lives, large and small,
and the places where it all happened

An Index

canning, 224
Caple, Kenneth, 162, 165, 172
Carnes, Mary, 119
Carpenter, Mrs., 121
Carroll, Gertrude, 88, 94, 119
catalogs
    Sears & Roebuck, 10, 29, 37, 56
    Montgomery-Ward, 10
celibacy, 57
Central Missouri State
    College, 34, 42, etc.
Central Place (322), 210
charavari, 59, 65
Chorus, 181
Christmas, 37
"Christ of the Andes," 54
Churchill, Winston, 46
churning, 129
Civilian Conservation Corps, 161
Clay Dog, the, 230
Clough, Dr. Norman, 104
College Avenue (Warrensburg), 47
Columbia, 87
Compton, Rose, 211
Connard Hill, 192
"Coolidge Custard," 23
coon, 41
Cooper Hill, 174, etc.
cottage cheese, 201
Courtwright, Geneva, 47
Craig, Prof. Ben, 46
Creamettes, 213
"Crip," 43
Crites, Earl, 187
Crites, Katherine, 187
Crow, Alva, 248
Crowder, Mae, 117
Cuivre River, 171
Czeschin, Mrs. L., 201

D

"date," 62
Davis, Slick, 88
Daylight Saving Time, 110
Decker, Mrs., 90
deer honeymoon, 234
deer hunting, 235
Denque Fever, 195
Denny, Lillian, 211

Department of Education, 43
Depression, 2, 19, etc.
Devault, Rainey, 201
dikes, 171
Dillon, Emmett, 185
Downs, Myrtle, 58
draft, wartime, 167
Drewel, Benjamin, 204
Drewel, Hilda, 188
Drewel, Lora, 188
Dry Fork Creek, 196
Dubrouillet, Zelda, 75
Duey, Don, 160
"Dumpy," 241
Duncan, Dell, 224, 226
Duncan, Gertha, 82
Duncan, Marian, 227
Duncan, Ted, 227

E

Eaton House Hollow, 120
Eliot, President (CMSC), 63
Ellis, Emmett, 131
Emmanuel Lutheran Children's
    Home, 109
Engler, Ruth, 214
English, Cliff and Eva Mae, 234
Enke, Harold, 174
"e-qui-nox-ial," 48, 54
Essman, George, 179
Essman, Mrs. George, 205
Etc. Club, 74, etc.
Euchre, 49
Express Flyer, 193

F

Famous-Barr, 226
Farris, Chester, 108
Fatima, 246
FBI, 133
Fent, John, 11
Ferguson, Lil, 96
Ferguson, Maggie, 97
Ferrier
    Buell, 93, 231, etc.
    Dan, 231, 238, etc.
    Fern, 231
fire brick, 231

An Index

An Index

An Index

''Teacher, Teacher,
I Done It! I Done It!
I Done Done It!''

was designed by The Nunn Group,
and photocomposed in Times
with titles in Deepdene

The Westphalia Press
The Dohman-Boessen House
Route 1   Box 96
Loose Creek, Missouri 65054